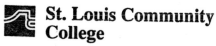

Lost Revolutions

Lost

The South in the 1950s

Revolutions

Pete Daniel

The University of North Carolina Press Chapel Hill and London for

Smithsonian National Museum of American History Washington, D.C.

© 2000 Smithsonian Institution

Manufactured in the United States of America

The paper in this book meets the guidelines for permanence
and durability of the Committee on Production Guidelines
for Book Longevity of the Council on Library Resources.

Set in Minion and Impact by Eric M. Brooks

Library of Congress Cataloging-in-Publication Data

Daniel, Pete.

Lost revolutions: the South in the 1950s / Pete Daniel.

   p.   cm.

Includes bibliographical references and index.

ISBN 0-8078-2537-9 (alk. paper) —

ISBN 0-8078-4848-4 (pbk.: alk. paper)

1. Southern States—History—1951–   2. Southern States—
Social conditions—1945–   3. Nineteen fifties.   I. Title.

F216.2.D36   2000

975.043—dc21   99-048066

Photograph on p. iii © Ernest Withers;
courtesy Panopticon Gallery, Boston, Massachusetts.

04 03 02 01 00   5 4 3 2 1

For Lisa and Laura

Contents

Illustrations

Acknowledgments

The Smithsonian Institution awarded me a Regents' Fund Fellowship for independent study in 1994–95, and the staff of the National Museum of American History has generously supported this book project.

The staff of the defunct Division of Agriculture and Natural Resources as well as my colleagues in the Division of the History of Technology have encouraged this project. Louis Hutchins worked with me on the "Science in American Life" exhibit and helped with research on fire ants. Smita Dutta, who worked on both the science exhibit and "Rock 'n' Soul: Social Crossroads," strongly supported my research and writing.

Many scholars who took part in the museum's fellowship program challenged my ideas and often suggested sources and ideas. Museum interns who helped on the book were Corey Brown, Kris Deroucher, Sarah Haviland, Margaret Hayden, Rebecca Lynch, Story Matkin-Rawn, Robin Morris, Lori Robbins, Maureen Sele, Sonya Hand Stover, Jaime Vazquez, and Andrea Woody.

The following people read and commented on portions of the manuscript: Karen Anderson, Tony Badger, Elspeth Brown, Elizabeth Eckford, Laura Edwards, Randy Finley, Glenda Gilmore, Janet Greene, Peter Guralnick, John Hartigan Jr., Laura Helper, Michael Honey, John Howard, Elizabeth Jacoway, Colin Johnson, David K. Johnson, Robert Korstad, Angela Lakwete, Charles McGovern, Hazel Bryan Massery, Grace Palladino, Charles Payne, John Pearson, Roy Reed, William T. Martin Riches, Amy Richter, Beth Roy, Edmund Russell III, Tim Tyson, Brian Ward, Jeannie Whayne, Harold Woodman, and Robert O. Zeller Jr. Dan Carter, James C. Cobb, Sara Evans, and Jacquelyn Hall, who read the complete manuscript, offered invaluable suggestions.

Many friends and scholars have helped by sharing information and allowing me to share ideas, including Andy Ambrose, Angie Blake, Vernon Burton, Ann Chirhart, Camy Clough, Kari Frederickson, Sylvia Frey, Hank Grasso, Hartmut Keil, John Kirk, James Lanier, David Less, Maida Loescher, Leslie Burl McLemore, Mary Panzer, Judy Reardon, Mary Reardon, Natalie Ring, Helen Rozwadowski, Lee Woodman, and Nan Woodruff. Jim Kelly contributed not only his ideas but also his childhood photograph, taken in 1953 in Sparta, North Carolina, which begins book 1.

The staff at the Red River Grill, including Matt Weiss, Josh Levin, Justin Polanin, and Aziza Nazir, have faithfully added happy hours to Tuesday evening discussions.

The following archivists and librarians provided extraordinary help: Beth Bilderback, Beverly Brannon, Andrea Cantrell, Dwayne Cox, Michael Dabrishus, Tom Johnson, Alice Hildreth, Michael Paulk, Linda Pine, James Rush, Mattie Sink, John Woodard, and Tara Zachary.

Drs. Jerome W. Canter, Brenda Dintiman, Neil Kahanovitz, and Joseph Lamb have attended to my health.

Kate Torrey and the staff at the University of North Carolina Press strongly supported this project. Only an author can fully appreciate the skill that editor Paula Wald lavished on the manuscript.

Graziella Tonfoni has contributed ideas and given enthusiastic support for the project.

Finally, I want to thank my family and friends for tolerating my obsession with this book.

Lost Revolutions

Introduction

After fifteen years of depression and war, in the fall of 1945 southerners anticipated a tranquil and prosperous future. Hedging against a postwar depression,
farmers had saved money, but they longed for tractors, pickups, and washing ·
machines. Defense workers regeared for peacetime and anticipated shelves
filled with consumer goods. Soldiers returning from the nightmare of war were
impatient to push aside trifling southern customs. As democratic war rhetoric
sharpened the sting of segregation, membership in the National Association for
the Advancement of Colored People (NAACP) increased. In 1944, the U.S.
Supreme Court struck down the white primary, opening up participatory
democracy to all citizens. At few times in southern history had the path to revolutionary change seemed so clear. The road into the 1950s, however, took
unexpected turns. The South that evolved in the twenty years after the war
emerged out of displacement, conflict, and creativity—not tranquillity.

The decline of labor-intensive agriculture, working-class cultural achievements, and the civil rights movement challenged elite white control and middle-
class sensibilities. In most instances, the revolutionary energy generated by
these interconnected movements was siphoned off. Washington bureaucrats
and lobbyists in the 1950s advised farmers to embrace science and technology,
to get big or get out. Machines and chemicals destroyed jobs, reconfigured the
landscape, and undermined the environment. In the two decades after the war,
some 11 million southern sharecroppers, tenants, and small farm owners left the
land, a demographic shift that had enormous implications.

When the last generation of sharecroppers arrived in towns and cities across
the country, they quickened cultural change and stamped it with their rural
ways. The collision between rural and urban cultures generated creative tidal
waves. Rock 'n' roll music and stock car racing sponsored by the National Association for Stock Car Auto Racing (NASCAR), two important manifestations
of working-class culture, were the backbeat to migration and the accelerating
movement to secure civil rights. Music and racing also helped alleviate the
mounting tension among people facing polar changes in their lives.

The civil rights movement troubled whites and gave hope to African Americans. To some southerners, integration was a manifestation of necessary
change, but it was also another adjustment to a world that had less use for
racism and discrimination. Many whites, however, inherited a flawed history
that conflated segregation, the Lost Cause, religion, and sex. Chained to segre-

gation and racial prejudice, state and local politicians revived antiquated rhetoric and portrayed themselves as victims of such handy enemies as the federal government and communism. They became defenders of a neo–Lost Cause.

It is impossible to know how many whites would have traveled down the road to equal rights in the 1950s if any white politician had risked martyrdom to find out. Nor did any white political faction champion compliance with the 1954 *Brown v. Board of Education* decision. Significant attempts to unite black and white workers foundered soon after the war, shattered by charges of communism. A timorous clergy avoided engagement, and indecisive white liberals were no match for ruthless segregationists. From the White House to southern governors' mansions to plantations, white leaders either remained silent or launched counterattacks against black and white activists.

The middle class emerged as a driving force that both supported and opposed the civil rights movement. The NAACP, a middle-class organization, explored a legal path to equal rights and inspired much of the civil rights activity of the 1950s. Citizens' Councils and other segregationist groups claimed memberships that included the best white people. Working-class blacks and whites also wrestled with civil rights, but leaders seldom solicited their opinions. The 1957 crisis at Little Rock's Central High School epitomized many of the race and class issues of the era as well as the failure of white leadership.

In early 1960, southerners discovered common ground as sit-ins attracted blacks and whites, men and women, from both the working class and the middle class. The institutions that guided civil rights efforts in the 1950s had no control over the students who sat at lunch counters in 1960. The Student Non-violent Coordinating Committee (SNCC) organized a grassroots movement to secure black voting rights, school integration, and African Americans' access to public space. Mississippi became the principal battleground of the civil rights movement, and the struggle culminated in the events of the summer of 1964.

The years between World War II and Freedom Summer were ripe with possibilities, but the postwar climate failed to produce political visionaries. In 1948, Dixiecrats embraced the past and the legacy of race and class that had defined so much of southern history. The *Brown v. Board of Education* decision fatally divided society and provoked whites to make a frantic defense of segregation. It would be ten years before Congress passed the 1964 Civil Rights Act and another year before it got around to protecting black voting rights. Southern whites twisted these laws to portray themselves as the victims and begrudged every black advance.

By the mid-1960s, both the rural and the urban South had changed in ways that frustrated, astounded, and often upset southerners. Nevertheless, the cauldron of racism continued to boil and search for vents. White Americans preferred to ignore the implications of segregation when at all possible. It was easier to celebrate Elvis Presley than Martin Luther King Jr., Ralph McGill than Ella Baker.

Lost opportunities littered the southern landscape in the years between World War II and Freedom Summer. One can only imagine how different southern history might have been if politicians, the press, the clergy, and local leaders had supported democratic reforms that bestowed full citizenship on African Americans. And one can only imagine how little would have been accomplished if a handful of blacks and whites had not taken risks to bring about the changes that did come.

BOOK I THE POSTWAR LANDSCAPE

1 Going among Strangers

It's no wonder the Revival Preachers are all preaching against going to War Work and begging people to coax their relatives back before they all go to Hell.

—*Mississippi farmer*

In 1994, Mississippi planter Frank Mitchener pointed across a stand of inch-high cotton plants to tiny jewels of reflected light at the edge of the field near the banks of a bayou. The effect came from glass slivers, he explained, the remains of windows shattered when tenant houses were bulldozed thirty years earlier. Before the Delta's cypress swamps were cleared for agriculture, Mitchener added, the Choctaw had lived on the same high ground beside the stream. Mitchener had often walked across the field with his grandson picking up Choctaw arrowheads and pottery shards mixed with snuff tins, bottles, and other bits of African American material culture. In the mid-twentieth century, advances in farm machinery, the development of synthetic chemicals, and government agricultural programs had doomed most agricultural laborers much as the lure of rich Delta land had tempted whites to banish the Choctaws a century and a half earlier. Most of the Choctaws and African Americans had moved on, but the vitreous reflections and artifacts were emblematic not only of the complex layering of the southern experience but also of the historical forces that had dispossessed the Choctaws, altered the landscape, and created and destroyed both slavery and sharecropping.

Rural change, urbanization, science, technology, racism, and popular culture were interlocking revolutionary components that swept through the South after World War II. The fabric of rural life was torn apart as millions of dispossessed farmers spilled out of the countryside and settled in towns and cities across the country. A landscape that had been dotted with small farms was reconfigured to fit machines and chemicals. The breakup of rural life had profound implications, for southern exiles transplanted rural culture wherever they settled. In urban jobs, the clock—not the sun—ordered their days. As the civil rights movement gained momentum in the mid-1950s, its potential excited blacks as much as its implications frightened whites. The simultaneous rise of agribusiness, stock car racing, rock 'n' roll music, and challenges to segregation generated immense constructive and destructive energy that forged both hope and fear, joy and sorrow.

The reflected light from the broken windows symbolized the long continuum of labor-intensive agriculture, including slavery. The cotton culture dominated southern agriculture for a century and a half, since land-hungry cotton growers during George Washington's presidency began clearing new ground across the fertile crescent that spanned the South's Black Belt and the Mississippi Delta.

The Civil War destroyed the grids that bound together the antebellum South, forcing all southerners, black and white, men and women, rich and poor, to reconstruct a society based on free labor. Former masters and slaves, as well as their white neighbors, understood not only the importance of controlling the sale and proceeds of their crops but also the potential of free labor. After the Civil War, planters and merchants devised imaginative strategies to control labor, credit, and marketing. This restructured but still labor-intensive cotton culture persisted until the mid-twentieth century. It then collapsed in a moment, in the twinkling of an eye, almost as quickly as a bulldozer could splinter a row of shotgun houses. The enclosure movement that drove millions of southern farmers from the land coincided with depression, war, migration, urbanization, and the civil rights movement. It was a time of intense emotional stress.[1]

Tractors, harvesting machines, and chemicals largely replaced the hired hands, tenants, and sharecroppers who had tended southern crops for so long. Most farmers' lives revolved around the cultivation of cotton plants, the annual routine of breaking the land, plowing, planting, cultivating, picking, and ginning. Other rural southerners, black and white, moved to the rhythm of different crops. Generations of black and white southerners drew their sustenance from the land and their values from rural routines and institutions. Although few were educated beyond being able to write their names, read a few Bible verses, and make basic calculations, they not only subsisted but also created a vibrant culture. The technological wave that swept farmers from the land also preserved remnants of their music, dance, and language on sound recordings and film. No matter how exploitative the system or how roughly rural people were jettisoned when machines and chemicals took their place, the rural culture bequeathed by the last generation of sharecroppers significantly reshaped U.S. culture. Lacking worldly goods and formal education, rural people improvised, broke the rules, experimented, and boldly stamped a southern imprint on music, dance, and language.

World War II job opportunities attracted many rural exiles to towns and cities. Government programs, mechanization, and herbicides continued to displace farmers throughout the 1950s and beyond. In 1940, 3 million farms existed in the South; thirty years later, only 1.2 million remained. The tenant ranks had been thinned from 1.5 million to 136,000 over the same years. The number of black farm operators declined from 680,000 to 90,000, and the number of black farm owners dropped from 142,000 to 56,000. At the bottom of the social scale, sharecroppers, who numbered 541,000 in 1940, were not even counted as a category after 1959, when their total sank to 121,000. This population shift had enormous implications, both for the southern countryside and for the towns and cities that absorbed the migrants.[2]

As southerners left rural areas, small-town businesses went broke, church congregations dwindled, and community vitality flickered and sometimes died. When migrants reached larger towns and cities, the more sedate residents often shuddered at their unpolished ways. They arrived in jalopies, quickly modified their homes and yards to suit rural tastes, and generally presented an untamed demeanor that elicited both loathing and guarded awe. It was the wildness of these migrants—their patched-up cars and clothes, passionate music, and lust for life—that would reshape U.S. culture. Both black and white migrants had to master not only hourly work but also urban segregation codes that were at once more lax and more confining than those in rural areas. In cities, blacks and whites competed for jobs, housing, recreation, and seats on public transportation, and the problem of the color line assumed pressing urgency. In rural areas, most folks knew each other and could make allowances, but in cities, segregation ruled all public spaces. Still, in the vastness of cities, as in rural areas, refuges existed where the color line blurred or vanished.

For many southerners, World War II was a great divide. The war challenged their provincialism, offered employment, and reshaped society. After the war, they could not fit their experiences or expectations back into the South of the 1930s. Many southerners, having traveled and tasted relative affluence during the war, became dissatisfied with the rural cycle of labor and debt that had previously characterized their lives; after the war, they stayed in cities and worked for a steady wage. Mississippi planter Cauley Cortwright labeled the war years a time of "dispersion" and recalled that black families who left for California, Chicago, New York, and Detroit "never returned after they moved out." Rural life also changed drastically, as segregation and challenges to rural values emerged as central issues among those who remained. The war also accelerated structural changes that had begun to take place during the 1930s. Despite labor shortages and rationed machinery, many farmers prospered during the war, and the wealthiest eagerly awaited further scientific and technological developments that would ease the demand for labor.[3]

In the South, then, the war hastened the development of a new agricultural structure, intensified urbanization, rejuvenated musical tastes, reshaped leisure, inspired union organizing, and launched a civil rights movement. The war, more than the New Deal, alleviated hard times for southerners, and during the war, the federal government, already enlarged to fight the depression, expanded and became ever more critical in reshaping southern life. The issue was not government intrusion—by 1940, commercial farmers, wage workers, and sharecroppers all took advantage of federal programs—but rather which group would benefit most.

The war accelerated rural consolidation and further entrenched the conservative forces that advocated management, science, and technology. A reconstruction era after the war would allow the application of science and technology to catch up to ideology. Larger farmers, in the meantime, feared that laborers would move before the structural change to mechanization could be completed, and landlords utilized their positions of community leadership and power to tighten labor control, combining vestiges of the dying system with elements of the new one. Despite higher commodity prices, farmers complained of rising labor costs and tried every stratagem to find cheap labor. One observer labeled the large farmers' labor obsession "a farm labor shortage hysteria." The need for labor varied according to commodity, season, and stage of mechanization.[4]

Planters pressured draft boards to exempt their best workers. In Coahoma County, Mississippi, the Agricultural Adjustment Administration (AAA) agent admitted that when a sharecropper left for defense work, the draft board would move him to the top of the list. In May 1943, McKinley Morganfield, better known as blues singer Muddy Waters, quit his job driving a tractor on the Stovall plantation near Clarksdale and moved to Chicago. His foreman, he remembered, "blew all to pieces" when he asked for a $.03 raise to $.25 an hour. Within a week of leaving, he received his draft notice.[5]

Military service instilled in some African Americans a determination to end discrimination. Amzie Moore was drafted in 1942 and served in Burma. Assigned to intelligence, he was ordered to tell African American soldiers that conditions in the United States would be better when they returned. He joined the National Association for the Advancement of Colored People (NAACP) while in the service and after the war returned to Cleveland, Mississippi, still in a fighting mood. He estimated that in Mississippi one black person was killed every week for nearly a year. He opened a gas station, beauty shop, and grocery store on highway 61 that became headquarters for civil rights efforts. Medgar Evers spent the war in France and England and then, despite his reservations, returned to Decatur, where he immediately began to encourage Mississippi's black veterans to register and vote. Aaron Henry came from a share-cropping family near Clarksdale, and he, too, cut his activist teeth in the military. These three black men would emerge in the 1950s as key civil rights leaders in Mississippi.[6]

During the war, southerners sensed that important changes were taking place that could alter their lives. They perceived a sharp break from the days of the depression and observed that the war was intensifying changes in society, especially regarding race relations. Indeed, race relations became the most visible element of conflict and change. By the summer of 1942, Bureau of Agricultural Economics field agents in the South uncovered different interpretations of the purpose of the war. Whites, investigator Edward Moe reported in August 1942, believed they were fighting to keep things "as they have been in America." They feared "a revolution" in race relations. Blacks, on the other hand, were reluctant to join the war effort unless their participation awakened "recognition of their equal rights, and being accorded those equal rights." Whereas whites muted their enthusiasm for the war because they feared social change, blacks withheld support because they insisted on social change as a reward for patriotism.[7]

During the war, friction along the color line exploded into six civilian riots, more than twenty military riots and mutinies, and between forty and seventy-five lynchings. Blacks challenged discrimination more openly, and whites countered ruthlessly. Fearing federal intrusion, southern political leaders berated the federal government, which had been increasingly involved in southern society since the beginning of the New Deal.[8]

But significant attempts were made during the war to confront segregation and racial discrimination. The Congress of Industrial Organizations (CIO) succeeded in uniting black and white workers, which alarmed white politicians and businesspeople. In Memphis, Tennessee, for example, aggressive leftist CIO organizers won bargaining rights at sixty work sites in and around the city. In Winston-Salem, North Carolina, the United Cannery, Agricultural, Packing, and Affiliated Workers of America–CIO supported a 1943 strike led by African American women at the R. J. Reynolds Tobacco Company that won bargaining rights a year later. The leftist-led unionization drive had political implications that made possible the election of an African American alderman in 1947. The power of such unions to challenge segregation and entrenched politicians alarmed the white elite. Although some labor leaders understood that the success of unions depended on uniting blacks and whites, many white workers jealously guarded their privileges and were uncomfortable in integrated meetings. Even as they benefited from defense jobs and government programs, many whites suspected that the federal government and labor unions were intrusive institutions that would ally with northern liberals to force changes in society.[9]

Discrimination came under attack from northerners who settled in the South and ignored traditions demeaning to blacks. They called blacks "Mr." and "Mrs.," paid higher wages, and supported equal rights. Northern white soldiers stationed at southern bases, bored by military routine, detested life in the South and seized on the race issue as a focus of protest. Northern black soldiers resented the South even more. "They come to fiercely hate Southern conditions," Moe reported. "They talk against discrimination on every occasion and encourage violence as a way out." In 1944, the Supreme Court struck down the white primary in *Smith v. Allwright*, giving blacks the opportunity to participate in the only meaningful ballot in one-party southern states. In South Carolina, John McCray immediately founded the Progressive Democratic Party and insisted that whites share political power. Southern whites had never been assaulted on so many fronts of the color line.[10]

Membership in the NAACP swelled on the rising tide of militancy. Ella J. Baker, a North Carolinian and Shaw University graduate whom the NAACP hired as a southern field secretary in 1940, played a major role in attracting new members. After leaving Shaw, Baker had spent more than a decade in Harlem. Living in New York had offered Baker the opportunity to explore her sense of style and develop her interest in politics and culture. She wrote for newspapers and served as national director of the Young Negroes' Cooperative League. On weekends, she strolled the Harlem streets dressed in stylish clothes, making small talk with anyone she encountered. Baker was not shy. For a time, she worked at the Schomburg Library, where, as she put it, she "began to learn some things." She searched out radical discussions. The Harlem Young Women's Christian Association attracted women such as Pauli Murray, Dorothy Height, Anna Arnold Hedgeman, and Baker, and the atmosphere crackled with curiosity and ideas.[11]

Baker seemed uninterested in either a permanent career or a confining marriage. Her ideology was toughened as she associated with New York radicals during the late 1920s and 1930s. Her energetic organizing throughout the South not only increased NAACP membership but also planted grassroots seeds that would grow during the next decade. From 1940 to 1946, she braved white hostility and black indifference, honing ideas and skills that would serve her well later on. For six months each year, she rode Jim Crow trains and busses, always insisting that if the law mandated that blacks be separate but equal, she expected equality. A small woman (she stood five feet, two inches tall), Baker used her commanding voice and fearless presence to cow insulting drivers and conductors. "I wasn't delicate," she later boasted.[12]

Ella Baker, 1940s. LC-USZ62-110575, *National Association for the Advancement of Colored People Papers, Prints and Photographs Division, Library of Congress, Washington, D.C.*

Baker understood the significance of both the vast migration provoked by the war and the friction along the color line as black and white workers competed for defense jobs, transportation, and housing. The NAACP's New York office tightly controlled its civil rights initiatives. Disappointed that the NAACP neglected the power of local chapters in fighting for equal rights and recognizing that NAACP head Walter White ignored her ideas, she resigned in 1946. But

Baker's impact on local chapters endured, and her popularity among southern NAACP members would serve her well when she returned to the South as a civil rights activist in the 1950s.[13]

Some southern whites were also active in challenging the color line. In 1925, twenty-eight-year-old Lillian Smith returned to northern Georgia after teaching music at a Methodist mission school in Huchow, China. She took over her family's Laurel Falls girls' camp and molded it to fit her own interests, particularly music, drama, dance, writing, painting, and sculpture. She hoped to guide the girls in her camp to understand, as she put it, "the dichotomies of our southern way of life." Sports and campfire songs gave way to frank discussions about sexual matters, childbirth, relations between girls and their parents, racial problems, and world events. Increasingly Smith devoted more time to writing and reading widely in psychology and literature. In 1935, Smith and her friend Paula Snelling began to publish what would become a series of radical journals over the next decade: *Pseudopodia*, *North Georgia Review*, and *South Today*. Contributors, encouraged by Smith, denounced segregation and dealt frankly with other controversial issues. In 1944, Smith published *Strange Fruit*, a disturbing and controversial novel about an interracial relationship. In her outspoken support of integration, she was far ahead of most southern whites.[14]

Both Ella Baker and Lillian Smith realized that the war created enormous stresses in southern society. Blacks and whites perceived a decline in morals, speculated about mechanization, fretted about returning veterans, condemned defense workers and cities in general, and feared that the nation would sink into a depression when the war ended. Many African Americans were confident that their war effort would erase the color line. Southerners sensed that their lives would be different following the war and were apprehensive about the future.

In Tishomingo County, Mississippi, located in the northeastern corner of the state, people left behind by the war complained that defense workers were throwing away money on liquor, sex, and gambling. A farm owner in his fifties learned that many workers had gotten by "with being half-drunk on the job" and were doing things that made "one's hair stand on end." He told of a neighbor's son who in his mid-twenties went to Mobile, Alabama, with his wife and two children to work in the defense industry. His wife had run off with another man, and he had been drunk ever since. "It's no wonder the Revival Preachers are all preaching against going to War Work and begging people to coax their relatives back before they all go to Hell," he observed. A middle-aged Farm Security Administration client charged that workers didn't behave "much better than hogs." There was universal agreement that the farther away people strayed from their roots, the less they could resist temptation.[15]

The concerns voiced in Tishomingo County found resonance in other areas.

Lillian Smith.
Hargrett Rare Book and Manuscript Library, University of Georgia, Athens.

A county agent in Pope County, Arkansas, summed up the conventional thinking about why people stayed in rural areas: "Not wanting to go among strangers & strange work & inside work & no fishing & visiting probably biggest reasons."[16] Although urban work was in some ways liberating, it enslaved laborers in an hourly routine and curtailed outdoor activity.

Some women remained at home and did farmwork (in Lafayette County, Mississippi, an interviewer found one woman "mowing lespedeza when I was there"), but an almost equal number of men and women left the countryside for urban jobs. Women's widespread migration, participation in the workforce, and spirit of independence challenged old stereotypes. Many of the women who found good jobs during the war were never again content to keep house. Women's work off the farm, like their on-farm egg and butter trade, supplemented income and opened up new opportunities.[17]

The war changed the status of women who remained at home in significant ways. Across the South, whites complained about the lack of both fieldworkers and domestic help. When the Clarksdale AAA agent heard in 1944 that cotton pickers would be demanding $2 per 100 pounds, he complained bitterly that many black women were loafing around town instead of working because they received money from their husbands in the service. They were no longer dependent on wage work such as chopping and picking cotton, ironing clothes, and doing housework. The interviewer asked whether it was not the case that more white women were loafing around than black. "Yes," he admitted, "but [you] can't do anything about that—many of them never picked cotton and you can't force white women to work." In January 1945, *Charleston News and Courier* editor William Watts Ball commiserated with his sister, Sarah B. Copeland of Laurens, South Carolina. "Everything is demoralized, the servant question here is certainly as bad as it is in Laurens," he reported. "Our cook comes, but not until 9:30 A.M."[18]

Just as farmers were eagerly buying machinery with their government payments and their earnings from higher commodity prices, those who returned from cities and the armed forces no longer tolerated what they considered backward farming practices and conditions. They had higher expectations. "We'll have to have electricity to get tenants—good tenants," the owner of a supply business in Harnett County, North Carolina, lamented. "They won't come otherwise; they want their electric refrigerator, radios, and washing machines and all that."[19] Mobility, then, acted as a school of consumer education, and for the first time, many southerners stepped up to sales counters with money in their pockets. Blacks and whites shared rising expectations.

Defense centers became great magnets that pulled in workers. The heavy influx of permanent residents into key southern defense areas strained services, for most southern cities were ill-equipped to handle even peacetime populations. Just as some farmers used federal programs and subsidies to restructure their operations, city governments looked to Washington to solve problems of urban growth brought on by migration. Southern cities expanded and improved their infrastructures using federal coordination and funds.[20]

Growing cities all faced similar problems. New housing required expansion of the water supply, sewage disposal, streets, and garbage collection. Workers expected public transportation to ferry them to work, shopping, and recreation. Children needed schools, working mothers sought child care, and everyone demanded adequate health care, which required new hospitals and additional doctors. Coordination was essential, especially in a war economy, to avoid shortages of food and fuel. These problems were further complicated by the fact that the working population moved from farm to town, from town to city, and from lower- to higher-paying jobs; had not been routinized to hourly work; and was divided by segregation laws.

Migrants confronted confusing urban problems, and they contributed to the chaos. Writer John Dos Passos keenly observed that city life and steady wages astonished migrants. Even a house trailer equipped with electric lights and running water, he pointed out, "is a dazzling luxury to a woman who's lived all her life in a cabin with half-inch chinks between the splintered boards of the floor."[21]

Whereas Dos Passos understood that even a house trailer meant upward mobility to rural migrants, *Washington Post* reporter Agnes E. Meyer, with obvious distaste and condescension, wrote that in the Gulf of Mexico region, "there is a type of war-worker from the country districts of Mississippi, Tennessee, Louisiana, and Alabama, the like of which I have never seen anywhere else." They were "illiterate" and had "transported to Pascagoula and Mobile their native habits of living." They preferred to live in the squalor of trailer parks and tents, she insisted, rather than moving into newly constructed apartments. Those from the mountains, she harshly judged, were the "most ferocious and unreliable of the lot." She was mortified by the story of a young man who "ran amuck after getting drunk, kicked holes in the walls, broke all the windows, and rammed his knife in the floor so hard that his hand slid down the blade, nearly severing the fingers." The next morning, he woke up in a girls' dormitory.[22]

Although in Meyer's opinion it would take time to "tame" such people and train them to work and live in harmony with their neighbors, most migrants adapted easily to urban life and eagerly developed their newly acquired skills. After taking a three-week welding course, Lena Porrier Legnon left a farm near New Iberia, Louisiana, and moved to New Orleans to join her husband at the Higgins shipyard. She boasted that "women were better than men welders. Neater welders." She rode the streetcar to work and at night danced and drank in the French Quarter. Unlike many women who worked at welding during the war and then gave it up, Legnon returned to rural Louisiana after the war and continued her trade into the 1980s. Cordell Jackson, who became a Memphis record producer after the war, worked during the war as a riveter at Fisher Aircraft in Fort Worth, Texas. Years later, she still took immense pride in the speed and precision of her wartime work. She also played stand-up bass in the Fisher Aircraft Band. Despite their skills, however, most blacks and women were kept at the bottom of the workforce.[23]

Southern cities found it easier to improve services that allowed them to function more efficiently than to solve other problems, especially racism. African American workers, particularly black women, endured discrimination at most job sites throughout the country. Southern segregation restrictions covered all aspects of public life. When blacks in Mobile violated the segregated-seating code on buses, police sometimes beat them and hauled them into court. In one instance, a black soldier from Brookley Field argued with a bus driver over segregated seating and the driver killed him. For black soldiers, the segregated buses were another battlefront, a manifestation of the "Double V" slogan

Lena Porrier Legnon (second from right) and friends at Marty Bourke's Bar, Bourbon Street, New Orleans, 1942. Courtesy Lena Porrier Legnon.

that reminded black Americans that they not only had overseas enemies but also had racist enemies at home. Many young African Americans fought a protracted war of attrition on buses as their misbehavior antagonized and sometimes provoked whites.[24]

Growing militancy from the NAACP and the National Urban League put pressure on southern city administrators to equalize separate black and white facilities. A 1944 Atlanta Urban League study revealed that although African Americans composed a third of the school-age population, only 20 percent of the school buildings were used for blacks; blacks received $37.80 per pupil, whereas whites got $108.70; public school property was valued at $887 per pupil for blacks and $2,156 for whites. African American students attended split shifts of three and a half hours, whereas white students received six hours of instruction a day. Similar discrimination existed in library facilities, health care, and other aspects of urban life. "The cost would be great," the *Atlanta Constitution* piously editorialized, "but Atlanta, searching its heart and conscience, can no longer hide the fact of this discrimination and cannot further support it."[25] By admitting discrimination and promising equal facilities, the *Constitution*'s editors perhaps heard the early legal footfalls that would challenge the separate-but-equal myth.

During the war, juvenile delinquency raised disturbing questions, especially when girls were involved. Reporter Agnes Meyer discovered in April 1943 that one of Mobile's "worst problems is the sex-delinquency of very young girls." The chief of police had arrested bold girls eleven years old who "pursue not only sailors and soldiers but war workers." Meyer learned that girls "are frequently the ones who buy contraceptives, and when one druggist refused to sell these articles to a group of very young girls, they informed him contemptuously that he was an old fogey." The Catholic bishop of Mobile, after observing that the problem of "sex offenses among minor girls is particularly shocking and grave," concluded, "We are fostering and encouraging a future race of gangsters and criminals." Such reports were not confined to the South, but given the region's obsession with the sanctity of white women, the trend portended major changes in the values of young women.[26]

Southern cities, then, grew during the war and were forced to confront the full spectrum of urban problems. The extent of the transformation, at least in defense centers and military posts, was staggering. In population growth, social relations, city planning, and, in particular, the use of federal funds to expand services, southern cities challenged rural areas for dominance. Before the war, these cities were dozing seaports or trade centers, but the war shook them awake. Faced with hundreds of thousands of new residents, cities at first buckled under the strain but with federal support built infrastructures that could sustain larger populations. This scenario was repeated in Mobile, Norfolk, Charleston, Brunswick, Pascagoula, and Beaumont, as well as in other cities less critical to the war effort. The demographic shift was significant, for people who had become accustomed to hourly wages, decent housing, better schools, adequate medical care, and other advantages of city living did not want to return to rural areas.[27] Urbanization and rural decline as well as the end of the white primary would eventually transform southern politics.

Returning veterans brought home the baggage of war, including shattered bodies, nightmarish memories, dreams of peace and prosperity, and, for most, an awareness that the world was more complex than they had ever imagined. The experiences of gays and lesbians provided them with both a sense of liberation and an awareness of their vulnerability. Although psychiatrists labeled gays and lesbians mentally ill and unfit for military service, many evaded military screening and some million served in the armed forces. Gay soldiers who had never been aware of the existence of a national gay and lesbian cohort discovered friendly bars and made fast friends. Army stage shows often featured cross-dressed men playing women's parts. During the war, most Americans either ignored or denied the presence of gays and lesbians in their midst, but in the fifties, homosexuality became a savage political issue.[28]

Harvey Goodwin performing at a defense rally at the Little Rock Auditorium, September 25, 1942. Harvey Goodwin Papers, Archives and Special Collections, University of Arkansas, Little Rock.

The fifteen years of depression and war sent tremors of change throughout the South, and by 1945, the region was unsteadily pondering its future. Blacks and whites were moving, some to southern cities newly updated to handle large populations, others to the north and west. Most would never return to farming. And the South would never return completely to its prewar customs. For better or worse, World War II reconfigured southern society.

The surface changes stood out in bold relief. The rural South withered, whereas urban areas blossomed. Machines and chemicals assumed iconic importance as agribusiness relied on capital more than labor. Migrating farmers took their rural ways with them and spread elements of southern culture across the country. The years were ripe with revolutionary possibilities.

But most southerners quietly adjusted to the status quo. A small band of white integrationists waited for an opportune sign, whereas liberals hung back, hoping for gradual miracles. Black southerners, weighing their options, impatiently waited and covertly organized for an assault on the color line.

2 Creation and Destruction

Side by side with the invention of machines that build and create have been machines that tear down and destroy.
—Lillian Smith

Whites who speak out for equality of opportunity, they are good citizens and heroes, but A NEGRO, when he speaks for equality of opportunity, or ending of segregation, he is impudent.
—James M. Hinton

The end of the war caught millions of southerners "among strangers." Stunned by depression, hardened in battle, and remolded for factories, many southerners were disoriented by the abrupt relocation from farm to factory, from civilian life to military life, and from war to peace. Away from their communities, they found the economically backward and segregated South indefensible; it was embarrassing to whites and contemptible to blacks. After the war, many chose to settle elsewhere and make a life outside the confines of segregation and sharecropping. Other southerners were halted in midstep, unsure whether to face the past or the future, agriculture or industry, segregation or integration, God or mammon.

But southerners could not return to the past, nor could most whites envision major changes in the social structure, so the struggle between segregation and integration and between rural and urban life would rage for decades, not months or years. Despite the war's lessons about intolerance, racism, and injustice, most white southerners still insisted on maintaining the color line to mark their privilege. Black ambitions collided with white intransigence. In the nine years between the end of World War II and the *Brown v. Board of Education* decision in 1954, black and white southerners negotiated the delicate issue of segregation. The awful legacy of Hitler's genocide, the collapse of colonial rule, and the lofty rhetoric of freedom and democracy could have opened political space for civil rights initiatives. For twenty years after World War II, however, southern white politicians defended segregation. No antisegregationist political faction rose to challenge the status quo. Whatever the mass of white southerners thought, they did not forsake segregation by word or deed.

Southerners, like other Americans, celebrated victory at the end of World War II, but the atomic fireball that vaporized Japanese civilians sent many Christians to their Bibles. Lillian Smith, whose 1944 novel *Strange Fruit* secured her literary reputation, commented on the larger implications of the atomic age. "Side by side with the invention of machines that build and create," she warned in 1946, "have been machines that tear down and destroy." People attempted to diminish the bomb's awesome image linguistically by labeling strong drinks, spicy candy, attractive women, and a host of products with names that playfully alluded to atomic power.[1]

After 1945, the shadow of the bomb provided a constant reminder of the possibility of annihilation. No matter how unlikely it was that an atomic bomb would be targeted at the rural or even urban South, southerners pondered prophesies of a wrathful God ending the world in flames. The bomb also underscored the fact that science and technology were significantly reshaping the world and that many southerners were out of step with modern times. Backward, segregated, and tied to one-crop agriculture, southerners were ambivalent about the future.

Postwar letters often contained references to the bomb that revealed that it was emblematic of postwar insecurity. Religious fundamentalists warned of increasing threats from cultural change, capitalists demonized unions, white southerners feared blacks' exercise of their voting rights, parents watched their teenage children escape from the living room thanks to the automobile, and some suspected that communism had infiltrated and undermined U.S. institutions. It was an article of faith among white southerners that black and white people lived happily in the South unless disturbed by outsiders. Pressures mounted from both inside and outside the South that should have forced whites to confront racial injustice.

Black voters presented a formidable challenge to white control. John H. McCray was an energetic crusader for equal rights and the vote for blacks in South Carolina. Born in Florida in 1910, McCray relocated with his family near Charleston when he was six years old. An excellent student, he graduated from Talladega College in 1935 and then worked as an agent for the African American–owned North Carolina Mutual Life Insurance Company until 1938. At that time, he moved to Columbia and started a newspaper, the *Lighthouse and Informer*. After *Smith v. Allwright* struck down the white primary in 1944, McCray founded the Progressive Democratic Party and pushed for black voter registration. McCray informed the head of South Carolina's Democratic Party that his organization would strive to end "the type of government our sons successfully fought against around the world." Jim Crow restrictions had prevented blacks from gaining "city employment beyond janitorial and garbage collecting capacities." McCray dejectedly concluded in March 1946, "So it is with the state of South Carolina."[2]

Barred from holding positions of responsibility in the white-dominated world, blacks had established a parallel society. Because white institutions customarily neglected the needs of African Americans, black institutions expanded to provide services. Many black funeral homes not only buried the deceased but also sold burial insurance and sponsored picnics and parades. Black churches became community centers that nurtured both body and soul. Since the founding of the National Negro Business League at the turn of the century, many black businessmen had carved out niches of prosperity and respectability, and they jealously guarded their segregated turf. Newspapers such as McCray's *Lighthouse and Informer*, insurance companies such as North Carolina Mutual, grocery stores, barber shops, restaurants, juke joints, funeral homes, and churches provided segregated havens free from white competition and white association. Segregation had benefits as well as staggering costs.[3]

Black Americans hoped that obtaining the vote would empower them to fight discrimination, just as being denied the vote at the turn of the century had stripped away such power. In the postwar South, African American voter registration rose dramatically, from some 200,000 in 1940 to 600,000 in 1946. Black voting, however, raised disturbing questions among white moderates who were grappling with the militant programs of the Southern Conference for Human Welfare (SCHW) and the Southern Negro Youth Congress and the interracial work of the Congress of Industrial Organizations (CIO). As historian Patricia Sullivan has observed, "A large segment of white southern moderates and old-line interracialists . . . met the heightened black consciousness and racial polarization of the war years by defending southern autonomy and the segregation system." She cites as examples a number of newspaper editors, among them Ralph McGill, Virginius Dabney, and John Templeton Graves.[4]

Junius Scales, a North Carolinian who joined the Communist Party in part because it was the only organization that advocated integration, analyzed the dilemma. "Those white liberals were mostly courageous, and they often took moral stances which expressed the true conscience of their time and place," he explained. But they lacked the will to confront the race issue. "What caused them to temporize and waver on issues involving Negro rights," Scales continued, "was the vested interest and depth, scope, and sheer virulence of the bigotry they opposed." Those who took a stand for integration were harassed, shunned, and sometimes subjected to violence.[5]

Left to right: *John H. McCray, Pete Ingram, J. C. Artemus, and James M. Hinton,*
April 25, 1948. John H. McCray Papers, South Caroliniana Library, University of
South Carolina, Columbia.

As most whites wavered, African Americans became increasingly impatient
and outspoken about segregation and white control over every aspect of their
public lives. Scales recalled the reaction of Bennett College president David
Jones in 1947 when Frank Porter Graham, the personification of North Carolina
liberalism, proposed the creation of a segregated University of North Carolina
School of Medicine. "I and my people would follow Dr. Graham to the ends of
the earth. We respect and love him," Jones began, "but, my *God!*" He asked
when white people would admit that segregation was criminal and destructive.
South Carolina National Association for the Advancement of Colored People
(NAACP) leader James M. Hinton complained in December 1947 to editor William Watts Ball about a *Charleston News and Courier* editorial charging that he
was impudent to suggest that blacks share the administration of Lander College, a black college in Greenwood, South Carolina. "Whites who speak out for
equality of opportunity, they are good citizens and heroes," Hinton chided,

"but A NEGRO, when he speaks for equality of opportunity, or ending of segregation, he is impudent." Hinton reminded Ball that $10 million had been budgeted for white state institutions of higher learning for the next fiscal year, whereas the state's only black school had been granted $800,000. Such discrimination would no longer be accepted, he insisted. Two months later, Ball confided to conservative journalist W. D. Workman Jr. that the *News and Courier* "has advised that the negro institutions be turned over to the exclusive management of the negroes." He claimed that the newspaper "is more than willing that the negroes have a chance to prove what they can do without interference with or control by white people."[6]

Although whites contested every attempt by blacks to gain political power, Mississippian Chalmers Archer Jr. argued that "whites badly wanted black people's acceptance." They sought assurance "that everything was fine with us." Black people might tell whites that they were content with segregation, but away from whites, they expressed their intense dissatisfaction. "They talked of escaping the maddening, smug assumption of white 'superiority,' and the transparent condescension of 'good' white folks who 'always loved black people,'" Archer explained.[7]

Segregation and its bitter fruits came under increasing attack as blacks secured their voting rights and challenged white control. White southerners often looked backward for inspiration—to what they regarded as their glory days. Over the years since the Civil War and Reconstruction, whites had created an elaborate mythology that not only glorified the Lost Cause but also defended the violent recapture of state and local governments and the implementation of legal segregation. White men had driven corrupt African Americans out of government, the story went, and made the South, and especially white women, safe from the depredations of black men. The story of the Lost Cause, Redemption in the 1870s, and the erection of the separate-but-equal barrier at the turn of the century had become chronologically and factually distorted. All versions came to the same conclusion: black men and white women should never occupy the same space on equal terms. White men, on the other hand, could share and dominate all spaces, including that occupied by black women. White men ruled both the boardroom and the bedroom.

Charles S. Reid, a prominent Woodbury, Georgia, businessman and short story writer, vividly recalled the end of Reconstruction in South Carolina as he pondered another assault on state powers. "It seems the Carpetbaggers again are in the saddle, or on the Bench," Reid complained to his friend William Watts Ball in July 1948. Reid was "just a kid" in 1876, "but the spectacle of the red-shirts . . . was quite indelibly impressed on my memory," he wrote. "A broad-brim hat, red flannel shirt, black trousers, the wearer mounted on a spirited

horse, all were rather impressive." Reid insisted that he did not hate blacks; he just did not want them to vote. "I am glad that we have the negro down here, with all his faults," Reid wrote in August, "rather than that great army of riffraff of imigrant [*sic*] crooks and scallawags [*sic*] they have in the north."[8] The heroic Red Shirts, according to Reid's narrative, drove out corrupt black politicians and their northern white accomplices and restored honest, and white, government. Denying African American citizens the vote, in his mind, was traditional rather than unconstitutional.

White southerners thus employed failed nineteenth-century political arguments in an atomic-age battle. They hoped that such rhetoric would disarm both southern liberals and northern civil rights advocates. But as the United States became more powerful, it hoped to impress and make allies of newly independent countries in Asia and Africa, and southern segregation tarnished America's image. Segregationists argued that diplomacy should play no part in determining state customs, nor did they concede that African Americans' patriotism had earned them equal rights. Instead, many equated President Harry S. Truman's civil rights agenda with that of the Radical Republicans during Reconstruction. Southern intransigence had worn down nineteenth-century reformers, and segregationists prepared for a twentieth-century reenactment.[9]

In the first years after the war, returning veterans, recently enfranchised blacks, and disenchanted whites united in support of reform. Several southern states, including Alabama, Louisiana, and North Carolina, elected liberal governors, and another group of liberal southerners went to Congress. In

May 1946, James Dombrowski, executive secretary of the Southern Conference Educational Fund (SCEF), confided to Eleanor Roosevelt that although recent elections "greatly encouraged" him, he detected a disturbing pattern. "The reactionaries have as their platform a negative stand—against the CIO-PAC (the reds) and rule by Negroes." A year later, he reported "a general retreat" from "the forward looking policies of the new deal." The postwar window that allowed southern politicians to transcend the race issue opened for only a moment. A counterattack based on anticommunism and racism either defeated or silenced politicians, clergymen, and editors who advocated tolerance. Henry A. Wallace's presidential campaign on the Progressive Party ticket in 1948 encountered violent southern opposition as adversaries associated him with communism and integration. The strong Dixiecrat showing in the election demonstrated once again the potential of racialized politics. By 1950, any candidate "tainted" with liberalism or integration stood little chance of election. Significantly, no southern political organization emerged to counter the Dixiecrats and their states' rights and segregationist followers. Politicians encouraged people to conflate communism, unions, and integration. Both politicians and businesspeople thrived on the demonization of communists and unions.[10]

Southern white discontent in 1948 initiated a protracted realignment that over twenty years would reconfigure national political alliances. Over time, Dixiecrats moved into the Republican Party, which in many ways came to resemble the segregationist-era conservative Democratic Party. Blacks, on the other hand, turned to the Democrats and abandoned the party of Abraham Lincoln. The 1948 Dixiecrat platform of states' rights, Mississippi political kingpin Walter Sillers admitted, "does not appeal to many of the voting class, and especially to a larger number in the South." On the other hand, "the racial issue, which certainly is very much alive and one of the most potent issues in the campaign, does appeal to them and arouses their interest and enlists their support." The Dixiecrats' dilemma, he added, came down to the fact that voters outside the South rejected the race issue and white southerners ignored states' rights. Segregationist leaders understood that if they could find a formula that mixed enough states' rights rhetoric with racial concerns, their message would appeal to a larger percentage of the white population. Sillers predicted a long struggle followed by eventual victory. "It may not come until more Negroes move north and bloody riots follow as a result thereof," he wrote in July 1948, "nevertheless, the victory will come and as a result of the movement started by Mississippi and now under way." Not even Sillers could foresee that the struggle for equal rights would still be going on half a century later. Truman's unexpected 1948 presidential victory was only a temporary setback for Dixiecrat ideology. Eventually

*States' rights rally, Birmingham, Alabama, July 17, 1948. Photo by W. D. Workman Jr.
W. D. Workman Jr. Papers, Modern Political Collections, South Caroliniana Library,
University of South Carolina, Columbia.*

segregationist politicians would solve their rhetorical dilemma by seizing on a
neosegregationist code that masked the old agenda.[11]

Whatever the inner thoughts of most whites were, only a small number
openly challenged states' rights and the color line. Three groups in particular
attacked segregation in the immediate postwar years. Leftist-led CIO locals
broke down segregation and demonstrated the power of a united workforce.
The SCHW allied with the CIO to end the poll tax and increase black and white
voter registration. The Highlander Folk School in Monteagle, Tennessee, abolished segregation in its labor-focused classes.[12]

These groups pushed an agenda that transcended the South's more tenuous
liberal tradition. Better race relations, an end to lynching, more job opportunities, and expanded voting rights, as Junius Scales pointed out, stopped short of
school integration or the equalization of social space. Representatives of the

more outspoken SCHW and SCEF met at the University of Virginia after the November 1948 election. This group, which included ten African Americans and a large percentage of women, signed a declaration demanding equal rights for all citizens and an end to segregation. The declaration called for equal access to all institutions, including schools and hospitals, equal pay for equal work, equal job training and employment opportunities, and equal access to housing and public transportation. New Dealer Aubrey Williams claimed that Truman's victory "changed the climate of the South. We must grasp this opportunity." The group visited Monticello, repeating Thomas Jefferson's words that "all men are created equal."[13]

Only a handful of southerners took such bold stands, and most blacks and whites publicly backed segregation regardless of their personal beliefs. Administrators at most southern white colleges and universities did not appear to share Jefferson's ideas of equality. Many used stalling tactics to discourage African Americans from applying to their schools. In February 1948, William H. Bell, a twenty-seven-year-old World War II veteran who was enrolled at the State Teachers College for Negroes in Montgomery, applied to Auburn University (at that time Alabama Polytechnic Institute). Registrar Charles W. Edwards informed Bell that the dean would be unable to advise him on admission until July. Edwards confided to a colleague that he suspected that the NAACP sought "to bring to a head an issue which has been developing now for eight or ten years." Bell later withdrew his application. The University of Alabama sent a form letter to African Americans who inquired about the possibility of applying to law school that was a masterpiece of deflection and mock candor. After reviewing separate-but-equal state laws, the letter concluded by warning the potential applicant that race relations would "suffer" if segregation ended. "The better elements of both races," it sermonized, "deplore anything that tends to retard or jeopardize the development of better relationships between the races."[14]

Occasional cracks appeared in the segregation wall. In January 1948, Donald Jones, an NAACP regional secretary, was "astonished to see three Negroes in the audience" at a Southern Methodist University chapel service, "Negroes who were students as I later learned." The dean of the School of Theology, Jones discovered, had made arrangements for the black students to attend the university "on the promise that no publicity would be given to it." Jones also learned from a student at Texas Tech College that defending segregation was no longer popular. "Now in our discussions," the student reported, "it is unpopular to defend segregation; and most often the defenders keep quiet entirely rather than have the majority of us jump down their throats."[15]

Across the South, white college students championed integration. From Durham, North Carolina, L. E. Austin, editor of the *Carolina Times*, informed

Walter Sillers. Walter Sillers Papers, Delta State University Archives, Cleveland, Miss.

the NAACP's Walter White in February 1947 that "a majority of the students at the University of North Carolina would welcome the admission of Negro students to that institution." Austin credited Frank Porter Graham, president of the University of North Carolina, for the university's "liberal spirit." He blamed continued support for segregation at nearby Duke University on "the type of reactionaries who have headed the school for the past quarter of a century or more." He urged White to push a test case.[16]

From Nashville, Fisk University professor Arna Bontemps reported in February 1948 that Christian students from black Fisk University and white Vanderbilt University met for fellowship on Friday nights and Sundays "on a basis of complete equality." Fisk professor E. A. Lanier used the Vanderbilt library and reported that students, professors, and staff "took his presence there without any strain to themselves whatever." One of Bontemps's informers speculated that "veterans with overseas experience are . . . a liberalizing influence" and also praised religious groups, the sociology department, and chancellor Harvie Branscomb. Vanderbilt's conservatism, Bontemps suggested, resided primarily in the board of trustees, "whose eyes are fixed rigidly on the past," and the faculty, which "stands in awe, if not in terror, of them." He expected no initiative from Vanderbilt supporting integration; instead, "I would expect ruthless opposition."[17]

Vanderbilt professor Donald Davidson, a renowned poet, author, and member of the agrarians, boasted of the institution's conservatism and actively fought to hold the color line. He also complained of changes that were sweeping Vanderbilt and other universities, including "the pressure of over-crowded classes, bureaucratic administrations, economic inflation, social confusion, uncertainty about the immediate future, vulgarization of education, etc., etc." To Davidson, such changes were creating a "mood of desperation." By 1947, half of the country's 2.5 million students were veterans, and Davidson likened the G.I. Bill of Rights, which funded veterans' tuition, to "a kind of death sentence or a disability-penalty" for faculty members. Classes that swelled from fifteen to forty-five students, he complained, "ended my own effectiveness as a teacher." Davidson detested Branscomb, who "quarreled bitterly with the History department about several matters," including "teaching too much Southern history." Branscomb then cut funding for the *Journal of Southern History*. In Davidson's opinion, Branscomb arrived on the job "with the purpose of cleaning out the 'reactionaries' and 'Neo-Confederates' at Vanderbilt." Branscomb was "achieving that by making things as unpleasant as possible for folks like [Frank] Owsley and me and by converting the university into an extension of the Duke-University-of-North-Carolina school of 'liberalism.'"[18]

Whereas Davidson defended segregation, many postwar liberals were well-intentioned toward African Americans but profoundly uninformed about black history and culture. Sarah Patton Boyle, like many white southerners, considered herself knowledgeable about her African American fellow southerners. In her autobiographical *The Desegregated Heart*, Boyle frankly recounted her tortured reeducation. Reared an Episcopalian among Virginia's first families, she had interpreted maids' and handymen's compliant demeanor and black people's deferential manners on the streets as proof of good relations between blacks and whites. Boyle married a University of Virginia professor and settled in Charlottesville. In 1950, Gregory Swanson, a twenty-six-year-old black man, entered the university's law school. Boyle assumed that her peers shared her goodwill toward Swanson and expected that Swanson would be elated to receive a welcoming letter from a faculty wife. After Boyle sent the letter, Swanson showed at best a cool reaction, and Boyle's friends shunned her. Ultimately, Boyle reeducated herself and fought a lonely battle for integration among the Charlottesville elite.[19]

As Boyle learned and relearned, the desire to keep black folk "in their place" and make their status appear ordained consumed whites. Segregation was based on assumptions and fears that for the most part evaded objective analysis. Interracial marriage between black men and white women, for example, persisted as a dreaded fantasy in the white mind. Wade F. Milam of Spartanburg, South Carolina, personified such thinking. He wanted blacks to be "treated fair, BUT," he emphasized, "we do not want [them] gradually working up to social equality." In Milam's estimation, social equality meant that "some low down white woman is allowed to find it rather respectable to marry a negro." Milam had heard rumors that tens of thousands of black men were headed south. "And into the mills they will go," he feared. Milam and many other white southerners assumed that if black men and white women occupied the same social space, intermarriage, or at least sexual relations, would result. Preventing that contact and what they saw as the ensuing "pollution" became a major preoccupation of many whites.[20]

By October 1948, when Milam voiced his fears about blacks entering the mills, the CIO's Operation Dixie had been undermined after a promising start. Begun in 1946, Operation Dixie, according to historian Michael Honey, sought to organize "the poorest and most neglected Southern workers, namely the tobacco and cotton-press workers of the Carolinas, West Tennessee, and Arkansas." Its initial success brought opposition, including a rival organizing drive by the American Federation of Labor and resistance from the business elite. Opponents employed racism and anticommunism as powerful rhetorical weapons. Birmingham steelworkers divided neatly between black NAACP workers and white Ku Klux Klan members. The Cold War intensified the effectiveness of anticommunism, which would become a staple political device. "You just could not do anything about the race relations," one union member admitted, "because that's the way the politicians got elected." In June 1947, Congress passed the Taft-Hartley Act, thwarting militant CIO organizers with a series of obstacles, including open-shop options and certification that leaders had never belonged to the Communist Party. More important, CIO leaders refused to use leftist organizers in Operation Dixie, undermined integrated locals, and broke off relations with the SCHW. Although the Highlander Folk School continued its integrated classes, few integrated locals remained. The interracial unionism that had flourished during the late 1930s and World War II had faded, as had the best hope for civil rights support among the southern working class. No other movement that would unite poor blacks and whites emerged.[21]

Many liberals assumed that the white working class blindly supported segregation and opposed unions. Lucy Randolph Mason, a legendary CIO organizer from Virginia's upper crust, understood that religious fundamentalists had a much more nuanced social and economic view. Like others who listened closely to the working class, Mason learned that economic self-interest existed side by side with religious faith and social custom. In April 1949, Mason cautioned a colleague who was drafting an article critical of some churches' anti-union message that many "evangelical (that is their choice of a word), holiness, and Church of God" congregations welcomed union organizers. Many CIO leaders, Mason observed, evidently expected white southerners to abandon God and Jim Crow when they considered their economic interests. "I know so many local churches in which the governing body and the minister are *of* the workers, rather than alien to them," Mason insisted, urging "some recognition of this side of the matter." Occasionally black and white workers joined ranks, but when they did, they usually faced hostility from both fellow workers and management.[22] The inability to understand the complexities of working-class white Christian segregationists hampered not only labor organizers but also civil rights activists. Fundamentalists seldom hid their misgivings about their black neighbors, but their religious faith and close association with blacks encouraged fair play. Unlike many middle-class whites, they often worked with blacks, sometimes lived near them, and knew them by name.

Mason understood that union organizing involved a great deal of civil rights work. She boasted to *Harper's* reporter Kent Ruth that "the CIO has done more to lift the economic status of the Negro and to increase understanding and good will between the two races than has any other institution, including the Church." The CIO taught black and white workers "that unless they stand together they are separately penalized." Management relied on prejudice "to arouse the fear of white workers."[23]

As the labor movement and white liberals became more conservative, African Americans increasingly spoke out and challenged white expectations. In June 1949, the Tuskegee Civic Association condemned the Alabama senate and house of representatives for calling on President Truman to rescind his civil rights agenda. Alabama legislators, the association charged, are "willing to sacrifice democracy in order to perpetuate segregation." It reprimanded the legislators for claiming that "the better thinking Negroes and whites concur in their utterances." The Tuskegee organization was "unequivocally opposed to segregation or anything that smacks of segregation or assigning the Negro to the position of a second class citizen." It called on Truman to stand firm on civil rights. "Any contrary position taken would in these times of mob violence be detrimental to the preservation of our democracy."[24]

Although white men controlled government appropriations, law enforcement, the local courts, and all county and state administrative offices, they made plans to deal with the grave threat of a possible U.S. Supreme Court ruling on school integration. By the early 1950s, white southerners suspected that the separate-but-equal shibboleth had frayed beyond repair. Even a cursory

Lucy Randolph Mason.
Rare Book, Manuscript,
and Special Collections
Library, Duke University,
Durham, N.C.

look at African American schools, housing, pay, and job opportunities revealed glaring inequities. Many white southerners also watched uneasily as school segregation cases that would be consolidated under the 1954 *Brown v. Board of Education* decision moved through the courts.[25] After weighing the odds, many whites surmised that the Supreme Court would end segregation. Still, on the off chance that the Court might simply upbraid them for providing inadequate schools instead of for having an outdated ideology, they hurriedly upgraded black schools.

As whites glanced over their shoulders at the federal courts, they also considered the implications of replacing black farmers with machines and chemicals. In Mississippi, the Delta Council, an organization that promoted agriculture and to some extent industry, discussed twin agendas. Although the Delta Council's 1952 report endorsed improving black schools "in principle," it suggested that this plan "should be studied more carefully." The Delta Council's Race Relations Committee reported "shifts in the Negro population to urban areas" over the past decade. Why should whites rush to build better black schools, the report asked, when "rural areas with a heavy concentration of Negroes at the present time may have few Negroes ten years from now"? Mechanical picking machines were already harvesting 14 percent of the Delta's cotton crop.[26] Capital was becoming more important than labor.

As the Delta Council coldly weighed the implications of the use of machines and chemicals, African Americans dealt as best they could with the reality of rural change. Chalmers Archer Jr. recalled the mean school buildings and lack of buses in Holmes County, Mississippi. Planters insisted that black children work in the fields. "Many of us remember how those pressures translated into tenant farmer evictions, food credit cutoffs, and peoples' relatives losing jobs in retaliation against those who simply sent their children to school." Archer resented the "hand-me-down history books from white public school children" that contained no mention of black people. He left the South, as the Delta Council predicted many blacks would, but not before earning an undergraduate degree at Tuskegee University and a Ph.D. at Auburn University. The Delta Council's concern for black schools was the result of the pending *Brown* decision, not a change of heart.[27]

As machines and chemicals pushed rural laborers off the land, the fight for equal rights accelerated. Planters would have been even more hostile to civil rights efforts if the demand for labor had not eased; nevertheless, their numerous references to the Reconstruction era contained the implied threat of violence. The migration of many African Americans from the South before and during the civil rights struggle weakened the political base that voting rights had created. The coincidence of an enclosure movement, fueled in part by federal intrusion through agricultural policy, and a civil rights movement, ignited by a Supreme Court decision and supported at least in theory by the federal government, scrambled federal, state, and local priorities. Southern white men, in control of politics and the economy, tried to dominate forces that might threaten their rule.

Whereas most southern whites numbly waited for a Supreme Court ruling on segregation, Myles Horton, head of the Highlander Folk School, in July 1953 began "a three year project for training labor, farm, church and other community leaders to assist in an orderly transition from a segregated to an unsegregated form of public education in the South." Four months later, he was in Atlanta when Governor Herman Talmadge gave a radio address pledging that Georgia would never have integrated schools. As Horton was traveling to a meeting, his taxi driver, who had supported Talmadge's speech enthusiastically, "tried to force a negro driver off a bridge." Horton understood that a great deal of effort would be required to change such people. A Highlander workshop a year later attracted African American teachers from Alabama, Georgia, and South Carolina, who "were full of ideas, plans and a great hope for the future of their children and their schools."[28]

The pending Court cases forced politicians into a neutral corner. During a radio interview in September 1953, Arkansas governor Francis Cherry refused to comment on the upcoming decision. Speaking as a former judge, he said the

Court should only look at the record. "That matter is under advisement by the Supreme Court of the United States; it doesn't *matter* what I think, or what anybody else thinks; we will abide by the decision of the Supreme Court because that's the law of the land."[29] Cherry's pronouncement left space for compliance once the decision arrived.

Tennessee governor Frank Clement stirred up many state residents in September 1953 when he announced over the radio that he expected that state schools, which had functioned "since the first flat boat brought early settlers into Tennessee," would "continue to operate and that we will continue to provide a free education for children of every race, creed or color." Letters poured in. Most came from middle-class whites. T. R. Montgomery of Memphis castigated the city's 200,000 blacks who "get almost free public housing and good loafing jobs and in some instances on relief rolls for great numbers of illegitimate children, and so on." Other whites repeated the familiar litany of complaints concerning lazy African Americans who relied on the federal government and black women who had children primarily to increase their welfare payments. Segregationists would later mask their racism behind charges of welfare abuse and illegitimacy statistics. School integration, Montgomery fully expected, would mean mixed marriages. "I do not want my great grand children to be kinky-haired bastards or yellowish high brown." Almost invariably, segregationists saw integration as pollution. Montgomery enclosed a copy of "The Kiss of Death," a pamphlet featuring a photograph of a black man kissing a white woman. "The Russians," the enclosure read, "regard every Negro in our midst as a weapon more deadly than the atomic bomb."[30]

Shocking stories, the equivalent of urban folk tales, circulated throughout the South and provided cautionary ammunition to segregationists. Some white women expressed repulsion at the prospect of mingling with blacks socially. "Our maker created them with black skin, kinky hair, flat nose and thick lips," Mrs. M. Lafayette Jones wrote to Governor Clement from Memphis. "We *cannot* have our children and our grand children, sit with them, mingle with them socially, and as they grow up probably marry a 'white negro' who, without *his knowledge* has enough negro blood in him to bring their first child *black,* as happened years ago, here in our town of Memphis."[31]

A ground swell of segregationist sentiment was directed toward Clement and other southern leaders. "Now, before so much of this happens," wrote Lella M. Galvoni from Nashville, "why don't you governors plan a *reservation* or *Negro Territory*? We had an *Indian Territory* you know!" F. K. Lashbrook wrote from Memphis that ending school segregation "would be the first step toward social contact and equality and from there on amalgamation and the downfall of our white, Anglo-Saxon civilization." Claiming to be "a profound student of history," Lashbrook reached back to antebellum defenses of slavery to justify segregation. Mrs. Martin C. Hunt of Knoxville suggested that both religion and the Constitution were being subverted. "Those urging the lowering of racial bars, under the guise of 'civil rights' & the 'Brotherhood of Man' (a communist slogan)," she determined, "have sadly misinterpreted our constitution." R. K. Pruitt wrote Clement from Dayton, Ohio, "I certainly trust that you will not fail the white people of Tennessee." Pruitt was hoping to move back to Tennessee in three years with his daughter, "and I sure don't want no negro boys sitting next to her."[32]

From Chattanooga, Kate Steel clearly articulated the fear of pollution. African Americans, she informed Clement, "come from homes where disease and vermin abound and baths are not taken too frequently." She also suspected that "the moral atmosphere of most negro homes is not good and the children from these homes can ruin white children by close contact." Communists, she believed, were behind integration and had convinced leaders that integration "was the democratic thing, the brotherhood thing, the *just* thing to do." To Steel, the situation was desperate. "I am ready to secede and fight the Civil War all over again," she threatened.[33]

As the time neared for the Supreme Court to decide the *Brown* case, liberal groups attempted to take positive action. The Ford Foundation had sponsored a study of black education by forty scholars headed by *Arkansas Gazette* editor Harry Ashmore. In August 1953, Greenville, Mississippi, newspaper editor Hodding Carter attended a meeting in New York to discuss when the report should be released. The group, Carter reported, "doesn't know whether to release the material until after the decision." In the end, *The Negro and the Schools*, an indictment of separate-but-equal education, appeared one day before the *Brown* decision was announced.[34]

By the spring of 1954, segregationists, with their imperfect understanding of the past and their emotional abhorrence of racial mixing, hoped that the Court would preserve separation. Blacks knew their history all too well and were emotionally primed to march into the future with equal rights. Within these segregated communities, many whites and blacks were prepared to work together to reconfigure southern society, and they expected enlightened leaders to take them to the Promised Land.

The civil rights movement paralleled a demographic shift of momentous significance, a variation of the biblical Exodus. Millions of southerners continued to leave the land of slavery and sharecropping and spread southern culture throughout the country. Although mobility did not resolve segregation, when rural and urban cultures collided, they generated energy that would transform urban life, leisure, and musical tastes.

3 Deprived and Mistreated

Why do big men like you sit around and study up something to hurt
a poor mule farmer?
—Mrs. J. O. Lawson

I am forty six years of age and all the Record that I Know of them havin
is to make the Rich Richer and the poor poorer.
—W. N. Andrews

Georgia novelist Harry Crews trenchantly recalled that the Springfield section of Jacksonville, Florida, "was where all of us from Bacon County went, when we had to go, when our people and our place could no longer sustain us." His rural neighbors considered the move to Jacksonville inevitable, and once there, he explained, "they loved it and hated it at the same time, loved it because it was hope, hated it because it was not home." They resented living "forever cheek to jowl." In the country, houses were far apart and the smell of trees and crops wafted over the land, but "the odor of combustion" choked Jacksonville. "They felt like animals in a pen," Crews wrote. "It was, they said, no way for a man to live."[1]

Crews's family joined the 11 million rural southerners who in the twenty years after World War II packed their worldly belongings and set out on a new life. A rural childhood shaped Crews, hardening him mentally and physically for the world outside Bacon County. His writing talent blossomed, in part because he left Bacon County and in part because he never abandoned rural values.

A vast network of federal, state, and local agricultural bureaucrats watched with pleasure as exiled farmers emptied into the country's Springfield sections. According to the U.S. Department of Agriculture (USDA) blueprint, the departure of marginal farmers would hasten the day when large farmers could expand, consolidate, and thrive using machines and chemicals. Federal policies became the legal basis for agribusiness, part of a new grid that, along with science and technology, would supersede labor-intensive agriculture.

The revolutionary structural changes that transformed the rural South began with New Deal agricultural policies that favored landowners. In the spring of 1933, millions of southern farmers started the season under the old system—sharecroppers and tenants bickering with landlords and every family planting all it could tend in the hopes of offsetting low prices. The Agricultural Adjustment Act, passed in May, caught farmers in the fields tending growing crops. For the remainder of the year, they witnessed the birth of a confusing and discomforting federal system that promised immediate reimbursement for plowing up portions of their cotton crop and higher prices for all commodities that autumn. The next year, the Agricultural Adjustment Administration (AAA) froze cropland by allotting acreage to landowners based on past production. Using a complicated formula based on supply and demand, the AAA licensed these landowners to plant a prescribed number of acres each year but denied allotments to tenants, sharecroppers, and wage hands. As farming evolved into agribusiness, the power to allot acreage became a crucial factor in farm survival. Local elites throughout the South quickly mastered and manipulated federal rules. By the fall of 1934, landlords had appropriated government payments; evicted unneeded sharecroppers and tenants; changed the status of others to wage laborers, denying them any claim on federal payments; and dominated local AAA committees. When disgruntled farmers failed to gain relief from county AAA committees, they complained to the USDA headquarters in Washington.[2]

Agricultural institutions also embraced the federal program. Land-grant universities, the federal Extension Service, farm journal editors, farm organizations, and county agricultural committees worked well with their servant, the USDA. Secretary of Agriculture Henry A. Wallace viewed agriculture through his experience as an Iowa farmer, farm journal editor, and advocate of science and technology. The AAA, if successful, would replicate Iowa-type farms across the land.[3]

Over time, both government agricultural programs and allotments became commodities that possessed inherent financial value. Since their introduction in 1933 as an emergency device to reduce surplus commodities, allotments evolved, in the words of one legal scholar, "into a new variety of transferable wealth." In all commodity programs, except for rice, the allotment was assigned to a farm and its owner. Rice allotments went to farmers who produced rice regardless of tenure. As allotments transformed from a temporary recovery device into a commodity, they grew in value. By the 1960s, for example, a tobacco farm gained $7,000 for each acre of tobacco allotment. Cotton and rice enhancements ran from $500 to $1,000 per acre. The original 1933 awards thus generated wealth for farm owners and their descendants, acting as "economic grandfather clauses," in the words of attorney David Westfall. Westfall observed that the largest landowners "received the lion's share of benefits." Eventually other USDA programs became commodified. Complex laws and farmers' leveraged position led large operators to offer "crops to be grown, growing crops, and/or harvested crops" as collateral, in effect creating a more expansive version of the crop-lien system.[4]

Throughout the 1940s and 1950s, the AAA and its acronymic successors, the Production and Marketing Administration and the Agricultural Stabilization and Conservation (ASC) committees, drastically cut allotments to raise prices and reduce the surplus. With their cropland frozen, farmers gradually intensified their inputs, expanding the use of fertilizer, irrigation, and chemicals. By 1975, cotton farmers produced an average of 453 pounds per acre, three times as much as in 1930. Other crops had comparable increases in yield.[5]

As one USDA office prescribed acreage cuts, other divisions explored how to increase production. This apparent contradiction was based on the belief that farmers could maximize their production per acre by using better seeds, herbicides, insecticides, and machinery. They were encouraged to idle their least productive land and intensify production on their best acres. By prompting well-capitalized farmers to take advantage of science and technology, the USDA supported programs that reduced production as well as programs that increased production.

Agribusiness ripened in the collusive atmosphere of government subsidies administered by local elites, land-grant university research, and corporate drumming. By the middle of the twentieth century, capital-intensive agriculture had largely reconfigured the southern countryside. Science, technology, and government agricultural policies administered by a corpulent and obfuscating bureaucracy destroyed the labor-intensive rural order born of Reconstruction. Only large farmers could afford tractors, combines, picking machines, and chemicals.

Through a powerful but almost invisible agricultural network that stretched from Washington to the thousands of county and local agricultural committees throughout the country, the bureaucracy sanctioned the ideology and strength of the white elite. Federal regulations empowered county committees to rule on crop allotments and labor disputes, and since these decisions were not published, they could be made with impunity. This system strengthened the white elite and obscured overt discrimination in bureaucratic vagueness. The USDA gained enormous power during the New Deal years, and it flexed its muscles by erecting a system that favored more educated and affluent farmers who invested in science and technology. County AAA committees were conduits for emerging agribusiness. The secretary of agriculture appointed state AAA committees, and in the South, the Extension Service dominated every level of AAA operations, often controlling the nomination and election of county and local AAA committees. Farm implement manufacturers and chemical companies were allies with the agricultural bureaucracy in transforming southern agriculture.[6]

Long-standing federal programs such as the Extension Service and experiment stations merged with the New Deal's mammoth AAA and other rural programs to federalize U.S. agriculture. Following the blueprint drawn by midwestern agricultural experts, the USDA envisioned a rural America of businesslike, mechanized, and efficient farms. USDA policies revealed an eagerness to please larger farmers and those who sold to them and a corresponding ill-disguised contempt for small-scale farmers. Such sentiment should not be surprising given the harmonious resonance between the racial and class biases of the southern white elite and those of USDA bureaucrats. The South's primarily labor-intensive, tenant-worked, and, by most measures, backward farms were out of step with the government plan. By pressing the federal mold on the South, the USDA squeezed out millions of tenants and sharecroppers, not because they were poor farmers but because they had no resources to fight a plan that damned them.[7]

Those who lived through this transformation saw it take place in increments—sharecroppers disappearing, neighbors selling out, crossroads stores closing, mule lots emptying, tractors tilling the land, Stearman crop dusters spreading the stench of chemicals, and church congregations dwindling. A way of life slowly faded away. To bureaucrats and their more refined constituents, most southern farmers were not a culture or even a resource but obstacles to the new order. Recognition of the richness of southern rural culture did not come until after sharecropping was safely doomed. The USDA portrayed sharecroppers, tenants, and wage hands as depraved victims of a primitive culture that would mercifully be eliminated by science and technology.

Although some farmers were more successful than others, most paid close attention to horticulture. They knew when to plant, weed, cultivate, and harvest. They studied the weather, insects, animals, and plants and exchanged their observations at country stores or on their front porches. They told stories, played music, traded work, helped neighbors through hard times, and worshiped. Most boasted that they worked hard, and many complained that landlords cheated them. What they lacked in formal education they made up for in knowledge about the seasons, animals, and plants. Some farmers could recall every crop year since they began farming and recite the weather, crop acreage, and prices. Such wisdom did not register on USDA scales.[8]

Rural people emerged from World War II deeply suspicious of what the future might bring. Many expected the depression to resume; some had hoarded money as a protection against hard times. To their amazement, good times con-

James Stringer prepares the soil on this Mobile County, Alabama, farm for planting cotton, April 1941. Photo by Forsythe. 16-N-1530, box 145, National Archives and Records Administration.

tinued, unleashing a pent-up demand for consumer goods. Women insisted on having "cooking utensils, dishes, linoleum, chairs, beds, and other basic items of furniture." Rural people sought electricity, running water, telephones, and paved roads. Installing red and brown "composition brick siding" became the most popular way to touch up unpainted tenant houses. Nearly all farmers dreamed of having a farm truck or pickup. The rural South was putting on a new face, or at least applying makeup to the old one.[9]

Cosmetics only covered the surface of the problems. Neither farmers nor bureaucrats acknowledged the human implications of the newly developed mechanical cotton harvester, self-propelled combine, and synthetic chemicals. The pace of mechanization and chemical use varied wildly across the South and depended on commodity, farm size, labor supply, and farmers' acceptance. The Delta and Pine Land Company (D&PLC), Mississippi's largest plantation, attempted to balance labor needs with machine purchases. By 1947, the English-owned plantation operated five mechanical cotton pickers (with ten more on

Field hands, Knowlton plantation, Perthshire, Mississippi, early twentieth century.
Boyd-Walters-Bobo Family Papers, Delta State University Archives, Cleveland, Miss.

order) and used tractor-pulled four-row planters, four-row cultivators, and two-
and four-row flame cultivators, which killed weeds with fire. Several hundred
mules remained on the plantation to supplement the machines. Management
took advantage of government programs, especially the commodity program
that allowed them to receive nonrecourse loans for storing cotton. "After paying
the loan and all accrued charges," according to the 1948 annual report, "we realized a net equity of $6,536.99." In 1955, the D&PLC placed 11,773 bales valued at
$1,974,356 under loan, more than any other plantation in the country.[10]

The old plantation system coexisted with the new, but increasingly landlords
substituted machines and chemicals for tenants and sharecroppers. In 1950, the
D&PLC's Early C. Ewing Jr. prophesied that "with the combination of breeding,
ginning technology, engineering, and cultural practices (especially weed control) the crop will soon be fully mechanized." By 1952, machines harvested
14 percent of the Mississippi Delta's cotton crop. As mechanical pickers became
more dependable and efficient and as herbicides cleared the fields of weeds, the
amount of labor needed for cotton production declined drastically. Mississippi
lost over 376,000 farmers in the 1950s.[11]

Agricultural policy had a significant racial dimension. Whites apportioned
paltry funding and inferior facilities to African Americans and then sneered at
their poverty. After Congress established segregated land-grant schools for
African Americans in 1890, it referred to them as "1890 schools" to mark them

as black. The disparity in funding between black and white land-grant schools mirrored separate-and-unequal educational funding throughout the South. In 1950, Alabama Polytechnic Institute (Auburn University) received $2,387,361 from federal, state, and local sources, whereas Alabama Agricultural and Mechanical College, the African American land-grant school, received $84,417. Such discriminatory funding typified all southern land-grant schools. Experiment station research funding was granted almost exclusively to whites. When blacks attended a field demonstration at the Auburn experiment station in 1950, the white agent warned them to bring their lunches. "We do not have facilities for handling negro farmers."[12]

The Extension Service, the logical agency to educate the rural population, largely ignored poor farmers and those who were likely to leave agriculture. It concentrated on selling the new system to those who had the capital to invest. Poor black and white farmers seemed unlikely targets. Black Extension agents, always subalterns, received less pay and fewer benefits. In Alabama, white agents earned an average annual salary of $5,331, whereas African Americans received $2,872, a disparity that held throughout the South. Home demonstration agents received lower pay overall, white women getting $3,864 and black women $2,805. The 4-H Club sponsored agricultural projects for school-age children, but the 46,000 black 4-H Club members were separated from the 330,000 white members. Blacks were excluded from the national 4-H camp held each year in Washington, the national 4-H Congress in Chicago, and the International Youth Exchange. No African American had ever won a national 4-H scholarship.[13]

Whereas the African American Extension program remained a small, isolated colony under white supervision, the white Extension program, experiment stations, farm organizations, state representatives, and county agents shared common interests and goals. State Extension leader P. O. Davis at Auburn University ghostwrote speeches for Alabamian Edward O'Neal, president of the American Farm Bureau Federation. When O'Neal inquired about his cotton allotment in April 1950, Davis quickly instructed the county agent in Florence to contact O'Neal "and help him to work out his problem." After returning from a meeting of the Cotton Council in Memphis in February 1950, O'Neal exclaimed, "What a wonderful organization they have! They treated me like a king. I saw so many of my old friends over there."[14]

The administration of farm policy was largely a man's world. Black and white women did demonstration work, but they were relegated to an auxiliary. In January 1950, Davis asked women demonstration agents for suggestions about how to improve the Extension Service. "Perhaps you could mention both the masculine *and* feminine members of your family in each letter," one woman commented, repeating the family metaphor that pervaded Extension Service

Cotton pickers, Delta and Pine Land Company plantation, Bolivar County, Mississippi, October 1941. Photo by Harmon. 16-AAA-7842-W, box 116, National Archives and Records Administration.

activities. Men, ever the patriarchs, controlled federal and state programs and farm organizations. When an Alabama farm woman criticized home demonstration presentations that featured the Farm Bureau agenda, her remarks were dismissed as the work of male Farmers' Union leaders. Since the woman only had a junior high school education, the home demonstration agent judged that she could not have written the reply herself.[15]

By 1950, mechanization, chemical applications, and federal acreage reductions were decimating the rural South. During the Great Depression and World War II, most rural exiles had been landless, but in the 1950s, 67,000 African American and 413,000 white landowning families abandoned the countryside, complaining bitterly as they watched their rural dreams dissipate. They damned the USDA bureaucracy, which in their minds had become cold, impersonal, and rule-bound. Calculations, allotments, and regulations—not hard work—determined whether farmers succeeded or failed. Unless a farmer served on a county committee, was high up in the Farm Bureau hierarchy, or

Mechanical cotton picker in Arkansas, 1947.
Photo by Hunton. 16-s-14965, box 116, National Archives and Records Administration.

had large holdings, he or she was simply at the mercy of a formula. The New Deal had created both a coldly inefficient bureaucracy and a rural structure that favored the elite, and agricultural policy subsidized the gleaming machines and synthetic chemicals that epitomized agribusiness.[16]

The election of Dwight David Eisenhower as president in 1952 and his appointment of Ezra Taft Benson as secretary of agriculture accelerated the spread of capital-intensive agriculture in the South. Benson agreed with the emerging agribusiness mentality that was destined to doom small and inefficient farmers. At first, Benson insisted on weaning farmers from federal programs and throwing them on the mercy of the market. Commodity price supports were set too high, he complained, and he advocated flexible supports that would lower prices for overproduced commodities. But during Benson's eight years as secretary, federal policies—not the market—pampered large farmers and destroyed millions of small farmers.

Benson's speeches and autobiographies, in their promotion of free enter-

Twenty-two mechanical cotton pickers ready to leave International Harvester's Memphis works in the biggest "drive-away" in the plant's history, December 1954. The machines paraded through Memphis with a police escort en route to Kennett, Missouri, where they were delivered to customers. Mississippi Valley Collection, University of Memphis Libraries.

prise, free association of clichés, blindness to African Americans, disregard for small farmers, and loathing of southern congressmen, suggest that he was a man not only poisoned against the South but also vastly ignorant of it. A devout Mormon, he insisted on prayers in cabinet meetings, and his family proudly entertained without offering coffee, tea, alcohol, or tobacco or playing cards. His rigidity was legendary, as was his inability to hold his tongue instead of making embarrassing statements. Benson, along with USDA bureaucrats and the Farm Bureau, envisioned a rural bourgeoisie that lived in neat houses, farmed with the latest machines, and purchased clothes, furniture, and appliances just like

Secretary of Agriculture Ezra Taft Benson (left) and Senator Alexander Wiley,
Wisconsin, drink cartons of milk from a vending machine located in the U.S.
Department of Agriculture in celebration of National June Dairy Month, 1958.
16-N-27086, box 40, National Archives and Records Administration.

urban folks. In the 1950s, however, few rural southerners, especially tenants and sharecroppers, could aspire to such a life-style.[17]

Benson quickly learned that although many farmers condemned federal farm programs, his free-market speeches hit a sensitive nerve. An Alabama banker warned President Eisenhower that Benson's policies would punish small farmers who relied on federal supports to survive. "My directors are frightened by what they hear from your Mr. Benson," he wrote in February 1953. They remembered farm failures and unrest during the depression.[18]

M. G. Mann, general manager of the North Carolina Cotton Growers' Co-operative Association, resented Benson's insinuations that farmers begged Washington for help. "You never hear the Secretary of Labor talking about labor representatives running to Washington for help," he fretted. "I do not recall that I have ever read where the Secretary of Commerce has referred to representatives of industry running to Washington for help." Farmers, just like laborers and businesspeople, relied on federal programs, Mann reasoned. Mann shared his misgivings about Benson with his congressman, Harold D. Cooley. "Just wait until I get Mr. Benson before the House Committee on Agriculture and 'watch the feathers fly,'" Cooley replied. "Unlike you, I have been unable to understand Mr. Benson from the very beginning."[19]

By late July 1953, Benson realized that his speeches had not been universally well received. "Many of our friends feel that we have talked enough about self-sufficiency and freedom," he cautioned Assistant Secretary Donald Paarlberg, "and that now is a good time to shift emphasis to safeguarding the farmers' interest and making farm programs effective in bringing the support and help which farmers need today and in the future." Benson had learned that although reliance on the free market sounded practical, it threatened programs that benefited large farmers, many of them Republicans. Although such farmers championed small government in principle, they depended on USDA policies to disperse acreage, stabilize prices, provide credit, and inform them of the latest advances in science and technology. Benson urged Paarlberg to keep this in mind for future speeches.[20]

It probably took Benson only a few months to fathom that what politicians said about farm programs bore little resemblance to the actual system. What had begun as an emergency New Deal program had metamorphosed into a vast system that subsidized farmers, bureaucrats, processors, experiment stations, and agricultural schools. The USDA had become an unwieldy bureaucracy that cultivated a wide band of support by dispensing favors to contradictory interests.[21] It suckled a mixed brood. The powerful, of course, pushed the runts aside.

Benson especially outraged southern cotton farmers. A short crop in 1950 resulted in a wartime embargo on cotton exports, but increased production the next year contributed to a huge Korean War surplus. In the fall of 1953, Benson drastically cut some 5 million acres from the national cotton allotment in an effort to control the surplus. When allotments were abandoned during the war, western cotton growers increased production and insisted that new allotment formulas include more western acreage. Mississippi congressman Jamie Whitten pushed for a quick secretarial decision to increase the national cotton allotment in part to ease year-end tenant contracting but also to outflank western politicians. Benson claimed that he lacked the authority to make such a decision.[22]

The conflict between labor-intensive farmers in the East and capital-intensive ranchers in the West reached a crisis in 1953. Cotton cultivation had been moving west since before World War II, and western Texas, Arizona, New Mexico, and California were well suited to growing irrigated cotton. Using chemicals, machinery, and irrigation, western farms produced high yields with a lower cost of production than labor-intensive farms in the East. Texas was a microcosm of these changes. In the eastern part of the state, farmers tilled cotton on small unmechanized farms, whereas larger capital-intensive ranches flourished in the western areas. In 1954 and 1955, the Texas ASC committee awarded 10 percent more acreage to expanding western producers. In 1956, the committee set aside 255,063 acres for small farms in eastern Texas. Four western growers, expecting annual increases, filed suit claiming that the 1956 state reserve had been allocated unfairly. A federal court ruled that the state committee's decision was final. Judge John R. Brown, ruling on another acreage case in the U.S. Court of Appeals, reasoned that the intrastate squabble had "much of the character of earlier cattle-sheep disputes of the Western range."[23] The allocation issue involved the future as well as the present. It centered on whether small farmers or highly capitalized operations would produce cotton.

Southern farmers complained about allotments to county agricultural committees and review committees. Hearings were not open to the public, and committees purged their files after five years. The magnitude of complaints suggests that farmers were extremely agitated. In 1954, some 6,000 review proceedings were held on the county level, and a year later, about 14,000 were held. Southern farmers bitterly protested their small 1954 allotments. "I have never heard as much complaint from cotton producers as at this time as a result of the individual farm acreage allotments," an observer reported from Georgia in December 1953. A revised allotment calculation that considered both historical farm acreage and the total land under cultivation led to drastic reductions for some farmers; the allotment for one farmer dropped from 230 acres to 80.[24]

Four Louisiana farmers expressed frustration with their acreage cuts. Alex Noflin, an African American, owned a 150-acre farm in West Feliciana Parish. He and four tenants were to share an 8-acre cotton allotment. "That," Noflin observed, "will be exactly 1.6 acres for each of us." Salvadore Miletello, who farmed near Maringouin, complained that his allotment had been reduced from 40 acres to 13. Ted C. Jackson, a farmer from Bains, was allotted 16.5 acres, less than half his previous allotment of 44.8 acres. "How these Cotton Allotments are figured is beyond my understanding and comprehension," Jackson admitted. His four black tenant families, who had twenty-eight children, were to share the proceeds of 16 acres. After his 31-acre allotment was cut to 18, Bunkie farmer Harry Himel stated that he doubted he could cover his machinery notes. "I have 17 head of people to feed on top of that," he added. A complaint from Arkansas farmer R. G. Lamb about his reduced allotments elicited the standard bureaucratic response. "We are fully aware of the problems with which some cotton farmers in some areas as well as many cotton farmers in other areas may be confronted in making the severe adjustments in cotton acreage that will be necessary under the present law," a USDA assistant secretary wrote.[25] Such a letter brought small comfort, nor was it intended to. USDA planners were well aware that their policies would force many southern farmers off the land.

Farmers who could exploit the contradictions of the USDA's ever-changing policies—the Korean War embargo, the absence of acreage controls for two years, and then the abrupt reinstatement of controls in 1954 and 1955—prospered. Farmers voted for acreage allotments in 1955, Mississippi politician Walter Sillers observed, but "every one who had the means to employ them, immediately set about through mechanical equipment, fertilizers, insecticides and irrigation, to increase the production on their reduced acreage to where the smaller acreage produced as many or more bales than was grown by them the previous year." Sillers labeled the federal government's failing efforts to dispose of the surplus "stupid blunders."[26]

Shrinking cotton, tobacco, and rice allotments threatened farmers who needed a minimum acreage to make planting worthwhile. Farmers often found fault with the county committees that distributed allotments or with county agents who apparently controlled the committees. Kentucky tobacco farmer James N. Cundiff judged that the Adair County agent had been replaced by "a much bigger crook." The county committee, he added, favored certain farmers, and the situation was "so rotten it stinks." Carl L. Burton became so disgusted with the county office that he quit farming and found a job in Louisville, 100 miles from his home.[27]

Many southern farmers suspected that county committees played favorites when allotting acreage. In 1954, J. True Hayes, a Dillon, South Carolina, farmer, complained to Ezra Taft Benson that the county ASC committee was corrupt. He requested access to ASC records to compare the tobacco acreage allotted to committee members, office staff, their relatives, and politicians to the acreage allotted to "the rest of us, who have no political pull or other unfair means of getting extra acreage." The USDA replied that allotment records were available but that harvested acreage, recorded on the same card, was not public information. "To put the two items of information together and then to classify them as confidential," Hayes complained, "is nothing more than a method of hiding and protecting the unfairness that has been practiced in the past." No one would trust the system, Hayes warned, until allotment information became public. Hayes finally won access to the records, but the results of his investigation are unknown.[28]

Farmers often faced unresponsive, condescending, and inept bureaucrats. In 1954, Mrs. Clyde V. Collier explained to the head of the Rogersville, Tennessee, ASC office that the office's incorrect reporting had canceled her 0.7 acre tobacco allotment. She dutifully produced her 1948 production records proving the ASC office's mistake. "He said there was nothing that he could do about it," she protested. "So I left with the thing not settled." After several more visits to the Rogersville office, she appealed to Benson, who referred her to the state ASC office in Nashville.[29]

To check on compliance, the USDA measured farmers' planted acreage. Even farmers who attempted to comply with allotments sometimes felt harassed. The local ASC committee told one Tennessee tobacco farmer in 1957 that he had overplanted by .02 acre. He protested and paid $6.00 for a remeasurement, which revealed a .01 acre overplant. The farmer then paid $4.00 to have the Loudon County ASC committee destroy the overage. Senator Estes Kefauver charged that this was not an isolated incident, implying that the measurement and destruction of tobacco had become a thriving local industry.[30]

Rice farmers also battled local committees over allotments, and in Arkansas, a county review committee received a rare reprimand for showing favoritism. In June 1955, the ASC forced the Jackson County review committee to reopen fourteen rice cases. The landlords in question had made fraudulent calculations to increase their allotments. The review committee originally overruled the county ASC committee, but the state ASC later overruled the review committee. The administrator ruled that the fourteen landlords were "placed at a distinct advantage" and recalculated their acreage.[31] It was rare for elite farmers to break ranks and expose fraud or favoritism.

As in cotton and tobacco farming, shrinking allotments strangled rice farmers and forced them to abandon farming. In Craighead County, Arkansas, according to the testimony of B. D. White, 326 rice farms had existed in 1954, but a year later, only 234 remained. "A big percentage of those farmers quit and folded up," White testified, "and moved their families north in order to obtain work in the factories." He insisted that his 80-acre allotment was the minimum acreage a rice farmer needed. White had put in two $5,000 wells and owned $30,000 worth of rolling equipment, including two tractors, a combine, and a grain buggy. White's capital investments supported his 350 acres of rice land, so the smaller his allotment, the more dire his economic predicament.[32]

Many farmers concluded that USDA bureaucrats both in Washington and locally had lost touch with rural conditions. In 1955, Elizabeth May described the conditions around Farmville, North Carolina, and urged Benson to visit and see "the pain on men's faces" for himself. They could not even afford a Bible, she complained. May also asked Benson to "reevaluate your idea that small farms are not economical and should therefore be abolished." Pauline Lowry painted a drab picture of "suffering" and "weeping" farmers near Kirkland, Tennessee. "The farming industry is fast falling to pieces," she observed. "We fear our land will soon lay untilled."[33]

At times, USDA inflexibility seemed capricious and spiteful. In 1957, Congressman Basil L. Whitener of North Carolina explained to the USDA's Marvin L. McLain that western North Carolina farmers customarily "raised a small amount of dark, heavy tobacco for their personal use." Since this tobacco never reached the market, Whitener thought it should be exempted from allotments. The USDA refused to budge, arguing that "the only practical way of handling it is to measure all tobacco on the farm and charge it against the allotment."[34] Such punitive regulations demonstrated the bureaucratic compulsion to control even the most innocent local custom.

Farmers also used imaginative, sometimes illegal, means to increase their allotments. On October 2, 1953, J. W. Paul, a Beaufort County, North Carolina, tobacco farmer, bought a relative's adjoining farm along with its tobacco allotment. Paul informed the ASC office of the purchase and asked that the allotment be transferred to his farm. The next day, Paul "reconveyed" the farm minus the tobacco allotment to his relative. For three years, Paul planted tobacco based on the combined allotments, but in January 1957, the county USDA office discovered the fraud. It assessed a penalty of $5,866.05, which Paul paid. In 1960, he filed suit for a refund, however, charging that "the penalty was the result of a retroactive act." Paul lost his case, not because of his argument but because he had not appealed first to the county review committee. "A dissatisfied farmer who has not exhausted the review board remedy cannot reach the courts," the judge held.[35]

During the early New Deal years when federal intrusion was new, people expressed hope that government programs would aid them. By the 1950s, however, bitter farmers condemned the very programs they had previously seen as their salvation. Mrs. J. O. Lawson from Covington, Georgia, had dreamed of owning a farm and achieving security in her old age. But in 1953, her husband had "taken a public job" and they had left the farm. "We have nothing after twenty eight years of married life and working hard to raise eight children the right American descent [sic] way to live," she complained to Benson. "Why do big men like you sit around and study up something to hurt a poor mule farmer?" Henry J. Smith began his letter, "I am not a farmer, just a soil slave." The Woodland, Mississippi, farmer owned some 45 acres, but, he charged, only the big farmers received favorable treatment. "If I'm not wrong the way I see the one gallus soil tiller, if there isn't something done for him in the near future, there soon won't be any of us left on the farms."[36]

Many southern farmers scorned policies that favored large operators. "The big, rich are getting bigger and the poor, little farmer is getting smaller," El Campo, Texas, farmer Norman L. Hicks declared in 1955. W. N. Andrews from Fort Payne, Alabama, agreed. "You stick with wealthy farmers," he complained to Benson in 1956. "You have bin in there three years," he wrote, "and you havent done one thang for little farmers." Many of his neighbors had left farming, he added. "I am forty six years of age and all the Record that I Know of them havin is to make the Rich Richer and the poor poorer." All around him, bankers, merchants, lawyers, doctors, and politicians were farming for a tax loss. After calling on Benson to resign, Andrews wrote, "I am sorry for you and may God Have mercy on you and forgive you." He signed the letter, "one of the many Deprived and mistreated farmers."[37]

Mrs. Leigh Kelly of Fort Smith, Arkansas, complained in 1953 that Benson visited only prosperous states. "Arkansas is a poor relation," she explained. The small farmers who raised chickens and cattle and grew fruit "can not compete with the doctor, lawyers, oil men etc. who are running model farms to take a loss on their income taxes. It is a case of the 'amateurs are putting the professionals out of business.'" M. E. Cousins Jr. from Enfield, North Carolina, also faulted those he called "fun farmers" who intentionally lost money to lighten their tax burdens. Real farmers, Cousins explained, worked "long hours and often work their wives and little children from daylight until dark"; "they live in tumbled down leaky houses, wear ragged and dirty clothes buy almost all the used cars and are not able to educate their children and often are not able to provide the bare necessities of life and have to be helped by their government."[38]

In February 1954, Texas farmer Gene R. Andrew argued that to make allotments equitable, the USDA should base them on a graduated scale like the income tax. The allotments of large farmers would be cut by a higher percentage than those of small farmers. If the administration wanted to help farmers, Andrew continued, it should "prevent the rich city doctors, lawyers, etc. who already 'have it made' from buying and farming from their office thousands of acres of the real farmers' land and creating the actual surplus that exists." Andrew requested that such farm owners be "sent back to the original occupations and farm production be given back to the farmer."[39]

The USDA promoted self-serving slogans that tied agricultural research to attempts to feed a starving world but seldom mentioned that the country grew more crops than it could sell or even give away and was paying enormous sums for storage. Few people questioned why rural women, historically self-sufficient, needed instruction in basic household duties or why 4-H Clubs continued to boost agriculture despite the dwindling opportunities for young people on farms.

W. O. Vaughn, a Murray, Kentucky, farmer, warned Benson that encouraging farmers to increase production per acre while at the same time reducing their allotments "reminds me of the FAT LADY who wanted to reduce, yet she stuffed with SWEET FOODS, STARCHY FOODS AND FAT FOODS, and could not understand why she was getting fatter." Vaughn saw farmers around him selling out to doctors, dentists, and businesspeople who were not farmers. They, in turn, took advantage of the Soil Bank and other programs that drove "many poor people out of homes." Vaughn, who boasted that he was a small farmer with no debts, insisted that farming should be left to farmers.[40]

In a neat five-page handwritten letter, Mrs. Aron Sanders, an Arkansas farmer, scolded Benson in January 1956 for ignoring small farmers. She was tired "of being slapped in the face with 'inefficient-marginal-socialistic-communistic' if we raise our voice for honesty and justice." The media, she complained, portrayed the small farmer as "a beggar and a leach" who "*sits* and waits for a big government check." Farm wives, the story went, increased the butter surplus by churning butter twenty-four hours a day. But the big milk companies created the butter surplus, not farm wives, she argued. Small farmers could not hire experts to "juggle our finances around and dodge income tax on the big farming scale." When the controversial Democrat-backed Brannan Plan was being debated, she remembered, "each and every one of you screamed socialism, communism." With great prescience, she predicted that the pending Soil Bank program was "only another plan to put more money in the big farmers pocket then ruin the rest of us."[41]

When acreage cuts and flexible price supports failed to control production, in 1956 Congress passed the two-tiered Soil Bank program. The Acreage Reserve paid farmers for cutting back on basic crops and for leaving the land idle. The Conservation Reserve compensated farmers for withdrawing cultivated acreage from production over a longer period.[42] Southern farmers eagerly, even greedily, signed up; indeed, the Soil Bank unleashed a wildcat fever in southern rural areas. In essence, it opened another cash window for those who controlled cropland. It demonstrated that idle land could be as valuable a commodity as cultivated land.

The Soil Bank, like earlier programs, tempted landlords to dismiss tenants, remove land from production, and pocket government money. A South Carolina farmer complained that local landowners, much like those twenty years earlier who had appropriated AAA payments, were forcing tenants off the land so they could place all of their cotton allotment in the Soil Bank. "To my mind," he wrote, "there is nothing more reprehensible." Assistant USDA Secretary Marvin L. McLain replied, as had USDA officials twenty years earlier, that tenant rights were safeguarded because it was "the responsibility of the county committees to determine whether or not the participation in the Program by a producer has or will result in a reduction of the number of tenants or sharecroppers on the farm." In effect, the rules gave local committees a free hand. The comfortable collusion between Washington and county committees stamped the federal imprimatur on local discrimination and outright illegalities.[43]

Texan Hollis W. Walton charged that the Nacogdoches County ASC committee knowingly allowed landlords to displace tenants. "I know of cases where colored people have been run off the place and then his land was put in the soil bank," Walton reported to Senator Lyndon Johnson. "Now, Mr. Senator, just because a man is colored shouldn't have any effect on his eligibility for what is lawfully his." When Walton's father was displaced, the ASC committee told him "he wasn't supposed to know" why his landlord made the decision. The elder Walton appealed his case to the state committee, but it backed the county committee. His father's appeal was exceptional, Hollis Walton explained. "Most of these farmers, upon receiving a communication from the ASC office they don't like will throw it down, give the office a good cursing, and go back to ploughing and forget it." To some extent, the USDA bureaucracy relied on such belligerent indifference in executing its policies.[44]

Tenants who rented land outright often manipulated the Soil Bank. Linda Flowers, who grew up in eastern North Carolina and became an English professor, recalled the story of a farmer who rented "every available acre a big landowner had for twenty-five hundred dollars, and the 'very next damn day,' as my father tells the story, put it in the Soil Bank for six thousand dollars, thus clearing a bundle without so much as cranking his tractor—and there was nothing illegal about it." In a similar case, an Alabama widow complained that her tenant placed rented land in the Soil Bank at "considerable profit" and even rented out the houses on the land. Since the Soil Bank was a "voluntary program," the USDA replied, no regulations restricted "the making of private arrangements between landlords and tenants."[45]

The sharp decrease in production caused by the Soil Bank created a ripple effect throughout the Cotton South. Cotton gins faced an autumn with less business, seed crushers at oil mills cut back accordingly, and implement dealers, store owners, and fertilizer suppliers all lost business. Unemployed workers at gins, oil mills, and other businesses joined farmers as migrants. W. G. Buie III, who owned a general store and gin, summed up the cycle. Benson's Soil Bank, he suggested, "has wasted millions of dollars and has accomplished nothing other than putting a lot of people out of work and slowing the pace of business and prosperity." He noted declining sales in fertilizer, automobiles, farm machinery, appliances, and furniture.[46]

When registration for the Soil Bank program began in February 1957, the program attracted such overwhelming support that counties often ran out of funds before all interested farmers could sign up. A. W. Todd, Alabama's commissioner of agriculture, painted a bleak picture of what farming had come to. Todd likened the plight of those who still waited in line after some 20,000 farmers signed up to the "indignities suffered by people on direct government relief." They stood in line for hours, Todd complained, "and when they finally reach the office, there is no money available." He had toured ten counties, he continued, "and it looked like the re-establishing of the 1931 soup lines."[47] The long lines, however, suggested that Alabama farmers were anxious to receive federal money for idling both their land and themselves. Something for nothing beat nothing for something.

At a time when the cry of free enterprise resonated throughout the land, the Soil Bank overtly paid farmers to take land out of production and loaf. If some farmers saw a contradiction between ideology and action, they bravely overcame it. Owners listened to federal Extension agents' advice about increasing production, signed up for the Soil Bank, invested in machines and chemicals, and intensely cultivated their planted acreage. Landlords or even tenants who could juggle federal programs prospered.

In 1958, farmers again flocked to USDA offices to sign up for the Soil Bank, and again the first-come, first-served policy and shortage of funds angered many farmers. Claude O. Vardaman, chairman of the Republican State Executive Committee of Alabama, observed that 37,000 farmers had signed up for the Soil Bank and 25,513 "were given numbers of their standing in line and told to come back later to sign up." George Hoback did not make the cut; the funds were exhausted before he reached the office. He chided Benson that the program reminded him of a farmer who had eight children but only enough food for four. The first to the table got all the food. In his opinion, "the hole thing should be thrown in the river." Some farmers who had placed their land in the Soil Bank the year before had sold their machinery, evidently intent on making a career of inactivity. When they were unable to enroll in 1958, they could no longer farm. A Texas farmer noted the injustice that one farmer could put all his acreage in the Soil Bank whereas another might not qualify "because he did not attempt to outrun his neighbor to the office."[48]

In March 1958, Mrs. A. A. Luckenbach succinctly explained her interpretation of farm policy to Senator Lyndon Johnson. "Everyone knows that the Soil Bank bill as presently written is meaningless for the small farmer as contrasted to the benefits derived by the large corporation type operation." The Eisenhower administration, she reminded Johnson, had favored "converting the farming in our country to that type."[49]

By the late 1950s, farmers who manipulated government programs were living better than ever. "The condition of the farmer during this period has grown from rags to riches," judged C. P. Quincy in March 1958. He had for forty years run a general merchandise store in Hertford, North Carolina. Farmers owned tractors, combines, and trucks, he remarked, but "they are never satisfied. . . . Their hands are outstretched for a give me." The USDA was a "laughing stock for millions of farmers because of the hand outs they receive with out efforts on their part." Farmers worked less than ever, he observed. "Our farmers have become such sportsmen that there is not enough fishing piers on the North Carolina coast to accommodate the farmers that visit them daily."[50]

Just as the Soil Bank tempted many farmers to idle their land, the storage of surplus commodities became big business and tempted farmers who had storage space. Fortunes were made, and when temptation was too great, reputations were lost to scandal. Storage costs for agricultural commodities grew from $73.2 million in 1952 to $408.6 million in 1958.[51] Even as the surplus increased, however, the federal Extension Service encouraged farmers to intensify production by adopting the use of machines and chemicals.

By 1959, many southern farmers suspected that something was drastically wrong with federal agricultural policy. All around them they saw both prosperity and failure, hard work and idleness. In May 1959, seventy-one-year-old E. Spech, a Frenchman's Bend, Arkansas, farmer, combined observation, analysis, and nostalgia as he summed up a quarter century of federal agricultural policy. The trouble had started when Franklin Roosevelt's New Deal created "a helpless inconsiderate spoiled set of farmers," he began. "They ruined us when they commenced paying us parity and subsidy. The fault is now we can't move without a handout." In earlier times, Spech recalled, farmers worked from sunup to sundown "and went home and found their wives with supper ready— clean clothes—bath water." Times had changed. Farmers' wives "are in society with a $4000 car running up and down the hiways," he complained. The children ran wild when their parents were away from home. Each morning the men headed for "some local restaurant for a cup of coffee while their wives sleep till noon." Spech complained that women attended the Home Economics Club to discuss "cooking and don't know how to boil water." He admitted that there were "a few good people left but they are like mound builders. They are passing."[52]

Farmers came to harbor a deep distrust of government bureaucracy even though they relied on it to survive. J. P. Kimbrell of West Point, Tennessee, condemned "those parasites who sit in easy chairs with their feet propped high on a $500 desk while they pour out jaw-breaking words about what they are going to do for the downtrodden farmer." The local bureaucracy had grown, he complained, and "occupies a fair sized building and is staffed by an army of so-called experts." Government interference with agriculture, he observed, "has always ended in catastrophe."[53]

In July 1959, Lubbock, Texas, farmer Grady West blasted bureaucrats, "swivel chair experts who never cured a ham, canned a vegetable, fed pigs, gathered eggs, milked cows, who think a 'cattle guard' is a man with a gun"; congressmen, "whose only exercise of judgment is back home in selecting flowery promises of things they know will never materialize"; and the farm program, "which has destroyed the very thing it proposed to save, which forced more than fifty million people off their land (just like the Indians were treated)." Shrinking allotments, he charged, had driven off farmers and denied veterans a chance to obtain farms.[54]

If Benson believed that his policies were returning farmers to reliance on the market, he was deluding himself. The market was not interested in the vast glut of commodities that U.S. farmers produced. Farmers eagerly took Soil Bank money and idled their land or explored several tiers of exchange. Enterprising tenants paid landlords rent, received federal payments from the Soil Bank, but never worked the land. Some landlords took federal money that they should have shared with tenants. Significantly, most of the money that changed hands came from the federal government. Agricultural policy constantly changed and upset farmers' calculations and planning. Programs became more complex and favored educated and well-capitalized farmers. A Texas oil mill manager complained in 1961 that farm programs had been around for thirty years, but "they are still as unstable and as unpredictable as they were at the beginning. Every year there is a change."[55]

African Americans struggled against not only machines and chemicals but also southern whites who encouraged them to migrate. After the *Brown v. Board of Education* decision in 1954, most whites hardened their hearts against their black neighbors, especially those who insisted on testing the color line. African American farm families in the South declined from 551,469 in 1950 to 267,008 in 1959. Over a million southern farm operators left the land in the 1950s. The small towns that dotted the South registered the loss in declining sales, empty sidewalks, and vacant rural houses. From the beginning of World War II to the end of the 1950s, half of the South's farm families left the land.[56]

The machines and chemicals that came along behind the refugees failed to usher in universal prosperity or peace of mind. The USDA deified science and technology and offered machines and chemicals as the South's salvation. Agribusiness swallowed up the South and created a farming system that bore a fateful resemblance to Henry A. Wallace's Iowa blueprint. Millions of fleeing southern farmers glanced back over their shoulders as they left the land, confused and bitter at their loss. A Springfield section waited for them, as it had for Harry Crews and his Bacon County neighbors.

4 A Rogue Bureaucracy

Pesticides are as vital to the efficient production of crops and livestock as aircraft or telephones are for modern transportation and communications.
— W. L. Popham

A dedicated bureaucrat anywhere is interested in nothing but the promotion of the goals of his bureaucracy, and he will without the slightest hesitation lie, cheat, or steal, or do anything else, to accomplish his bureaucratic goals.
— J. Lloyd Abbot

After World War II, machines revolutionized agricultural production throughout the South. The tractor, combine, and mechanical cotton harvester were icons, long-dreamed-of engines of change that by the 1950s allowed employers to substitute capital for labor. Mechanization in the cultivation of some crops had progressed far when synthetic pesticides offered the final alchemy. The USDA bureaucracy, which policed allotments and administered federal policy, shared with land-grant university agricultural engineers and planners a vision of an antiseptic countryside purged of weeds and insects as well as what it considered backward farmers. These scientists and administrators believed that nature, even human nature, was flawed. Nature simply was not good enough, and advertisements promised weedless and insect-free lawns and fields. Science and technology, championed by corporations and nurtured by state and federal subsidies, marched through the cotton, tobacco, rice, and sugar fields, acting as powerful agents of capitalism charged with increasing production and driving out inefficiency.[1]

With tractors breaking the land and cultivating crops, herbicides replacing the spring and summer work of most field hands, and mechanical cotton-picking machines supplanting human pickers during the autumn harvest, the labor-intensive seasonal work of men, women, children, and mules in the cotton culture gradually ended. Machines and chemicals displaced farmworkers, who took their understanding of husbandry with them.

Those who remained in the rural South lived in a mist of pesticides that infused the countryside. U.S. Department of Agriculture (USDA) bureaucrats, singularly eager to embrace chemical solutions to insect and weed pests and hide their unhealthy consequences, concealed findings of excessive chemical residues in milk and meat. Single-minded, ambitious, and eager to curry favor with anyone higher up in the USDA organizational hierarchy, in Congress, or among chemical company boosters, the Agricultural Research Service (ARS) leadership shamelessly and sometimes unethically promoted pesticides. Earlier scientific research on biological control fell away. If USDA bureaucrats were unwavering, even punitive, in enforcing the minutiae of crop allotments, ARS scientists worshiped pesticides as a plague-ending god with the fervor of the newly converted.

After agricultural chemicals helped push farmworkers off the land, they invaded the bodies of those who remained as well as, through residues, those who left. The haste to use synthetic chemicals left inadequate time for research into long-term effects. By the mid-1950s, chemical residues, like nuclear fallout, were inescapable. Rural southerners previously had endured dangers from agricultural applications of Paris green, arsenic, lead, and other chemicals, but synthetic chemicals worked more insidiously. Government residue research and guidelines addressed only the acute effects of such pesticides. The short-term effects of chlorinated hydrocarbons such as DDT seemed benign, at least to humans, but the long-term effects would emerge in time. Indeed, scientists are still debating the question.[2]

Primitive guidelines for setting residue limits in meat, milk, and other foods provided assurance that if used properly, synthetic chemicals posed no threat to humans, but the USDA never made public its discovery of widespread illegal levels of residue in milk and meat. During a decade gripped by fears of Soviet subversion, the USDA cloaked chemicals in benign verbiage and brazenly claimed that the very survival of the country depended on the use of pesticides.[3]

Synthetic chemicals seemed far superior to Paris green, a paint pigment that had been used as a pesticide since the Civil War; lead arsenate, which had been developed in the 1890s; and nicotine, pyrethrum, derris, lime sulfur, and bordeaux mixture, which had emerged before World War I. The USDA recommended the use of calcium arsenate to kill boll weevils in 1916 and added sulfur dust and nicotine in the 1920s. The fight against agricultural pests benefited from intense research during World War I aimed at developing countermeasures to chemical warfare, which ultimately killed some 90,000 people. Following the war, the Chemical Warfare Service and the USDA's Bureau of Entomology further blurred the boundaries between human and insect research. Making insects its new enemy, the Chemical Warfare Service continued to conduct research based on the understanding that lethal insecticides were potentially harmful to humans.[4]

The aerial application of chemicals also emerged from warfare. In 1922, the Army Air Service, in part to utilize surplus airplanes, joined forces with the Bureau of Entomology and developed aerial techniques for spraying cotton to kill boll weevils. By 1925, Huff, Daland & Company biplanes, designed specifically for aerial chemical application, had sprayed 90,000 acres in Louisiana, Arkansas, and Mississippi. Three years later, C. E. Woolman bought Huff, Daland's dusting service, which became the Delta Air Service and later, shorn of its spraying operation, Delta Air Lines. Meanwhile, the USDA continued its research on agricultural chemicals, including nicotine sulfate and calcium cyanamide. The chief of the Chemical Warfare Service suggested in 1924 that his agency coordinate efforts with the Army Air Service to spray the countryside for boll weevils, mosquitoes, flies, and grasshoppers. His ambitions unmasked the symbiotic agenda of research on poisons lethal to people and research on poisons that targeted insects.[5]

Chemicals posed risks not only to the pilots and ground crews who handled them but also to the crops and animals near target fields. By the mid-1920s, the government had established limits on the amount of chemical residue allowed in some foods, but occasionally chemicals struck more directly. At dawn on August 15, 1937, for example, Arkansas farmer Stedman Dodson observed an airplane applying arsenic to a neighbor's cotton crop. He "saw something white" settle on his pasture, and later in the day "one of his mules got sick and one of his cows was down." Both died. When Dodson's neighbor returned home that night, she found two sick cows in her pasture. Another neighbor reported that the pilot "never did shut off" the spray and doused the entire neighborhood.[6]

Southern farmers respected the dangerous poisons they used, although few took the proper precautions. Since most farmers could not afford to hire a crop duster, they applied chemicals with hand-cranked sprayers or more sophisticated mechanical contraptions. Those who were careful wore bandannas over their noses. The presence of chemicals posed dangers even to the most cautious, however. Novelist Harry Crews recalled a harrowing incident that occurred in the 1930s. As an infant, Crews put some lye in his mouth. When his mother saw that he was bleeding from the mouth, she shouted to his father, who stopped his tobacco spraying to rush him to the hospital. "When they got back home," Crews wrote, "the yearling cows were dead, lying already stiff by the barrel of lead poisoning." His father stoically resumed spraying and after dark buried the tainted cows. "He was afraid to butcher them because of the poison."[7]

Synthetic chemicals promised an end to such risks. During World War II, scientists made important discoveries of synthetic chemical formulations that, in various concentrations, could be turned against human or insect enemies. DDT (dichloro-diphenyl-trichloroethane), a chlorinated hydrocarbon that at-

Field hands dust cotton with calcium arsenate using hand-operated dusters, Tallulah, Louisiana, about 1935. 16-G-264-1430-F, box 264, National Archives and Records Administration.

tacked the nervous system of insects, was first synthesized in 1874. It emerged after the war as a miracle chemical that promised relief from the threat of typhus and malaria. Scientists synthesized other chlorinated hydrocarbon compounds, including aldrin, benzene, chlordane, endrin, heptachlor, and toxaphene. Captured German scientific records revealed research on organophosphates that led to the development of such chemicals as parathion, chlorthion, Diazinon, phosdrin, and TEPP. The fight against foreign enemies quickly became syntactically linked with the struggle against insects and weeds. After the war, the metaphors of extermination were easily applied to the civilian battle against such pests.[8]

The herbicide 2,4-D (2,4-dichlorophenoxyacetic acid) also emerged from wartime laboratories. Although 2,4-D originated as a plant stimulant, scientists discovered that increased doses caused plants literally to grow themselves to death. In 1945, after the end of wartime secrecy permitted publication of scientific studies of 2,4-D, the American Chemical Paint Company successfully applied for a patent and marketed the herbicide as Weedone and Weedust.[9]

With no long-term experiences to draw on and no indication of acute effects, people accepted the conventional wisdom that synthetic chemicals were safe for humans. Meager testing of the health effects of DDT and 2,4-D did not prevent both miracle chemicals from being rushed into production. Preliminary testing during World War II had raised enough health questions that the military regarded DDT use as a war measure. But as the war was ending, DDT became available to the general public on August 1, 1945, and in October, the USDA informed farmers that it presented no danger to humans. Assistant USDA Secretary Charles F. Brannan claimed that "a great deal of experimental work has been done" on DDT and that "it is safe to recommend the use of certain types of DDT insecticides for the control of certain insect pests." The first postwar *Yearbook of Agriculture*, which appeared in 1947, contained a number of articles that recommended the use of synthetic chemicals, especially DDT, to kill insects.[10]

The public seized on the promise of a pest-free environment. Fog banks of DDT hung over small towns and cities, killing mosquitoes, bees, and other insects indiscriminately. People armed themselves with hand sprayers to combat flies and other household pests. Farmers doused their homes, barns, livestock, and crops. Herbicides promised not only weed-free fields but also perfect lawns. Advertisements encouraged homeowners and farmers to declare war on weeds and insects. Despite DDT's lethal impact on insects, most people accepted assurances that it was benign to humans. Chalmers Archer Jr., who grew up on the edge of the Mississippi Delta, recalled that in the late 1940s and early 1950s, white health department workers would enter African Americans' homes and "spray every nook and cranny, including the kitchens and beds." In his 1992 memoirs, Archer speculated about the harmful effects of living in an environment laced with DDT.[11]

By 1951, U.S. farmers were spending $38 million a year on sprays and dusts, and nearly 6,500 pilots were applying chemicals to crops, only some 800 less than the number of pilots who flew for commercial airlines. In 1958, farmers sprayed 92 million acres with pesticides, and 20 percent of the acreage was treated by aerial applicators. The age of miracles seemed at hand.[12]

Chlorinated hydrocarbons did not differentiate between beneficial and pestiferous insects, and their harmful effects persisted long after application. Within three years of the introduction of DDT, insects such as houseflies were developing resistance. As the target pests gained resistance, research discovered long-term problems for wildlife that stored DDT in body fat. As environmental and human implications shadowed nearly all pesticides, chemical companies invested in research on new compounds. Selective but more toxic organophosphates and carbamates ultimately would replace chlorinated hydrocarbons.

U.S. Department of Agriculture chemist J. E. Fahey dissolves the chemical residues on apples sprayed with DDT, 1946. Photograph by Knell. 16-G-N-8384, National Archives and Records Administration.

Immediately after World War II, though, a wave of pest control optimism propelled by glowing advertisements and USDA endorsements broke across the country. By the time Rachel Carson published *Silent Spring* in 1962, southern farmers were relying extensively on synthetic pesticides and were shocked that Carson considered them potentially harmful. Southern agriculture had meanwhile metamorphosed into a capital-intensive industry that relied on hybrid seeds, vast fields of one crop, machines, and enormous amounts of chemicals.[13]

Synthetic chemicals, like so many advances in science and technology, epitomized the paradox of creation and destruction. Herbicides presented complex problems because of their selectivity. The herbicide 2,4-D, for example, destroyed broad-leaved plants but spared those with narrow leaves. Rice, corn, and wheat farmers utilized 2,4-D to control weeds, but the chemical caused broad-leaved plants such as cotton, tomatoes, spinach, cabbage, cucumbers, squash, strawberries, ornamental shrubs, and flowers to, in effect, self-destruct. Problems arose when 2,4-D intended for rice fields drifted onto nearby cotton fields. The USDA received a number of complaints in 1948. That year, drift from 10,500 pounds of 2,4-D sprayed in two Louisiana parishes left a wide swath of damage in vulnerable cotton fields, completely destroying 297 acres and heavily damaging 471 acres.[14]

Because drift was unavoidable, a body of liability law emerged enabling a farmer whose crop was harmed to seek damages from either the farmer who owned the crop that was dusted or the aerial applicator. Most states licensed pilots and required applicator companies to carry insurance and undergo inspections. Such laws sought to balance the rights of aerial applicators, farmers who contracted for spraying, and neighbors. Establishing negligence became the crucial legal element. As late as 1962, legal loopholes in Mississippi allowed rice growers' neighbors to claim drift damage long after the suspect crops had been harvested.[15]

The risk of litigation did little to curb farmers' enthusiasm for pesticides. In Arkansas, the Chapman Chemical Company, hoping to recruit rural customers, demonstrated the aerial application of 2,4-D dust. Rice growers eagerly used 2,4-D to destroy the coffee bean plant, a broad-leaved weed that reduced the quality of threshed rice. On July 1, 1947, the Elms Planting Company hired the Chapman Chemical Company to spray 2,4-D on its rice crop. The dusting took place on a windless day, and the experienced pilot applied most of the dust to the target field. Neither the Elms Planting Company nor the Chapman Chemical Company realized that 2,4-D dust "possessed the quality of floating for great distances when cast in the air, even for miles." Nonsynthetic dusts used earlier to control pests either did not possess this volitant quality or, more likely, did not have 2,4-D's lethality. In this case, 2,4-D damaged a cotton crop three-quarters of a mile from the rice field. Both the Elms Planting Company and the Chapman Chemical Company denied culpability, but the court ruled that they shared liability. Such episodes led the U.S. Civil Aeronautics Administration to ban 2,4-D dust in June 1948; liquid 2,4-D continued to be used, however.[16]

According to USDA bulletins, even in calm conditions, 2,4-D in liquid form drifted 1,350 feet when sprayed from an altitude of 20 feet and 550 feet when released from an altitude of 10 feet. Chemicals could ride the turbulence from planes, travel on breezes, or exploit atmospheric conditions, drifting far from the intended field. A 3-mile-an-hour breeze could carry a droplet 8 miles when applied from 10 feet above a field. In Arkansas, Franklin Heeb learned that taking precautions did not necessarily prevent damaging drift. Heeb carefully selected a spraying service for his rice crop, checked the wind conditions, and made sure that the pilot flew at the proper altitude. A woman watching the

Cotton spraying by airplane near Lubbock, Texas, August 1950. Photograph by Putman.
16-G-Texas-47062, box 115, National Archives and Records Administration.

plane from a nearby farm testified that "the spray from the plane was just like a fog at her house." Even though she closed her windows and doors, the drifting pesticide made her feel ill. Despite his precautions, Heeb had to pay his neighbors for damages to their cotton crops.[17]

Chemicals also threatened domestic animals. On July 23, 1950, Raymond W. Nunn sprayed a mixture of 2,4-D and 2,4,5-T along the Southwestern Bell Telephone Company right-of-way in Scott County, Arkansas. The phone line ran through J. A. Smith's pasture, and when his three cows died, he sued. Smith had seen poisoned animals, he testified in court, and his dying cows clearly had been poisoned; they frothed at the mouth and their legs were "opposite to the ground wouldn't touch the ground, just held out, swelled as tight as an animal could be blown up." A veterinarian agreed that poison had killed the cows. The telephone company argued that as an independent contractor, Nunn bore all responsibility, but the court ruled that Nunn and the telephone company shared liability.[18]

Ten years later, farmers were still reporting poisoned livestock. Hoyt B. Lamm complained to North Carolina congressman Alton A. Lennon in September 1960 that he had had some "bad luck." He had tied his cow in the pasture at eight in the morning, and when he returned from selling tobacco three hours later, the cow was dead. At first Lamm was mystified, but after asking around the neighborhood, he discovered that his neighbor across the road had recently sprayed his cotton crop. Lamm also learned that another neighbor had lost some chickens. "Dusting by plane may be all right where you have big fields," he judged, "but it is as dangerous as Atom bomb on small farm like we have down in Robeson County." Texan C. S. Baker complained to Senator Lyndon B. Johnson in October 1960 that three of his cows had died after herbicides were sprayed on a nearby cotton field. "There have been several cattle killed in this county by this defoliant they are using," he warned. Rachel Carson reported in *Silent Spring* that livestock were often attracted to 2,4-D-wilted weeds that were not their natural food, sometimes with fatal results.[19]

Increasing public concern about chemical dangers to domestic animals and wildlife prompted both regulation and testing. Congress in 1947 passed the Federal Insecticide, Fungicide, and Rodenticide Act intended to protect consumers from residues and fraudulent claims by chemical companies. The testing bureaucracy never seemed capable of keeping pace with proliferating chemicals. Still, some results were disturbing. In North Dakota in 1950, Fish and Wildlife Service research on toxaphene, chlordane, DDT, and 2,4-D demonstrated that all were lethal to wildlife and fish. Tests on 2,4-D revealed that it killed "all emergent Dicotyledons and 75% of all emergent Monocotyledons." D. H. Janzen, regional director of the service in Minneapolis, reported that wildlife personnel were "gravely concerned." Janzen had heard that a North Dakota resident had died during the summer "as a result of being exposed to an insecticide applied by airplane although the cause of death was listed as heart failure." Attributing death to a chlorinated hydrocarbon pesticide proved difficult, however, since in most cases any health effect was cumulative.[20]

Court cases relating to 2,4-D and other chemicals raised serious questions not only about damage to plants and domestic animals but also about fish and wildlife kills. Elwood Rosenbaum, a commercial minnow dealer, charged that when the Kentucky Aerospray Corporation sprayed his neighbor's tobacco field with Toxatone (toxaphene), the chemical killed 150,000 to 170,000 of his minnows. Mrs. Victor Fuller and her daughter, who were standing near the pond at the time, fled inside their house to escape the fumes. A chemical analysis of the water in the pond showed the presence of toxaphene at 1.5 parts per million, three times enough to kill all the fish in the pond.[21]

Such fish kills were indisputable proof of toxicity, but long-term effects were more subtle. Because DDT and other chlorinated hydrocarbons were stable chemicals—that is, they did not break down—their effectiveness continued for months, even years. Stability also allowed them to lodge in fat and move up the food chain to predators that took in concentrated DDT from their prey. Ultimately scientists discovered the effects of pesticides on American bald eagles, peregrine falcons, and pelicans, birds at the top of the food chain. Physiologists learned that pesticides altered birds' metabolism; DDT residue in females lowered the level of hormones in the bloodstream, which caused thin eggshells. When birds sat on their nests, they cracked the shells. For roughly fifteen years after the war—until Carson's *Silent Spring* was released in 1962—chemical companies, the USDA, and many farmers ignored warnings that these and other chemicals posed dangers to animals and even humans. The same callous denials that later would dominate the debate over cigarette smoking persisted among manufacturers, promoters, and consumers of chemicals. By the time Carson warned of the invisible dangers of radioactivity and chemicals, atomic testing and the widespread application of chemicals had long been accepted as benign.[22]

Encouraged by the USDA's endorsement and saturated with advertisements, the public eagerly embraced chemicals to control insects and weeds. The USDA's Agricultural Research Service, created in 1953, absorbed the Bureau of Entomology and Plant Quarantine. ARS administrators shared with many other USDA leaders a midwestern land-grant university background and a conviction that the application of science and technology to agriculture could conquer all problems. Following the appearance of DDT and other chlorinated hydrocarbon insecticides after World War II, ARS scientists increasingly backed chemical rather than biological control of insects. The ARS shared with advocates of mechanization a dream of capital-intensive farm units that utilized the latest products. Encouraging the widespread use of chemicals would increase the influence and size of the ARS. The top tier of ARS administrators prescribed chemicals indiscriminately, usually without full knowledge of the circumstances and seldom with any thought of side effects.

The claims made by chemical companies and boosted by journalists proved irresistible to consumers. The June 1950 issue of the *Southern Farmer* contained, along with a full-page Hadacol advertisement promising a cure for many maladies, a series of articles on agricultural chemicals. "The new agricultural chemicals have an almost miraculous effect on farm pests," one article claimed. "They not only entirely wipe out the boll weevil; they also kill practically every other insect in the cotton field." The article concluded that "the boll weevil can be utterly destroyed by 3-5-40, properly applied." M. J. Funchess, dean and director of the School of Agriculture at Auburn University, had biting words for this supposed panacea. "Such a suggestion is based on ignorance alone," he judged. "No person who knows anything about the problem would make this type of proposal." Boll weevil infestation extended in a 1,500-mile arc across the South, and to spray the perimeter and all the fields inside it would smother most of the South in pesticides. Such articles confused farmers, Funchess warned, but "in a so-called free country I guess there is nothing we can do to stop it." Funchess delighted in dashing utopian chemical dreams, but his was a lonely critical voice among agricultural leaders.[23]

When crises challenged its claims that chemicals were benign, the ARS solicited support from other government agencies. A Sarasota, Florida, newspaper reported in October 1956 that malathion sprayed to combat a Mediterranean fruit fly infestation had affected people with asthma and caused skin rashes. The ARS immediately requested "a reassuring statement from the U.S. Public Health Service." A *Business Week* columnist reported in September 1957 that sixty persons near Glen Alan, a small Mississippi community near Greenville, were suffering from a "high fever" of 105 degrees and "asthmatic breathing, various flu-like symptoms, and some pneumonia." The local doctor suspected that "spraying cotton fields with an insecticidal mixture containing zylene" had caused the outbreak. With indecent haste, a Mississippi Extension entomologist and a representative of the Public Health Service that same day "concluded that the condition was in no way related to the use of insecticides." The ARS promptly notified the *Business Week* correspondent of the investigation and referred him to Wayland J. Hayes Jr., a Public Health Service toxicologist and dedicated chemical supporter. Ultimately the outbreak was attributed to the Asian flu.[24] Still, the Sarasota and Greenville episodes became part of an accumulating body of lore that questioned chemical safety.

By embracing and defending chemicals, ARS leaders not only abandoned health concerns but also entered the domain of bureaucratic dereliction. Federal guidelines allowed for no residues in milk, but by 1948, studies uncovered traces of DDT in 25 percent of milk samples. Food and Drug Administration (FDA) scientist Paul A. Clifford, who directed a national survey of residues in milk in 1955–56, reported "the presence of toxic residues in 62 per cent of the milks." "A limit to the sensitivity of all chemical and bio-assays" caused Clifford to extrapolate an even more startling conclusion: "It seems reasonable to infer that pesticide traces occur in *all* market milks." The organic-chloride pesticides, Clifford continued, "concentrate in the fat component of contaminated milk." He warned that butter probably contained "a concentration of near 20-fold."[25]

Clifford's report raised troubling questions for administrators at the ARS. T. C. Byerly, assistant director of livestock research, suspected that the report, if

U.S. Department of Agriculture chemist H. D. Mann analyzes milk from cows that had been fed hay sprayed with a pesticide, September 1946. Photograph by Forsythe. 16-G-N-8243, box 262, National Archives and Records Administration.

made public, could lead to "a great deal of public clamor." If the FDA enforced the law, it could "seize all our milk as adulterated and dump it." Byerly suggested that the ARS could file for a tolerance on pesticide residues in milk, although that option would necessarily publicize the residue problem. "So long as there is the present use of pesticides," Byerly admitted, "it would be naive to suppose that any of our foods are without traces of them." Still, Byerly saw "no cause for alarm" in the Clifford report as long as the public remained ignorant of milk pesticide residues. "Such attention has been directed with respect to DDT, with respect to antibiotics and with respect to fall-out," Byerly complained.[26] Like many USDA bureaucrats, Byerly saw such matters as public relations problems strangely disconnected from public health. Neither Clifford, Byerly, nor for that matter any scientist in 1957 fully understood the health implications of pesticide residues in milk or meat, but ARS leaders realized that the Clifford report showed that they were not in compliance with the law. They did not pursue the even more troubling question of whether or not pesticide residues were increasing.

ARS and FDA personnel reviewed the Clifford report but refused to publicize it. Instead of furnishing the report to farmers or even to Extension agents, ARS deputy administrator M. R. Clarkson circulated it only to Extension entomologists and state Extension leaders with the warning that it was "not intended for general distribution." Wary of public exposure, Clarkson and other ARS bureaucrats longed for a pesticide that "will not result in toxic residues in food." Instead of taking action on the issue, Clarkson suggested to Byerly that the Clifford report "be sent to files." Fearing that appropriation requests for residue research or tolerance applications would alert Congress to pesticide residues, Byerly and his colleagues opted to do nothing. By burying the report, the ARS accepted unlawful chemical residues in milk, failed to educate farmers about the problem, and purposefully deluded the public.[27]

The enormous increase in the use of agricultural chemicals also created residues in meat. When lobbyist Herrell DeGraff, who represented the cattle industry, arrived at the USDA's meat inspection division on January 29, 1959, Swift and Company, the American Meat Institute, and the American National Cattlemen's Association had already briefed him on USDA residue studies. DeGraff stressed that cattlemen would tolerate neither "legal sanctions" nor "bad public relations that would inevitably follow publicity concerning a pesticide contaminated meat supply." He expressed special concern about the publicizing of the discovery of residues in Swift and Company's baby food products.[28]

During the 1950s, the amount of pesticide residues in meat samples increased, far exceeding the 7 parts per million tolerance for DDT. John McCoy of the USDA's meat inspection division discovered not only that animals accumulated DDT in body fat but also that ingesting large amounts "at one time" could be fatal. He inferred that "such contaminated fat constitutes a major hazard if ingested by humans." Since the USDA handled meat inspection, it was charged with enforcing the 7 parts per million tolerance for DDT. Meat inspections revealed "especially high residues through the South," and additional tests of southern meat plants uncovered "previously unknown highs of residues." One beef carcass assayed "not less than 1,000 ppm of benzenhaxachloride [sic] (probably lindane) plus not less than 700 ppm of DDT." This led a scientist to comment, "This animal must have been eating straight insecticide." Because it took a week to finalize test results, the carcass went to market long before the results were known. The laboratory head stated that "if any considerable amount of that fat was eaten, some folks must have had digestive distress for a day or two." He also confessed that such chemicals might damage the liver. Inspection,

T. C. Byerly. 16-G-N-3074, *National Archives and Records Administration.*

then, did nothing to protect human health. The public unknowingly consumed potentially harmful insecticides.[29]

T. C. Byerly, who had buried findings of chemical residues in milk, met with DeGraff and dismissed the residue problem. Byerly argued that "alarming residues" were "probably exceptional," that it was the USDA's responsibility to ensure "wholesomeness of meat," and that "chlorinated hydrocarbon residues in meat have not been demonstrated to be a public health problem." As with milk residues, Byerly feared that "publicity might result in public demand for drastic action harmful to the meat industry." DeGraff agreed to share his report with only three people, advising them that Byerly "considered the residue problem serious but transitory." If the public could be kept in the dark until more benign chemicals were developed, Byerly assured him, the problem would disappear as if it had never existed. DeGraff deemed the cattle industry "fortunate indeed that men of such sound judgment as [Ervin L.] Peterson and Byerly are sitting on the problem in Washington."[30]

Deception stretched far beyond the USDA's meat inspection division, the ARS, and the FDA. In 1959, Donald Paarlberg, White House liaison for USDA issues, admitted internally that the discovery of pesticide residues was a poten-

*M. R. Clarkson, 1962.
16-G-BN-16708, National
Archives and Records
Administration.*

tially explosive issue. Paarlberg confessed that some meat samples "contain residue exceeding the tolerance level by ten, fifty, or one hundred times." He was relieved that no deaths had been attributed to pesticide residues. The problems, Paarlberg continued, "are known to a limited number of persons in scientific circles, in the regulatory agencies, and in the food trade." One journalist knew "the essential facts and has thus far refrained from releasing them." Paarlberg, like other bureaucrats, feared "an outbreak of sensational journalism" far more than the effects of pesticide residues on humans. He believed that if chemical residues became public knowledge, a domino effect would undermine consumer confidence, harm corporate food producers, and stunt chemical sales. He advocated research to develop less toxic chemicals and to determine the effects of pesticides on human health. If such steps were taken, he hoped, "a bad news break would not catch us flat-footed." Assistant USDA Secretary True D. Morse concocted a bureaucratic statement to blur the residue problem: "For meat, tests reveal residues occasionally in samples representing animals from widely scattered areas and raised under a great variety of conditions." In the end, neither the White House nor federal bureaucrats publicized the residue problem. As long as they could delude the public, they considered the problem under control.[31]

Despite its barrage of reassuring claims, the ARS failed to halt all unfavorable publicity. In 1960, reporter Hart Stilwell sensationalized pesticide dangers in a *True Magazine* article, "Farm Fallout Can Kill You!" Stilwell boldly suggested

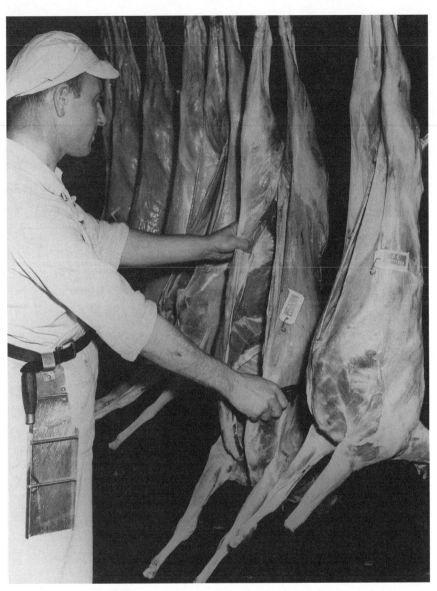

Peter Hlatky inspects "U.S. Retained" carcasses set aside for special examination, July 1948. Photograph by Forsythe. 16-G-N-10201, box 239, National Archives and Records Administration.

that "we and our unborn children, together with much of our fish and game — face a future of sterility, deformity and a possible tremendous upsurge of cancer, because of poisons being flung almost heedlessly about the country." He graphically described an area the USDA had sprayed to kill insect pests. "It was as if an invisible H-bomb had struck. Nothing moved. All was silence." *True* readers learned that chlorinated hydrocarbons "settle in abnormal quantities in the sex organs of women." Accepted beliefs were inverted, Stilwell suggested. "Little Johnnie eating his apple a day to keep the doctor away is probably being poisoned. . . . The mother nursing her precious baby may be poisoning it." He listed a frightening number of deaths caused by chemical use.[32]

Stilwell interviewed those who worked most closely with the chemicals — namely, the pilots who applied them to crops. The Civil Aeronautics Administration reported that poison ingestion had been a factor in six or seven of the year's fifty-five fatal crop duster crashes. When Arnold L. Murdock Jr. crashed in an open field in California after his vision blurred, his hands went numb, and he became nauseated, his doctor suggested that the symptoms were caused by his fear of chemical poisoning. Stilwell listed other crop duster accidents, many fatal. The ARS regularly received reports that chemicals were responsible for crop duster crashes. In July 1960, pilots spraying phosdrin in Kern County, California, "had either been made ill or had shown dangerously low cholinesterase levels in the blood and had been 'grounded.'" Low cholinesterase levels inhibit the transmission of nerve impulses. The Federal Aviation Administration launched a study of pilots who handled pesticides to determine if some chemicals were too toxic for aerial application. The ARS recommended that applicators be instructed in "label recognition" and that banning a chemical should be "a 'last resort' approach." Neither pilot safety nor the possible effects on people nearby concerned ARS bureaucrats. They wanted to spray.[33]

By 1957, 4,500 pesticides had been approved under the Federal Insecticide, Fungicide, and Rodenticide Act. The market for pesticides increased enormously due to the development of synthetic chemicals, rising from $40 million in 1939 to $290 million in 1956. DDT production increased from 37.9 million pounds in 1953 to 124.5 million in 1959. The residue problem never came into sharp focus, but even ARS bureaucrats realized that the dangers involved more than public relations. When Bette Haney interviewed Justus Ward, head of the ARS's regulatory division, in 1960, he was forthcoming about pesticide registration until he discovered that Haney worked for Rachel Carson. He then abruptly ended the appointment.[34]

When at last in 1960 the U.S. Department of Health, Education, and Welfare set zero tolerance levels for some chemicals, ARS assistant administrator W. L. Popham whined about the impact on agriculture. "Pesticides are required in modern agricultural production practices," he wrote to ARS administrator Byron T. Shaw. "Pesticides are as vital to the efficient production of crops and livestock as aircraft or telephones are for modern transportation and communications." Without chemicals, he predicted, production would fall and crops "would be of low quality and unwholesome because of worms and rot." The choice, Popham argued, was either to withdraw pesticides or market commodities that were not in compliance. DDT, for example, would require a complete ban to achieve zero tolerance, as would heptachlor and perhaps aldrin. To scientists such as Popham, it was as if agricultural practices prior to the creation of synthetic chemicals had never existed.[35]

ARS spray campaigns extended far beyond fields and pastures into cities. Suspicious of chemicals and doubting government assurances of safety, Margaret Till, a seventy-year-old Memphis woman, warned the USDA that she did not want her yard sprayed for white-fringed beetles. "I enjoy the birds and the squirrels and the pet cat that live on my place and besides these, five young grand children will visit me this summer and play in my back yard," she wrote. "I want to keep it safe for them." She kept her roses healthy by spraying them only when they needed it, Till boasted. "I am satisfied with the results so I say again, keep your men and their equipment off my premises." Another Memphis woman sent Senator Albert Gore a clipping of an article quoting Audubon Society president John Baker comparing dieldrin, which was being used in the city's spray campaign, to radioactive fallout.[36]

By 1961, the USDA budget for plant disease and pest control came to $25 million, including $2.5 million for fire ant eradication, $1.5 million for pink bollworm control, and $3 million for witchweed control. The USDA also handled over $316 million in classified research for the U.S. Department of Defense. Over half a million dollars went to the Bureau of Entomology and Plant Quarantine and the Bureau of Agricultural and Industrial Chemistry. None of the documents relating to the defense projects identified a specific topic; they listed only a vague title and personnel.[37]

By promoting chemicals as their atomic bomb and aerial application as their strategic strike force, ARS bureaucrats evangelistically spread their pesticide gospel. USDA films such as "Battle of the Beetles," "Total War against a Farm Pest," and "The Fire Ant on Trial" portrayed insects as deadly enemies deserving annihilation. Some pesticide projects had little or nothing to do with the production of food and fiber. Large-scale spray campaigns to combat spruce budworms, gypsy moths, Japanese beetles, bark beetles, Mormon crickets, mosquitoes, and grasshoppers targeted large areas of the United States. Envisioning themselves as powerful generals in a national insect war, ARS administrators hungered for a major southern insect enemy.[38]

The Argentine fire ant, after a carefully orchestrated campaign, emerged as the South's scourge. More than any other spray campaign, the fire ant eradication program epitomized the ARS's ability to generate support from farm organizations, pressure both state and federal lawmakers to appropriate funds, disregard environmental warnings, and falsify chemical dangers. The fire ant

*W. L. Popham, 1960.
16-G-BN-10460, National
Archives and Records
Administration.*

campaign eerily fit the 1950s obsession with foreign agents, gigantic insects, bureaucratic bullying, and unintended consequences.[39]

In 1918, one species of Argentine fire ant (*Solenopsis richteri* Forel) disembarked from a ship in the Mobile, Alabama, harbor. Between 1933 and 1945, another species (*Solenopsis invicta* Buren) arrived in Mobile and spread rapidly. Two Auburn University entomologists experimented on killing fire ants with chlorinated hydrocarbon insecticides—toxaphene, DDT, benzene hexachloride, aldrin, and chlordane—and in 1949 reported their results in a bulletin. All killed fire ants. In Louisiana, Federal Extension Service entomologist Kirby L. Cockerham reported in 1952 that the fire ant had "become a serious pest" and was "spreading rapidly and causing great damage, inconvenience and alarm among the people." His reports varied little from year to year, however, suggesting that fire ants were a pest but no threat to agriculture or wildlife.[40]

In their haste to test poisons, entomologists neglected to study the life cycle of fire ants. Like bees and wasps, fire ants belong to the insect order Hymenoptera and metamorphose through egg, larva, pupa, and adult stages. A mature ant colony contains a queen, workers, and winged males and females called alates, sexuals, or reproductives. During warm weather following a rain, alates fly from the colony and mate 300 to 800 feet in the air. When the female falls back to earth, she tunnels into the ground and in a month produces her first brood. The new colony develops as the queen lays eggs and workers forage for food and build a mound. A mature fire ant colony produces an extraordinarily large number of sexuals. Entomologists failed to realize the implications of the immense sexual energy driving fire ant colonies.[41]

Most rural southerners agreed that fire ants had vicious stings and built bothersome mounds. Until the mid-fifties, however, fire ants were just another pest. The Argentine fire ant's transformation from being a minor pest to being a major predator epitomized agricultural institutions' ability to create projects to suit their ambitions. Earl L. Butz, who served as an assistant USDA secretary in the fifties, admitted that Washington officials often "generate pressure from the country on themselves."[42] In this case, ARS personnel, cattlemen, entomologists, and the Farm Bureau generated the pressure. The invention of the imported fire ant as a major threat to southern agriculture marshaled the efforts of local, state, and national farm organizations; county agricultural agents; state Extension Services; county agricultural committees; ARS bureaucrats; state and national politicians; chemical companies; and land-grant university scientists and administrators. This combined institutional power drowned out voices of protest.

Skeptical southerners scoffed at the general alarm. "Give every one a crow bar and a can of kerosene oil," an Alabama farmer suggested in March 1957. "Take the crow bar and make a hole in the ant bed and pour a qt. of oil in it." An eight-year-old girl from Mobile recommended that anteaters be imported "from South America to eat the fire-ants." A woman who had discussed the problem with neighbors facetiously suggested "reading portions of the Congressional Record to the ants and having them laugh themselves to death or to sause the mounds in good ol' corn likker." She liked the idea of using flamethrowers even better.[43] Although none of these suggested remedies would have eradicated fire ants, at least they would not have left a legacy of environmental damage.

J. Lloyd Abbot, a Mobile nurseryman who kept a sharp eye on the campaign, scoffed at the claim "that the insect had to be eradicated to save the American farmer from a monster which was a threat to agricultural production." Abbot traced the impetus for the campaign to disgruntled Alabama cattlemen who wanted "to be given some insecticide by the state and federal governments which the cattlemen were not entitled to and should have to buy for themselves."[44] The ARS staff must have known that spraying pastures would increase the levels of pesticide residues in milk and beef.

The fire ant eradication campaign fit neatly into Cold War ideology. The foreign ant, like communist subversives, was undermining the security of the country and should be eradicated—not simply controlled. Ambitious ARS generals would use airpower to spread the most deadly chlorinated hydrocarbons—heptachlor, dieldrin, and aldrin—over areas infested with fire ants. ARS literature traced the fire ant's spread on maps that called to mind the invidious spread of communism. Spokesmen shamelessly employed the most potent vocabulary of the day to win support for the program.[45]

Newspapers and magazines helped overcome the public's lingering doubts about the need to eradicate the fire ant menace. A July 1957 article claimed that fire ants not only ate cabbage, eggplant, potatoes, okra, and ungerminated corn but also attacked newborn pigs, calves, muskrats, young birds, and people. "The farmer with fire ants swarming over his property," the *Shreveport Times* warned, "can tell hair-raising tales of fields sucked dry of life and newborn stock eaten alive." Fire ants made "quick work of the succulent membranes," the article continued, and the ant "gobbles at the tender stems beneath the surface and sucks the plant juice." Children could not play outside, and housewives "cannot hang out the laundry without fear of the painful sting." Threats to the young, the tender, and the succulent created powerful images of danger.[46] Given that fire ants fed primarily on insects, these inventive articles clearly drew on sources that were intent on constructing a fire ant enemy. With each retelling of the story, the fire ant became more vicious.

Such popular images of fire ant depredations conflicted with Auburn entomologist Kirby L. Hays's April 1957 research in Argentina, the fire ant's home habitat. "All specialists consider these ants to be beneficial," Hays reported, "and cannot understand the concern of the North American farmers." He found no livestock deaths and learned that cultivation discouraged infestation. Neither specialists nor farmers in Argentina considered the fire ant "to be of economic importance." Hays's report could have created problems for eradication advocates, but it never gained widespread circulation. It did raise serious questions about fire ant research in the United States, which seemed to rely more on lobbying and imagination than on scientific research.[47]

Armed with sweeping congressional authorization to cross state lines and spray on private property, plus $2.4 million in federal funds and matching state funds, the ARS drew up ambitious battle plans. In December 1957, when ARS eradication plans became public, Assistant Secretary of the Interior Ross Laffler warned Secretary of Agriculture Ezra Taft Benson that dieldrin was twenty times more toxic than DDT and would be devastating to fish and wildlife. Laffler's words had no effect, nor did other warnings.[48]

In its responses to critics, the ARS made disingenuous if not fabricated claims, in one case suggesting that "domestic Tom cats are probably more harmful to birds than the overall effects of the economic poison now being used by the USDA against the fire ant." In fact, chemicals were killing large numbers of wildlife. In Decatur County, Georgia, where 48,000 acres had been treated as of March 5, 1958, Fish and Wildlife Service personnel discovered that the ARS had used airplanes—not ground application as required—to spray dieldrin "in every possible situation." Representatives from several government agencies stumbled over each other investigating both wildlife losses and the death of cattle. Despite the wildlife carnage, neither the Fish and Wildlife Service nor the ARS publicized their findings. In April 1958, Auburn entomologists checked a 3,600-acre test plot for wildlife deaths. "A large number of dead quail, songbirds, frogs, fish, rabbits, and other animals were collected from the area following treatment. None were found in the unsprayed check area."[49]

Mobile nurseryman J. Lloyd Abbot unleashed a flurry of letters in June and July 1958 urging Auburn officials to expose the spray campaign. "A dedicated bureaucrat anywhere is interested in nothing but the promotion of the goals of his bureaucracy," he wrote to the president of the university, "and he will without the slightest hesitation lie, cheat, or steal, or do anything else, to accomplish his bureaucratic goals." Abbot's warnings went unheeded despite one heroic forty-five-line Faulknerian sentence specifying deceptions by state and federal control personnel.[50]

Despite ARS efforts to stifle criticism, by the summer of 1958 the fire ant campaign faced strong opposition. Articles in fish, wildlife, and conservation periodicals documented wildlife kills. By this time, Rachel Carson had committed herself to writing a book on pesticide dangers and easily tapped into the growing network of opponents inside and outside the government. In early October 1958, Clarence Cottam, director of the Welder Wildlife Foundation, visited the ARS offices in Washington. Twenty years earlier, Cottam had started his career at the USDA with the U.S. Biological Survey. He then moved to the Fish and Wildlife Service when it took over the survey and in 1953 resigned over a conservation dispute. Cottam had an excellent reputation and could not easily be dismissed or dissuaded. A few weeks after his ARS visit, he declared the fire ant program "immature and irresponsible" and added that "it is like scalping to cure dandruff—quite unnecessarily severe." A month later, he learned that ARS personnel had intimidated other government scientists. When dead animals were found in one test area, he discovered, ARS fieldworkers made "entirely unfounded" allegations that they had been shot "for study purposes."[51]

To counter adverse publicity, the ARS produced a film, "The Fire Ant on Trial," which, among other fabrications, charged that fire ants attacked wildlife and that chemicals were benign. When Fish and Wildlife Service personnel previewed the film, an acrimonious argument exploded that led to substantial changes in the film. Members of the Washington Audubon Society, including Carson, viewed the film and complained to Secretary of Agriculture Benson that dieldrin and heptachlor "are recognized, beyond possibility of denial, as extremely toxic even in minute traces." Continuing criticism led W. L. Popham to admit that the ARS had "a public relations job beyond anything we have en-

Clarence Cottam.
99-1084, record unit 7231,
Waldo LaSalle Schmitt Papers,
1907–58, Smithsonian Institution
Archives, Washington, D.C.

countered before." After *Reader's Digest* carried an article questioning the fire ant campaign, the Maryland state entomologist suggested that the ARS publish articles defending the program in the *Saturday Evening Post, Reader's Digest, Life,* or *Coronet.* These articles should contain factual material, the entomologist conceded, "but give emphasis on the use and need of pesticides in conservation work."[52]

More and more, the ARS discovered that its lack of research and disregard for wildlife had flawed the fire ant campaign. In December 1959, the ARS announced that it had cut the per acre application formula for dieldrin and heptachlor from two pounds to one and a half. By this time, 1.5 million acres had been treated with the stronger mixture. An incredulous Cottam pounced on this statement. "Who was profiting from the excess use of poison?," he demanded. "Had an adequate research program preceded rather than succeeded this program," Cottam fumed, "there would have been a tremendous saving of public funds and I am convinced a saving of much wildlife that has been unnecessarily destroyed." Later Cottam condemned the "arrogant bureaucracy of federal leadership that, too often, is less concerned with public service than with power, authority, and prestige."[53]

The Alabama legislature in 1960 refused to appropriate funds to continue state support of the fire ant program, and Texas and Florida followed the next year. Criticism and funding cuts tempted ARS leaders to commit even greater excesses when they testified in April 1960 before the Senate Agriculture Appropriations Subcommittee. Georgia senator Richard Russell observed that a controversy "rages" about livestock and wildlife kills. Byron Shaw vigorously defended the program. He claimed that "the death of a lot of fish in some of these areas is due to fire ants that washed into the lake and the fish have eaten it." A skeptical Senator Russell asked if the guilty fire ants were "filled with your poison and then taken in by the fish." Shaw's claims of fire ant attacks on fish were groundless. Still, ARS spokespersons minimized reports of fish and wildlife kills.[54]

Russell produced evidence to undermine Shaw's claim that ARS personnel had "never gone on to anyone's property without their expressed request." When M. R. Clarkson declared that fire ants had been eradicated on the 1.6 million acres treated to date, Senator Spessard L. Holland of Florida noted that "there are more new infestations than there were before you started." The ill-considered campaign had not taken into account the life cycle of fire ants, insect resistance to chemicals, and insects' ability to adapt quickly to such threats. Although the poison killed most ants in treated areas, those that survived quickly reproduced and moved to untreated areas. Paradoxically, the ARS eradication plan actually encouraged fire ants to spread.[55] The scenario proved worthy of a fifties science fiction film. The fire ant quickly acquired resistance to chemicals and became more voracious, whereas its enemies were devastated.

Despite fierce criticism, the fire ant program endured. From 1957 to 1962, the ARS treated 20 million acres mostly with dieldrin and heptachlor, and during those years, the infested area grew from 90 to 126 million acres. The use of heptachlor was phased out in 1960 when the FDA canceled tolerances for heptachlor residue in pasture grasses. After briefly using Chlordecone (kepone) to kill fire ants in the late 1960s, ARS control personnel sprayed Mirex over 120 million acres. In 1969, when a Conway, Arkansas, motel manager reported a single fire ant mound, the ARS sprayed Mirex over 4,500 adjoining acres. Mirex also came under scrutiny from environmental groups because of its persistence and bioaccumulation. In 1979, the Environmental Protection Agency approved Amdro, a more expensive formulation that seemed to present fewer environmental problems.[56]

Its failure only inspired the ARS to seek more funding for spraying, and incessant lobbying kept the spray campaign alive despite its sorry record. The fire ant campaign was a small but telling chapter in the post–World War II rush to exterminate pests, create perfect lawns, and control other aspects of the environment with chemicals. In this war, nature became the enemy. The scenario became so common that it was predictable: a promising chemical is approved without adequate testing, critics are labeled alarmists, insects build up resistance, the pesticide raises serious environmental concerns and is reluctantly

Byron T. Shaw, 1948.
Photograph by Forsythe.
16-G-N-10296, National
Archives and Records
Administration.

banned, and a new chemical is introduced as a panacea. Despite Carson's warnings, the rapid spread of fire ants during the ARS eradication effort, and the troubling residue issue, lobbyists and the ARS kept the fire ant issue alive. In Arkansas, for example, government bulletins, the state legislature, and the press sensationalized fire ant depredations into the 1990s. Tales of swarming ants devouring pigs, sheep, and calves resonated with myths from the 1950s. Instead of acknowledging the ecological damages of the futile battle against fire ants, Arkansas politicians blamed the Environmental Protection Agency for banning pesticides.[57]

The $156 million spent on control between 1957 and 1990 not only aided the fire ant's spread but also possibly triggered evolutionary changes. In 1973, scientists in Mississippi discovered the first multiple-queen colony. Although it is unclear what caused this profound evolutionary change, protection against chemical warfare seems the most logical explanation. The fire ant has slowly expanded its range over 250 million acres in eleven southern states and recently has been sighted in California. The fire ant's spread has been aided by the march of civilization: cleared fields, pastures, lawns, golf courses, and other open, sunny spaces have given the ant a home. It is as if the fabricated fire ant of the 1950s has become a reality, for instead of eradicating the fire ant, chemical warfare created a more powerful and resilient fire ant. A festival celebrates its notoriety, and advertisements for the FireAnt computer promise that "never has a portable this light delivered such a powerful sting."[58]

Rachel Carson in *Silent Spring* attacked the notion of chemical remedies for nature's pests and at first threw chemical advocates off balance. In October 1962, B. F. Smith, executive director of the Delta Council, warned council members of Carson's "new and frightening" book. A month later, Smith wrote Delta Council members that *Silent Spring* "is resulting in a wave of hysterical outcryings" against chemicals. "Book reviewers, hunting and fishing writers, newspaper columnists and even preachers," he complained, "have joined in the chorus." Smith enclosed with his letter "a kit of factual information on agricultural chemicals." He also thoughtfully included a copy of Monsanto's pamphlet "The Desolate Year," which could charitably be described as a hysterical account of a world without chemicals overrun by insects.[59]

When members of the Delta Council board of directors met on November 27, 1962, they had already dismissed *Silent Spring*. W. M. Garrard Jr. proudly reported that the 3,402 cotton-picking machines in the Delta and the 312 machines in the hills harvested 68 percent of Mississippi's cotton crop. Herbicides controlled most weeds, insects succumbed to aerial warfare, and farmworkers moved around the Delta to chop weeds when heavy rains washed away herbicides.[60]

As Garrard suggested, farmers relied on machines and chemicals, and few challenged the Delta Council's conventional wisdom that only chemicals stood between them and plague. But in September 1963, the revered and powerful Walter Sillers, longtime Speaker of the Mississippi house of representatives and a Delta Council officer, confided to Archie Lee Gray, the executive officer of the Mississippi State Board of Health, that he had serious reservations about agricultural chemicals. "I am receiving complaints daily concerning the pollution of the air from large and continuous volumes of poisons put out by airplanes," he began. "Many think these poisons are doing about as much harm to people as they are to the insects." Sillers dreaded riding through the Delta because "the country-side is polluted with great volumes of insecticides and/or defoliations." The chemicals, he explained, "affect my eyes, nose, throat and ears, and if I be suffering from a cold or virus the aggrevation [*sic*] thereof and ill effects are quite annoying and unpleasant—and perhaps injurious." Sillers did not make a formal complaint but suggested that chemical pollution be studied "quietly and without fanfare or publicity."[61]

Gray admitted that agricultural chemicals, especially in the Delta, "have given us much to worry about." He too had received "many complaints from people, particularly in the Delta section, very similar to your description of the effect of these chemicals on you personally." Based on complaints and personal experience, Sillers suspected that pesticides were creating major health problems, but even he was reluctant to take on the agricultural establishment.[62]

Rachel Carson dramatized chemical dangers and sparked the rise of the modern environmental movement, but the intervening years have not eroded the public's confidence in chemicals. The lost war against fire ants should have been cautionary, a warning against hubris and unintended consequences. Instead, it typified a mind-set that substituted faith in science and bureaucratic expertise for common sense. A cadre of interest groups constructed an ant menace, wasted millions of dollars, poisoned the environment, denied killing wildlife, and prompted fire ants to expand their range and develop resistance and survival strategies. Federal bureaucrats withheld information about residues in milk and meat that could have endangered peoples' health. In these cases from the early years of synthetic chemicals, biblical injunctions against pride and hypocrisy along with praise for the ant's industriousness seem particularly applicable.

BOOK II LOW CULTURE

5 Fast and Furious

I bumped a lot of guys, put a lot of guys in the fences, but I never did get mad enough to try to kill somebody out there, like hit 'em in the driving door or something like that.
— Tim Flock

Basically, we'd run 'em sideways and backwards and about any way you wanted to see one, in whatever position you wanted to see it in. We could get 'em in that position and still save 'em and not wreck 'em a lot of times.
— Junior Johnson

In the countryside and small towns that dotted the postwar South, southern families—rich and poor, black and white—shared customs, religious beliefs, and pastimes. People were judged by hard work more than success, church attendance more than piousness, and good deeds more than good manners. They preferred their working-class culture to highfalutin pretensions and airs. "Redneck," "woolhat," "hillbilly," "coon," "coonass," "clodhopper," "linthead," "nigger," and "white trash" were some of the epithets used to demean poor southerners. With their penchant for inversion, they often changed the word placement or intonation to turn such degrading epithets into terms of endearment or provocation.

During the middle decades of the twentieth century, an unlikely renaissance swept through southern society, generated primarily by the working class. As World War II broke down rural isolation, savvy race promoters and record producers would recognize the explosive talent embodied in the southern working class. Southern music and stock car racing, two outlets for this energy, not only gained cultural significance but also provided a release for the enormous tension generated by urbanization and the civil rights struggle.

"Working-class culture," to some an oxymoronic expression, encompasses the worldview and habits of lower-class people, their speech, religion, music, work ethic, and pastimes. "Lowdown culture," which seems a better label, is an ambivalent term edged with pride and denigration. While the working class wore their lowdown status with pride, pretentious people looked askance at

their rough edges and untamed enthusiasms. Southerners made their conces-
sions to segregation, for they lived in a complected society where a broad spectrum of pigments registered as only black and white and where whites retained
enormous privilege. Still, preferences of association in work and leisure continually violated all codes.[1]

The white middle class and elite aspired to more polished behavior and
habits, attended less fundamentalist churches, often sent their children to college, and sneered at country music, blues, stock car racing, wrestling, and other
enthusiasms of the vulgus. Each community constructed a cautionary "white
trash" class at the bottom of the social spectrum. While few would raise their
hands to claim membership in the lowest class, everyone knew someone else
who qualified, someone a little farther down the road. As Alabama native Rick
Bragg observed, "If you really do grow up as what some people call white trash,
you grow up knowing that it might all turn to shit at any second." When whites
failed so miserably that their perceived filth and squalor objectified them as
garbage, they entered a social black hole that threatened to swallow anyone
who came near. When reporter I. F. Stone and two English correspondents had
cocktails at the Helena, Arkansas, country club in September 1958, they got a
lesson in southern class boundaries. A woman turned to Stone and observed of
poor whites, "Why some of them are so low that niggers won't associate with
them."[2]

Many southerners doubted the need for education. Men and women passed
down to their children the knowledge and skills they had learned from their
parents and practiced throughout their lives. Black and white farmers raised the
same crops, worshiped the same God, received the same rainfall, and shared the
same basic vocabulary. Without formal English instruction, southerners developed playful speech. Both African Americans and their white neighbors lacked
access to education and became grammatical heretics, lapsing into syntactical
aberrations and malapropisms that suggested to some ignorance rather than
calculated insolence. Southern segregation laws were insufficient to block the
exchange of counterfeit linguistics. Because black and white people were often
neighbors, music, language, dress, religion, Saturday night partying, and even
yard art were an alternating current that moved between neighbors, communities, counties, and states. Especially when it came to exchanging something offensive to the upper class, racial barriers collapsed. Lowdown southerners bent
both grammatical rules and musical notes to their purposes. William Alexander Percy revealed the upper class's contempt for lowdown people in his description of his father's campaign for the U.S. Senate in 1912. As his father spoke,
Percy observed "the ill-dressed surly audience, unintelligent and slinking. . . .
They were the sort of people that lynch Negroes, that mistake hoodlumism for

wit, and cunning for intelligence, that attend revivals and fight and fornicate in the bushes afterwards."[3]

The postwar years witnessed vast changes in southern society, and more working-class southerners acquired mainstream manners and avoided glaring comportmental outrages. As prosperity lifted them to respectability, they buried their lowly origins. Whites who had gained respectability most recently guarded their status most viciously. Still, a large element of black and white southerners remained untamed, ignoring conformist pressure to acquit themselves in a way that made respectable people comfortable. Black and white musicians, stock car drivers, and their fans were on the cutting edge of wildness. In the dense, loud, and sexually charged dance halls and the wild and frenzied infields and grandstands at stock car races, southerners found the space to reclaim their wildness. While polite people discovered ways to sublimate such temptations, at least on the surface, lowdown southerners proudly exhibited their bad manners. "It was common, acceptable, not to be able to read," Rick Bragg observed, "but a man who wouldn't fight, couldn't fight, was a pathetic thing." Bragg's male relatives, he wrote, taught him "much of what a boy should know, of cars, pistols, heavy machinery, shotguns and love, all of which, these men apparently believed, can be operated stone drunk." Although respectable people condemned such behavior, some envied their uninhibited cousins and suspected that politeness and polish came at a cost. Respectable families might attend football, basketball, and baseball games, but stock car racing gave them pause.[4]

Southerners manifested an inordinate interest in automobiles. With aggressive drivers, fast cars, and wild fans, automobile racing became the ultimate working-class sport. Stock car racing attracted a segment of southern society that was proudly boisterous. In a decade when many frustrated middle-class Americans were searching for lost meanings, lowdown southerners wallowed in authenticity.

With the decline of rural life and the migration of blacks and whites to cities in the North and South, lowdown culture relocated and evolved. Whatever their misgivings about being uprooted, migrants to cities found jobs, housing, and opportunities that infused them with optimism. Having worked outdoors in harmony with the seasons most of their lives, they resented confining hourly jobs that demanded discipline and regularity. Each day they faced the whip, chair, and pistol of corporate management that punished them for displaying any residue of wildness. They chaffed at punching a time clock and other constraints that challenged their will, and they longed for escape, if not retribution.

Polite society condemned farmers as volitionless and culture-bare, even after they moved to towns and cities. Their vile language and hard living repulsed sophisticated urbanites. Tales abound of uncouth southern migrants, black and white, arriving in respectable neighborhoods and immediately lowering the value of property and propriety. Their display of material culture seemed meretricious and their language insipid. Such people, the conventional wisdom went, lacked intelligence, swilled liquor, used foul language, dressed poorly, craved sex, and lapsed in personal hygiene. But their pride, industry, and inventiveness belied the stereotype. The last generation of sharecroppers possessed enormous creative energy both while they farmed and after they left the fields and infiltrated towns and cities. They would bend U.S. culture to their purposes.

Musicians had always used their talent to evade both farmwork and hourly jobs. In the juke joints and honky-tonks that stretched across the South, blues and hillbilly music soothed workers bored by routine, beset by hard times, or troubled by hard love. At least since the Prohibition era, some southerners had escaped routine work by hauling illegal liquor from isolated stills to urban centers. Because trippers, as these drivers were called, were loath to become public figures or leave records, their careers were shrouded in mystery and legend. Musicians and trippers not only escaped routine but in some cases earned far more money than their less-talented or adventurous friends and relatives.[5]

During World War II, southerners became more affluent, and many bought their first automobiles with defense earnings or soldiers' pay. Southerners subscribed to the notion that an automobile largely defined its owner, and they modified their cars to reflect their particular vanities. The car craze was largely a male obsession. Southerners created a unique racing culture that not only reconfigured machinery but also attracted rabid fans.

The men and women involved in stock car racing were tough and resourceful. "It was rough and rowdy," South Carolina driver Jack Smith recalled. "It was a lots of boys just getting out of the service—they had been over there four or five years in them wars." He estimated that 70 percent "had been involved, in what we called trippin' whiskey, haulin' whiskey, maybe makin' a little bit of whiskey." Many promoters and track owners, he speculated, had earned their investment money in the liquor business. Smith hauled liquor for the thrill as much as the financial return. "It was dangerous," he boasted. "Some people I think likes to live dangerous."[6]

Trippers needed fast cars to outrun the law. Many drove 1939 or 1940 Fords, cars that not only could be fitted with readily available (though expensive) racing parts but also had ample trunk space for liquor. Although a liquor car may have looked like a stock car, it had better brakes, a modified engine, a beefed-up transmission, and a heavier suspension. Driving souped-up cars on mountain roads and matching wits with the law honed trippers' driving skills and gave

Group of men standing beside a moonshine still near Ellijay, Gilmer County, Georgia. GIL-1, *Vanishing Georgia Collection, Georgia Department of Archives and History, Atlanta, Ga.*

them immense experience in driving fast. Losing a race with the law meant going to jail. Legends grew about trippers' speed and tactics. Children from the Georgia mountains turned the game of cowboys and Indians into trippers and revenuers; the trippers were the good guys.[7]

Many drivers found racing preferable to dull, low-paying jobs or even to tripping. The people who turned their attention to automobile racing were unusually skilled mechanics and drivers. A handful of mechanics who could build engines and tune suspensions created a legacy that in many ways parallels that of the drivers. Some mechanics roped off a bay in their filling stations and reserved it for race preparations. Others had national reputations and vast experience as full-time racing mechanics. Red Vogt, an Atlanta mechanic whose magic touch aided bootleggers, revenuers, and racers, had been a crew member in Indianapolis 500 races in the late 1920s. After World War II, he built cars that competed in the modified series. When the National Association for Stock Car Auto Racing (NASCAR) started its Grand National series, Vogt built cars for Red Byron, who won the first championship. "All of us run second unless his car crashed," renowned mechanic Smokey Yunick admitted. "His cars never broke and were always fastest." Mechanics saw racing differently from drivers. "I want to race other mechanics with drivers," Yunick observed. Before money dominated the sport, mechanics "wanted to race each other, to see who could build the fastest car." During World War II, Yunick had served as a B-17 pilot. He was as brash and fearless as the drivers. Before the 1968 Daytona 500, technical inspectors removed the gas tank and other parts from his car and found nine violations. Yunick, the story goes, started the engine and as he drove away without a gas tank shouted, "Better make it ten." According to another story, when inspectors attached their seal to the engine of Yunick's car to prevent tinkering, the next day, the seal was the only part that was the same.[8]

In the post–World War II South, racing fans were the hard core of lowdown culture, men and women who had grown up hard and were making a transition from farm to city, from sun-time to clock-time, and from family-centered rural communities to chaotic urban neighborhoods. Reporter Max Muhlmann, who covered racing from 1957 to 1964, observed that the fans at the Charlotte, North Carolina, fairgrounds "were good folks, low-income people who worked on cars or used machinery, farmers and a lot of rural people, people who worked with their hands." Such fans happily lost themselves in an orgy of dust, liquor, and noise.[9]

Fans created a folklore not only about drivers and mechanics but also about themselves. They may have appeared tame during the workweek, but their weekend activities could never be harnessed. For stock car fans, every race weekend became a carnival of drinking, eating, and debauchery. Women were as interested as men in escaping their workaday routines. The racetrack offered an unpoliced space for uncivil behavior and vile language and an escape from television laugh tracks, humorless bosses, and plastic surroundings. The farther people moved from the country and its cycles into hourly work and consumer culture, the more they needed a fix of racing, wildness, fun, and laughter. Ultimately even people who had no memory of rural life or less savory lowdown habits embraced racing, country music, and the accompanying scene, as if their respectable jobs created a need for such spectacles.[10]

While some amusements included reminders of work routines, stock car racing taught other lessons. At first glance, race cars circling a track in dozens or hundreds of rotations might suggest an assembly line or some other repetitive job. Stock cars, however, often bumped or crashed into each other, interrupting the cycle, destroying sponsors' investments, and sometimes injuring drivers, not a scenario that a factory owner would want employees to internalize. Nor did fans behave in ways that would return them to the job alert. Although races might take the edge off of fans' frustrations and even make them more compliant, skilled drivers at the edge of control constantly suggested that escape was possible for those with enough talent or nerve. A race weekend not only turned the proper world upside down but also turned fans against themselves. It was carnivalesque with a vengeance.[11]

Drivers and mechanics as a rule were not well educated or well mannered,

Left to right: *Red Vogt, Bill France, and Red Byron.*
*International Speedway Corporation/*NASCAR.

but all were proud, many were extremely resourceful, and some were brilliant. They intimidated competitors, abused their automobiles (and those of rental companies), drank both on and off the track, flirted with women, fornicated, and fought over any slight. "My wife hated racing," Smokey Yunick explained. "To her racers were bums, trash." Motel owners and rental car agents often refused their business. In a 1965 *Esquire* essay on driver Junior Johnson, Tom Wolfe observed that stock car races were "immediately regarded as some kind of manifestation of the animal irresponsibility of the lower orders."[12]

Tim Flock, a two-time Grand National champion in the 1950s, insisted that modern stock car racing started after World War II "in a cow pasture right outside Atlanta, Georgia." Drivers would bet against each other, with up to $20,000 changing hands. Others were willing to pay to watch. Retired driver Ned Jarrett recalled tales of promoters who "would hang the green flag out" to start the race and then leave with the gate receipts. The race would continue until the drivers realized it should have been over, "and so they'd stop and find out there was no money there for them." Race promoter Bill France brought order to such contests.[13]

Twenty-seven-year-old William Henry Getty France arrived in Florida from

Red Byron driving a modified race car at the three-quarter-mile speedway at Charlotte, North Carolina, in the 1950s. Courtesy Don Hunter.

Washington, D.C., in 1935, opened a service station in Daytona Beach, and occasionally drove in local races. After World War II, Big Bill France saw the possibilities of organizing the outlaw races that were springing up throughout the South. On December 14, 1947, three dozen men met at the Streamline Hotel in Daytona Beach and agreed to form a sanctioning body for stock car racing. Red Vogt, the respected Atlanta mechanic, suggested they call it the National Association for Stock Car Auto Racing. Only U.S.-manufactured cars were eligible. France, who had been helping promote races since the late 1930s, became president.[14]

At first NASCAR competed with at least four other sanctioning bodies that sponsored national championships for stock cars. Before 1950, most race cars had substantially modified engines and suspensions to increase speed and improve handling. Most of the NASCAR races involved such modified cars, but in June 1949, France sponsored a 150-mile race at Charlotte for new "strictly stock" cars, and 13,000 fans showed up. The lineup for the race included 10 Fords, 6 Oldsmobiles, 4 Hudsons, 3 Lincolns, 2 Buicks, 2 Chryslers, 2 Kaisers, 1 Cadillac, and 1 Mercury. Fonty Flock later complained that his Hudson was exceedingly slow. "All I did was ride around playing the radio and waving at the girls in the stands." Other drivers pressed too hard, and their new cars expired. Flock finished second, never passing a car. Jim Roper won in a Lincoln. The "strictly stock" race was quickly renamed the Grand National, a term borrowed from elite British horse racing. France's showroom series transformed automobile racing. Grand National stock cars, resembling the automobiles fans owned, suggested respectability, whereas the older but faster modified cars were linked to the rowdy past and hauling liquor. A fan who saw a Ford or Chevrolet victory on Sunday might be moved to buy a similar car on Monday, a temptation not lost on the automobile industry. The consumer potential proved enormous.[15]

Over the years, Bill France's empire spread across the country, and he became the czar of stock car racing. He tolerated no disloyalty. When drivers Tim Flock, Lee Petty, and Red Byron competed in an unsanctioned race at Bruton Smith's Charlotte track in 1950, France stripped their points earned in earlier races, probably causing Petty to lose the Grand National championship and Flock to lose the modified series. France made his point. He later beat down other attempts to organize drivers or challenge his will. The power that France exerted was different from that of antebellum planters or textile mill owners. Cajoling, threatening, and punitive, Big Bill France brilliantly mixed the smile, the handshake, and the clenched fist. When France turned the empire over to his son, William Clifton France, in 1972, NASCAR was sanctioning 1,600 races in thirty-four states and some in Europe. France campaigned for George Wallace in his 1972 bid for the presidency and was generally recognized, in the words of one of his employees, as "the John Wayne of the South." He brought undreamed-of prosperity to stock car racing. With the help of sponsors, France hammered at drivers' rough edges, discouraged their public fighting, and generally kept them on a short leash. Whatever political notions, if any, these wild men had in the early days of racing, prosperity made them Republicans.[16]

The Daytona race, which used the beach and the parallel highway, anchored France's empire, but in 1948, South Carolinian Harold Brasington went to the Indianapolis 500 and returned to Darlington with a dream for a paved stock car track. The circuit that emerged lacked Indianapolis's length but exuded its own asymmetrical mile-and-a-quarter charm. One end narrowed to avoid a minnow pond, and the other widened because the road grader driver dozed off in mid-turn, or so the story goes. On September 4, 1950, Darlington hosted a 500-mile Grand National race, and 20,000 fans cheered Johnny Mantz to victory in a 1950 Plymouth. He won $10,510. Darlington was the only completely paved NASCAR track in 1950, the first southern superspeedway. When the track first opened, Smokey Yunick recalled, it had one toilet, a single spigot for drinking water, and one telephone. In his estimation, Darlington "was a chicken-shit facility run by a bunch of farmers." As late as 1957, reporter Tom Higgins recalled that most tracks had wooden grandstands and "the restrooms were military latrines out in the woods."[17]

Southern 500, Darlington, South Carolina, 1950. Photographs by W. D. Workman Jr.
W. D. Workman Jr. Papers, Modern Political Collections, South Caroliniana Library,
University of South Carolina, Columbia.

Countless stories circulated about the first generation of stock car drivers. All were rowdy and uneducated former trippers, the legend goes. They emerged from their families and communities as larger-than-life heroes primarily because their origins had been so humble. The communities they came from respected their determination and skill. The fact that more respectable folks looked down on the racing community only swelled their pride. A disproportionate number of drivers came from the Carolinas and the Georgia and Virginia mountains.[18]

The Flock family of Fort Payne, Alabama, personified the skill, nerve, and wildness that created such legends. After Lee Preston Flock died, his wife, Maudie Josie Williams Flock, affectionately known as Big Mama, reared eight children on her own. The family moved in installments to Atlanta to live with Carl, the oldest boy, who worked for his uncle, Peachtree Williams, in what was called the "liquor business." Carl also competed in speedboat races, winning, among other titles, the 1933 national outboard championship. He ultimately got

out of the liquor business and became a Florida businessman. Reo Cleo Flock, named for the automobile, ran away from home at age nineteen and became a parachutist with an aerial barnstorming troupe.[19]

In Atlanta, the younger boys helped with their uncle's liquor business. Bob Flock, born in 1918, made his first liquor trip from the Georgia mountains near Dahlonega to Atlanta when he was sixteen years old. During the depths of the depression, $30 to $40 a load was big money. He also won over 300 of the wildcat races at tracks in the area. Although Bob also drove in what became NASCAR's Grand National series, he preferred the faster modified races.[20]

Fonty Flock followed in Bob's footsteps, hauling liquor and racing modified cars (winning the series in 1949) before pursuing his Grand National career. He bragged that as a tripper he deliberately baited lawmen to chase him. In addition to his driving skills, Fonty was known for his outrageous behavior. He made a fashion statement by sporting a thin mustache and boldly racing in Bermuda shorts. He retired after being injured at the Southern 500 in Darlington in 1957. Ethel Annette Flock was born in 1920. After marrying, Ethel Flock Mobley often raced modified cars, and in her one Grand National appearance, the 1949 Daytona race, she finished eleventh to Tim's second but was ahead of both Bob and Fonty.[21]

Tim Flock, born in 1924, was the youngest child. His mother wanted to protect him from both tripping and racing. He became an itinerant worker, driving trucks, working in hotels, and selling liquor (legally). When World War II began, he joined the army but was discharged because of a bleeding ulcer. He then took flying lessons. "I'd fly under bridges . . . did touch and goes on the top of moving trains, and landed on back roads," he remembered. While employed as a taxi driver in Atlanta in 1947, he convinced his brothers to take him to a race at North Wilkesboro, North Carolina. It was not in his nature to stand on the sidelines, so he began racing. On June 20, 1949, Tim won his first race at Greensboro, North Carolina. By the time he called Big Mama to report his victory, she had already heard from Fonty, who had won a race at Birmingham, Alabama, and Bob, who had won at Columbus, Georgia. In 1949, the Flocks moved to North Carolina to be near more racetracks. Tim recalled that racing in the fifties was rough. "I bumped a lot of guys, put a lot of guys in the fences, but I never did get mad enough to try and kill somebody out there, like hit 'em in the driving door or something like that." When a reporter asked Flock if dirt track racing was a good living, he replied, "Yes . . . but not for nervous people." In 1952 and again in 1955, Tim won the Grand National championship.[22]

To make a living in the late forties and early fifties, drivers sometimes competed in three races a week. Ned Jarrett recalled that most races were 100-mile events on short dirt or paved tracks. He would arrive at four in the afternoon, practice for a few hours, and race at eight. He might race at Columbia, South Carolina, on Thursday night, Charlotte on Friday, and Hickory, North Carolina, on Saturday. As late as 1955, the NASCAR Grand National tour included only three paved tracks—Darlington, Raleigh, and Martinsville, Virginia.[23]

Promoters in the fifties encouraged any gimmick that might attract the crowds and eagerly embellished rumors of driver feuds, wild behavior, fights, and crashes. One of Tim Flock's car owners, Ted Chester, bought him a monkey whom he named Jocko Flocko and convinced Tim to let the monkey ride with him in the number 91 Hudson. They installed a tiny seat on the passenger side of his race car so that Jocko Flocko could look out. On April 5, 1953, Jocko raced with Tim at Charlotte and, with appropriate promotion, continued his career until May 30. During a race at Raleigh, Jocko escaped from his seat belts, panicked, and ended up on Tim's shoulder. Tim pitted and handed the frightened monkey to his crew. During his career as Tim Flock's codriver, Jocko helped earn $3,945.[24]

Fonty Flock and Ethel Flock Mobley, standing by Tim Flock's number 91 car, probably at Lakewood Speedway, Atlanta, Georgia. International Speedway Corporation/NASCAR.

In 1954, Tim Flock quit racing in disgust when his car was disqualified after he won the Daytona race and opened a filling station in Atlanta. In 1955, he went to Daytona as a spectator and ended up driving Carl Kiekhaefer's hot new Chrysler 300. Because the Chrysler had an automatic transmission, Tim could not accelerate out of the corners, and Fireball Roberts won the race, only to have the victory taken away from him over a rules infraction. Tim Flock inherited the win. After a manual transmission was installed in the Chrysler 300, Flock won eighteen races in 1955 and managed to overcome Lee Petty's points lead to win his second Grand National championship. By the season's end, all three Flocks were driving for Kiekhaefer, who in 1956 expanded his team to six drivers. According to Tim Flock, Kiekhaefer played favorites, and after winning at North Wilkesboro on April 8, Tim quit the Kiekhaefer team and finished out the season with other rides.[25]

At its wildest, racing was a round of all-night parties, on-track drinking, and late-night cavorting with women. Although many drivers and crew members attended the wild parties, other drivers and mechanics lived a far less romantic life. They worked on their cars, hauled them to the track, qualified, raced, and then hauled them back home to work on them for the next race. Jarrett recalled that when he raced modifieds, he continued to help manage his father's lumber and sawmill business.[26]

Although most women of the era stood by their men, Sara Christian and Louise Smith joined Ethel Flock Mobley as race car drivers. Sara Christian, whose husband, Frank, was reputedly not only in the numbers and liquor business but also a good mechanic, competed on equal terms with men. In 1949, she won NASCAR's Woman Driver of the Year award, completing the year thirteenth in the points standing, and she won six of the seventeen races she entered. Christian finished fourteenth at the "strictly stock" race at Charlotte in June 1949. At a forty-lap race at Daytona in July 1949, Louise Smith overturned early in the race but with the help of spectators "uprighted" her car and finished twentieth, two positions behind Christian. Mobley finished eleventh. On September 11, 1949, Christian finished sixth, Smith sixteenth, and Mobley forty-fourth in a 200-mile race at Langhorne, Pennsylvania.[27]

Louise Smith was born in Greenville, South Carolina. Her father and brothers were automobile mechanics, and she learned to drive by age seven. When racing started around Greenville, she entered a race, and her reputation as a fast driver spread. She not only drove fast but also drank, cursed, and fought with men. She expected no special treatment. Still, Smith realized that her presence on the track goaded men. "The men are gentlemen off the track," she judged, "but when you are in a race with them, they are all for themselves, and they don't concede anything." Smith retired in 1956.[28]

As NASCAR races became more organized in the 1950s, women disappeared from the cars and eventually were banned from the pits. Various sources claim that women were excluded because of unspecified safety concerns, because they caused a distraction, or because of jealousy. Their exclusion from competition paralleled other attempts to marginalize women in the 1950s. Women's only official role in racing became that of race queen. In the early years, neither promoters nor drivers had been organized enough to ban women, further testimony to the democratic nature of early stock car racing. Consigning women to the bleachers and the floats left the garages, pits, and tracks a male preserve. In the minds of some men, banning women from competition increased NASCAR's respectability. In the fifties South, decent women did not rub shoulders with uncouth men. Women fans, however, continued to find drivers and races irresistible.

African American driver Wendell Scott brought another kind of diversity to NASCAR. When a race promoter in Danville, Virginia, was seeking a black

Sara Christian, Lakewood Speedway, Atlanta, Georgia, 1949.
International Speedway Corporation/NASCAR.

driver as a device to lure fans, a local policeman recommended Scott, who was on probation for hauling liquor. Born in 1921, Scott was at home in the low-down culture of racing, but because he was black, he was taunted by white fans at his first race at the Danville fairgrounds in 1947. Drivers' reactions varied from acceptance to outright hostility and violence. At least one track, Darling-

Sara Christian in her Olds '88, Lakewood Speedway, Atlanta, Georgia, 1949.
*International Speedway Corporation/*NASCAR.

ton, refused to allow him to compete. In the 1950s, the white fraternity of stock
car drivers was not exactly liberal on matters of race, but Scott learned to survive whatever torment came his way without resorting to fighting. He did well
on the dirt tracks across the South. In the early 1960s, he moved into Grand National racing. Although he never secured a major sponsor, year after year he put
together a respectable effort. In 1961, he finished thirty-second in the points. He
was a solid mid-field competitor, finishing twenty-second in 1962, fifteenth in
1963, and twelfth in 1964. On December 1, 1963, Scott won his first and only
Grand National race at Jacksonville Speedway. Although Buck Baker got the
checkered flag, Scott clearly had won, and a recheck of the scoring showed that
he had lapped Baker twice and actually had completed 202 laps. NASCAR officially declared Scott victor several weeks later. It was widely believed that Baker
was initially granted the "victory" so that Scott would not appear in the win-
ner's circle with the white race queen.[29]

Junior Johnson considered Wendell Scott "a very well mannered gentleman"
who loved racing but had no financial support. "I don't know if I could have
lived underneath the strain that Wendell lived under and kept on racing," Johnson admitted. Jarrett observed that although his "equipment . . . really was not

Louise Smith. International Speedway Corporation/NASCAR.

as good as some people he was competing against," Scott remained competitive because of his skill as a car builder and a racer. Drivers often shared parts with him. Both Johnson and Jarrett admitted that some drivers were less than polite to Scott. It was remarkable that Scott could compete at all, especially after the backlash against the *Brown v. Board of Education* decision in 1954 intensified debate over the issue of segregation.[30]

Out of the dust and grime of the dirt track era emerged stories that recounted and sometimes embellished the fast and furious lives of drivers, mechanics, and fans. A handful of 1950s stock car drivers became legends, including the Flocks, Junior Johnson, Curtis Turner, Fireball Roberts, and Joe Weatherly. Junior Johnson was born in 1931 in Wilkes County, North Carolina, the son of Robert Glenn Johnson Sr. and Lora Money Johnson. Tom Wolfe's *Esquire* article and a subsequent film on Johnson increased his already substantial fame. Johnson's father, like many of his neighbors, farmed and made liquor. "About everybody who lived around where I lived was either involved in it one way or the other," Johnson explained of the liquor business. Glenn Johnson and his three sons, L. P., Fred, and Junior, operated a major illegal liquor business. When Junior was four years old, federal agents found 1,113 cases of illegal liquor

Wendell Scott stands in front of his 1961 Chevrolet. Courtesy Don Hunter.

in the Johnson home. They poured out 7,100 gallons and broke all 6,678 Mason jars. After hiding out for eight months, Glenn Johnson turned himself in and received a four-year sentence. He had been hoarding low-priced liquor waiting for the price to rise.[31]

Glenn Johnson's family continued in the liquor business. In 1953, federal agents found 1,200 pounds of sugar near the Johnson home and brought bootlegging charges against Junior, Fred, and Glenn Johnson. They were found guilty and sentenced to eighteen months in prison. They appealed, and a three-judge panel overturned the convictions. Even as they fought the charges, which Junior considered unfair, the family continued making and transporting liquor. Junior told reporter Bob Zeller that he sometimes made three trips a night, operated four stills, and had up to twenty-five people working for him.[32]

Junior quit school in the eighth grade, by which time he considered himself grown. He did not start out planning to race automobiles. From the time he was ten until he broke his arm at age fourteen when a farm tractor overturned, Johnson learned baseball under the tutelage of a retired professional pitcher. By the time his baseball career ended, he was playing against boys four and five years older in the leagues around Wilkes County. After he could no longer pitch because of the pain in his arm, he concentrated on learning to drive. Already at

Junior Johnson, 1963.
Photograph by Bill Wilson.
Courtesy of the Atlanta
History Center.

age fourteen, he was hauling liquor for the family business. He studied driving as seriously as he had studied baseball. "I basically could outguess what the car was going to do," he explained. When the North Wilkesboro Speedway opened near his home, he began racing. Sponsorship was unheard of, so a group of young men would pool their money in order to enter a race. In the early days, Johnson recalled, they raced "for the fun of it, more than anything else." The racers partied as hard as they drove. "You know, seeing who was the best partier was just as important almost as seeing who was the best driver." Jarrett remembered that many drivers would "just get together and either celebrate a victory over the past weekend or celebrate one they thought was coming up the next weekend."[33]

Curtis Turner, Fireball Roberts, and the Flocks headed Johnson's list of top competitors of his generation. They had "nerve," which in Johnson's estimation had to be used wisely. "You need to save all your nerve and skills and stuff till it's real important." In a close race, other drivers knew that Johnson would summon his nerve and never back off. Pondering why drivers felt compelled to race, he admitted that "it was like we was all crazy." Since they made little money, "we did it mostly for fun to start with because we all enjoyed the challenge." Fans came at first to see "a bunch of fools," he joked, but the skills of his generation of drivers astounded them. "Basically, we'd run 'em sideways and backwards and about any way you wanted to see one, in whatever position you wanted to see it in," he continued. "We could get 'em in that position and still save 'em and not wreck 'em a lot of times." Johnson explained that any sense of danger was offset "because you're controlling everything. . . . You can either slow down or go however fast you want to." The point of racing, he insisted, was "to prove to the other guy you're better than he is."[34]

Drivers sometimes deployed brutal tactics. In 1959, while racing Lee Petty for the lead at Charlotte, Johnson was forced off the track with a flat tire after Petty incessantly banged his bumper. Johnson pitted, changed the tire, and after returning to the race deliberately forced Petty into the wall. The incident brought out the Charlotte police. "H'it was dog, eat dog," Johnson explained to author Tom Wolfe. "That straightened Lee Petty out right smart." Many drivers believed in such swift justice. Drivers in the fifties "were competitive people with tempers," Jarrett explained. "It was not uncommon on a Saturday night at Hickory Speedway to have two, three, or four fights during the night," he recalled. "One, most of the time, would outshine the others." Johnson recalled that "they liked to fight about as good as race. . . . They'd stop the race and fight." NASCAR had rules, but drivers negotiated racing etiquette with humor, arguments, fights, and on-track retribution.[35]

Even as his racing career was flourishing, Johnson was arrested in June 1956 for firing his father's liquor still and sentenced in November to two years in a federal prison plus a $5,000 fine. The agents caught him red-handed, and he accepted the verdict and served eleven months. In 1958, federal agents brought charges against the entire Johnson family. His brothers Fred and L. P. went to jail, and their mother was fined $7,500. Junior was not convicted. For the Johnson family, making and hauling liquor was not only their business but also a way of life. Racing was Junior's leisure activity, whereas tripping was his living.[36]

In retrospect, Johnson considered prison "one of the best things that ever happened to me." It taught him discipline. Before prison, he explained, he "was a pretty well hardheaded, set type individual. When I came out of prison, I weren't that way, and I never have been since." The guards did not care who he was or where he had come from. When they gave orders, he remembered, you either followed them "or you paid, paid dearly." Johnson still reflects before he speaks, gives concise replies to questions, and offers no small talk. His concentration, both as a driver and as a car owner, was awesome. This was not a man to tangle with, as Lee Petty discovered.[37]

In his 1965 essay on Johnson, Tom Wolfe suggested how Johnson transcended the sport. "Junior Johnson is one of the last of those sports stars who is not just an ace at the game itself," Wolfe judged, "but a hero a whole people or class of people can identify with." Johnson retired from racing in the mid-sixties when he was thirty-four years old and became a car owner. His race cars won 139 races and 6 championships. In 1995, at age sixty-five, he sold his racing team and retired. As a tripper who never got caught on the road, as a faithful son who served time for firing his father's still, as a driver who wisely used his nerve, as a successful businessman, and as an owner whose cars won often, Junior Johnson personified the contradictions and genius of southern culture.[38]

Fireball Roberts shared both Johnson's penchant for keeping to himself and an association with baseball. Roberts earned the nickname "Fireball" as a baseball pitcher in his teens. Introverted, moody, preoccupied, and contradictory, Roberts became one of the great drivers of the 1950s and early 1960s. Born in Apopka, Florida, in 1929, Roberts attended two years of college at the University of Florida. He dropped out in 1950 to race full time.[39]

During the early fifties, Roberts drove in modified and Grand National races, and in 1958, he won both the Rebel 300 and the Southern 500 at Darlington. The next year, he teamed up with mechanic Smokey Yunick. "Fireball was wild, drunk all the time, chased women all the time," Yunick recalled. In Jarrett's estimation, he was one of the most gifted and smartest drivers of the era. In May 1964, Roberts crashed at the Charlotte 600, and his car burst into flames. He died from burns on July 2.[40]

At the time Roberts died, Jarrett explained, drivers protected themselves from fire only by dousing their racing outfits in "a solution of boric acid and other ingredients." The clothes were then hung on a fence to dry. "They'd look like you got drunk and throwed up and then wallowed in it," he continued. Fireball Roberts was allergic to the flameproofing agent. At the time of the accident, Roberts was wearing a "tailored uniform that had zippers on the sleeves, zippers on the side, and zippers on the legs." When Jarrett pulled Roberts from his flaming car, he could not get the uniform off quickly, Jarrett explained, and "that's what cost him his life, in my opinion." A day later at the Indianapolis 500, another fiery crash claimed two victims. Research intensified to develop flameproof uniforms and fuel cells that would not rupture in a crash.[41]

Ned Jarrett, born in 1932, grew up near Hickory, North Carolina, played high school sports, and worked with his father in the lumber and sawmill business. In 1952, as the community eagerly awaited the completion of the new racetrack being built at Hickory, twenty-year-old Jarrett decided to try racing. He staked his brother-in-law $100 in a poker game for his half interest in a race car. In his first race, Jarrett finished tenth, competing against, among others, Junior Johnson and Ralph Earnhardt, the father of modern NASCAR driver Dale Earnhardt. Jarrett could not recall any driver or crew member in the fifties who was not a member of the working class. Many, he admitted, were involved in the liquor business, especially those who raced at North Wilkesboro, Hickory, and Charlotte.[42]

Fireball Roberts, 1958. Photograph by Bill Wilson.
Courtesy of the Atlanta History Center.

Over the years, Grand National "strictly stock" cars evolved into race cars, in part to improve safety but also because speed won races. Ford products benefited from factory performance parts, which explains why trippers and modified car drivers were partial to them. In 1955, Chevrolet came out with a V-8 engine and, along with the Chrysler 300, offered Ford powerful competition. In 1956, team owner John Holman reinvigorated Ford's racing efforts, and the other major manufacturers followed by providing substantial backing to other teams. When their advertising campaigns stressed safety a year later, the Big Three ended direct sponsorship of racing. Once the drivers and owners had tasted the benefits of factory-backed racing technology, however, they continued to search for speed. In the 1960s, factory support reemerged and drove technical advances that enhanced speed. Over time, both speed and safety concerns grew and, Jarrett revealed, became strangely linked. A stronger and safer

Smokey Yunick, 1963. Courtesy Don Hunter.

suspension, for example, increased cornering speeds. "Just about every part of the car that they've improved over the years for safety has helped make them go faster," Jarrett stated.[43]

Curtis Turner emerged as one of the most talented and outrageous drivers of the 1950s, particularly on dirt tracks. Jarrett admired Turner's ability to drive even a hard-to-handle race car through a corner. By "throwing the car sideways and spinning the wheels and throwing up the rooster tails," Turner awed fans at dirt tracks and the famous beach course at Daytona. In Jarrett's mind, Turner, Junior Johnson, and, more recently, Dale Earnhardt were natural-born race drivers. Jarrett modestly admitted that his style was not so spectacular: "I learned that a race car would run faster straight than it will sideways."[44]

Curtis Turner was born in 1924 in the southwestern Virginia mountains. His father, Morton Turner, owned a sawmill, made liquor, and earned a reputation as a "tripper." By the time he was ten, Curtis had learned to drive, and at fourteen, he dropped out of school. By saving the money he made from hauling his father's liquor, Turner bought several sawmills of his own; he had a knack for investing and then losing money. Turner had rugged good looks, stood six feet, two inches tall, and weighed 220 pounds. In 1946, he began racing at Mount

Curtis Turner, 1966. Courtesy Don Hunter.

Airy, North Carolina. Over time, he became perhaps the best dirt track driver of his era, although he was as likely to crash as to win. Driver Ralph Moody put it simply: "He didn't give a damn for nothing," the highest compliment a low-down southerner could be paid. Smokey Yunick summed up Turner's style when he stated, "I spent a lot of time with Curtis drinking, chasing women, racing, raising hell, teaching people how to turn around in the middle of the road at 60 miles an hour, putting cars in swimming pools." Turner dressed in silk suits, drove a Lincoln Continental, hung out with Hollywood stars, and claimed that in the mid-fifties he spent $6,000 a month. "Curtis went through his money like it was water," Tim Flock recalled. Before one race, a group of drivers, Turner and Flock in the lead, paid a farmer $100 to borrow his mule and then pushed it up the steps of a motel to the second-floor balcony, where it greeted surprised guests. Unlike many drivers of his generation, Turner rarely fought. He would knock competitors out of the way on the track and then disarm them after the race by inviting them to a party.[45]

It took all of Turner's charm to placate an enraged Tiny Lund after Turner carelessly knocked him out of the lead at an Atlanta race. After the race, Lund found Turner washing off grime beside the infield lake and pushed him into deep water. A gasping Turner reminded Lund that they had raced and partied together, that they were friends. A crowd gathered, and Lund recalled that some of them were urging Lund "to drown him and part of 'em to save him." Such incidents not only grew in the telling but also inscribed the unwritten rules between competitors.[46]

Joe Weatherly, Turner's sidekick, was born in Oak Grove, Virginia, in 1922. After serving in World War II, he raced motorcycles before turning to stock cars in the early 1950s. In 1953, he won fifty-two races and the modified championship. Turner and Weatherly often relaxed together offtrack, and their outrageous behavior became part of the folklore of stock car racing. Turner recalled that on one race weekend, they basically destroyed two "U-Drive-It" cars, one of which Weatherly drove one into a motel swimming pool. Then they went from room to room until they found one unlocked and vacant, went inside and bolted the door, and spent the night in someone else's room. During the Daytona Speed Week, Turner and Weatherly threw parties at which drivers and crews reputedly consumed $5,000 worth of liquor, goaded topless dancers, and violated several of the Ten Commandments. Such stories preserved the texture of wildness and lowdown behavior that epitomized the racing world of the fifties. Among other victories, Weatherly won the Rebel 300 at Darlington and the National 500 at Atlanta. In 1962 and 1963, he won the Grand National championship. He died in 1964 in a race accident at Riverside Raceway in California.[47]

Turner was reputed to have won and lost several fortunes in his lifetime. He and promoter Bruton Smith developed the mile-and-half Charlotte Motor Speedway, which opened with the World 600 in June 1960. They ran into numerous problems during construction. When the earth-moving contractor demanded payment and blocked the unpaved portion of the track with his machines, Turner appeared with a shotgun and cleared the track. Turner ultimately overextended himself and lost his share. The Charlotte Motor Speedway joined the updated Daytona track, which opened in 1959, and Darlington as NASCAR's superspeedways, and the trend toward larger and larger spectacles was well under way. By 1960, NASCAR's southern tour included eight paved tracks. The number of fans who enjoyed stock car racing seemed limitless.[48]

Jacque Passino, who once headed Ford's racing program, had problems with unruly drivers. From his corporate point of view, which focused on winning races and gaining good press and public relations, some of the drivers were "just classy barbarians." Passino might well have had the best car, but then, he complained, "you put this dumb bastard in your car." He was especially leery of

Joe Weatherly.
Courtesy Don Hunter.

Turner and Weatherly. Once the race started, they were likely to do anything. "They were just out having fun. I never really put too much faith in either of those guys because you never knew how long you were gonna have them running." They had probably partied all night the night before, and he dreaded telling Ford executives that they had lost "because all these guys were at an allnight party." Passino failed to understand that Weatherly and Turner, among others, used Ford as a medium for pursuing their own interests, and their destruction of automobiles was purposefully disrespectful of Ford and other manufacturers. Their passion for outrage defied such sponsors. Many drivers were practical jokers and partiers, but their humor was lost on Passino. He wanted to tame them for commercial purposes, to make them predictable, presentable. To Weatherly and Turner, racing meant more than allowing a Ford to win on Sunday so that Fords would sell on Monday. They were part of a racing troupe that jested, turned the rules upside down, and mocked authority. Tim Flock recalled that he would party all night before a race and even drink during the race. "We'll take it down the straightaway and let Lord Calvert take it through the turns," he joked. At one race, members of his pit crew were stumbling drunk when he made a pit stop. Once the untamed part of racing died, drivers became icons of capitalism, identified as much with the product as with their own names.[49]

Passino, of course, wanted predictability, dependability, and victory. Tamed, articulate, and successful drivers could sell cars and plug sponsors. Turner loved racing, but the races were only one part of his life. Investing money, pursuing women, partying, and driving big cars vied with racing. For him, it seemed, losing a fortune was almost as much fun as amassing one; destroying a car gave almost as much pleasure as winning a race with one; mangling a rental car in a friendly public road race not only was fun but also added to his legend.

The fiercely competitive racing culture was characterized by a disrespect for authority that had been the underpinning of the bootlegger culture and of the worldview of the working class. Those who inhabited racing's outlaw world, whether in a lowlife dive, a race car, or the grandstands, shared contempt for elite standards. Fans thrilled as they watched loud and powerful race cars in the hands of aggressive drivers teetering on the edge of control. The race cars themselves appeared transgressive to spectators whose own automobiles had stock mufflers, engines, tires, and suspensions. Fans took to racing in part because drivers personified both wildness and success, transgression and acceptance, and were people much like themselves who had become stars. The folklore of southern stock car racing is thick with 1950s heroes. Untamed and uncouth, these heroes tore a wide swath of outrage through the decade.

Many race fans in the fifties mirrored the drivers in that they had grown up hard, had country credentials, worked at filling stations or in other low-paying jobs, and knew the sting of poverty. Attending races reaffirmed their status as outsiders, outlaws. They scorned polite society and were in revolt against the constricting forces that threatened to tame them and rob them of their spontaneity. They were rude, violent, uncouth, and proud of it. And most of them were white men. Rare photographs of black race drivers exist, but unfortunately their legends and fans have never been put forward as part of the larger fabric of racing. Only Wendell Scott rose to the top level of competition.

Attending races eased the taming process by providing an outlet for behavior that was becoming ever more unacceptable in polite society. In more recent times, the riotous infields and nonstop partying desperately reaffirm the tradition, if not the substance, of outrage and wildness. The original compulsion for revelry has been eased with materialism, just as the racing environment has been transformed by immense grandstands and souvenir stands hawking hats and T-shirts. Since the first Darlington Labor Day Southern 500 in 1950, the infield crowd became the annual yardstick of wildness, and each year, the crowd constructed some new outrage to compete with the past. The most recent stabbings, shootings, fights, seductions, and drinking bouts were embellished to match former narratives. It was a bloodshot weekend. Jarrett spent a night in the Darlington infield in the early 1950s, and he recalled that there were "lots

Car sponsored by William Cave Johnson Sr., owner of an automotive repair shop in Clarksville, Tennessee, at the New Providence Speedway in Clarksville, August 20, 1954. Johnson's son stands beside the car. The driver is not identified. Looking Back at Tennessee Collection (Montgomery County 090), Tennessee State Library and Archives, Nashville.

of opportunities" to get into trouble. "They were not bashful with sex, and, of course, they'd be some quickly put together country music groups, lots of drinking, card playing. It was pretty wild." An infield jail detained the most savage. The stories of a beautiful Lady Godiva roaring through the infield on a Harley before lapping the track and disappearing rivaled tales of whore hearses, all recalled over bourbon and beer and the music of Merle Haggard. Country music became anthematic of NASCAR, as reflected in a host of songs that celebrate racing.[50]

The wild stories continue, but now they spill from motor homes, apartment-sized rental trucks, and recreational vehicles whose owners are far removed from lowdown culture. The Darlington infield has been divided into an Azalea Terrace, the President's Suite, and a Fourth Turn Club that features a gigantic corporate hospitality tent. Confederate flags still wave over the bellied and bronzed fans, but for the most part, present-day fans lack the violent edge of their predecessors. Many lowdown fans, not accidentally, have been priced out of the $500-a-ticket Azalea Terrace. Many race fans, at best neo-lowdown, are more affluent, but they still treat themselves to redneck weekends. These fans are making a transition from factory work to service jobs to corporate employment, but they nevertheless crave illicit pleasures and uninhibited behavior. For half a century, NASCAR has been a palliative for working people in transition. They crave the noise, smell, and danger of racing.[51]

The very landscape of racing has changed so radically that whatever lowdown "purity" existed in the early days has largely vanished. Modern grandstands boast not only adequate restrooms and numerous concession and T-shirt stands but also executive suites. Two hundred and fifty corporations support the racing teams as well as 15.4 million fans and a television audience of 130 million. What started out as informal races in pastures by trippers has evolved to the point that NASCAR racing is indistinguishable from advertising. The rough edges have been filed off. Even the most vicious driver, in deference to his sponsor, speaks carefully, if not grammatically, as he praises God, sponsor, and crew. Sponsor dollars force drivers to resist the temptation to curse publicly or blame other drivers, and a $10,000 fine discourages fighting. In the 1950s, drivers were icons of rebellion and resistance. They didn't give a damn, according to the most lavish praise. They would do anything. Perhaps the ultimate sign of taming came in the 1970s when NASCAR sanctioned a preaching service before the races. Weekend wildness, the working class's respite from drudgery, has been inherited by the middle class, which has a different catalog of discontents.[52]

Drivers, crews, and spectators in the 1950s were working class, hard-core, lowdown. Despite the wildness and the outlaw image, most were God-fearing family people. No matter how outrageous their behavior on the track or in the infield, they were, Jarrett insisted, "just good down-to-earth people" who cared for each other. The drivers "found a challenge that they wanted to pursue." Some were bootleggers and some were wild, he admitted, but they were all there for the challenge, "to try to outrun someone." In Jarrett's mind, drivers, crews, and families were a close community that might fight and disagree but loyally supported each other. In their wildness, they not only refused to bow to elite culture but also mocked it. As late as 1968, a columnist for *Road and Track*, a magazine that favors Ferraris over Fords, Formula 1 over heavy metal, succinctly denounced NASCAR. "The rules are ridiculous, the vehicles are neither stock automobiles nor proper racing cars and NASCAR puts on its races with all the hokiness of an Elvis Presley movie. And with about as much class." But the good old boys wanted acceptance. Attempting to remain lowdown in an increasingly affluent racing culture presented challenges and exposed contradictions. "You can say it's lost its soul," Junior Johnson philosophized. "But it's making a lot of money."[53]

Facilities have improved, more fans come from the middle class, drivers speak articulately, television carries all of the races, and drivers have gained national and international fame. Retired drivers such as Ned Jarrett, Benny Parsons, and Buddy Baker share their insights with television and radio audiences. The cars still go in a circle, Jarrett points out, but nearly everything else has changed. The creative elements of lowdown culture eventually became tamed and commodified but not before establishing a racing series that has gained worldwide respect. Drivers and fans in the 1950s bent culture to suit their purposes, but as NASCAR closes small tracks and cuts ever bigger deals, commercialism bends lowdown culture to its purposes. After a 1988 interview, Junior Johnson paused along the pit road at the Dover, Delaware, track. After surveying the decaled cars, flashy sponsors, and executive suites, he shrugged his shoulders and said, "It's all been tamed now."[54]

6 Rhythms of the Land

In the beginning, people from all over the country came to Memphis,
came down that river and docked somewhere along there and came to
Beale Street. . . . Beale Street was the black man's haven.
—*Rufus Thomas*

I will say unhesitatingly that if God gave me anything at all, anything at all,
he gave me the intuitive powers to not read minds but to feel souls.
—*Sam Phillips*

Southern rural music—blues, country, gospel, work songs, and field hollers—evolved from the everyday trials, tribulations, and hopes of southern farmers. Country people often spent their lives within a community, but their cultural landscape extended beyond county and state lines. Even before Victrolas and radios became commonplace, traveling musicians transmitted the latest popular music to the most isolated crossroads. They traveled along an invisible network composed of the shifting and overlapping itineraries of minstrel and vaudeville shows, one-night stands in small towns, street corners, brothels, juke joints, and honky-tonks far removed from any tracking system.[1]

Whether it was blues, country, or gospel, rural music was dynamic and evolving. The younger generation of musicians might well have learned how their ancestors played, but its presentation addressed contemporary concerns and provided a commentary on family, love, tragedy, and frustration. When farming failed, rural refugees gathered their earthly belongings and moved to towns and cities, where their music became the seed of a mid-century revolution. Rural African American music, sacred and secular, urbanized and electrified, ripened into rhythm and blues. At almost the same time, a faster beat infected hillbilly music and, drawing on African American sources and its own vitality, flowered into rock 'n' roll. Although spirited debate over the origins of these musical genres continues, blues, black and white gospel music, and hillbilly music all had rural roots. Much of the music of the latter twentieth century thus goes back to rhythms of the land and embodies the essence of rural life and memory.

The last generation of sharecroppers replaced their blasted rural dreams with urban hopes and frustrations. The culture that had served them so well in the country evolved to fit city spaces. Across the country, the collision of rural music with the energized urban beat reshaped the cultural landscape. Southern musicians profoundly influenced musical development in the twentieth century, not because they embodied pure European or African traditions but because they dynamically exchanged and incorporated their vast musical knowledge. During the middle decades of the twentieth century, an unlikely renaissance swept through southern society. Black and white musicians were part of a vibrant cultural exchange that produced jazz, blues, country, gospel, rhythm and blues, rock 'n' roll, and soul music.[2]

Memphis and its surrounding countryside cultivated a disproportionate number of musicians, and their experiences suggest that they shared a compulsion to travel, an ambition to master all forms of popular music, and an eagerness to perform and record despite receiving little compensation for their creative work. Ashley Thompson, for example, grew up at the turn of the century near Ripley, Tennessee, and performed with whites and blacks throughout the South. In 1928, Thompson and his friend Noah Lewis joined their old acquaintance Gus Cannon in Memphis to make a record. In this session, Thompson sang "Minglewood Blues" and "Big Railroad Blues" for Cannon's Jug Stompers. They performed on a work-for-hire basis, waiving royalties and copyright protection. "I got $7.50 a song," Thompson remembered; he took home $30 for the four-song session. Sam Chatmon, who lived near Bolton, Mississippi, formed the Mississippi Sheiks along with members of his extended family. Their songs "Sitting on Top of the World" and "Corinna" sold millions of copies, he recalled, but "I ain't got a penny, not nairn." He received a lump sum at the recording session. "Wasn't no royalties in them days," he noted. "He give you $20 and you'd go on back home and forget it."[3] As members of the black working class, Thompson and Chatmon measured their payments against assumed corporate profits.

Arthur Crudup personified the tribulations of a poor creative artist. Born in Forrest, Mississippi, in 1905, Crudup wrote, performed, and recorded songs while working day jobs in Indianapolis, Chicago, and the Mississippi Delta. In 1949, while farming in Mississippi, he insisted that the landlord cheated him out of over $1,500. In 1954, when Elvis Presley launched his career by recording one of Crudup's songs, "That's All Right, Mama," Crudup was headed for Florida to join the migrant labor stream. When he died in 1974, Crudup was still claiming $60,000 in back royalties.[4] Such musicians as Thompson, Chatmon, and Crudup, along with hundreds of others who came from the Memphis countryside, made significant contributions to the musical revolution that swept Memphis in the mid-1950s. If a complete list of musicians from the 150-mile radius around Memphis could be compiled, it would be enormous.

The vitality of fifties Memphis owed a huge debt to the city's rural refugees. When rural options were exhausted, farmers turned to what they deigned public work, and Memphis was the largest mid-South city. Rural people did not move because they yearned to live in northern or southern towns and cities. They moved because of the depression, because landlords evicted them in order to pocket their share of New Deal payments. They moved when the defense industry boomed during World War II, when draft notices arrived, and when tractors, picking machines, and herbicides replaced them. The collapse of labor-intensive agriculture triggered not only the spread of southern music but also its transformation. Something significant happened in the 1940s and 1950s when the last generation of sharecroppers arrived in towns and cities. Although many parents viewed public work and dense urban housing with distaste, their children arrived in Memphis and other cities immensely excited about their prospects. To young refugees, cities and towns offered a lifeline. As they matured, many found security in day jobs, but they dreamed of creating music.[5]

When country folks moved to towns and cities, they encountered complex urban segregation codes. The strictures against interracial socializing presented contradictions that were puzzling to many teenage rural exiles of the 1950s generation. Born in depression, weaned in war, and restless to make their way, southern working-class teenagers often overstepped racial boundaries as they explored city life. Many whites had an uncontrollable appetite for African American music and style. Likewise, social currents flowing out of World War II and challenges to the color line spurred African Americans to test segregation laws. Parents may well have been worn out by depression and war, but their children were hungry for adventure.

As much as any city, Memphis became a mixing bowl of rural migrants and their urban working-class cousins. Post–World War II migrants found a city in transition. In the first forty years of the century, the black population rose from 49,910 to 121,498. By 1960, 184,320 of the city's 497,524 residents were African Americans. Prior to World War II, African Americans in Memphis had better housing in less restricted sections of town than African Americans in such cities as Richmond and Atlanta. "We lived in patches," Blair T. Hunt, principal of Booker T. Washington High School, recalled. "There was no big black belt, no solid black belt anywhere in this city of Memphis." During the thirties, New Deal programs aided public-housing construction, but projects were often built on the ruins of recently razed black communities. African Americans had inadequate health care and poor, though proud, schools. Buses, theaters, hotels, restaurants, auditoriums, and even factories were segregated. As the city grew and pressure to integrate schools and public accommodations increased during the 1950s, city planners used freeway construction and urban renewal as tools to destroy black neighborhoods and enforce residential segregation. Just when the confluence of black and white music challenged segregation, white leaders began to police the color line more energetically.[6]

Memphis offered workers a growing variety of employment. In addition to jobs involving construction, the river trade, and the cotton industry, the Firestone Tire and Rubber Company opened a factory in 1937. After the war, International Harvester located a mechanical cotton harvester plant near Memphis that hired many rural refugees to make machines that would drive more farmers off the land. The city's promising interracial labor movement of the late 1930s and World War II, however, faltered in the shadow of the Cold War and anticommunism. Integrated unions had furnished an institutional framework for blacks and whites to challenge segregation and fight for higher wages and benefits. Many whites reacted bitterly and sometimes violently to the U.S. Supreme Court's order to integrate public schools in the 1954 *Brown v. Board of Education* decision. By 1954, most Congress of Industrial Organizations (CIO) leaders who had insisted on integrated unions had been purged, so most unions took no stand on school integration. Because many whites equated civil rights efforts with communist activity, white union members risked ostracism or retaliation if they supported integration. Many African Americans voted in Memphis, but powerful political boss E. H. Crump exerted enormous control. Reform candidates, with CIO support, defeated Crump's ticket in 1948. States' Rights Party candidate Strom Thurmond, however, outpolled Harry S. Truman in the 1948 presidential election, indicating that the Dixiecrat message of vehement segregation and anticommunism had found eager disciples. It would take years for African Americans to gain proportional power in the city. Still, black voter registration in Memphis increased from 18 to 31 percent of the total voter registration during the 1950s. "The fact that blacks could vote in Memphis," historian Michael K. Honey concluded, "created a situation quite in contrast to the fascistlike reaction against desegregation and unionism in many parts of the South during the fifties."[7]

Black workers found that segregation and discrimination were as tough in Memphis as in the surrounding countryside. When riding city buses, blacks were forced to pay the driver and then reenter the bus through the backdoor and had to sit or stand behind white passengers. Whether they worked at the large Firestone plant, at International Harvester, on the riverfront, at furniture factories, or in the various jobs connected with the cotton trade, blacks found few opportunities for advancement into skilled jobs. Restrooms, locker rooms, and dining rooms at these jobs were segregated.[8]

Despite discrimination and a decline in integrationist support, many African Americans joined unions and rose to leadership positions. At Firestone, Clarence Coe spent years fighting discrimination by using whatever leverage the cio offered. Some white workers at the plant belonged to the Citizens' Council or the Ku Klux Klan, and any white worker who broke ranks and treated blacks with respect risked isolation. Despite unionization and constant complaints about discrimination, Coe stated, Firestone did not completely integrate until 1974.[9]

George Holloway worked for International Harvester. Despite being a leader of the United Automobile Workers (uaw), he experienced constant discrimination. In 1948, during bargaining sessions at the Chisca Hotel, Holloway had to enter the hotel by the freight elevator. For years, he recalled, Harvester representatives "would use the word 'nigger' at every grievance meeting." In the union hall, Holloway protested the separate restrooms for blacks and took his complaints to the top ranks of the uaw. Whites in the Memphis local detested the national uaw's stand on equal rights and berated national executives when they attempted to enforce it. Holloway often felt that his union activities endangered his life. As Honey has argued, black workers such as Coe and Holloway fought for civil rights by insisting on equal treatment and equal opportunity. Unfortunately, the negative reaction to Truman's civil rights initiatives, the rise in Dixiecrat popularity, and fear of school integration after the *Brown* decision made interracial cooperation increasingly difficult.[10]

For black migrants from the countryside, the Memphis workaday world bore a terrible resemblance to what they had left behind. Leroy Boyd moved to Memphis in 1945 when he was twenty-one years old and a year later began a job at Federal Compress hauling cotton bales to a warehouse. His supervisors, he explained, were "right off those plantations." Like Coe and Holloway, Boyd joined the union and fought for decent working conditions.[11] Workers such as Coe, Holloway, and Boyd carried on a war of attrition against segregation and discrimination. White workers tenaciously opposed them with every tool at hand, fearing that skilled black workers would undermine their privileged positions.

Although Firestone, International Harvester, Federal Compress, and other companies were sites of African Americans' running battles for equal rights, other places existed where African Americans were insulated from most discrimination. Black institutions such as churches, funeral homes, businesses, and musical establishments along Beale Street offered a haven from white surveillance. Despite their meanness on the job, many whites, especially youngsters, were keen on black music.[12]

Integration came slowly to Memphis, in part because the local National Association for the Advancement of Colored People (NAACP) chapter did not confront the segregationist city fathers. Tennessee's Pupil Placement Act, passed in 1957, permitted black students to attend white schools, but local school boards continued to stall. It was not until 1960, after sit-ins swept through the city, that the Memphis NAACP chapter filed a desegregation complaint. The city downplayed the sit-ins, but by the end of the year, white business leaders agreed to end segregation on buses, in libraries, and at the zoo. Without warning or preparation, the Memphis board of education announced on October 2, 1961, that thirteen black children would integrate a white elementary school the next day. Some angry whites withdrew their children, but otherwise, token desegregation came peacefully.[13]

In Memphis, as in other places, musicians and athletes often did more to undermine segregation than community leaders. Musician Jim Dickinson credited 220-pound Louisiana wrestler Sputnik Monroe—who had a white skunk line in his hair, "hot" and "cold" tattooed above his nipples, and arms like Popeye—with integrating Memphis public arenas. Many whites considered Monroe white trash and cheered his opponents. Monroe challenged the color line with impunity and drew an enthusiastic African American following. He often strutted down Beale Street preening for his fans. When he performed in Ellis Auditorium, segregation laws dictated that whites sit downstairs and blacks in the balcony, and management insisted that whites compose 50 percent of the audience. Dickinson reported that segregation dissolved at Monroe's matches, however; "greed took over and they had to let more blacks in to where eventually the audience was integrated. They had to let them come downstairs." In Dickinson's opinion, Monroe "had more to do with integrating the Memphis audience than anything that was litigated by the city fathers."[14]

Whereas Sputnik Monroe blatantly challenged segregation, the radio encouraged what amounted to invisible integration. Some radio stations, immune to segregation laws, carried all types of music. "If some Southerners could have segregated the airwaves," blues musician B. B. King wrote, "they would have." In October 1948, white-owned WDIA became the first radio station to feature an all-black team of disc jockeys. High school teacher Nat D. Williams became the dean of African American DJs, joined by Rufus Thomas, Ford Nelson, A. C. "Moohah" Williams, B. B. King, and others. They mixed blues and gospel and included live music. WDIA became more than a radio station; it was also a community institution that promoted racial goodwill. By 1956, twenty-eight stations in the country had all-black programming, and most were in the South. As late as 1960, blacks owned only four radio stations.[15]

At night after WDIA signed off, white disc jockey Dewey Phillips, who joined

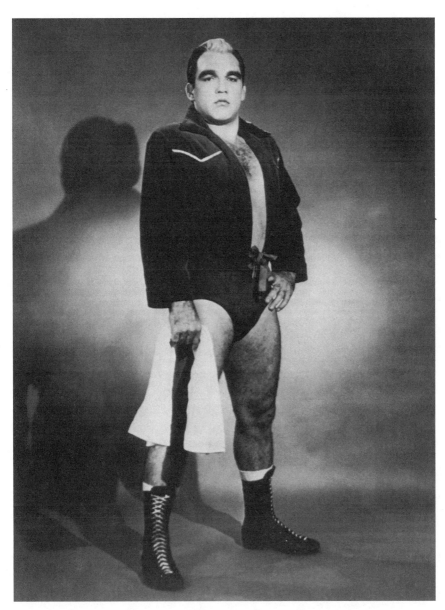

Sputnik Monroe. From the personal collection of Bernard J. Lansky.

WHBQ in October 1949, symbolically desegregated white programming from nine to midnight. He mixed country, rhythm and blues, gospel, and later rock 'n' roll on his *Red, Hot, and Blue* program. Phillips understood both the city's unique musical endowment and the communications revolution that would spread it. He spoke in a frantic blur, mixing metaphors, commercials, and nonsense. Phillips ignored categories and played what he considered the best contemporary music, which strayed far beyond conventional white tastes. In 1956, thirty-year-old Phillips went on television with his *Phillips' Pop Shop* program, which took improvisation to a new level. For six months, he rode a wave of popularity before the station syndicated the less spontaneous and more mainstream *American Bandstand*. Radio, recordings, television, and live performance allowed music to flow almost unimpeded through the city. White teenagers in particular felt an almost illicit thrill when they heard African American music on the radio or in some cases at black clubs.[16]

Rigid segregation could not silence radio stations or jukeboxes or prevent record stores from stocking all types of music. In July 1946, John Novarese, Joe Coughi, and Frank Berretta opened a record store on Poplar Avenue named Poplar Tunes. It became a "one-stop" shop for jukebox distributors, who formerly had been forced to call on each label outlet in the city. Disc jockeys such as Dewey Phillips would drop by almost daily to chat and look for new material. Record producers, aspiring musicians, and music-savvy consumers, nearly all white males, moiled around Poplar Tunes, making it not only a regional information exchange but also a powerful force in shaping the musical tastes of the mid-South. Eventually Coughi was instrumental in founding Hi Records and bringing in black band leader Willie Mitchell to arrange and produce records. Novarese and Coughi also booked concerts. As independent labels declined, Novarese judged, music's "zeal" died. The hungry independents had been the ones to take the chances.[17] As with auto racing, increasing popularity and commercialization in the music business tamed creativity.

Among the other record shops in the city, none was more eccentric than Reuben Cherry's Home of the Blues on Beale Street. He stocked records that attracted both black and white customers. Cherry wore his pants high, parted his hair in the middle, and sported a thin mustache. In Jim Dickinson's mind, Cherry, Phillips, and Monroe were figures "on the margin of society in Memphis." When Cherry died, his family attempted to erase virtually all traces of his life, destroying nude photographs of women he had collected in various Memphis hotel rooms and a thick, blank book titled "The Sex Life of Reuben Cherry."[18]

Memphians enthusiastically supported live music. Across the Mississippi River in West Memphis, the Plantation Inn employed the cream of Memphis's black musicians. The Cotton Club and Danny's attracted a wilder clientele. Lax, or at least selective, law enforcement in West Memphis opened the fleshpots to young whites who flocked over the bridge from Memphis. For twenty years after World War II, Plantation Inn owner Morris Berger cultivated a diverse clientele that varied from underage thrill-seekers to movie stars. All the patrons were white; all the musicians black. If transgressions occurred at the Plantation

Inn, they comprised underage drinking, stimulating dancing, and the thrill of hearing an excellent black band. A high school girl would arrive from a prom with perfect hair and wearing a formal dress, a corsage, and white gloves and, according to Morris Berger's daughter-in-law Bettye Berger, leave disheveled, barefoot, corsageless, "perspired, and probably smooched." The Plantation Inn set the standard for dance music, and the bands that played there in the late 1940s and 1950s—the Phinas Newborn Sr. Band, Willie Mitchell and the Four Kings, and the Ben Branch Band—had a significant influence on musicians, black and white.[19]

In the 1930s and 1940s, Phinas Newborn, after working all day, played drums at night at Memphis clubs and sat in with visiting bands. He also occasionally went on the road with Lionel Hampton. His sons, Phineas (who changed the spelling of his name when some girls made a comment about his "fine ass") and Calvin, grew up in the Orange Mound section of Memphis. Both Phineas and Calvin took piano lessons, but after two years, Calvin switched to guitar because his brother, who would become an outstanding jazz pianist, monopolized the keyboard.[20]

After Phinas Newborn formed his own band, including both sons, it became the house band at the Plantation Inn for four years. The band mastered a wide variety of music to please the customers, who often requested the latest hits as well as old favorites. Calvin recalled that his income from the Plantation Inn allowed him, even in high school, "to wear Lansky Brothers suits" and have his shoes shined every day. Calvin and Phineas's coming-of-age in Memphis demonstrated the role of public education in shaping musical talent and the opportunities available to young musicians. "I feel that when Beale Street died," Calvin reflected, "like the real Memphis music died." In his mind, the "omnivarious" music of his youth dwindled to blues and rock 'n' roll. "The real Memphis music is jazz," he insisted.[21]

Willie Mitchell, another Plantation Inn band leader, learned to play trumpet at Melrose High School. Like many youngsters his age, he jammed with musicians on Beale Street. At age fourteen, he started his own band. Mitchell attended Rust College in the late 1940s and served in the army from 1950 to 1952. The band he led at the Plantation Inn after returning from the army, he boasted, was "probably one of the most popular bands in this area." In the late 1950s, Joe Coughi approached Mitchell to work at Hi Records, and he later began arranging for the label.[22] The triumphs of the Newborns, Mitchell, and other black bands were closely followed by the Memphis black community. Many can still recall the city's most prominent black bands and session musicians and a wealth of musical experiences that stretched far beyond the schools and Beale Street.

Fred Ford recalled the city's musical diversity. Born in 1930, he grew up in Memphis's Douglas community. Youths from all over the city converged on Beale Street, which Ford described as "a hotbed of youngsters that just loved to play." They hung around the New Daisy and Palace Theaters hoping to find work. Sunbeam Mitchell ran a hotel and club and regularly housed and fed visiting musicians. In Ford's youth, he explained, "people from different eras" gathered on Beale Street or at Sunbeam Mitchell's late at night to exchange licks, and "the torch got handed down." When Beale Street was razed in the late 1960s, Ford lamented, the generational meeting ground disappeared. After what Ford referred to as urban renewal, youngsters no longer sat at the feet of their elders, no longer jammed, and did not even have "any place to sit down and talk about it." In Ford's youth, Memphis was a musical feast.[23]

Nearly all musicians, black and white, shared a knowledge of church music and a love of gospel singing. Churches varied enormously in their choice of music, which ranged from unaccompanied quartets to various combinations of organs, guitars, drums, and cymbals. A variation of what pleased the Lord on Sunday morning had pleased the Lord's followers the night before, for religious music's cadence and beat, under a different guise, praised the devil on Saturday night. As historian Martha Bayles has pointed out, Elvis Presley, Jerry Lee Lewis, and Little Richard Penniman all grew up in the Pentecostal faith. Presley's fondness for gospel music is better known than the fierce struggles of conscience that both Lewis and Penniman endured in singing the devil's music. White and black southerners had a similar affinity for religious music.[24]

Willie Gordon and James Blackwood, both born in rural Mississippi, represented the black and white gospel traditions. Because Gordon suffered from asthma, his mother sought better health care by moving the family first to Vicksburg and then to Memphis. Shortly after moving to Memphis, Gordon's mother became ill and died, and a couple from the church the Gordons attended raised Gordon. He attended Booker T. Washington High School, and his musical talent earned him a fellowship at Rust College. Gordon listened to blues, of course, but it was religious music that captivated him, for he believed it was "biblically inspired" and had a "higher nature." After a tour in the army from 1950 to 1953, Gordon returned to Memphis and organized the Pattersonaires, a gospel group named for the pastor of the New Salem Missionary Baptist Church. Gordon also came under the spell of the legendary W. Herbert Brewster, pastor of East Trigg Baptist Church and a prolific hymn writer. Gospel music alone could not support Gordon, so he also held a day job, first working at a restaurant, then for the *Memphis Commercial Appeal*, and then at the Veterans Hospital. Although he continued to battle asthma, Gordon's day of rest was filled with frantic activity. He played for Shiloh Baptist Church's Sunday school, New Salem's worship and afternoon services, and Second Baptist's Training Union. "Then I'd come back to New Salem for the evening service at 8:00, and then the 'Shadows of the Cross' at 9:00. Then I'd end up going to Reverend Brewster's at 11:00."[25]

The road James Blackwood traveled to Memphis proved longer and quite different from that of Willie Gordon or the younger musicians who turned to blues and rock 'n' roll. Born in Choctaw County, Mississippi, Blackwood started singing in church when he was seven years old. In 1934 when he was fifteen, James and his brothers, Roy and Doyle, and Roy's son, R. W., formed the original Blackwood Brothers quartet. After performing regularly on Mississippi radio stations, they moved to Shenandoah, Iowa, where they worked for the Stamps-Baxter music company, performing live broadcasts that attracted a million listeners. Willie Gordon recalled that when he visited Iowa with the Rust College choir, some locals had never seen a black person.[26]

After ten years in Iowa, the Blackwoods pined for the South and in 1950 moved to Memphis, where they appeared on a noon radio show on WMPS. Country artist Tammy Wynette later told Blackwood that while she was enrolled in beauty school in Memphis, she and her girlfriends would "sit in the studio while you were broadcasting." Elvis Presley attended the same church as James Blackwood, the First Ascendent of God Church, and was admitted free to his concerts. Blackwood recalled that when the quartet toured northern cities, thousands of people "who had migrated from the South to these industrial centers in the North" would attend their concerts. Gospel music reached an immense national audience through radio, recordings, and concerts. Throughout his life, Blackwood maintained a keen interest in black gospel music, often performing for black audiences and sharing the stage with black performers.[27]

At mid-century, then, Memphis contained an explosive diversity of musicians. The air was filled with sounds ranging from nationally popular music to rhythm and blues, upbeat country, and gospel. Despite some DJs' propensity to mix black and white music, a distinct musical color line segregated country and much popular music from blues and rhythm and blues.

Samuel Cornelius Phillips, who would go on to found Sun Studio and record a stunning array of blues and rock 'n' roll performers, attempted to erase the musical color line. Born in 1923 near Florence, Alabama, Sam Phillips was one of seven children. After dropping out of school, he became a local radio announcer, moved to WLAC in Nashville, and in 1945 arrived in Memphis. Although he was not a musician in the formal sense, Phillips had a keen ear for music and heard it changing. He became a Memphis radio announcer and technician and engineered national hookups of big band music from the Skyway at the Peabody Hotel. But his ear was attuned to a different sound, for all

The Blackwood Brothers. Left to right: *Dan Hurley, James Blackwood, R. W. Blackwood, Bill Lyles, and Jack Marshall. Courtesy James Blackwood.*

his life he "had heard the innate rhythms of people that had absolutely no formal training in music, didn't know one note from the other."[28]

In 1950, Phillips opened a recording studio at 706 Union Avenue. He sensed that underneath the Beale Street beat and the club music, something revolutionary pulsed. He recorded African American blues and rhythm and blues artists such as B. B. King, Joe Hill Louis, Rufus Thomas, the Prisonaires, Junior Parker, Roscoe Gordon, Jackie Brensten, Ike Turner, James Cotton, and Howlin' Wolf — a virtual who's who of African American performers, most of whom had grown up within a 150-mile radius of Memphis. Whites often taunted Phillips about his association with black performers. He sold his recordings to other labels such as Chess and RPM until 1952, when he started his own label, Sun Records.[29]

In 1953, Rufus Thomas gave Phillips his first Sun Records hit with "Beat Cat." Born in 1917, Thomas took advantage of the diverse musical opportunities in

Sam Phillips. Courtesy Showtime Archives (Toronto) and Colin Escott.

and around Memphis. In high school, he joined the Brown Brevities, a vaude-ville group. In the 1930s, he toured with F. S. Wolcott's Rabbit Foot minstrel troupe out of Port Gibson, Mississippi, and, like other black performers, re-membered having to stay in private homes because he was barred from white hotels. Entertainment jobs did not pay the bills, however, and for twenty-two years, Thomas held a day job at the American Finishing Company, a textile mill. When he started there in 1941, he recalled, "they had that colored water and the white water." He condemned the notion that "white and black can't work to-gether" as "one of the biggest lies ever told." Thomas's enormous love of Mem-phis was edged with bitterness over the destruction of Beale Street, which he de-scribed as "the black man's haven."[30]

B. B. King, another of Phillips's artists, was born in rural Mississippi in 1925 near Itta Bena and brought country blues to the city. As a youngster, King ea-gerly listened to blues records on his aunt's Victrola. "As a little kid," he recalled, "blues meant hope, excitement, pure emotion. Blues were about feelings." As mechanization intruded into fieldwork during World War II, King became a tractor driver, a job he likened to "being in an elite bomber squadron." A minor accident with a tractor prompted him to give up farming and move to Memphis, and for the first time, he saw paved streets, large buildings, and city buses. "I found Beale Street to be a city unto itself," he marveled. In 1948, he brazenly introduced himself to Sonny Boy Williamson, auditioned, and appeared on his *King Biscuit Time* radio show. King recalled the late 1940s as a time when "black music was on fire." He had grown up with country blues but was also influenced by T-Bone Walker, Louis Jordan, and Wynonie Harris. He appeared on WDIA and played extensively in the countryside around Memphis. In 1952, the twenty-six-year-old King recorded "Three O'Clock Blues," which hit the top of the *Billboard* rhythm and blues chart. This hit launched a career that for nearly a half century kept King on the road doing as many as 330 shows a year, "a commitment," he declared, "that's serious, solitary, and damaging to the idea of a full-time love."[31]

Although Sam Phillips was not known for being overly generous with royalties, he did give aspiring musicians such as Rufus Thomas and B. B. King an opportunity to record. For rural people, dealing with record producers followed a familiar pattern. Landlords controlled crops, credit, and annual "settlements," and record producers wielded similar power.[32] Out of dissatisfaction with their royalties or the desire to find better opportunities, many of Phillips's blues artists moved on, as did whites later.

Phillips focused on rhythm and blues performers because he recognized that the faster beat captured the ongoing evolution of blues. He heard other hints of change in upbeat country tunes. Blues and country music reflected the cadences and experiences of rural life, whereas rhythm and blues and upbeat country suggested the more rapid pace of urban life. Young white musicians, in particular, were drawn to upbeat Hank Williams and Bob Wills songs. In Phillips's mind, country performers were, in their own way, edging toward rhythm and blues. He suspected that a white crossover musician was waiting to be discovered.[33]

Phillips searched among the last generation of sharecroppers and their urban cousins, rebellious high school students and young working-class musicians who were adventurous and hungry. He knew instinctively that any breakthrough would come from an unself-conscious youth who felt at ease with African American music and style. Paradoxically, such a musician would probably come from a family that accepted segregation, and, in the estimation of polite folks, embodied the worst of lowdown traits.

As much as anyone, Phillips understood the contradictions of southern working-class people. He heard the stories of unrefined rural migrants, black and white, threatening more polished, reserved, and polite city dwellers, who seldom looked beyond accent, dress, and decibel level. Older city residents despised the loud music, vicious dogs, and offensive oaths; the inattention to wardrobe and grooming; and the eager consumption of beer and hard liquor and conspicuous display of empty cans and bottles in the yard. This untamed streak fascinated Phillips, and he had the gift of being able to isolate and nurture the creative genius of such people. Because he harbored such sentiments himself, Phillips understood that rural migrants brought to the city not only their rough manners but also music that embodied and embellished their hopes and dreams.

Sam Phillips listened to the hopefuls who dropped by Sun Studio. He cut acetate records for self-conscious young musicians who were willing to pay to hear themselves. In the summer of 1953, a bashful Elvis Presley paid $3.98 to Sun receptionist Marion Keisker to record two ballads. Phillips dropped a passing compliment, and Keisker noted his name and phone number. In January 1954, while working as a truck driver, Presley recorded two more tunes, and on June 26, Phillips called Presley to tell him he had arranged a session with guitarist Scotty Moore and bass player Bill Black.[34]

By this time, Scotty Moore was on his second marriage and playing at honky-tonks around Memphis with the Starlite Wranglers. Moore grew up in rural Crockett County, Tennessee. He detested school, loathed farming, and lied his way into the navy at age sixteen. His guitar accompanied him through action in both China and Korea. In 1952, he took a job at his brother's dry-cleaning business in Memphis. Bill Black, a neighbor, worked at Firestone and played bass with the Starlite Wranglers. Phillips had mentioned to Moore that the singer was Elvis Presley, a name Moore later described as "out of science fiction." Presley showed up at Moore's house the day before the session, according to author Peter Guralnick, "wearing a black shirt, pink pants with a black stripe, white shoes, and a greasy ducktail." His outfit was not that of the average white truck driver. Neither Moore nor Black was impressed—with his clothes or his musical ability.[35]

The next day, the trio arrived at Sun Studio at seven in the evening to record. Either relieved to finish the uninspiring session or desperate to catch Phillips's attention, Presley started clowning around with "That's All Right, Mama," the song Arthur Crudup had recorded for RCA seven years earlier. Black and Moore joined in the fun, and an incredulous Phillips emerged from the control room, he later recalled, feeling "like someone stuck me in the rear end with a brand new supersharp pitch fork." In that moment, Elvis Presley transcended his musical inhibitions; he crossed the line.[36]

Elvis Presley onstage in Little Rock with Scotty Moore. Larry Obsitnik Collection, Special Collections Division, University of Arkansas Libraries, Fayetteville.

WDIA disc jockey Dewey Phillips dropped by Sun Studio the next day, and Sam Phillips played the tape of "That's All Right, Mama." After both men listened, lost in thought, Dewey Phillips agreed to play the song. Presley was at the movies when Phillips queued up the record around 9:30 or 10:00 P.M. Telegrams and phone calls began flooding the studio as soon as the song ended. Phillips called the Presley house and told Gladys Presley to get her son out of the movie theater and send him to the studio. Although listeners were unsure whether Presley was white or black until he revealed his Humes High School background on the air that evening, they knew immediately that they liked this music.[37]

Presley's first record epitomized the union of black and white music: Crudup's rhythm and blues song was on one side and Bill Monroe's country "Blue Moon of Kentucky" was on the other. But Presley's record was neither black nor white, neither rhythm and blues nor country. Presley tried to explain this to Marion Keisker when she asked him who he sang like; he told her, "I don't sound like nobody." Sam Phillips had found what he was searching for— "the blues with a mania." Such alterations in musical style were not unique to Memphis. Wherever rural southerners settled across the country, a spontaneous invention of music akin to rock 'n' roll occurred.[38]

After recording five singles, Phillips sold Presley's contract to RCA. Phillips then devoted his resources to molding the talents of an improbable group of young white men and women who walked into Sun Studio, including Carl Perkins, Jerry Lee Lewis, Johnny Cash, the Miller Sisters, Charlie Rich, Barbara Pittman, Sonny Burgess, Roy Orbison, Billy Lee Riley, and Stan Kesler.[39] Many of the Sun performers who followed Presley had strong rural roots. The white artists who recorded at Sun brought not only the musical heritage of the rural South but also the influence of radio, recordings, and film.

Carl Lee Perkins was born in Lake County, Tennessee, in 1932. "I'm sad to say," he confessed, "that I came from a family of people who didn't own any of that rich flat Mississippi River land. . . . We were just known as sharecroppers." His father rationed the use of the battery-operated radio, which brought in such programs as the *Grand Ole Opry*. Perkins also went to movies on Saturdays at the Strand Theater in Tiptonville, where he admired the cowboy singers in Westerns. He worked in the fields with John Westbrook, a black man who taught him how to pick 300 pounds of cotton a day, a lesson he vividly remembered fifty years later. Perkins recalled "forty and fifty black people picking and chopping in the field with me." In the long afternoons, the singing would start, "that music without guitars." Singing made the time seem to pass more quickly and lifted the workers' spirits.[40]

It was not until he went to school and students laughed at his ragged clothes that Perkins noticed he was poor. "And that's when I realized that life wasn't equal, it wasn't fair for me." Westbrook sold him a guitar for $3 and then taught him three chords. "He did a thing with that third finger," Perkins remembered. "He'd push that string. It was," Perkins smiled, "a blues lick." Like the cotton-picking lesson, it remained vivid in his mind half a century later. Such kindnesses as those of Westbrook to young Perkins were part of the complex web of

Carl Perkins.
Rock 'n' Soul Project.
Courtesy Carl Perkins.

southern rural life. Westbrook was a major figure in Perkins's life, a man who unselfishly taught him how to work and how to play guitar. Perkins learned early that music was his ticket out of sharecropping, and he worked hard at his musical career "to keep from having to go back to the cotton field." By age fourteen, he was working at a dairy, writing songs, and performing at several local nightspots with his brother, Jay.[41]

Perkins was living in Jackson, Tennessee, when he heard Presley's "Blue Moon of Kentucky" on the radio. His wife, Valda, said, "Carl, that sounds like yall," referring to the Perkins brothers. Recognizing that the airing of the song legitimized the kind of music he was performing, he and his brothers, Jay and Clayton, drove their old Plymouth to Memphis, walked into Sun Studio, and begged Sam Phillips to listen to them. After they performed a few uninspiring covers, Carl Perkins sang "Movie Magg," his "song about a boy taking his girl to the movie on a mule called Magg." This upbeat rural saga appealed to Phillips. He told the Perkins brothers to contact him when they had another such song. "I think I wrote probably two or three songs on the way back to Jackson," Perkins joked.[42]

In February 1955, Phillips issued Perkins's "Movie Magg" and "Turn Around" on the Phillips Flip label. Ten months later, Perkins sat on the steps of his apartment building and composed "Blue Suede Shoes," a song inspired by his observation of a young man berating his date for scuffing his shoes. Perkins's immense songwriting talent had been shaped by his rural upbringing, the ever more accessible popular culture of his day, and his insight into how the two collided. Perkins offered an ambiguous description of rock 'n' roll music: "It's slurred notes, it's bent notes, it's not hardly a note, it's somewhere between, it's moving around." Like many early rock 'n' roll performers, Perkins did not read music. Instead of apologizing for this, he used humor: "Somebody asked Chet [Atkins] one time did he read music; he said, 'Yeah, but not enough to hurt my picking.'"[43]

Billy Lee Riley doubted that he would have ventured into Sun Studio alone. Music promoter Jack Clement recorded Riley's "Trouble Bound" in a garage studio and took it to Phillips, who released it in May 1956. Born in Pocahontas, Arkansas, in 1933, Riley spent his early years moving with his family around the northeastern part of the state. His father sought work as a house painter but often sharecropped to put food on the table. Billy Lee Riley gave a telling description of cotton sharecropping: "We'd plant it with a two-row planter pulled by horses, mules. Then we would chop it, pick it, and starve to death in the wintertime." When he was five years old, the family lived in the Red Row section of Osceola, Arkansas. Riley's father bought him a harmonica when he was six and a DDT-damaged guitar three years later.[44]

Life on Osceola's Red Row was cruel; Riley later caustically referred to it as "the good old days." All his neighbors were "fighting to live, fighting to survive," but they were generous with what they had. "Our neighbors on both sides were black, and I'd go to their houses when I was a kid and eat with them, and they'd visit our house." Red Row was near the city dump, and Riley remembered that fights would break out over food scraps. The Riley family could not afford respectable shoes and clothes, and after being "humiliated by the ones that had more," he and his sister quit school. Like other poor southerners, the Rileys used the Sears and Roebuck catalog as a wish book. "We'd sit there every year and tally up everything we wanted before school was supposed to start," he remembered. "We would have it all down, man, and it never came true. I always wanted a mackinaw jacket. . . . And I never had nothing, never had a coat, never had a pair of boots."[45]

In 1946, the family moved near Forrest City and sharecropped. Because no houses were available, they lived in a tent. Although he deemed that year awful in many respects, he also recalled that it "was the best year for me in music, because that's where I really learned the blues and learned to appreciate it and learned to play it and write it." On a black family's porch, "they were blowing harmonicas and one guy's playing a homemade guitar, and they were playing washboards, and they were really doing what turned me on." One of the first songs he wrote, "How Come We All Ain't Got the Same?," was inspired by his childhood. One line asked why some people "got all the comforts" while "all I

Left to right: *Malcolm, Amos, and Billy Lee Riley. Courtesy Billy Lee Riley.*

got is pain." He saw only two classes in those days: "The ones that had every-thing and those that didn't have anything."[46]

Falsifying his age, Riley joined the army in 1949 and, after being encouraged to enter, won a talent contest in which he sang Hank Williams and Lefty Frizzel songs. After leaving the army in 1953, he moved back to Arkansas and formed the KBTM Ranch Boys, a country band that played on the radio and at dances. In 1955, he moved to Memphis ("the only place where anything was happening") and opened a restaurant, which lasted three months; he then worked as a meat cutter.[47]

After making his first record at Sun, Riley worked hard to produce a hit. In December 1956, he recorded the memorable "Flyin' Saucer Rock and Roll" with his band, dubbed by Sam Phillips the Little Green Men. When Phillips decided to push Jerry Lee Lewis's "Great Balls of Fire" in late 1957 instead of Riley's promising "Red Hot," Riley got drunk and trashed Sun Studio. Instead of calling the police, Phillips arrived with a bottle of liquor and retreated with Riley to the control room. At dawn, Riley left the studio convinced by Phillips that he would be the next great rock 'n' roll star. Riley's experience demonstrated not only Phillips's regard for his musicians but also his power to decide their fate— whether to have Riley arrested or drink with him while offering up fantasies of stardom, whether to toss him out or use him and the Little Green Men in future sessions. Riley never attained stardom, but as much as any 1950s performer, he gloried in playing rock 'n' roll music. Over the years, Riley recorded not only rock 'n' roll but also blues and country songs.[48]

Charlie Rich, from a more middle-class background than Perkins or Riley, grew up in rural Arkansas; at times, his father managed a Delta plantation and, at other times, retreated to a small farm on Crowley Ridge. His mother played piano ("white gospel church-type music"), and his father sang in a quartet and played guitar. Like most rural southerners, Rich listened to the *Grand Ole Opry*, but he also remembered hearing "your Perry Comos and that sort of thing."[49]

Rich remembered field songs, gospel music, and Saturday nights when C. J. Allen, a black sharecropper, would call at his family's house and join his father in "drinking a little sauce" and playing blues. Allen, Rich remembered, "played a nice blues piano." Rich's mother, who frowned on the Saturday night sessions, started him on piano lessons in the third grade, but Allen, who Rich considered "like a member of the family," continued to teach him the unwritten Saturday night chords. Photographs of Rich and Allen show that the two men were very fond of each other. Rich, Riley, and Perkins were gracious and generous in their praise for their black teachers. After Rich served in the air force from 1952 to 1956, his uncle set him up in farming "'cause he figured it was the only thing I knew how to do, which I didn't." In addition to farming, he was playing the local "chitlin' circuit," singing blues, country, "or whatever the situation called for."[50] Rich's farming did not prosper, but his music did. He, too, became a Sun artist.

Stan Kesler, who began recording with Phillips in the mid-1950s, grew up on a farm near Abbeyville, Mississippi, one of nine children. Some of his brothers

Billy Lee Riley. Courtesy Billy Lee Riley.

"played guitars, fiddles, mandolin, and so forth," and from age six or seven, he was interested in music. Growing up in North Mississippi, Kesler listened to blues and gospel music, but he later claimed that "my favorite, my kind of music, was country music. I mean I loved the Grand Ole Opry; I loved Bill Monroe, Eddie Arnold, the hillbillies of the time." After graduating from high school, Kesler served two years in the marines, during which time he started playing lap steel, or Hawaiian guitar, as they called it then. When he left the marines in 1947, he and his brother started singing around Abbeyville, but a year later, like so many others, he moved to Memphis to seek better opportunities. Kesler went to work for Sears and Roebuck and lived in Mrs. Snearly's

C. J. Allen and Charlie Rich. Rock 'n' Soul Project. Courtesy Charlie Rich.

boardinghouse. Other musicians lived there, and led by drummer Clyde Leoppard, they formed the Snearly Ranch Boys. They played the "little school houses, little beer joints, wherever we could set up and play, we'd play and we'd travel around Mississippi, Arkansas, Tennessee, around small towns, little theaters, and schoolhouses, and put on shows."[51]

Country musicians, Kesler recalled, had started picking up the beat. Bob Wills and the Texas Playboys' western swing and Hank Williams's "Hey Good Lookin'" and "Move It on Over" inspired him. After hearing Elvis Presley sing "That's All Right, Mama," Kesler went to see Phillips, who hired him to play steel guitar at recording sessions. Presley's first record, it seems, served as a beacon that attracted hungry and talented country boys intent on pursuing musical careers. Kesler became part of the Sun house band and played with Perkins, Charlie Feathers, the Miller Sisters, and others. He cowrote "I'm Left, You're Right, She's Gone" and later wrote "I Forgot to Remember to Forget" and "Playing for Keeps" for Presley. In the mid-fifties, he switched from lap steel to bass, symbolically completing his move from country to rock 'n' roll. "All the guys I worked with were from similar backgrounds," Kesler recalled. "They came out of the country, out of Arkansas, Mississippi, and Tennessee. Most of 'em were farm boys."[52]

According to Perkins, most Sun performers came from "a circumference of a hundred and fifty miles around this town, Memphis, Tennessee. . . . The guys that played that blues mixed with bluegrass with a gospel feel."[53] They understood farm life and rural metaphors and had discovered music at a young age. All freely admitted and some even boasted that black people had influenced their musical tastes. By a strange coincidence, they converged on Sun Studio, where Sam Phillips not only recognized their raw talent but also understood how to cultivate and nurture it.

Phillips's country upbringing and his association with African Americans both as a child and as an adult paralleled the experiences of most young musicians who entered his studio. Although he was only ten years older than many of these musicians, he saw himself as a father figure. "They were exposed to many of the same things that I was," Phillips said. "I knew how to deal with 'em." He was at once demanding, forgiving, aloof, engaged, and demonically driven. His eyes radiated hypnotizing energy. He was not modest about his achievements. "I will say unhesitatingly that if God gave me anything at all, anything at all, he gave me the intuitive powers to not read minds but to feel souls."[54]

Phillips's recollection of these musicians is tinged with both condescension and admiration. They came to Sun, he remembered, almost hat in hand—insecure, "snaggletoothed," prematurely bald, and carrying beat-up instruments. In Phillips, they found a mentor who could, like a plantation owner, manipulate their rural work ethic and transform the rough seeds of their music into a lucrative crop of records. They were just as concerned as their parents had been about whether they were receiving a fair settlement. In other respects, Phillips resembled a cult leader as he brooded in the Sun control room, demanding a conversion experience from country to rock 'n' roll.[55]

Perkins recalled that Phillips would "step out from behind that little old glass window, and he'd say . . . 'Do it again. Do it one time for Sam.'" Perkins would then "walk out on a limb, I'd try things I knew I couldn't do. . . . I'd say, 'Mr. Phillips, that's terrible.' He said, 'That's original.' I said, 'But it's just a big original mistake.' And he said, '*That's what Sun Records is.* That's what we are.'"[56] Over time, Phillips and these country boys became a cult, and they have been elevated—Elvis Presley above all—to a hallowed place in American music. The shared rural heritage was the core of Sun, whose label featured a rooster crowing at the morning sun. Phillips's genius in provoking several dozen black and white musicians to record songs that changed national, even international, musical tastes made him one of the most significant music producers of the mid-twentieth century.

The Sun legend overshadowed the careers of other musicians who achieved a degree of popularity but never became stars. Even recording for Sam Phillips at Sun did not guarantee stardom. Although Malcolm Yelvington, Charlie Feathers, Warren Smith, Sonny Burgess, and Barbara Pittman did not gain the national fame of Presley or Perkins, they shared in the creation of rock 'n' roll music. Paul Burlison, Johnny Burnett, and Dorsey Burnett, the Rock and Roll Trio, won first place on the *Ted Mack Amateur Hour*. After several years of touring, Burlison returned to Memphis and worked as an electrician until retirement.[57]

Many of the generation of white Memphis musicians who came of age in the fifties were from the country, but the next generation grew up in Memphis. Jim Dickinson, who moved with his family to Memphis from Chicago in grade school, personified the new perspective. At first, he was seen as a newcomer. He credited Alex Tiel, a black man who did yard work, with not only coaching him out of his Yankee demeanor but also introducing him to southern music. Unlike rural whites who mixed with blacks at work and play, suburban kids such as Dickinson saw black people as exotic and black music as subversive, transgressive. Dickinson was fascinated the first time he heard a jug band in downtown Memphis. A drunken white couple was dancing to the music. His father dragged him away.[58]

At Baylor University, Dickinson discovered folklore and learned that many "legends" were still living in Memphis. Until he went to college, he did not realize that his musical influences—Dewey Phillips, Elvis Presley, B. B. King, the Plantation Inn, and Sun Records—were unique. Dickinson called the 1950s Memphis experience a "racial collision." In the 1950s, "the races were reaching for each other culturally, and the music collided." In his mind, rock 'n' roll was "the idea of a true dyed-in-the-wool southern redneck playing racially offensive black music." Black music, he explained, had been generally considered "trash music."[59]

Whereas the first Memphis musical explosion came primarily from black and white musicians largely influenced by rural traditions, the next phase originated in the city's eastern suburbs among white kids who saw black music as transgressive and among urban black kids who grew up under the influence of Beale Street, good high schools, and the church. Musicians David Porter, Al Jackson Jr., Andrew Love, Booker T. Jones, and William Bell, for example, attended Booker T. Washington High School.

Jim Stewart, the conduit for the new musical expression, was born in 1930 and grew up on a farm seventy miles east of Memphis near Middleton. After graduating from high school in 1948, he moved to Memphis, looking for "better jobs, better opportunity, and a better way of life." After spending two years in the army, he graduated from Memphis State University, took law courses, and got a job at First Tennessee Bank. Stewart played fiddle in a country band that performed at the Eagle's Nest in the mid-fifties, and Elvis Presley, Bill Black, and Scotty Moore sometimes played at intermission. Stewart remembered "that excitement when Presley would hit the stage." Rock 'n' roll, he mused, was "a form of freedom of expression" that transcended the music of the big band era and even country.[60]

In 1958, Stewart produced several records on the Satellite label, and then his sister, Estelle Axton, joined him and they made records in a Brunswick studio. Several years later, Stewart and Axton converted an abandoned theater at the corner of McLemore and College Streets into a recording studio. Rufus Thomas and his daughter Carla, backed by Thomas's son Marvell on piano and sixteen-year-old Booker T. Jones on saxophone, made a recording at the studio. It was a hit. An astounded Stewart realized that his studio, located in the heart of the black community, was surrounded by musical talent. David Porter bagged groceries across the street, Gilbert Caple lived nearby, and a procession of curious young musicians wandered into the studio, both to browse the record shop Axton had set up in the lobby and to explore the recording business. Since another studio claimed the Satellite label, Stewart and Axton created their own label, naming it Stax after the first two letters of each of their names. Estelle's son, Packy, Steve Cropper, Donald "Duck" Dunn, and Wayne Jackson had formed a group called the Royal Spades, which played mostly rhythm and blues. These and other black and white musicians sat in on sessions, and a distinctive sound emerged from Stax Studio. "We didn't have any problem finding the talent," Stewart admitted; "we couldn't record anywhere near all that came in."[61]

By 1962, Stewart had gathered a rhythm section composed of Duck Dunn, Steve Cropper, Booker T. Jones, and Al Jackson Jr., and he added Gilbert Caple, Floyd Newman, Wayne Jackson, and others as the Memphis Horns. Stewart surreptitiously recorded "Behave Yourself" during a jam session, and, deciding it was good enough to release, recorded what became the legendary "Green Onions" for the flip side. The musical atmosphere at Stax Studio sizzled with creativity and experimentation, and the studio epitomized the dream that music could bring black and white people together. For a time, it generated an impressive list of hits from such artists as Otis Redding, Sam and Dave, Booker T. and the MGs, the Staple Singers, Carla Thomas, and others. It was not until Otis Redding and other band members died in a tragic airplane crash in December 1967 and Martin Luther King Jr. was assassinated in April 1968 that the spirit of cooperation dwindled. In one sense, Stax came along as a logical progression after Sam Phillips first recorded black artists and then whites, always separately. Stewart successfully encouraged black and white musicians to create music together. The Stax experiment remains one of the most significant examples of black and white musical collaboration.[62]

The musical revolution that seized Memphis and then the nation had its roots in the surrounding countryside. It was conducted by creative but often uneducated people who were not constrained by elite taste. Other cities experienced similar musical revolutions, but Memphis was unique. Something in migrants' musical heritage, their spirit, and their abrupt flight from the countryside disposed them to explore Beale Street, listen to radio stations, inspect freelance studios, patronize clubs, and haunt music stores. They hungered to make music. During the 1950s and 1960s, there was enormous pressure to conform, but Sam Phillips and Jim Stewart nurtured young musicians' untamed streak and encouraged them to take risks. "Sam was after the unknown," guitarist Scotty Moore declared.[63] At Sun Studio, the rhythms of the land collided with the beat of the city, and at Stax Studio, blacks and whites joined forces, and the energy redefined American music. A surprising number of the performers recognized immediately anywhere in the world came from Memphis and its environs. For a moment at mid-century, lowdown southerners rewrote popular culture. It was a time many people look back on as the Golden Age.

7 A Little of the Rebel

We would dress like the blacks did. That was kinda the in thing to do,
and a little bit of the rebel.
—*Charlie Rich*

They would say, "Little girls don't play guitars."
—*Cordell Jackson*

The explosion of rock 'n' roll and later soul music was part of a cultural revolution that recoded music, language, dress, dance, and values. Whereas Sun Studio produced separate expressions of black and white musical creativity, the decline of Stax Studio after 1968 marked the fading dreams of racial cooperation. The intervening years were filled with great hope—and greater confusion. Rhythm and blues evolved into rock 'n' roll at the same time that the U.S. Supreme Court handed down the *Brown v. Board of Education* decision, and soul music rode the wave of civil rights triumphs and failures. Except among musicians and athletes, however, the color line remained largely intact. In their desire to gain musical insight, musicians created a blueprint for racial cooperation that was lost on both political leaders and most whites.

In a decade of enormous tension, the music that flowed from the genius of black and white southerners resonated with youths throughout the country and ultimately the world. However much music overlapped in black and white culture, the fusion did not register with most whites, some of whom contemptuously referred to rhythm and blues and rock 'n' roll as "nigger music." Many adults saw rock 'n' roll's fast beat, obscure lyrics, frantic performances, unorthodox wardrobe, and hectic dancing as lewd, lowdown, transgressive.[1]

Onstage, Elvis Presley not only moved suggestively but also wore clothing and mumbled phrases associated more with African Americans than with whites. The clothes worn by Sun's white performers departed radically from those of country performers. Many country musicians early on hung up their starched Sunday suits or bibb overalls and donned cowboy outfits that transformed them into reflections of nomadic heroes of the silver screen. Until the mid-fifties, many southern country/hillbilly musicians performed in the basic

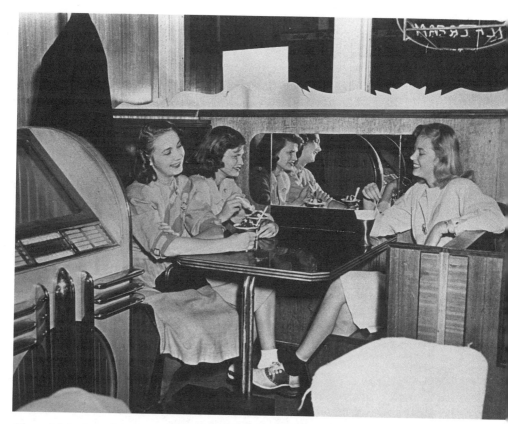

Three girls in Sutton's ice cream parlor, Vicksburg, Mississippi.
Photograph by Charles Faulk. Charles Faulk Papers, Special Collections
Department, Mitchell Memorial Library, Mississippi State University.

cowboy uniform. Others who could not afford such glitter dressed in casual slacks and shirts. In a photograph taken around 1954, a young Elvis Presley is flanked by guitarist Scotty Moore and bass player Bill Black, both of whom are wearing western shirts and string ties. Presley stands in the foreground dressed in clothes bought from Lansky Brothers on Beale Street of a style usually worn by African Americans. "We would dress like the blacks did," Charlie Rich admitted. "That was kinda the in thing to do, and a little bit of the rebel."[2]

Lansky Brothers specialized in the stylish, unconventional clothing that Elvis Presley sensationalized. At first, the store sold primarily to African Americans, but, Bernard Lansky observed, when "whites started seeing what they were wearing . . . they used to come in here and buy the same thing." Black and white fashions, he judged, were "getting closer and closer." Presley had a fondness for pink and black, Lansky noted, "and everybody saw Elvis wearing it and everybody wanted pink and black." Jerry Lee Lewis, Carl Perkins, Roy Orbison,

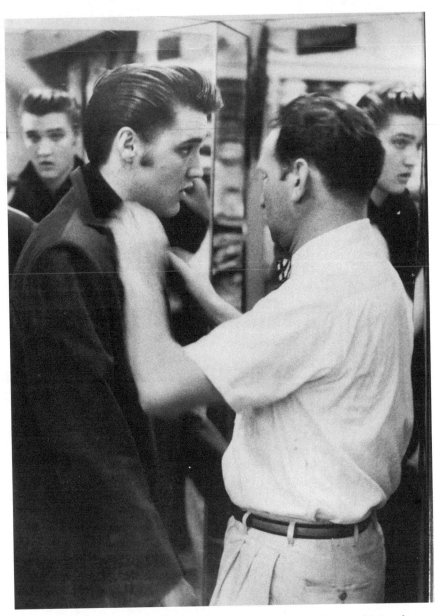

Elvis Presley and Bernard Lansky. From the personal collection of Bernard J. Lansky.

Charlie Rich, Johnny Cash, and even Pat Boone bought clothes from Lansky's, as did B. B. King, Isaac Hayes, and many black bands and gospel groups.[3]

Presley's grooming, automobiles, motorcycles, and even furniture conveyed eccentric tastes, as well as a kinky and more unsettling edge. His hair was ample and often looked greasy, and he spent an inordinate amount of time combing it. Jimmy Denson, a neighbor, recalled that Presley passed through a zoot suit phase in high school and oiled his ducktail haircut with brilliantine. Bill Black's brother observed that when Presley showed up at parties, women fussed over him. "All these guys with crew cuts and muscles," he added, "resented a pretty boy." When Presley performed on the popular radio show *Louisiana Hayride* in the fall of 1954, he showed up, according to Peter Guralnick, "wearing a pink jacket, white pants, a black shirt, a brightly colored clip-on bow tie." On the road in Lubbock, Texas, in February 1955, Jimmie Rodgers Snow said he performed in "a chartreuse jacket and black pants with a white stripe down the side." In Snow's estimation, Presley primarily attracted girls. Boys sometimes "reacted very violently in many areas because, I suppose, of the way the girls acted." With his music, clothes, eye shadow, and suggestive body movements, Presley challenged racial and gender conventions.[4]

Presley's stage presence, his moving, shaking, and sneer, was unlike that of country or big band performers. His motion was not straightforward sexual hunching but an awkward splay-legged and pigeon-toed swivel. In 1955, historian Bill Malone, then a student at the University of Texas, saw Presley in Austin. He was shocked both by Presley's "physical gyrations" and by "the screaming response of the young women who rushed the stage." Among country performers, he noted, neither men nor women "were permitted to exhibit sensual feelings in public." At a hearing on the monopoly dispute between ASCAP and BMI before the House Judiciary Committee, songwriter Billy Rose denigrated BMI-licensed rock 'n' roll music, suggesting that it made possible Presley's "animal posturings." Scotty Moore observed that most guitarists "would stand flat-footed and play and pat the foot." Presley wore "big-legged britches," Moore pointed out, and he "kind of stood on the balls of his feet." When he kept time, "the britches would start shaking." Moore first noticed the "screaming and hollering" at an Overton Park concert in Memphis.[5]

Drummer D. J. Fontana realized that Presley's clothes, long hair, posture, sneer, footwork, and sideburns suggested rebellion to some people, vulgarity to others. Working with Presley allowed Fontana to use licks he had learned while drumming for burlesque shows, in which the women performers expected him to "catch their leg movements, their tassel movements, their rear end movements." Fontana used the beat to accentuate Presley's movements. "I just played an accent wherever his legs were or wherever his rear end was, and I just learned to catch all that by watching these girls strip." Not surprisingly, Fontana did not regard rock 'n' roll as particularly sexy. He admitted that it was "different because of the tempo, and the beat; it was a strong back beat, and that made the kids want to dance and jump up and scream and holler, but as far as being sexy, we didn't think it was."[6]

Although Presley electrified women fans, his appeal to men refracted. Scotty Moore insisted that Presley was heterosexual, even homophobic, and rumors of anything else were "horseshit." "Let's face it," Moore added, "the man was damned near too pretty to be a man." Presley had admired actor Tony Curtis's use of mascara and heard that it accentuated the eyes in photographs. Whatever Presley's reasons for wearing eye shadow, peoples' reactions to it varied. When Presley appeared at the Grand Ole Opry in October 1954, a worldly Chet Atkins declared: "I couldn't get over that eye shadow he was wearing. It was like seein' a couple of guys kissin' in Key West." In the estimation of the Rolling Stones' Mick Jagger, the androgynous side of rock 'n' roll originated with Elvis Presley. Older people feared Presley, Jagger suggested, because they saw him as "an effeminate guy." In photographs of Presley, "the eyes are done with makeup, and everything's perfect." The Rolling Stones became androgynous "straightaway, unconsciously." With his Lansky Brothers' wardrobe and his Tony Curtis eyes, Presley represented both a surrogate black man and a transvestite. Androgyny, then, was yet another manifestation of 1950s culture. Part of the Presley magic was his plasticity, which enveloped diverse listeners and trapped their loyalty. Presley's music and style sent out beams across a broad spectrum.[7]

Elvis Presley was years behind Little Richard in style and presentation. By the time eighteen-year-old Richard Penniman made his first record in 1951, he had been performing in women's dresses for several years. He gravitated toward gay culture and credited Billy Wright and Esquerita with influencing his wardrobe, makeup, and music. Stage shows, minstrel shows, and snake oil salesmen, according to Little Richard, often hired gay performers. This world coexisted alongside fiery preachers, themselves slickly groomed, and Bible Belt intolerance. Coming from a religious background, Little Richard felt the tension. He, like Jerry Lee Lewis, would alternate between rock 'n' roll ecstasy and religious guilt and repentance. In the early 1950s, musician Johnny Otis described Little Richard's act at the Club Matinee in Houston as "just beautiful, bizarre, and exotic." At the end of the act, Little Richard announced, "This is Little Richard, King of the Blues," then thoughtfully added, "And the Queen, too!"[8]

In 1955, Bumps Blackwell at Specialty Records recorded Little Richard. During a lunch break, Little Richard sang the bawdy words to what became "Tutti Frutti." Songwriter Dorothy LaBostrie cleaned up the lyrics, and after three takes in fifteen minutes, Little Richard had his first hit. Blackwell insisted that Little Richard's hair was a foot high. "His shirt was so loud it looked as though he had drunk raspberry juice, cherryade, malt, and greens and then thrown up all over himself." Loud and transgressive, Little Richard defied nearly every fifties taboo and still became a star.[9]

Despite Presley's androgynous impact and Little Richard's more vigorous assault on convention, very few women broke into rock 'n' roll and none became as prominent as women who performed country or soul music. Sam Phillips recorded Maggie Sue Wimberly in 1955 and the Miller Sisters, Jean Chapel, and Barbara Pittman in 1956. Although Presley could dress like a black man, shake suggestively, and use makeup, southern society would not tolerate a woman grinding against a guitar onstage. Songwriter and producer Cordell Jackson remembered the conventional wisdom in Pontotoc, Mississippi, during her childhood. "They would say, 'Little girls don't play guitars.'" She recalled that when she played, men would "just walk off." Women remained largely offstage as rock 'n' roll fans, consumers but not producers. They were not allowed to generate male frenzy by exhibiting their bodies or manipulating an instrument onstage. Women did lose themselves in screaming frenzies at concerts, and they danced with abandon when opportunity allowed. But even as fans, young women upset their dates, who both feared and admired their passionate reactions to the musicians and the music.[10]

The Presley style exerted a powerful influence on young people. Bobby Manuel, who later played guitar at Stax Studio, recalled that he was twelve when he first heard Elvis Presley. Since Presley lived on Lamar Avenue close to his mother's florist business, Manuel occasionally saw him riding his motorcycle. Respectable boys dressed in khakis and wore short hair, but Presley had "just tons of hair and all the leather and the boots and everything." Impressed, Manuel and his friends bought "semi-leather jackets" at the local drugstore, which started to deteriorate after only a few weeks. Girls' reaction to Presley convinced Manuel to play guitar instead of saxophone. Later he reflected that much of the fascination with rock 'n' roll came from the sexual charge it delivered. Whereas Manuel saw sexual energy in girls' reactions to Presley, his parents labeled the screaming and dancing girls "silly."[11]

It was not just screaming young girls who upset more conservative people but also adults who lapsed in decorum. "During the past 15 years we have seen our nation accept immorality and sin as commonplace," Martelle Willis from Warren, Arkansas, wrote to the editor of the *Arkansas Gazette* in 1957. "Our ladies and girls parade the streets in garbs that would have had them jailed 20 years ago." Churches had become social clubs, she despaired, and women "appear on the streets in shorts and smoking cigarettes while accompanied by two or three children." Such "wicked" behavior had prompted God to destroy Sodom and Gomorrah and send the Great Flood, she warned.[12]

As southern young women learned about birth control, they gained a measure of sexual freedom. In some cases, white men claimed that white women's use of birth control resulted in less interracial sex. Robert Armstrong Andrews observed changing courting rituals on Edisto Island, South Carolina. When he was a young man, he wrote to *Arkansas Gazette* editor Harry Ashmore, "I was a victim of the *mystique* . . . that there were nice white girls, bad white girls, and colored girls who were willing. Everybody I knew had the same idea." These ideas had changed, he insisted, because of "twenty-five different kinds of contraceptives." He knew of no interracial births on Edisto Island in twenty years, "not because the white men have declined in virility, but because the white girls, all the way from the shanty in the swampland to the colonnaded . . . big white house have learned that sin doesn't necessarily mean babies."[13] Interestingly, Andrews credited women for taking the initiative in contraception, another example of the profound changes among southern women.

The sexual revolution that began during World War II caught the attention of Jack Johnston, a Georgia Baptist preacher and newspaper editor. During the late 1940s, Johnston's articles were obsessed with race and sex and were sometimes "more appropriate to a men's wash room than to a church study." African American men, he imagined, "want to have our women and wipe out the white race." White men sometimes raped black women, Johnston admitted, but he suspected that such rapes occurred less frequently. "Our white girls are a lot freer now. These little fourteen year old girls. They know how to take care of themselves now." Without pausing to condemn fornication, he continued, "Way it is now, where boys don't have to go over to niggertown."[14] Johnston suggested that any willing female, even a fourteen-year-old white girl, could be used by white men.

However contraception altered courting rituals, rock 'n' roll and its attendant style were driving forces that drastically changed the way young people passed their time. Automobiles freed courting couples from the family room. They drove around town making appearances at drive-in restaurants or dances or found privacy at drive-in movies or in lovers' lanes. Their mobility gave them the opportunity to escape parental supervision. Couples had always found ways to be alone, but automobiles offered both mobility and a comfortable courting environment with a radio and couchlike seats.[15]

Although most people did not realize it, heterosexual and homosexual cultures overlapped in public spaces such as bars, restrooms, and parks. As historian John Howard has revealed, by parking their automobiles in Atlanta's Piedmont Park, heterosexual couples inadvertently drew attention to homosexuals who shared the park. City authorities installed bright lighting to discourage both straight and homosexual couples from frequenting the park. Homosexuals also contested other public spaces throughout the city. In 1953, Atlanta police used a one-way mirror to observe patrons in the Atlanta Public Library restroom and arrested twenty men for having homosexual encounters. The judges in the case were draconian. The names of those who were arrested were published in local newspapers, nearly all of them lost their jobs, several were banished from the city, some were put under the guidance of ministers, and all pled guilty and paid fines. "As heterosexual courtship assumed a new visibility and legitimacy in the public sphere," Howard revealed, "homosexual men shared in that visibility, but became all the more illegitimate." Many of the men arrested in the public library case had earlier fled rural areas and small towns to seek a less repressive community in Atlanta. The city, at least most of the time, offered welcome invisibility for sexual experimentation.[16]

The rural nature of the South, its class system, and segregation created a distinct gay and lesbian culture. As in other parts of the country, most southerners accepted neighbors and friends whom they might have labeled as "sissies" or "old maids." Rural and small-town people might have whispered or giggled about "queers," but they seldom took public action. As long as people played a role in the community and were discreet about their sexual preferences, they could live "normal" lives. Any number of upper-class white men had black male lovers, but how far down the class structure such relationships extended is uncertain. In the midst of the homophobic and Bible Belt South, gays and lesbians found space, even in rural areas. Although most southerners considered them perverts and thought they were damned, southern lesbians and gays offered neighbors enough ambiguity to guarantee their acceptance and security.[17]

Wartime mobility had encouraged gays and lesbians to form communities throughout the South. In Richmond during and after World War II, Bob Swisher has reported in *Southern Exposure*, "cruising went on unchallenged in the men's rooms and the men's grills in the basements of most of the hotels, in the Greyhound bus station, and in most of the movie theaters along Broad Street." Two bars, Marroni's and Sepul's, catered to gays. In Sepul's back room, men could listen to a jukebox and dance. "On Halloween some men came in drag," one person recalled. As a rule, gay blacks remained segregated from the white gay community.[18]

The mobility of men and women during World War II allowed vastly expanded contact among gays and lesbians. Since women entertainers were scarce on military bases, men often cross-dressed to provide humorous stage shows for the troops. Women in the military, however, faced official displeasure when they impersonated men. Being soldiers to some extent insulated gays and lesbians from persecution. Since men and women were separated in the military, homosexual bonds of affection could flourish. In life or death situations, sexual preference made little difference. Tolerance varied wildly, but in many cases, officers who valued their gay and lesbian soldiers protected them from investigations. When homosexual troops returned home, they found it difficult to adjust to civilian society.[19]

The Cold War obsession with security often focused on the gay and lesbian community. The Johns Committee spent nearly a decade tracking Florida integrationists, communists, bootleggers, and homosexuals. When state senator Charley E. Johns failed to uncover a vast communist conspiracy, he launched a ruthless investigation of homosexuals that ultimately ruined many lives. Remus J. Strickland epitomized the rogue investigator, using entrapment, one-way mirrors, guilt by association, coercive interrogations in hotel rooms, seizure of clinical records, and other abuses of civil liberties. He attacked professors and students at the University of Florida, Florida State University, and Florida Agricultural and Mechanical University, as well as government workers. As Johns and Strickland gathered testimony, they shamelessly posed prurient questions and encouraged suspects to describe sexual acts in detail. Although some refused to supply any information, others gave names. Some young men claimed that because they were unable to seduce women, they had turned in desperation to gay men for sexual relief. Faced with Strickland's evidence, several dozen professors quietly resigned from the University of Florida in the winter of 1959. Similar secret investigations and disappearances plagued other campuses. Even after Strickland left his position in 1963, the investigations continued until 1965, when the legislature finally withdrew funding.[20]

The 1964 Johns Committee report, "Homosexuality and Citizenship in Florida," featured a cover photograph of two men kissing, photographs of bondage and a posed restroom encounter, and twenty small photographs of naked young boys. The report estimated that the gay population of Florida was 60,000, announced that sixty-four teachers had been decertified on morals charges, and included a "Glossary of Homosexual Terms and Deviate Acts." The graphic report offended many Floridians and created concern that sex offenders or minors might acquire the report.[21]

Even author Lillian Smith was wary of receiving public censure for her private life. Since Paula Snelling began work as a counselor at Smith's summer camp for girls, she shared not only Smith's literary interests but also her personal life. Smith and Snelling became lifelong companions, but they destroyed nearly all evidence of their intimacy. "I am sorry my letters are burned," Smith wrote Snelling in June 1952, "that is my ambivalence. My shame about something different and completely good." Throughout her life, Smith confronted the contradictions inherent in segregation and the requirement that white women deny their sexuality. Her autobiographical *Killers of the Dream*, published in 1949, described with passion and clarity her struggle against southern racial and sexual proscriptions, including the judgment "that a terrifying disaster would befall the South if ever I treated a Negro as my social equal and a terrifying disaster would befall my family if ever I were to have a baby outside of marriage."[22]

Smith's frankness about race and sex resonated with the concerns of many other southern white women. "By the time we were five years old," she explained, "we had learned, without hearing the words, that masturbation is wrong and segregation is right, and each had become a dread taboo that must never be broken." The parts of her body, therefore, were segregated, and "you cannot associate freely with them any more than you can associate freely with colored children." The body also had to be kept pure, so no alcohol should invade it. Smith suggested that prohibition, like racial segregation, protected people from the "stronger temptations" that inebriation might unleash. Such honest observations about segregation and sexuality offended some readers, but to many southern women, Lillian Smith became an inspiration, an icon.[23]

In the mid-1950s, as Smith worked on her novel *One Hour*, she speculated on the potential impact of Dave, a clergyman in the book. "I know a number of young ministers intimately enough to know quite a bit about their love affairs, and their somewhat perverse and 'abnormal' affairs." Smith's use of symbols and myth in *One Hour* upset her psychoanalyst friend Lawrence Kubie. Smith could not understand Kubie's scientific preoccupation or his reaction to dancing. Kubie "despised dancing," asking, "'How can any woman fling her arms and legs around, letting her legs do what her arms should do and arms do what legs should do?'" Smith "cringed in a kind of mammoth distaste" at Kubie's comments, she confided to a friend. Kubie had stopped attending the ballet. "Above all I was depressed by the manner on the theme of bisexuality, and by the cackles of excited fairy laughter that would arise in the audience as their response to their homosexual risibilities were touched off," he wrote to Smith. Acknowledging that he sounded "dreadfully uncharitable," he labeled gays in the audience "a small group of sick people" who banded together "in order to avoid facing the reality of their own illness." He also claimed that he could not think of a single dancer "who is not a screwed up human being, whether male or female."[24]

Despite her own relationship with Snelling, Smith privately made biting comments about same-sex relationships. She clearly understood the dangers of being attacked as a homosexual. In the 1950s and 1960s, most southerners had little tolerance for known homosexuals. In 1961, for example, Eleanor Roosevelt implored Smith to help in the case of a Georgia man who had been sentenced to thirty-five years in prison "for acts of homosexuality." Admitting that she was "grieved and shocked" and that such prejudice was "strong and ugly," Smith replied that she did what she could to help in her writing. "We are working in Georgia at present on the problems of segregation and mental illness," she explained; "if we add homosexuality to these, we shall really have a hornet's nest."[25]

Despite a seemingly pervasive Puritanism regarding deviance from heterosexual behavior in the South, many black and white residents in small southern towns exhibited unexpected ribaldry and appreciation for at least mildly transgressive rituals. "Womanless Weddings," folk dramas of unknown origins, featured a town's male residents in both female and male roles, which necessitated cross-dressing. These ceremonies, always segregated, raised money for churches, civic groups, or other community endeavors and customarily were performed in school auditoriums. Town residents laughed at the spectacle of men, including the town fathers and ministers, dressing and acting as women. The characters usually included a pregnant and unattractive bride, an irate and armed father, a dim-witted groom, an inventive minister, and buxom attendants who delivered ribald commentary. Neither the participants nor the audience attributed untoward motives to the cross-dressed men. Because the script consisted of corny dialogue, the humor was based on watching prominent men act silly while dressed as women. In Lewis Nordan's novel *The Sharp-Shooter Blues*, one character commented on an incident during a womanless wedding in Arrow Catcher, Mississippi: "Remember that year Mr. Rant was the bride in the Womanless Wedding and got so drunk he fell off the stage in a floor-length gown? I like to died laughing." Womanless weddings, which continue to be performed, were distinct from minstrel shows, which were also staged in small southern towns.[26]

Photographs taken in Wilson, Arkansas, in 1950 show some white men cross-dressed as beauty contestants occupying the same stage as others in blackface. Whether the program featured this mix or whether several casts appeared onstage simultaneously for photographs, the suggestive mingling of "black" men and white "women" went to the heart of transgression. The small-town white audience of men, women, and children seemed intent on the action. In real life, the appearance of black men and white women in the same social space would have set off an explosion of emotion and, no doubt, retribution. But to Wilson's white citizens, the occasion was festive and humorous. Only the straight announcer seemed uneasy. A photograph taken at the 1952 New Year's Eve party at Atlanta's elite Nine O'Clock Club shows a crossed-dressed man offering a toast and a black pianist, probably his accompanist. Several photographs from Delta State University in Cleveland, Mississippi, feature young men enjoying themselves in women's clothes.[27]

Obviously, many southern men flirted with transgressive behavior. In a society that placed a premium on masculinity and whiteness, white men easily assumed roles that demonstrated their mastery of both women and blacks. A stage full of white men posed no threat regardless of what might transpire on it. Black dandys leering at scantily clad white women could have provoked alarming violence in real life, but onstage, white men turned such a scenario into

Cast of a "Womanless Wedding," 1940. Courtesy Mary Panzer.

side-splitting humor. Since they controlled the household, local and state politics, the economy, and race etiquette, white men could violate and enforce all
barriers with impunity. Cross-dressing and other risqué behavior, of course,
were not limited to whites. Blacks also staged "Womanless Weddings" to raise
funds, and minstrel and other stage shows often featured cross-dressing. Since
such productions were categorized as entertainment, did not challenge white
institutions or propriety, and in many white minds confirmed black depravity,
most whites paid them little attention. Still, the coexistence of license and con-
straint complicated southern social life. As segregation came under attack and
white men's fears of political intrusion mounted, transgressive behavior became more threatening but also more thrilling.

In Memphis, a thriving lesbian community developed around softball teams
and working-class culture. Most of these women never told their parents or
openly admitted their sexual preference. They hung out in friendly "mom-and-

Stage show, Wilson, Arkansas, 1950. Lee Wilson & Company Archives,
Special Collections Division, University of Arkansas Libraries, Fayetteville.

pop bars" and juke joints, where they danced, flirted, and fought. Some women
dressed "butch" and risked arrest for cross-dressing. Police sometimes raided
gay and lesbian parties; one Memphis woman's police record noted that she was
"suspected of homosexuality" and "involved with lesbians." After one woman
was arrested, her boss suggested that they invite some men to their next party.
Women's softball games offered what many lesbians considered the best meeting place. "I think that softball fields," one woman remembered, "were the only
place that most of us felt comfortable." Large crowds attended the games, and
the level of competition was excellent. Memphis's lesbians remained largely underground but still managed to find space for meeting, competing, and form-
ing the basis of a community.[28]

In such ways, southern society in the 1950s was remarkably unsegregated.
Blacks and whites lived, worked, and sometimes played together, and closeted
gays and lesbians were integral members of society. As long as African American men were cordoned off from public spaces where they might encounter

white women as equals and as long as gays and lesbians remained in the closet, straight white southerners lived in comfortable delusion. It shocked whites to learn that blacks were unhappy; it surprised many southerners to discover that gays and lesbians felt cheated that they had to hide their sexual preferences.

Even at the fringes of polite Memphis society, creative people strained at fifties conventions. Bettye Berger's experiences revealed the tension between the customary expectations of women and new opportunities. She grew up in rural Tennessee and at age seventeen visited her sister in Memphis, where she fell in love, soon married, and eventually had three children. "My dream," she recalled, "was to have a white house with a baby, pushing it in a little stroller." The dream lasted eight years. She then resumed a modeling career, and her husband gave her an ultimatum: "Stop modeling or we get divorced." Divorce followed. Berger boldly called Sam Phillips with an idea for a business, but instead he hired her as a disc jockey at his 1,000-watt ("a thousand beautiful watts") WHER all-woman radio station. The DJs sometimes made mistakes, Berger admitted,

Nine O'Clock Club, Atlanta, Georgia, New Year's Eve, 1952.
Courtesy of the Atlanta History Center.

but they had fun. When one announcer began, "This is WHER, and now the news from abroad," a man laughed so hard he ran his car into a telephone pole. At least, that was the story that circulated.[29]

By the time Elvis Presley became popular, Berger was divorced, working, listening to Dewey Phillips, writing songs, and dancing at clubs around Memphis. When Berger did a television advertisement for Honeysuckle Corn Meal, Presley called her at WHER and asked her out. She begged off, explaining that Sam Phillips was recording one of her songs that night, but Presley insisted that they meet at midnight at the Chisca Hotel, the site of Dewey Phillips's *Red, Hot, and Blue* program. Berger recalled that at first glance Presley came across as "a motorcycle rider," which "wasn't very nice" and suggested "fingernails not too clean." Presley arrived in black pants, a black shirt, black boots, and a captain's hat. They went to his house on Audubon Drive, where Berger met his mother and admired his teddy bear collection and they sang spirituals. They talked until sunrise, and then she went home, showered, and reported to work at 8:30. It was not their last date.[30]

Two students. The Broom, 1960. Delta State University Archives, Cleveland, Miss.

Chorus line.
Box 1, Record Group 21, folder 13, Delta State University Archives, Cleveland, Miss.

Because she wrote music, dated musicians, modeled, spun records on WHER, and was part of the club scene, Berger witnessed a wide spectrum of Memphis social life. After she married Louis Jack Berger, Plantation Inn owner Morris Berger's son, she worked at the Plantation Inn. She often dropped by Poplar Tunes to buy records for her husband's jukeboxes. Later, she booked musicians and continued her independent life. The course of Berger's life intersected with music at every turn, and she became a keen observer of its flow through Memphis.[31]

Berger was a decade older than fifties teenagers who carefully monitored the radio, jukeboxes, records, and television dance shows for style clues. Before *American Bandstand* swept local shows aside, many communities hosted teenage dance shows such as Dewey Phillips's short-lived program in Memphis. In Little Rock, Arkansas, 120 miles from Memphis, high school students showed up each afternoon to dance on *Steve's Show*. Nearly every afternoon during the 1956–57 school year, tenth-graders Hazel Bryan and Sammie Dean Parker dressed in their poodle skirts, crinolines, and rock 'n' roll shoes and danced on television. Dancing, Bryan remembered, "was a really, really big part of our lives." Like most teenagers, Bryan paid little attention to the cultural influence of African American musicians. Unlike many white teenagers of the fifties, however, both Parker and Bryan were forced to pay attention to school integration in 1957 when they ended up in the middle of the crisis at Central High School.[32]

Singing rock 'n' roll and wearing Lansky's styles or motorcycle leather transgressed the color line and middle-class taste and appeared to be a calculated affront to polite white society. Seditious white rock 'n' roll musicians presented themselves as surrogate African Americans. Rock 'n' roll music, language, and dress moved black culture into the mainstream at the very time that white southerners were emotionally confronting the civil rights movement and trying to preserve segregation. Horrified southern white politicians and their racist allies saw in rock 'n' roll music a powerful threat to segregation and, they were quick to point out, to southern white womanhood.

This style, this rebellion, troubled many whites who were already preoccupied with other threats to the color line such as blacks who came to bat each weekend in television baseball games. Shrill segregationists often drowned out more moderate voices. The official organ of the North Alabama Citizens' Council, the *Southerner*, charged that "the utter beast is brought to the surface" by rock 'n' roll. This music could have monstrous consequences, the *Southerner* insisted, including the spread of communism and integration. Asa E. Carter, who headed the North Alabama group, started a campaign to ban rock 'n' roll records from jukeboxes, charging that the music eroded the morals of American youths with its "degenerate, animalistic beats and rhythms." Across the country, pastors and other cultural arbiters condemned rock 'n' roll as a threat to polite society and occasionally publicly broke records.[33]

Many white southerners objected not just to rock 'n' roll but to all violations of the color line. Some whites found offenses where none had existed previously. In Wetumpka, Alabama, seventy-five carloads of Citizens' Council members, irate at a drive-in showing of *Islands in the Sun*, starring Harry Belafonte and Joan Fontaine, cut off power, blocked the access road, chased journalists who had arrived to cover the incident, and beat up a photographer. "Niggers may run wild in Montgomery," one protester announced, "but Elmore County is going to take care of itself." In Pine Bluff, Arkansas, whites boycotted a drive-in restaurant, demanding that two black carhops be fired and replaced with white girls. Owner Tommy Priakos had employed black carhops for four years with no trouble and refused to fire the two Agricultural, Mechanical, and Normal College students.[34]

Black carhops, probably in Columbia, South Carolina. John H. McCray Papers, South Caroliniana Library, University of South Carolina, Columbia.

In Jackson, Mississippi, Archibald S. Coody waged a protracted battle against communists, Jews, and blacks, a tribute to his hero, Theodore Bilbo. "Everywhere you see *niggers*," he protested to a friend; they were "on TV shows, baseball, football, prize fights, etc." One of Coody's friends had visited his son in New York, and they had attended a baseball game. "He said the first man up to bat was a Negro, the 2nd a Negro and the 3rd a Negro," Coody recounted. "He told his son, 'let us get out of here, this is no place for a white man.'" The son protested that he had paid $8 for the tickets, but his father dragged him away, arguing that it was worth $8 "to learn where not to go." Whether or not the son was attempting to demonstrate that integrated contests were hardly controversial, the father was irate.[35]

The widespread acceptance of black performers, especially by young white women, as much as the beat of rock 'n' roll, challenged white segregationist ideology. Robert B. Patterson, secretary of the Mississippi Citizens' Council, wrote a friend in March 1955 describing a Louis "Satchmo" Armstrong concert at the

University of Mississippi. "It was my pleasure (?) to see and hear 'Satchmo's' inter-racial orchestra consisting of two blacks, two whites, and two yellows, entertain a packed house of co-eds and male students; mostly co-eds," he wrote. "You should have heard the co-eds shriek when the yellow boy soloed on his slide trombone. During the show Louis addressed his white orchestra members by their first names and hugged them affectionately, etc." White women's emotional response to the integrated Armstrong orchestra disturbed Patterson, for in his mind it suggested more than an affection for the music. The screaming white women obviously cared more for the music generated by the integrated orchestra than for the segregation code. Although Patterson enjoyed Armstrong's music, he did not relish the color line transgressions.[36]

Worries about women's sexuality were not restricted to whites. Nat D. Williams, the first African American disc jockey on Memphis's WDIA, described the reaction to Elvis Presley's appearance at the 1956 WDIA Goodwill Review. Some 9,000 people attended, and such top artists as B. B. King, the Moonglows, the Magnificents, Ray Charles, and the Five Blind Boys performed. Presley remained in the wings until someone pushed him onstage. The audience exploded. Williams reported that the "teen-age girls in the audience blended their alto and soprano voices in one wild crescendo of sound that rent the rafters and took off like scalded cats in the direction of Elvis." It took "several white cops" to restore order. "How come cullud girls would take on so over a Memphis white boy," Williams pondered, "when they hardly let out a squeak over B. B. King, a Memphis cullud boy?" He wondered whether the reaction reflected "a basic integration in attitude and aspiration which has been festering in the minds of most of your folks' women-folk all along."[37]

Nat Williams, like Robert Patterson, feared that men were losing control of women's sexuality. Young black women's blatant infatuation with Presley shocked Williams, just as white girls' screams for Armstrong's orchestra upset Patterson. The teenage craze for fifties music and its idols, especially among young women, challenged the color line in ways that were particularly disturbing to men. Respectable black and white women were expressing sexually loaded emotions in public, and these emotions were crossing the color line. Given that fear of interracial dating and sexual relations dominated many white conversations at the time, symbolic integration through music aroused strong sentiments. School integration, a strong possibility after the *Brown v. Board of Education* decision in 1954, would open up a social space where black and white young people could meet as equals. Rock 'n' roll music and a dance floor crowded with black and white youths terrified adults because it offered a space to negotiate an end to the color line.

Concerts and dances for whites restricted blacks to the bandstand and whites

Elvis Presley and B. B. King, Ellis Auditorium, Memphis, 1955.
© *Ernest Withers. Courtesy Panopticon Gallery, Boston, Massachusetts.*

to the audience, but at one concert at the University of Mississippi, that spatial division proved inadequate. Muddy Waters, who was a tractor driver in the Delta before leaving for Chicago during World War II, returned to his native state in 1960 to play at a dance at the University of Mississippi. At the dance, women students were out of control. As they twisted in short skirts, Waters remembered, "their little white panties [were] showing." The alarmed university organizers turned off the lights and sent the band outside to await their check in the rain. It was bad enough that the Miss America factory tolerated the twist at all, but when gyrating young white women forgot themselves and lost their respectability before a black band, white men acted to restore propriety.[38]

Ole Miss student Sandra Scarbrough attended the notorious Muddy Waters dance, as well as many other dances. Dancing to a black band was extremely popular at the University of Mississippi. "You always sort of moaned if there was a white band," she admitted, "because the black bands were so much better." Students drank enormous amounts of liquor, and at times, their "behavior . . . was very loose. I mean really." In her estimation, women were becoming more liberated sexually, although she doubted that they had abandoned their suburban middle-class dreams of having a houseful of children.[39]

As Scarbrough suggested, black music—gospel, blues, rhythm and blues, and dance music—had always been popular among southern whites of all classes. During the 1950s and 1960s, bands such as the Hot Nuts in the Carolinas and the Red Tops in Mississippi enjoyed regional fame. The Red Tops played out of Vicksburg and featured a drum, three trumpets, four saxophones, one guitar, and a lead singer. The band sometimes earned $1,000 a week playing college dances in Mississippi and Louisiana. Since the band performed without sheet music, audiences assumed they did not read music, but in fact the band's performances were carefully arranged and rehearsed. The Red Tops wore dark red coats and bow ties, and they choreographed stage acts and skits that kept them in constant motion. They played requests for old favorites, current hits, waltzes, fox-trots, rock 'n' roll, and even "Dixie." Lead singer Rufus McKay often evoked tears with his rendition of "Danny Boy." Band leader Walter Osborne required punctuality, neatness, and sobriety, and he hired a lawyer to implement a partnership agreement. Nearly all band members were family men who held day jobs. Trumpeter Willard Tyler used his income from Red Top performances to educate his four children.[40]

Blacks and whites were intimately connected through music, and away from prying eyes, the color line blurred. Sandra Scarbrough's adolescence in a small Mississippi town suggests the complexities that haunted segregation. Scarbrough grew up in Meadville, Mississippi, thirty miles from Natchez. After her mother died in 1954, she negotiated her teenage years largely under her grandparents' guidance. Long before she could drive a car, Scarbrough's boyfriend, Mike McElroy, and his brother, Warren, took her to the Blue Flame, a black juke joint next to bootlegger John Clark's house in nearby Bude. The blue interior, she recalled, was dominated by a huge bubbling blue jukebox filled with rock 'n' roll records. Warren started dancing. She had never seen anything like it. "I just

Sandra Scarbrough and Archie Campbell. Courtesy Sandra Scarbrough Kramer.

couldn't wait to learn to do it," she said. In high school, she often went to black juke joints. But McElroy rarely took her to Cooter's Park, a country bar in Mc-Comb, because the white guys would hit on her and he would have to fight them. The people in such white bars "were just the wildest people I've ever known in my life," she remembered. The dances she learned at the Blue Flame were, in her opinion, "very sexual." In that sense, she admitted, "the elders were correct."[41]

The atmosphere among high school students in Meadville was charged with music and sexual tension. "Sex was everywhere, and it's a wonder none of us got pregnant," Scarbrough admitted. "Only the terror of God and your father kept you from doing it." From the time she was fifteen, she spent many weekends in Natchez, "sin city." She and her friends went to the Beverly Club, which had a white band, or strayed "under the hill" to the Black Cat, which had a black band. Across the river in Vidalia, the Rex Showboat tempted them, but the "Vidalia gangs" were tough. In Ferriday, there were "the real, real raunchy places where Jerry Lee Lewis played." After McElroy took her home to Meadville, he and his brother would return to the Wagon Wheel, "'cause that's where they would get their 'bad girls.'" Scarbrough, a member of Meadville Baptist Church, would squirm through Sunday services. "You'd go out on Saturday night at the Beverly Club, and then you'd come in and rededicate your life on Sunday morning," she explained. Religion raised other questions in Scarbrough's mind. "We were really taught Jesus loves the little children of the world, red and yellow, black and white," she noted, and given her Saturday night experiences, she could not easily dismiss those words. Later, she became an activist in both the civil rights movement and the women's movement.[42]

Mississippi was a dry state, so juke joints and roadhouses provided bootleg liquor. "Many places now have a dance hall in the back and many of them with rooms connected," a former deputy sheriff of Sunflower County stated in 1960. "Teen agers go to these places, drink and dance, with unlimited opportunity to do just as they please." He campaigned to protect young people from such temptations. "Many a good mother would faint," he predicted, "if she could see some of the places open to their sons and daughters." He also judged that Mississippi had "more drunks" and "more wrecks" than states that sold liquor legally.[43]

The wild nightlife enjoyed by both whites and blacks coexisted with prohibition and drinking, sexual repression and freedom, religious guilt and secular release, and whites' insistence on rigid segregation and preference for black bands. University of Mississippi students embraced African American music and dance and doted on black bands, but they ignored the implications of such mixing. Scarbrough could not recall a single college discussion on civil rights. She also remembered her reception when she enrolled in an economics class. The professor "proceeded to say out loud in the class that economics was not for women."[44]

At nearby Rowan Oak, novelist William Faulkner observed the frenzy over rock 'n' roll, although in his fiction he largely ignored southern music. In 1957, he complained that "there is not one place in fifty miles that I have found where I can eat any food at all without having to listen to a juke box."[45]

In her novel *Heartbreak Hotel*, Anne Rivers Siddons described fifties social life and tension at Randolph University, a fictional version of Auburn University. When a woman student suggested that there might be more to life than dancing, her friend replied, "Well if there is, I don't want to know about it yet." Siddons summed up the young woman's understanding of race and music: "The affairs of the black race, save their music, were as alien to her as the comings and goings of aborigines, or ants, or hartebeests." Siddons, who had attended Auburn in the 1950s, included at least one autobiographical incident in *Heartbreak Hotel*. Like Maggie, the novel's heroine, while working at the campus newspaper, the *Plainsman*, Siddons had written "a fairly mild essay" urging tolerance after a riot broke out when Autherine Lucy was admitted to the University of Alabama. She was fired from the newspaper.[46]

Auburn maintained the public image of a quiet agricultural school, and strict rules kept women properly dressed and chaperoned. In 1946, Dean of Women Katharine Cater asked for more privacy for women sunbathers after "a number of rather unpleasant incidents when passers-by stopped to see the girls who were not so fully clothed as they should have been." After a pep rally on October 16, 1947, men launched a panty raid, and Cater's dormitory defenses proved inadequate. She wrote a thorough report to Auburn president Ralph B. Draughon detailing the property destruction and the affronts to women students. Appended to Cater's memorandum was a list of two dozen suspects and fifty-five incidents, including "many boys drinking," "kissed girls—tried to kiss others," "very ugly talk," "chased girls in rooms," and "kissed by drunkard." Cater estimated that the property loss amounted to $1,333.60.[47]

Behavior had not improved by the late 1950s, although Cater welcomed a lecture by writer Katherine Anne Porter in 1959 as a wholesome academic influence. Cater, however, was not happy with reports of drinking among students, especially among women students. In March 1959, she warned Draughon of what she considered deteriorating behavior among students. Two freshman girls had gotten drunk at a fraternity party, and one had become ill; both had been "punished." An off-campus fraternity party had degenerated into a drunken brawl that had left the area in "terrible shape." Many fraternities sent pledges to nearby Opelika to "buy as much as several hundred dollars worth of liquor." At another off-campus fraternity party, "the Negro house boy was brought to the dance. He, too, was given drinks and was intoxicated. There was much fraternizing among some of the boys, the house boy, and the Negro band." Cater did not elaborate on her notion of fraternizing, but obviously the color line was in danger even at Auburn. "Later at the fraternity house the drinking continued," Cater reported, "and a girl who was there told me that some very ribald songs were sung. She was so embarrassed that she resolved never to go to that fraternity house again." One of the head residents at a girls' dormitory reported that "on three occasions when she answered the telephone, boys who did not identify themselves asked if there is a girl around who would like to go out and have some beer."[48] Although white college students in the fifties preferred African American bands and even "fraternized" with them at times, such behavior was a long way from taking a stand for integration.

Lillian Smith closely observed the young women she encountered. In 1956, she had harsh words for Vassar students. "They shun wisdom, vision, love, compassion, hope." Smith noted that above all else they sought "security from hope. If they have hope, then they will have to assume the responsibility that lies before them. But as long as one is hopeless, one need do nothing, be nothing: hopelessness can pay high dividends (especially in the world we call art, literature, etc. etc.)."[49]

Southern students were no better, in Smith's estimation. "There were the young white and colored girls together, eating together, sleeping in the same dorm, often sharing the same room," she wrote of a 1957 Young Women's Christian Association conference at Spelman College. "They felt pious as—hell." Some of the white girls had gone against their parents' wishes to attend; others had slipped away. Smith told them that they had to create a new South, had to take action. The young women boasted of tolerance and blamed their parents' generation for segregation. "I used to say it too, long ago," Smith confessed. "I was really a rebel; these children are sort of playing dolls with it." Despite Smith's chiding that both "white and Negro girls have been too sheltered," such meetings indicated that civil rights had moved up a notch on the collegiate agenda.[50]

Smith had high expectations, but music and dance sometimes prompted confrontations that strained both generational and religious boundaries. During chapel services at Wake Forest College on November 21, 1957, alarm clocks went off at 10:15 A.M. during the choir's rendering of "Come Thou Fount of Every Blessing," and the entire student body walked out to protest a dance ban imposed at all Baptist-supported schools by a vote of the Baptist State Convention the day before. Students walked across the grass, a violation of school tradition, and gathered on the terrace beside the snack shop, where they turned up the jukebox and protest-danced for an hour to such favorites as "Wake Up Little Susie" and "Whole Lot of Shakin' Going On." Some of the women students dressed in black and pinned a red "D" on their sweaters. "It's my scarlet letter," one explained; "I dance. I'm a sinner." That night some students bunny-hopped across campus, others burned an effigy of convention president J. C. Canipe,

Students dancing. The Broom, *1959. Delta State University Archives, Cleveland, Miss.*

and still others danced in the parking lot of a nearby shopping center. Irate Baptists sent letters to several professors rebuking their indifference to the revolt. "For a riot," one administrator judged, "it was mature." In a larger sense, the convention's overwhelming support of a dance ban underlined the abrupt shift in musical tastes and the power of rock 'n' roll music. *Life* magazine found the demonstration newsworthy, and a double-page photo showed dancing students. The dance ban, of course, transformed the shag and bop into transgressive pleasures that "radicalized" even demure Baptist students. For many, it was their first protest.[51]

As the Wake Forest College demonstration showed, even protests against strict elders could be pulled off with good humor and wit. In the minds of the students, dancing had no association with African American culture. History has not recorded what their Baptist elders thought. It would be a mistake, then, to conclude that rock 'n' roll music magically converted either white or black youths into integrationists or made young women wanton. Ideological change seldom occurs so directly. Some of the same white youths who cheered Louis Armstrong, B. B. King, Little Richard, or Chuck Berry also enthusiastically cheered segregationist politicians. Still, black and white musicians gained immense fame and influence, and they undermined a wide spectrum of racial stereotypes.

Women, who were practically excluded from rock 'n' roll performance, screamed and danced with such untamed passion that men were confounded.

Rock 'n' roll unlocked women's emotions, but it also threatened men's control. The combination of music, religion, and civil rights, as Sandra Scarbrough suggested, contained transformative power. No doubt many dancing women evoked the transgressive "D" in male minds. The contradictions in the notion of Christian brotherhood in a segregated society, the prohibition of dancing, music's blurring of race, and an emerging civil rights movement created enormous tension throughout southern society.

It is difficult to determine how much power rock 'n' roll music exerted in reshaping racial ideology, whatever its potential. When blacks performed before white audiences at the very edge of the color line, their proximity conveyed no overt civil rights message. It took the 1960s sit-ins and probing television cameras to humiliate or sensitize white southerners, and even then, many remained ambivalent or hostile. Over the years, marches, sit-ins, violence, and legislation have forced radical changes in southern society.

The culture that produced significant trippers, record producers, and musicians has been damned as fundamentalist and illiterate. Indeed, prejudice against both African Americans and poor whites remains rife, even accepted, as the new millennium begins. But fifties creativity did not spring from unintelligent and untalented people. The southerners who fostered the racing, music, and style that transformed international culture had been largely invisible before radio and recordings offered them an outlet. The trek of 11 million farmers to the urban frontier coincided not only with the rise of radio and television but also with the country's hunger for new musical and cultural forms.

Rhythm and blues, rock 'n' roll, and soul eroded class and racial barriers, for neither class nor race could contain the musical energy. If the essence of this culture could have been distilled into a political force, southerners might have been able to face their own racial demons. Even as southern music grew in popularity, the music industry tamed its spontaneity, bled its interracial message, consumed its profits, and commodified its style. Like stock car racing, rock 'n' roll became diluted for mass consumption. Before they were tamed, the last generation of sharecroppers transformed world culture, and their fast cars and bent strings continue to transmit a spirit of rebellion.

BOOK III FATAL DIVISIONS

8 Brothers of the Faith

In Christ there is no East or West,
In Him no South or North;
But one great fellowship of love
Throughout the whole wide earth.
Join hands, then brothers of the faith,
Whate'er your race may be;
Who serves my Father as a son
Is surely kin to me.
—*John Oxenham, "In Christ There Is No East or West"*

Our political leadership might have come forward and led us, our newspapers
could have been more constructive, our churches might have proclaimed the light
with a little more heat, but nobody filled the vacuum until the White Citizens'
Councils got under way and the politicians saw they could make hay on the issue,
and then the main chance was gone.
—*Wilma Dykeman and James Stokely*

After depression, wars, the demise of labor-intensive agriculture, atomic threats, and fears of communist infiltration, finally on May 17, 1954, the U.S. Supreme Court handed down the *Brown v. Board of Education* decision. It assumed central ideological importance. It came down even as millions of dislocated southerners were searching for a new start away from farming. It came down less than two months before Elvis Presley and a group of white country boys began singing their way to fame.

If farming, stock car races, rock 'n' roll, and weekend madness were the domain of working-class southerners, preserving segregation became the cause of middle-class and elite whites. Southern whites who had recently entered the middle class, in particular, feared that integration would threaten their status, privilege, and upward mobility. Although working-class southerners certainly joined segregationist organizations, the middle class dominated them. Among white southerners of all classes, a substantial well of goodwill for African Americans coexisted with apprehension over an integrated future. The *Brown* deci-

179

sion ultimately rent the fabric of southern life, for no national, state, or local leader captured the spirit of interracial cooperation.

African Americans saw in the *Brown* decision a new breath of freedom. It would have astonished insensitive white southerners to read Pauli Murray's letter to her friend Lillian Smith a week after the decision. "I do not know where you are, but I can bet you wept on Monday last and throughout the week," Murray wrote on May 25. "I did, unashamedly." For Murray, who at the time had suspended her legal practice to write *Proud Shoes: The Story of an American Family*, it had been "a long road." Murray praised Smith for "the understanding and healing you have brought during the battle." To Murray, the *Brown* decision was intensely personal. "I was witnessing a climax of the long steep climb out of black slavery—when teaching a slave to read and write was a crime—toward an unequivocal declaration of the constitutional right to equal educational opportunity, a struggle that defined my family's role in the history of their time." Her grandfather had taught school in the first days of freedom. "My aunts had borne the brunt of enforced segregation in impoverished Negro schools for more than half a century," she explained, "enduring humiliations from their white superiors while striving to overcome the stigma of inferiority and give incentives to Negro children during the darkest days of racial *apartheid*." To Pauli Murray, the *Brown* decision "seemed almost like a benediction."[1]

Fourteen-year-old Leslie Burl McLemore heard the news of the *Brown* decision on the radio in Walls, Mississippi. While chopping cotton the next morning, he and his friends excitedly debated whether to attend the white Catholic school in Walls or the Horne Lake school. He recalled, "We really thought that we would be able to, starting in September." In 1954, McLemore was attending elementary school in nearby Hernando, but there was no public school building for African Americans. "We had some classes in a Methodist church, and the rest of the classes were in two different Baptist churches." When he graduated from elementary school in 1956 and spoke as valedictorian of his class at the DeSoto County Courthouse in Hernando, it "was the first time that black people had ever used the courthouse as a public facility, when they had not been there for some charge in court." After waiting for nearly 100 years for the Supreme Court to acknowledge the disparity between black and white opportunities under segregation, Pauli Murray, Leslie McLemore, and many others expected that the federal government would actively enforce the Supreme Court decision.[2]

Most African Americans, much like Pauli Murray and Leslie McLemore, expected the *Brown* decision to end school segregation. White activist Virginia Durr, who was living in Montgomery at the time, recalled that "it was regarded by the black people I knew here in Montgomery as the second Emancipation

Proclamation." Several excited black constituents wrote to Tennessee governor Frank Clement urging him to support the decision. "I am a Negro and I have never believed in segregation," Carrine Newton wrote from Memphis. "I am happy that the Supreme Court is allowing my people a chance." Fellow Memphian Josephine Winbush urged Clement to assemble the best black and white minds to discuss implementation.[3]

Whatever preparations liberal organizations, editors, clergymen, and politicians had made before *Brown*, the decision still left most white southerners breathless. No national, state, or local leader offered suggestions for how to dismantle half a century of segregation laws and customs. Moderate whites haltingly called for acceptance of the Court's decision, whereas segregationists minced no words in their strident opposition. During the summer of 1954, southerners searched for some way to either implement or avoid the Supreme Court decision.

During the summer of 1954, the *Brown* decision hung heavy in the air as southerners waited in vain for leaders to plot a course of action. On June 1, the Southern Regional Council's George S. Mitchell warned Fisk University president Charles S. Johnson that no local groups willing to discuss *Brown* had "sprouted" in the South. Mitchell doubted that many whites favored the decision, and he resisted lending organizational support to those who were lukewarm. The battle for the hearts and minds of white southerners had begun. From the outset, caution hampered whites who favored integration. "Our political leadership might have come forward and led us, our newspapers could have been more constructive, our churches might have proclaimed the light with a little more heat," activist writers Wilma Dykeman and James Stokely charged a few years later, "but nobody filled the vacuum until the White Citizens' Councils got under way and the politicians saw they could make hay on the issue, and then the main chance was gone."[4]

By 1954, few successfully integrated organizations had survived in the South. The Southern Regional Council and its state affiliates encouraged blacks and whites to discuss integration, but after *Brown*, such meetings provoked criticism. The Southern Conference Educational Fund confronted segregation but suffered from anticommunist attacks. Because the promising interracial labor movement had collapsed in the South by the early 1950s, no effective link between civil rights and unions remained. Many corporate leaders used racial rhetoric as a means of labor control to divide black and white workers.

Churches offered the best hope for easing the transition from segregation. Despite the wide range of denominational thought on race relations, Lillian Smith targeted "the ministers, and the laymen and laywomen" as the South's primary candidates for enlightened leadership. "This is the #1 problem: how to develop leadership down here," Smith wrote to Henry Hart Crane in April 1956. She dismissed politicians and editors but held out hope for the church. "If the ministers speak out bravely, quietly, persuasively they can give direction to the feelings of millions of white southerners who don't know what to do or where to turn." Southern churches had been burdened with guilt, she believed, but by making a bold stand against segregation, they could "take on new spiritual life."[5]

Southern pastors, as Dykeman and Stokely have suggested, could have played a crucial role in the years following *Brown*. Church steeples dominated southern towns and cities and punctuated the countryside. Most white southerners were Protestants, but Jewish communities flourished throughout the South, and numerous Catholics, especially in Louisiana, lived peacefully with their Protestant neighbors. Nearly all southern Christians agreed on certain fundamentals of faith, among them the inviolability of the Bible, the Trinity, the Virgin birth of Jesus, and his resurrection. Congregations found ample biblical passages and doctrines to dispute, and they splintered, seceded, and merged with the intensity of microbes, producing a great diversity of beliefs.[6]

Religious teachings usually complemented community ideology. Indeed, churches codified community beliefs, and ministers' sermons wove together platitudes, gentle cautionary tales, and condemnation of Ten Commandment sins. Although strong-willed and charismatic ministers sometimes challenged convention, a minister who called money changers to account or raised questions about segregation rarely kept his pulpit. Most parishioners expected to hear a sermon on Sunday that left them content with their piety and pleased with their neighbors. Even while striving to follow the example of Jesus, the church reflected the community, with its aggregation of sins and shortcomings.

Many southern Protestant ministers, especially those in more cosmopolitan areas, had attended college and seminary and were better educated than their flocks; they seldom worked with their hands. Because ministers visited shut-ins, attended meetings, prepared sermons, showed sensitivity to worthy causes, and were in the company of women more often than in the company of working men, to some extent they became feminized. The social distance between pastors and parishioners in the legion of working-class fundamentalist congregations was shorter, for these ministers often held day jobs.

Long before the *Brown v. Board of Education* decision in 1954, many southern religious leaders questioned segregation. What historian Mark Newman has referred to as the "progressive elite" of the Southern Baptist Convention disseminated a moderating message to Baptists through sermons, newspapers, and reports. To undermine legal segregation, the progressives relied on the New Testament and Jesus' disregard for social distinctions. Segregation and racial violence also hindered foreign mission work. The executive secretary of the Foreign Mission Board stated that the *Brown* decision would "strengthen American influence in many countries and will reduce some obstacles to missionary work among the races." The Southern Baptist Convention issued statements supporting the decision and distributed pamphlets and articles urging obedience to the law.[7]

Most Southern Baptist periodical editors interpreted the decision as an opportunity to practice Christianity by extending full citizenship to black brothers in Christ. Some Upper South editors praised the decision, admitting that it was overdue, and reported the favorable reactions of readers. Pastors suggested a prayerful response and called attention to the Golden Rule, but their congregations were torn between the word of God and their belief in segregation. Both South Carolina and Mississippi editors issued short, sharp, and unfavorable statements.[8]

Nearly all white southerners worshiped in segregated churches and accepted the framework of legal segregation. The editor of the *Alabama Baptist*, equating the Court decision to "reconstruction days," wrote that it "has jarred to the foundation a Southern institution." Still, many leading Baptists urged laypeople to accept public school desegregation "thoughtfully and calmly." A theologian presciently warned that Baptists should not allow politicians to stir up prejudice and promote violence. Most of the pastors who were sounded out in Baptist periodicals urged caution. Young white southerners often accepted the Court's decision to integrate schools more readily than their elders. Nineteen Tennessee Methodist students attending a meeting in the North Carolina mountains wrote to Tennessee governor Frank Clement that the *Brown* decision "should be accepted with poise and serenity."[9]

The school integration issue heightened a number of other concerns. Both pastors and laypeople fretted about what they considered collapsing morals; temptations surrounded them. When the Revised Standard Version of the Bible appeared in 1952, many Christians clung to the King James Version. Martin Luther Hux, the college-educated pastor of Temple Baptist Church in Rocky Mount, North Carolina, created a furor in 1952 when he threatened to burn a copy of the Revised Standard Version. He protested that the new translation of the Bible, among other faults, denied the Virgin birth. In the weeks after the *Brown* decision, the *Biblical Recorder*, a North Carolina Baptist periodical, denounced films, television, magazines, and comic books for encouraging untoward behavior. It condemned the Academy Award–winning film *From Here to Eternity* for glorifying a non-Christian life-style, including imbibing liquor and committing adultery. A Yale Divinity School survey, the magazine reported, had discovered that children in the New Haven area watched thirteen hours of television each week and listened to two hours of radio. In Fayetteville, North Carolina, civic, educational, and church groups established a Committee for Control of Harmful Comics to protect children from "unwholesome, crime-breeding comic books." Young comic book readers were also "subjected to numerous erotic pictures under the guise of 'love stories.'"[10]

The *Brown* decision came only weeks before the annual Southern Baptist Convention assembled on June 2, so the initial response had barely cooled when the convention heated up the issue dramatically. During the first week of June, some 15,000 messengers representing 29,496 Southern Baptist churches in 23 states with a total membership of 7.8 million gathered in St. Louis for the Southern Baptist Convention. At the Friday evening session, messengers deplored the rise of juvenile delinquency and encouraged Congress to ban radio, television, and print liquor advertisements. Then they approved a statement drafted by the Christian Life Commission that endorsed the Supreme Court's *Brown* decision, declaring that it was "in harmony with the constitutional guarantee of equal freedom to all citizens, and with the Christian principles of equal justice and love for all men." The report called on "Christian statesmen and leaders" to use wisdom and prevent "new and bitter prejudices." Debate lasted only half an hour, and two messengers spoke on each side of the question. Only 50 of the 9,000 messengers present at the session opposed the resolution to end segregation.[11]

Methodists, Presbyterians, and other denominations joined the Baptists in supporting *Brown*. The Southern Presbyterian General Assembly, assuring people that interracial marriage would not follow, went even further than the Baptists by calling for blacks' admission to churches and colleges. Some Catholic bishops in the South immediately supported the removal of racial barriers in schools and hospitals.[12]

Where the progressive elite led, the flocks of laypeople did not always follow. It took courage to break with segregation and risk the loss of friendships and community ostracism. Whereas ministers might be excused for their effusive notions of brotherhood, segregationists honed tools to punish errant congregants. Reverend Arthur C. Allen stated in June 1954 that the *Brown* decision "most emphatically showed the hand of God in it." Laypeople in his Memphis church, however, did not share his vision. Some members of his congregation, he lamented, "have been taught wrong things about God and righteousness and complain of God's work and goodness as manifested through this decision."[13] Indeed, for many parishioners, integration symbolized not Christian brotherhood but a manifestation of evil. Film, television, magazines, comics, and liquor were minor concerns compared to mixing with African Americans, whom they considered morally offensive.

In November 1954, Mississippi newspaper editor Hodding Carter notified Danville, Virginia, pastor Harry M. Wilson that he knew of no white pastors who had spoken out against segregationists. "Perhaps I am pessimistic," he worried, "but I am afraid that we are in for some tough times in the deep South over the Court's decision." Reverend Wilson confided to Carter that the editor of the *Danville Bee* was attempting "to drive a wedge between the pastors [who supported *Brown*] and their congregations." The South was passing through a trying time, Wilson agreed. He predicted that because of segregation and discrimination, "a social revolution was unavoidable." Wilson had no patience with ministers who remained quiet. "If the minister is expected and required to be neutral—to conduct himself as if he were in agreement with the general attitude toward the question of equal citizenship for the colored people—he has no recourse but to resign and to leave the ministry altogether."[14]

Some white pastors were apprehensive about their role in encouraging brotherhood with African Americans. Daniel L. Durway, pastor of the First Presbyterian Church in Des Arc, Arkansas, observed in January 1957 that the majority of his congregation "are quite opposed to feeling any brotherliness toward the negro." Having preached at the church only seven months, he hesitated to make anything other than guarded statements against segregation for fear that "my entire ministry here would be brought to an end." He confessed that this might sound like "rationalization" rather than "conviction." Walking a thin line between accepting segregation and fighting it, he insisted that he had his "own way" of "changing the attitude of 'keep the negro in his place' to one of 'love thy neighbor as thyself.'"[15]

As pastors took the pulse of their congregations, other white southerners tried to incorporate *Brown* into their gradualist ideology. Frank Porter Graham, former president of the University of North Carolina and an interim U.S. senator who was defeated in 1950, personified the liberal dilemma. Over the years, Graham and like-minded whites had supported the abolition of the poll tax, black voting rights, fair employment, state and federal laws against lynching, and integration in higher education. Such achievements, Graham had hoped, would win widespread support for integration and "make unwise and unnecessary the use of compulsory federal power." After the *Brown* decision, he expected southern whites to accept integration calmly and encouraged churches, civic organizations, and women's groups to discuss the implementation of the decision. No white leader stepped forward to organize such meetings.[16]

Southern liberals such as Graham had been comfortable urging caution, concern, and gradualism, but faced with Court-ordered integration, they feared being swallowed up in segregationist quicksand. Graham was drawn into a revealing correspondence with Elizabeth DeVane Worth of Raleigh, who pointedly inquired on June 21 whether he approved of "mixed marriages between whites and Negroes." In his July 2 response, Graham equivocated, observing that people insisted on both "the preservation of racial integrity" and "the privacy of personal associations and friendships." Worth interpreted Graham's remarks to mean that he favored intermarriage. Apologizing for the length of her July 7 letter (at the start of page 5), she wrote that "it is not a subject that can be covered in 25 words or less." In his reply, Graham elucidated his moderate position. "I have been denounced as a supporter of 'Jim Crow' by some extremists in the North and I have also been denounced as a 'nigger lover' and a foe of the South by the extreme States Righters in the Deep South," he explained.[17] The moderate position, as articulated by Graham, invited such attacks because it equivocated on issues that segregationists saw as iron law.

Junius Scales, an active member of the Communist Party until his arrest in 1954, observed that he split with liberals over the race issue. "I found a gulf beginning to separate me from the majority of white liberals," he recalled, "who were eager to avoid a confrontation on the 'race issue;' shied away from a chance to fight segregation even on favorable ground; and were, all too often, ready to seek a 'solution' by promising a future fight which usually did not take place." Still, he stated that liberals were "mostly courageous, and they often took moral stances which expressed the true conscience of their time and place." Scales surmised that they equivocated in the face of the "depth, scope, and sheer virulence of the bigotry they opposed." Few liberals were willing to suffer the retribution exacted for favoring integration.[18]

White southerners who supported *Brown* found themselves isolated and shunned. The publisher of Lillian Smith's *Now Is the Time*, a short justification for abolishing segregation published in 1955, removed the book from stores. She suspected that drugstores, dime stores, and other outlets for paperbacks "did not want the book in their stores." In the book, she gently explored the historical and psychological roots of segregation and encouraged whites to confront racial problems. "During this silent time," she wrote of the years after Reconstruction, "the consciences of gentle people went to sleep." She urged whites to avoid using expressions that demeaned African Americans and to reject clichés about integration. Smith concluded the book with twenty-five questions and answers concerning culture, intermarriage, law, religion, economics, and communism.[19]

Life and *Time* refused to publish Smith's response to William Faulkner's states' rights stance on segregation, and the *Atlanta Constitution* never printed her letters to the editor (or those of Paula Snelling or any of Smith's relatives). Editor Ralph McGill had assumed a satanic guise in her mind. Smith was also furious that she had never been asked to appear on television to discuss segregation. "The demagogues are asked; the lukewarm phony liberals are asked; but no real liberals in the South who have thought things through," she complained in 1956. *Strange Fruit* and *Killers of the Dream* should have granted her national stature and exposure. "Is it jealousy? Is it that I am a mere woman and my opinion is not worth anything?"[20]

At last, Smith received a media invitation. On October 2, 1957, she appeared on Dave Garroway's NBC *Today* show with Senator James Eastland. Garroway had promised her a five-minute introductory statement, and she had spent five days preparing it. Garroway cut out her opening statement but, she fumed, "let Senator Eastland give his on mongrelization." Although he had promised to draw her out on segregation, Garroway asked only two brief questions and then cut her off. NBC, she discovered later, had received a barrage of telephone calls from southerners who did not want her to appear at all. "It is, to me," she wrote to Lawrence Kubie, "one of the most shocking experiences I have ever had." The *New York Times* refused to print her letter of complaint. "The 'line' on me is that I am 'a queer,' a fanatical 'old maid who lives by herself up on a mountain' etc.," she confided to Kubie. "Hodding Carter in one of his columns called me 'a sex-obsessed old spinster.'" She labeled such treatment "smothering."[21]

In the summer of 1959, Smith's novel *One Hour* was published. It was a complex story exploring sexual fears and fantasies, science, and mob behavior. Her other publishers had been "almost 'deferential,'" she confided to her agent. "But not these savages at Harcourt's." She tried unsuccessfully to interest Hollywood in it and blamed the book's cool reception on her publisher, Bill Javonovich, who had admitted to her that *One Hour* "shook him up." Smith censured him for not pushing the book and failing to convince book review editors of its importance. "People are so shocked by the rigging of quiz shows," Smith stated. "I don't know anything more rigged than present-day reviewing and those best seller lists." She was still raging at Gerald Sykes's negative *New York Times* review, which she attributed, in part, to the fact that she had intervened to get him a reading of his play, but it had been rejected. She also cursed the *New York Times* book editor who had assigned Sykes the review, hoping that he might "fall off the subway platform, or something, and get it that way!"[22]

Wilma Dykeman shared Smith's frustration with the press and television. In November 1957, she and her husband, James Stokely, published *Neither Black nor White*, a book that explored southern opinion on race relations. They were largely frozen out of the media. Dykeman confided to Smith that they had "become enormously discouraged to discover that those very channels one would expect to be at least partially open for *all* white Southern viewpoints are, in fact, just as timid as those channels in our midst which are so vulnerable to their neighbors' opinions and pressures." People continually asked when white southerners would speak, Dykeman mused. "When Southerners *do* speak, who hears?" She had assumed that "another Southern voice on the side of human dignity" would have been welcome. In New York, she had expected at least several invitations to appear on television and more attention from the press. "Some of the deep South newspapers have already begun to hurl their pens at us," she wrote. Even their publisher, Rinehart, seemed uninterested in sending out review and complimentary copies.[23]

To compile material for *Neither Black nor White*, Dykeman and Stokely had toured the South interviewing people about their thoughts on the race problem. "In the century of the atom bomb," they wrote, the *Brown v. Board of Education* decision "set off a chain reaction which has resulted in a social fission of startling proportions." Their book incorporated a wide spectrum of southern thought. "The difficulty of trying to be a true moderate in the South today is almost insurmountable," a university professor confessed. "If you speak, you're often a traitor to one side and no good to the other." A North Carolina woman complained to Dykeman and Stokely that white supremacists isolated anyone who supported integration. "Outsiders are given the impression that no really conscientious, bona fide Southern citizen can possibly disagree with segregation," she told them. "But many of us do disagree, and who's to say we're less Southern than someone who can shout louder and angrier?"[24] The liberal position, as Frank Porter Graham and others were discovering, had become untenable. *Brown* had stripped away the illusion that had allowed moderates to champion harmony and slow progress. In the summer of 1954, segregation became polarized; it was either/or, not maybe/sometimes. With the exception of some preachers and brave loners, few white southerners admitted being integrationists.

Predictably, Smith warned Dykeman of Ralph McGill, who "lies and distorts and will stoop at anything to hurt me or one of my books." She suspected that he "probably had evil reasons" for writing a favorable review of *Neither Black nor White* in the *New York Times*. "You will have to remember, or perhaps learn," she cautioned, "that Ralph McGill, Hodding Carter and Harry Ashmore are not going to willingly see that the writers who are really against segregation are promoted." Being shunned by the media, Smith acknowledged later, hurt her deeply. "What is hard for me, being a proud bitch, is being asked in the true southern way through the back doors of the South."[25]

Being ostracized gnawed at Lillian Smith, and she detested the gloomy portrayal of white southerners that spread across the country. "I think of the creative work going on down here," she countered, "the fine sermons against segregation, against mob violence, against disesteem for the Supreme Court which so many of our young preachers have preached." Southern women, in particular, she stressed, were working for better race relations. In her estimation, novelist William Faulkner and such editors as Ralph McGill and Hodding Carter—"gradualists and separate-but-equalers"—were encouraging segregation by posing as the only moderate voices of the South. "We have a desperate need for lone voices to be heard; for individuals to speak their own thoughts not the voice of the Monster, the archaic one who lives deep down in our collective unconscious." No clear voice put issues in perspective. "This confusion is caused largely by white men, not by white women," she insisted. Blacks and whites in the South needed hope, and she needed to be heard.[26]

After Hodding Carter's "The Court's Decision and the South" appeared in the September 1954 issue of *Reader's Digest,* many southerners praised it as a moderate testament. As editor of the Greenville, Mississippi, *Delta Democrat Times* and a prolific author, Carter had a large following across the South and the nation. Although his ideas differed remarkably from those of Frank Porter Graham, both were labeled as liberals or moderates. "Within the Christian ethic and the democratic tradition, the Supreme Court could not have acted otherwise," Carter wrote of *Brown.* "Its morality," he cautioned, "was sounder than its legalisms." A casual reader might overlook Carter's telling equivocations. Integration, he hedged, would proceed slowly if at all in areas with large African American populations. In Greenville, he claimed, a wide gulf of illiteracy and crime separated the black and white communities. "The rural Negro's living standards, though rising, are still low," Carter advised his readers, "and he is still easygoing in his morals, as witness the five to ten times higher incidence of extramarital households and illegitimacy among Negroes than among whites in the South." Carter admitted that there was a "sex fear" among southern whites and predicted "some ugly racial gangsterism." Carter did not advocate the integration of Mississippi's schools, reasoning that the percentage of blacks was too great for it to succeed.[27] Despite Carter's caution, many readers viewed him as a leading southern moderate. Perhaps he was. Many moderates embraced deliberation and paternalism, although Carter's remarks on what he saw as black shortcomings clearly went beyond platitudes.

An African American who wrote Carter from Richmond, Virginia, signing his letter "C. W. R.," dismissed Carter's argument that a high percentage of blacks in an area prevented integration. In response to Carter's claim that a higher rate of illegitimacy existed among blacks than among whites, C. W. R. charged that Carter ignored whites who had abortions. Whites, he continued, often attended black clubs and were fond of black entertainers. "The southern whites seem to get a lot out of having some near-illiterate maid teach and help raise their babies," he chided Carter, "but can't conceive the educated Negro teaching them in school. 'Wow, you sure are a mixed up race.'" C. W. R. agreed

Hodding Carter.
Hodding and Betty
Werlein Carter Papers,
Special Collections Department,
Mitchell Memorial Library,
Mississippi State University.

that interracial sex was the crucial problem. It was natural, he asserted, that black men and white women were attracted to each other. "The real fear, as everyone realized . . . is the white female staying out of reach of the Negro man."[28]

Silence, in the estimation of segregationists, meant either agreement or weakness, and they dominated discussions. Unlike moderates, they were not shy about expressing their opinions or denouncing those who disagreed. Southern politicians, programmed for racial politics, vowed that segregation would endure. Shrill groups of whites throughout the South threatened to fight violently to preserve segregation; there was talk of a sinister communist plot as well as anti-Semitic whispers. In newspapers and letters, the image of mixing black and white blood recurred again and again. Because some whites associated African Americans with dirt and disease, they shrank in revulsion from possible pollution. Racist clichés a century old poured out in letters and speeches as whites attempted to deny the implications of *Brown.*

A streak of insecurity tinged with fear ran through white society, for allowing African Americans into schools on an equal basis devalued the special claims of all whites. Whites were the heirs of racial ideas that predated the country's founding, were refined during slavery, and were redefined on a more sweeping scale by turn-of-the-century geneticists, popularizers, and politicians. White southerners constructed a self-serving historical narrative of the Reconstruction era and the efforts of black Americans in the 1890s to achieve voting rights and political power. Whites trivialized black politicians, portrayed them as inept cartoon figures, and demeaned their political achievements. Clinging to their notions of superiority and unmindful of past black achievements, most southern whites in the 1950s could not comprehend black aspirations. Although many whites boasted that they "knew the Negro" well, in fact, as Dykeman and Stokely pointed out, "it has not occurred to them until recently that the Negro might have a whole area of thought and experience that was blocked off to white knowledge."[29]

In every southern hamlet, self-proclaimed experts on racial etiquette professed the essentials of segregation as they understood it. Outspoken segregationists gained a new status after *Brown*. "Talking nigger or nigra had changed from a custom to a necessity for acceptance in most circles by 1956," Mississippi congressman Frank Smith observed, "and among certain groups the loudest and the strongest talker could achieve a status otherwise unattainable." Still, the color line wavered depending on how blacks and whites in a community defined their spaces. Many white southerners had perceived no threat in the halting changes along the color line after World War II, but the *Brown* decision dissolved the illusion that segregation would always endure. If whites thought that all blacks would wait patiently for white action, they miscalculated. National Association for the Advancement of Colored People (NAACP) leaders pushed for immediate compliance. Integration, whites feared, would allow black males and white females to share the same social space—as equals. In the minds of many white men and women, this would automatically lead to interracial sex and children of "mixed" blood. There would be no interlude, according to this line of thought, but an immediate interracial orgy. Evidently, white men and black women would stand by wringing their hands.

After 1954, white southerners who had just emerged from poverty and local elites felt most threatened. Historian Nancy MacLean has revealed that membership in the Ku Klux Klan in 1920s Athens, Georgia, consisted primarily of recent arrivals into the lower middle class. They could still feel lower-class gravity pulling at them, so they attempted, according to MacLean, "to distinguish themselves—particularly through their moral codes—from the ordinary workers they viewed as beneath them." Those least likely to belong to the Klan were "unskilled workers, landless rural people, and the very wealthiest residents." After the *Brown* decision, the Citizens' Councils attracted whites from all classes, but there is little evidence that impoverished whites flocked to join with the best white men. Given the potential threat integration posed to the elite's divide-and-conquer labor-control tactics, it is no wonder that the best white men rushed to join. Members of the the shaky middle class also looked to the Citizens' Councils to prop up their insecurities.[30]

The *Brown* decision elicited little introspection among southern whites, who in most instances viewed black society through an unfocused lens. Unable to accept the idea that blacks had dreams, aspirations, and, most important, opinions, whites allowed smiles, nods, and rumors to nourish their stereotypes and fantasies of black complaisance. They assumed that the dutiful cooperation of their household help, chauffeurs, and yardmen signaled contentment among all African Americans. In their travels around the South in 1956, Dykeman and Stokely heard "the familiar chuckle over the Negro's happiness and good humor." Whites fancied that blacks had been happy on the auction block as well as in the shabby segregated schools they attended in the 1950s. If their black servants and neighbors were laughing, whites reasoned, "how could we be mistreating them?" Whites' unquestioning acceptance of black contentment, Dykeman and Stokely reasoned, was "because it was necessary for us."[31] The laughter never sounded the same after *Brown*.

Many white southerners expressed a fondness for their black neighbors even as they uncharitably maligned them. Mrs. Hugh C. Day was perplexed by the *Brown* decision and admitted to Tennessee governor Frank Clement on the day after the decision that it "has made all of us in our family just about sick, and I must say that is putting it mildly." She had descended from a slaveholding family, she boasted, and her grandfather had fought in the Civil War. She worked in a Memphis doctor's office, where she endured Yankee patients belittling southern prejudices. "We like the negro race," she assured Clement, "and we are Christians." By deftly marshaling slavery, Civil War memories, Yankee meddling, religion, culture, and politics in her defense of segregation, Day revealed how completely segregation encompassed her life.[32]

Many white southerners were blind to the contradictions in their images of African Americans. Athens, Alabama, attorney W. W. Malone, after blaming race problems on "the old hag, Harriet Beecher Stowe," expressed a deep distaste for black people. "There is something about the Negro that is repulsive," he averred. But Malone, as did many other southern males, professed an abiding affection for blacks in general and for the "good oldtime black mammy" who cared for him as a child in particular. Sixty-nine-year-old Hattie Daly, a North Carolina schoolteacher, recollected that her mother had written passes allowing slaves to visit neighboring farms. Daly still farmed tobacco with black tenants. "They are my friends and co-workers," Daly insisted, "but not my social equals. I have never treated one as such and never will. They know their place and stay in it." Daly feared racial pollution. "Mix white and black paint and see if the white is unbesmirched," she suggested. "Social equality O' how they crave it," she wrote.[33]

Young southern white women also wrestled with the contradictions exposed by *Brown*. Margaret Trotter, a twenty-one-year-old student at the University of

Tennessee, warned Governor Clement that she and her sorority sisters were "upset over this segregation question." Trotter considered herself a "good Christian girl" who attended Sunday school and church and read her Bible. "*Nowhere*," she stressed, "does it mix races, or even say they should be mixed." Then she turned on the family's ungrateful maid, who "has been with us since I was two years old." The family paid her well, gave her time off, furnished transportation, and allowed her to take food home. The maid repaid this goodwill with spite. "She steals money, food and besides what we give her, gets angry and sasses us all or deliberately breaks something, usually an irreplaceable antique." She had even "borrowed" Trotter's fur scarf at Easter without asking permission. Far from being the story of a faithful mammy, this account of the Trotter maid's scorn for her employers was a cautionary tale. That such a woman or her children might sit beside a white Trotter in a classroom would be intolerable.[34]

Whereas Margaret Trotter wrestled with her maid's faithlessness, other southern women went quietly about their business. There was a lull before public opinion swung behind obstinate white leaders who made segregation a sort of loyalty test. In the summer of 1954, the Extension Service held a school for men and women employees in Fayetteville, Arkansas. Despite temperatures that soared over 100 degrees during the entire session, Alabamian Margaret E. Poole enjoyed the outing. "I was surprised to see so many colored students—there must have been fifty (50) or more," she reported. In the cafeteria line one day, an Arkansas county agent commented to her, "I'll bet you Alabama girls never thought you'd stand in line to eat with negroes." Poole reported this factually without any embellishments, as if she considered it more of an adventure than a burden.[35]

Most white southerners flinched at integration. Respectability depended on their claim to whiteness, or so they had been coached. Removing the color line would devalue that badge of superiority. Mrs. L. G. Baker, a Pine Bluff, Arkansas, grandmother, asked President Dwight D. Eisenhower in May 1954 if he understood that respectable married Christian white women "deeply resent the insult handed down by the U.S. Supreme Court's decision on segregation." A white woman who had legitimate children, she explained, would now be "classed with a negress who has children with out marriage, some negros some half white." Baker disclosed that she rented land and did not even own a television, "but we have honor, pride and decency that money nor politics can't buy."[36] Segregation, she implied, protected her respectability. School integration not only would mix black and white students but also could allow black property owners, professionals, and many of the working class to rise above Baker's status.

Africa, a mythical Dark Continent, loomed large in the southern mind. "For to suppose that you can permit these descendants of jungle races to share in your councils and society without deterioration of culture," Harry P. Gamble pontificated from New Orleans, "is merely silly." Keeping democracy alive was hard enough, Gamble warned, "without adding the burden of veneered jungleism." But his bottom line remained sex. "Even the few mooneyed persons who think (though they are not thinking at all) that you can have the negro in your parlor without his edging toward the bedroom, will fade out."[37] Despite the availability of scholarly accounts of Africa, southerners such as Gamble apparently relied more on Hollywood films than on history.

In the summer of 1954, black hopes wrestled with white fears. A river of interracial sexual fantasies flowed through the South. Segregation had been built on such sexual fears at the turn of the century, and demagogues, race riots, lynchings, and the racist press had policed the color line and reiterated time and again the separate place of black men and white women. White men invariably controlled this discourse. Although they wielded enormous power, white men still feared that illiterate, unskilled, and impoverished black men could dominate them. They were uneasy with black males and magnified and coveted their sexual power. Author Lillian Smith suggested that many white men had a strong sexual attraction for black men and that such transgressive feelings and the resulting frustration drove them to violence.[38]

Fearing that white women were likewise attracted to black men, white men insisted that white women needed protection, needed to stand above it all on a pedestal. Perhaps they also feared black women, who they portrayed as more sexually aggressive than their pedestaled wives. Despite having wealth, status, and education, many white males still harbored both resentment and jealousy of black men. In a fair fight, white men feared, blacks would win. Every black baseball player who stepped to the plate, every black musician who performed before a white audience, every black actor projected on the silver screen, every NAACP lawyer who won a case, and, in time, every black person who marched for equal rights challenged white domination. In a world of total white privilege, the figure of the aggressive and untamed black male assumed fantastic proportions. White men had great power to preserve their privilege and status, but their insecurity bred intimidation and violence. Segregationist groups found eager recruits among southern white men who perceived in the *Brown* decision a grave threat to their status and their white manhood. No significant white countermovement challenged them.

9 Restrained Segregationists

My maid, a very intelligent negro, says they prefer segregation, but do want equal educational opportunities.
—Minnie McIver Brown

We learned all about the white race, and their depravity while serving in private homes, hotels, restaurants, on steamboats, Pullman, and dining car services.
—F. W. Avant

Nothing unmasked white elites' desperation to maintain power and control as much as their bitter reaction to African Americans petitioning for civil rights. Judge Thomas Pickins Brady, whose "Black Monday" pamphlet circulated widely in the months following *Brown*, suggested using updated tactics from the Reconstruction era. "While it is true we do not have an H-bomb and force and violence have no place here—still we have a destructive force at our command," he boasted. Mississippi Farm Bureau leader Boswell Stevens impatiently called for community and county meetings, presumably organized along the lines of county agricultural committees. A state representative reprimanded Stevens on May 25, 1954, for being "so indiscreet as to offer the facilities of the Farm Bureau." Unabashed, Stevens continued to use his Farm Bureau position to support segregation in addition to dipping into his own pocket.[1]

Stevens's segregationist activities had significant implications. The American Farm Bureau Federation represented both businesspeople and farmers throughout the country and retained a powerful lobbying presence in Washington. The organization originally grew out of local support for county agents, and its power resided in county and state elites. During the 1950s, Alabamian Edward O'Neal was president of the American Farm Bureau Federation, and Secretary of Agriculture Ezra Taft Benson favored most of the organization's policies. As head of the Mississippi Farm Bureau, Stevens could spread his segregationist agenda to every county in the state. It is unclear how closely the memberships of Mississippi's Citizens' Councils and its Farm Bureau overlapped, but both organizations represented those who were considered the best whites in the community. Stevens's active work on behalf of the Citizens' Coun-

195

cil suggests that organizations like the Farm Bureau that had extensive structures could easily be adapted to perpetuate segregation. The best white citizens, however, needed a respectable organization to lead a public assault on the *Brown* decision.

Robert B. Patterson, a former football player at Mississippi State University, a World War II veteran, and manager of a Leflore County plantation, framed the *Brown* decision in grandiose terms. His widely circulated May 18, 1954, letter to the editor bristled with images of patriotism, manhood, and anticommunism. "If red blooded southern Americans submit to this unconstitutional 'judge made law' and surrender our Caucasian heritage of sixty centuries," he direly predicted, "the malignant power of communism, Atheism, and mongrelization will surely follow." Patterson mobilized widespread support for an organization of white citizens to oppose integration. After a July meeting in Indianola, he christened his creation the Citizens' Councils and enlisted Mississippi community leaders to lend it respectability. Tightly organized from the top down, councils recruited upstanding citizens. Membership appeals portrayed the National Association for the Advancement of Colored People (NAACP) as a well-organized radical organization bent on destroying the (white) southern way of life. The nascent Citizens' Councils also distributed hate literature that ranged from racist diatribes to anti-Semitic nonsense. Leaders tapped into fears of vast conspiracies and encroachments by blacks, Catholics, and Jews.[2]

The founders of the Citizens' Councils distanced themselves from the secretive and violent Ku Klux Klan and poor southern whites in general. Only the best white citizens belonged, they claimed, and from the beginning, public relations became a crucial part of the agenda. In 1955, Walter Sillers, the speaker of the Mississippi house of representatives, who did not belong to a Citizens' Council, praised council members. "They are all outstanding, upright white citizens of Mississippi and they have the interest and welfare of the white people at heart." The councils had not been organized "to do anybody any harm," he stressed, "but to protect the white people of Mississippi from the vicious attacks and forced integration by negroes and other races under the force of federal court decrees." Sillers portrayed powerful southern white leaders as victims of both federal force and the NAACP.[3]

Southern segregationists varied remarkably in background, motivation, and temperament. The Citizens' Councils shared the white-supremacist beliefs of a host of other organizations, including several reincarnations of the Ku Klux Klan. In December 1955, labor leader H. L. Mitchell estimated that 568 local segregationist cells with a membership of over 208,000 existed throughout the South. A group could be found to fit every prejudice, every retaliatory impulse. What made other segregationist organizations different from the Ku Klux Klan was the bedsheet-free veneer of respectability, the dubious status conferred by demonizing the Supreme Court and the NAACP, and middle-class pride. Segregationist organizations publicly enforced their agenda by shunning, boycotting, or threatening their victims. These organizations could always lay hushed meetings, midnight rides, and clandestine violence at the doorstep of the invisible Ku Klux Klan.[4]

A number of segregationist organizations emerged after the *Brown* decision. Louisiana hosted the Southern Gentlemen as well as the Federation for Constitutional Government, which had branches in several other states, including Tennessee. Both Citizens' Councils and White America, Inc., thrived in Arkansas. In addition to Citizens' Councils and the Ku Klux Klan, South Carolina bred eight county or local segregationist groups that claimed 40,000 members, and the North Carolina Patriots became the leading Tarheel segregationist organization.[5]

In late December 1955, representatives of the Citizens' Councils, North Carolina Patriots, Defenders of State Sovereignty, and other segregationist groups met in Memphis to discuss strategy. The meeting also attracted a number of Klansmen. A speech by U.S. senator James O. Eastland set the tone, and John U. Barr, a New Orleans manufacturer's representative and National Association of Manufacturers spokesman, attended as head of the Federation for Constitutional Government. The leadership of the Federation for Constitutional Government teemed with right-to-work supporters, some of whom had been active in founding the Southern Gentlemen and Citizens' Councils in Louisiana. The merging of segregationists, right-to-work partisans, and businesspeople at the meeting suggested the intricate racial tactics used to divide black and white workers, to encourage right-to-work legislation, and to discourage unions. Citizens' Council intervention had stymied several unionization drives. Some white workers at the Firestone, Ford, and International Harvester plants in Memphis belonged to the Citizens' Council, as did steelworkers in Birmingham. Management cleverly fused the notions of unions and integration to create a fantasy of a communist threat that would unite white workers. Malcolm Dougherty, a Baton Rouge Farm Bureau leader, had sponsored the Louisiana right-to-work law in 1954 and, much like Mississippi's Boswell Stevens, used his Farm Bureau position to recruit for the Citizens' Councils and the Southern Gentlemen. Leander H. Perez, the powerful Louisiana politician who controlled Plaquemines and Saint Bernard Parishes, had been active in several segregationist organizations and was a member of the Federation for Constitutional Government's legal committee. Much of the drive to preserve segregation, then, focused on labor control. The *Brown* decision gave businesspeople another tool to fight unions.[6]

Southern universities sheltered some of the most adamant segregationists. Vanderbilt University professor Donald Davidson and University of North Carolina Medical School professor Wesley Critz George assumed leadership roles in their states' segregationist organizations. Davidson's segregationist beliefs had deep roots in southern tradition, whereas George utilized genetics, heredity, and history. Both men experienced anguish about possibly jeopardizing their academic standing and risked isolation from their more liberal colleagues.

Born in Campbellsville, Tennessee, Donald Davidson attended various private academies as his schoolteacher father moved from job to job. After joining the faculty of Vanderbilt University in Nashville, Davidson became a member of the fugitive or agrarian group, which included John Crowe Ransom, Robert Penn Warren, Allen Tate, and some dozen others. The fugitive literary production went largely unappreciated by the Vanderbilt administration, and lacking a Ph.D., Davidson waged a protracted battle with school administrators who denied the significance of his scholarly work. Influenced by his mother, Davidson enjoyed playing guitar and listening to music; he often attended the Grand Ole Opry. His only novel, *The Big Ballad Jamboree*, remained unpublished during his lifetime. Davidson understood the tension between the modern Nashville sound and older rural music. Whether influenced by his wide reading, his agrarianism, or his upbringing in Tennessee, Davidson defended segregation. His calm public disposition cloaked seething tension, frustration, and bitterness.[7]

John Donald Wade, who had collaborated with Davidson at Vanderbilt in preparing the agrarian manifesto, *I'll Take My Stand: The South and the Agrarian Tradition*, had sent him chatty letters from Marshallville, Georgia, about gardening, the weather, visits with old friends, and a trip to Athens, where he had taught after leaving Vanderbilt. In August 1954, he had other things in mind. The "race thing" especially upset him. "What can it mean?," he mused. Many whites had "cleared out for foreign parts" when the Civil War ended. "For what such parts could we clear out now?," he brooded. "*Must* we, then tell the South good bye,—I mean, if not by our leaving it, just as surely by its leaving us?" The "entire reputable world," he despaired, was attempting "to convince us that what we took to be the highest virtue is in truth the worst of vices. Lordy me, Lordy me!"[8] Although Wade was writing about segregation, he just as easily could have been mourning the end of the agrarian South, for the crisis over school integration coincided with agricultural transformation and the depopulation of the countryside. The South was leaving in every direction.

I'll Take My Stand, in one sense, was the last will and testament of agrarian segregationists. Davidson and his friends subscribed to a doctrine that elevated both agrarian life and segregation. By the 1950s, of course, millions of farmers

Donald Davidson. Photographic Archives, Vanderbilt University, Nashville, Tenn.

were leaving the land, capitalists were encroaching on the rural South, and segregation was under attack. Davidson would have been more comfortable in an earlier age that rewarded his literary production and praised his stand on segregation. "He remained a complex person," historian Paul Conkin has concluded, "sweet and genial towards friends, a devoted and superb teacher of creative writing, a periodically active lyrical poet, an increasingly well-informed folklorist, a sometimes balanced and acutely perceptive essayist, a talented historian, a perceptive observer of the new country music industry in Nashville, and, each summer, a faithful New Englander during his residence in Vermont."[9]

Davidson's stay at Bread Loaf, Vermont, in 1955 was not altogether pleasant and illustrated the increasingly tenuous place of southern segregationists among northern liberals. Davidson complained to Wade that poet Robert Frost "has been quite ugly in his talk on the segregation question. He has made a point of nagging me, in what I would call a rude and arrogant way, under circumstances that put me at a disadvantage." At a cocktail party, Frost suggested to Davidson "in a rather dictatorial way, that the South had just better give up and take the Negroes right into our educational bosoms (or words to that effect)." Frost declared that the South had no hope of winning against the Supreme Court. The South had lost before, and it would lose again, Frost prophesied. "Since I was a guest on all these occasions," Davidson fumed, "the most I could do was to stand my ground politely, and try not to lose my temper. I bantered him a little. But nothing was any good." Frost had crotchety moods, Davidson admitted, "but this one is the worst I have encountered."[10]

Even before the incidents at Bread Loaf, Davidson had been a founder and president of the Tennessee Federation for Constitutional Government (TFCG), an organization that sought to use legal means to defend segregation. The TFCG was run as a corporation, according to Davidson, with a "relatively small executive committee (carefully chosen)." He feared infiltration by "undesirable elements." Davidson was not confident that the TFCG would prevail. "Probably now," he admitted on November 23, 1955, "we have an influence out of proportion to our actual numbers." The focus on legal action had limited appeal in Tennessee, but Davidson had no stomach for economic punishment, boycotts, and violence.[11] The TFCG attracted economically secure white southerners, people more willing to contribute money than physical action.

Davidson corresponded with a wide spectrum of segregationists across the South, and he marveled at "the facility with which information can be interchanged around and among the various state organizations." Given the press releases of the Mississippi Citizens' Councils and the segregationist television spots and pamphlets that flooded the South, Davidson correctly assessed the segregationist movement of the 1950s as thoroughly modern in its use of media and imagery. Still, Davidson complained, "the pressure from the NAACP and the radicals of the North never lets up, and is always extreme, always has the official or semi-official backing of government, and influences both political parties." He did not see any southern whites as important enemies. Behind it all, he speculated, were socialist and communist influences. He wanted to broaden the debate beyond the question of integration or segregation to show that the *Brown* decision was "the result of a chain of tendencies."[12]

Henry L. Swint, a Vanderbilt history professor and friend of Davidson's, confided to historian Frank Owsley in 1956 that "the abolitionists are finally going to win." Most Americans, he thought, favored the end of segregation, and the

Brown decision and other events indicated "a movement toward nationalism and centralization which cannot be matched in our history." Davidson's group, he judged, "is fighting a losing battle, whatever the propriety or morality or advisability of it." But Swint speculated that once integrationists won, they would abandon the cause, as had abolitionists after the Emancipation Proclamation. "The Negro was not made the social, political, or economic equal of the white man by that decree," he judged. "Nor will he be by this one."[13]

Much like Tennessee, North Carolina enjoyed a reputation for moderate leadership, despite a history of anti-union violence, educational mediocrity, and staunch dedication to segregation. Soothing clichés tinged with paternalism portrayed North Carolina as progressive, even though by most criteria it lagged far behind northern states. After the *Brown* decision, state leaders timorously tested public opinion before settling on a middle course.[14]

North Carolina's counterpart to the Citizens' Councils did not emerge until the spring of 1955, and among its leaders were a half dozen members of the state's advisory committee of the Federation for Constitutional Government. The inspiration for the North Carolina Patriots may well have sprouted from Wesley Critz George's letter to the editor of the *Durham Herald* in November 1954. A North Carolina native, George received his Ph.D. from the University of North Carolina in 1918, and after further studies at Princeton University and Walter Reed Hospital, he returned to Chapel Hill to teach at the Medical School. In his letter, George employed conventional racist thought, genetics, and his interpretation of history. School integration would bring blacks and whites into close social contact, he feared, and this would promote interracial sex. "That in the course of time will result in the destruction of the white and colored races and the substitution of a mulatto race," he predicted. He insisted that human reproduction followed the same rules as animal reproduction. Blacks had less "intellectual ability and creativeness" than whites, he charged, and Africans had never produced a great civilization. He urged concerned whites to begin a petition drive to register their opposition to integration.[15]

George's letter triggered a wave of responses, most favoring his position. "Am ready & anxious to sign the petition," Felix Hichenson wrote. "My colored cook has said repeatedly 'I sure do wish they would leave the colored schools alone.'" Minnie McIver Brown of Chadbourn relied on her household worker for information. "My maid, a very intelligent negro, says they prefer segregation, but do want equal educational opportunities." In February 1956, Tarboro Patriot H. H. Palmer described his friendly relations with neighboring blacks. "I have yet to find the first negro who would indicate he approves of the ruling," he reported, "or who has any confidence in the NAACP." Palmer expected problems from the "ministers and the rag-tag-bob element" among teachers.[16]

Wesley Critz George.
Southern Historical Collection,
Wilson Library, University of
North Carolina, Chapel Hill.

Mary B. Gilson of Chapel Hill, however, was not amused by George's ideas. "I think you must have been feeding on Madison Grant, Stoddard and some of the other pseudo-scientists," she lectured him. Gilson declared that no reputable scientist would make claims of white superiority. "Give Negroes a chance for economic and educational mingling with the Great White Race," she chided him, "and you will see that our aloofness has kept them from exercising their potentialities." She also scolded him for subscribing to "apartheid." Jennifer Hauk Ogle found George's piece offensive and accused him of being someone who wrote "about human beings as if they were cattle—no doubt for the sole purpose of supporting his own backward racial prejudice." On the subject of breeding, she sneered, "I have had many Negro friends whose line I would much rather see carried on than yours."[17]

Most correspondents, however, supported George. Dallas E. Gwynn, who later became a power in the North Carolina Patriots, boasted, "It makes me proud indeed to learn that there are still a few members of the faculty that haven't fallen victim to the insidious, sickly sentimental eye-wash that many so-called 'educators' have been espousing in recent years." Respondents strongly associated segregation with manhood and integration with weakness. One correspondent described integrationists as "filthy," "reprehensible," "slimy," "scum," and "trash."[18]

George discovered that not all African Americans shared what many whites saw as their household help's unanimity on segregation. F. W. Avant, an African

American physician from Wilmington, scolded George not only for his ignorance of blacks but also for "race hatred and bigotry." Avant composed ten typewritten pages that mixed autobiography, history, and ridicule. Avant challenged the clichés that whites understood black people and that black servants were content. "We learned all about the white race, and their depravity while serving in private homes, hotels, restaurants, on steamboats, Pullman, and dining car services." African Americans, he proudly added, had achieved fame and fortune in a number of areas, and he devoted several pages to black history. Blacks would have achieved much more, he insisted, if they had not been hindered by Jim Crow laws.[19]

Avant disparaged George's fear of race mixing. "We have black, brown, red, yellow, and white people in our race," and the reason for such diversity, he explained, was that "white men have practiced the after-dark, undercover, social relations . . . to such an extent that it is a rather difficult problem to determine 'Who is Who' in our social status to-day." By focusing on the point at which black and white merged, Avant struck at the heart of George's biological-supremacy ideas. Many legally black people passed for white, and African Americans "recognize our white relatives in high and lofty places in our civic life." He and his wife had once been seated in a theater balcony along with other African Americans, he explained to George, when a white usher told his wife "that she was in the wrong place, and that she would have to go down to the orchestra circle." Taunting George with his wife's apparent whiteness, Avant implied that she could easily have moved downstairs to the orchestra and polluted the unknowing white audience. Laws proved useless in enforcing what the eye could not detect. George evidently did not reply.[20]

An African American woman who did not sign her three-page handwritten letter challenged George's assumption that blacks were instigators of sexual intimacy. "Why not tell your youth why are there so many half white and mulatto Negro women?" Black women endured constant sexual harassment from white men, she complained. "I have passed by hundreds of white men in my life and they winked their eyes," she wrote. "But to keep from being disgraced I kept my mouth because Negroes have no protection." She then compared black women's constant harassment by white men to the Till case. Fourteen-year-old Emmett Till had been murdered in Mississippi allegedly because he whistled at a white woman. "How many wolf whistles come from white men?," she taunted.[21]

The North Carolina Patriots officially organized in the spring of 1955. Whereas the Citizens' Councils sprang from the heart of the Mississippi Delta, where most of the state's African American population lived, the Patriots originated among businesspeople, not planters, in North Carolina's Piedmont. An attorney, an insurance agent, a chemical company executive, and three textile executives founded the Patriots. A third of the charter members lived in Guilford County, and most of the members were aspiring businesspeople and politicians. George became the first president, and Dallas Gwynn of Leaksville and Robert E. Stevens of Goldsboro were vice presidents. The other officers were from Greensboro. The Patriots publicized neither their membership list nor the number of members.[22]

Unlike the Mississippi Citizens' Councils, the Patriots did not employ economic sanctions or advocate violence but instead circulated press releases, letters, and segregationist literature. Meetings were sparsely attended, and leaders fretted about the poor public response and flagging membership. Reporter Chester Davis investigated the Patriots for the *Winston-Salem Journal-Sentinel* in June 1956. He found George a soft-spoken, sincere man. "He is not a demagogue," Davis observed, but "Dr. George cherishes his beliefs with an idealism that is fanatic in its fervor." He compared the Patriots' conservative leadership to the post–Civil War Ku Klux Klan. "During the Reconstruction years after the Civil War, that organization, headed by prominent state leaders, fought to preserve the status quo." The original Klan, he cautioned his readers, had turned to violence.[23]

As a university professor and scholar, George lent academic credibility to the Patriots. Speaking at Dartmouth College on October 12, 1956, George expounded on his racist ideas, especially genetics. School integration, he insisted, would result in "greater social intimacy" and "promote interbreeding and the protoplasmic mixing of the races." White people had "creative talents and abilities that have not been demonstrated to any considerable extent by the Negro race," he claimed. George challenged the notion that blacks had extraordinary musical gifts. "One hears of the Negroes' musical talent," he scoffed, "but the piano, the organ, the violin, the flute and harp, great musical compositions that thrill and soothe the human soul are creations of the white man, not of the Negro." His address combined the zeal of the true believer, the scientific imprint of the scholar, and the conventional wisdom of an earlier generation.[24]

The Patriots distributed George's Dartmouth speech widely and were careful to identify him as a professor in the School of Medicine at the University of North Carolina. His university connection and standing among scholars gave weight to George's writings. Still, the Patriots and segregationists in general discovered that their message did not play well in North Carolina. Whether it was because the program was too moderate (as opposed to the semiviolent and vicious Mississippi Citizens' Councils), too academic (George cited sources, albeit scant ones), or too radical (Tarheels preferred the middle ground of inaction), Patriot arguments fell on thin soil.[25]

Despite George's academic credentials and the citations in his pamphlets, he found little scholarly support for segregation. Replying to a Davidson College professor's request for a list of a dozen books on segregation, George admitted difficulty. "Very little writing of books specifically designed for the support of segregation has been done," he confessed. Most scholarship opposed segregation, "promoted by university departments of sociology, etc., and supported by grants and fellowships financed by the wealthy foundations that have gone radical." He could only come up with three segregationist works.[26]

Lacking academic ammunition, the Patriots distributed inflammatory photographs of black men and white women interacting in social situations. Newsletters from segregationist groups often contained images of interracial couples dancing, kissing, or enjoying themselves socially. The images no doubt were intended to arouse white fantasies and fears of interracial sex. A New Orleans correspondent sent George a photograph of a white woman sitting with a group of black men who was tentatively identified as actress Ava Gardner, a North Carolinian. In Mississippi, Walter Sillers also showed interest in such photographs. He commented on a photograph of Adlai Stevenson arm in arm with boxing champion Joe Louis, who had "referred in a contemptible manner" to white southerners. Another photograph of Dwight and Mamie Eisenhower on a Harlem tour also caught his eye.[27] Segregationists eagerly collected such photographs and stories as documentary proof of black and white social mixing. Such transgressive images provoked both disgust and excitement.

Paul D. Hastings, a member of the North Carolina Patriots executive committee, told George that 1956 would be a crucial year in the school integration struggle. To counter the expected NAACP demand for integration, Hastings suggested implementing a membership drive (the Patriots already claimed a hundred new members a day), sending school boards and government officials Patriot literature (he was sure they had been "flooded with integration material"), and backing "the interposition movement for all that we are worth." Despite Patriot speeches and mailings, Hastings was disappointed that few Tarheels had heard of the organization. He was also annoyed that a newscaster had charged that "our organization was looked upon by some as a country club Klu Klux Klan [sic]." George's scribbled marginal comments revealed caution: "Don't over do," "use restraint or we arouse opposition."[28]

As in other states, North Carolina blacks were tiring not only of segregationist organizations but also of cautious white politicians. On August 8, 1955, Governor Luther Hodges called for voluntary segregation. Kelly Alexander, head of the state's NAACP, rejected the governor's ploy. Hodges pushed the plan clearly misunderstanding most black Tarheels' views of either voluntary segregation or his justification of it. Hodges's address at a gathering of the African American

North Carolina Teachers' Association elicited "only a brief, polite ripple of applause," he remembered. In November 1955, students at North Carolina Agricultural and Technical College in Greensboro responded to Hodges's speech with "a discourteous snicker" and "a shuffling of feet." Hodges was mortified. Later he learned that the students had been offended by his pronunciation of "Negro." Hodges lacked the introspection to decipher the deeper meaning of such behavior. Like most whites of his generation, he expected polite clichés to soothe black people. Behind the muted applause, snickering, and shuffling of feet, pressure was building among African Americans to end such humiliation. In September 1955, Benjamin E. Mays, president of Morehouse College, may have had Governor Hodges in mind when he wrote that white leaders' disregard for the *Brown* decision "is an invitation to lawlessness all over the place." Black leaders, he complained, were ignored.[29]

As brave ministers and laypeople stood their ground, the Patriots attempted to undermine them with an oppositional message. Ministers were "influential in advocating integration," Hastings insisted. "Many of our laymen feel that the best way to quiet these preachers down is by getting the lay members of our church informed as to what is involved in the issue." He proudly reported that fifteen ministers had been forced to leave their churches and boasted that the same tactics were used to fight unions through the church.[30] Hastings cleverly combined anti-union and anti-integration activities. He sent Cannon Mills owner William C. Cannon a document claiming that United Automobile Workers head Walter Reuther had donated $75,000 to the NAACP. Distributing this information among workers, Hastings suggested, "would keep more textile workers from joining the unions than everything else put together." The Congress of Industrial Organizations textile union in Spray, North Carolina, he reported, had contributed $25 to the Patriots. "We have a large membership in the Rockingham County Chapter from the mills in Leaksville, Spray, and Draper." Hastings believed that nearly all white workers favored segregation. But no one could fathom what was beneath the surface of the pool of silence among most working-class whites.[31]

Neither the university, the clergy, nor the press mounted a concerted movement to implement integration. Nor did all Tarheel editors favor even token integration. Bill Sharpe, editor of *The State* magazine, complained that the press presented views at odds with most white people's beliefs. He charged that "the fotched-on bias of our editors is a disgrace." Sharpe deeply resented the portrayal of segregationists as ignorant. "A lot of readers have little opportunity of knowing that in addition to that of themselves and their neighbors, the determination to resist integration is held by someone besides ignorant snuff-dipping rednecks." Sharpe implied that segregation was too important to be left to the working class. He described an alarming scenario in which integrationist university professors isolated students who agreed with their views, subsidized their graduate education, and pushed them into academic positions, "where they perpetuate the vicious circle." J. Bruce Eure of Whiteville, North Carolina, suggested to George that liberal professors "should be ferreted out and discharged for the best interest of the true people of the South." Newspaper editor Reed Sarratt, on the other hand, complained that faculty members were too apathetic on the race issue. "By leaving the field to the politicians we are inviting demagoguery and all that accompanies it." Professors needed to speak out. "Otherwise," he warned, "the people of North Carolina might conclude that Dr. George speaks for the University faculty."[32]

The Patriots faltered, for without the support of whites in the unindustrialized and heavily African American eastern part of the state, they remained a Piedmont-bound group. William D. Anderson attributed the Patriots' collapse to "apathy among the rank and file of the whites in the eastern and western . . . sections of the state." In the east, "the whites consider themselves perfectly capable and competent to handle things on a local level and the western counties have practically no negroes and therefore, aren't in the least concerned." Eastern North Carolina, then, varied dramatically from the Mississippi Delta, which boasted of highly organized Citizens' Councils.[33]

On August 25, 1956, at the Patriots' annual meeting, George reported a depleted treasury, declining membership, and general disorganization. "This tended to paralyze any action, good or bad," George admitted, "and was the cause of regrettable friction among our people." In the spring of 1956, he sadly reported, "there came a sharp, unanticipated drop in the rate of inflow of new members." George likened the integration impulse to a "fever in the body politic," and he predicted that if the Patriots could "keep the patient alive while the infection subsides, I think the fever will pass." He declined to serve again as the organization's president and suggested that a younger man take the reins. He sounded a retreat, not a call to arms.[34]

In August 1957, when North Carolina began token integration under the Pearsall Plan, many Patriots lost enthusiasm, and the organization went into a steeper decline. Patriot leaders blamed the press, the clergy, and college professors for eroding support for segregation. University of North Carolina professors, George complained, indoctrinated students. The high percentage of integrationists on the faculty "is not mere accident," nor was the press's support of gradual integration "mere chance." The university, he surmised, was the center of radical action on the race issue.[35]

After the Patriots disbanded in March 1957, Reverend James Dees emerged as the state's segregationist leader. In October 1958, a year after schools had been integrated in Charlotte, Winston-Salem, and Greensboro, Dees wrote, "We are not ready now—nor ever—to submit our children to the jungle of integrated schools." A month later, he established the Defenders of States' Rights, Inc. Dees pointed to communists, the NAACP, and liberal ministers as the sponsors of integration and warned that integration would produce "a mulatto culture." A number of Patriots moved to Dees's group, including Gwynn and George. In February 1958, Citizens' Council leader W. J. Simmons, learning of the vacuum of segregationist leadership in North Carolina, asked George if he would object to a Citizens' Council movement in North Carolina. George assured him, "I am in favor of anything honorable that will help to prevent integration."[36]

The Ku Klux Klan also attempted to fill the void left by the collapse of the Patriots. On January 18, 1958, Grand Wizard James Cole, a Free-Will Baptist minister who lived in South Carolina, led an ill-fated rally in Robeson County, which had a large Lumbee population. Cole planned to warn the Lumbees not to mix with whites, a message the volatile Lumbees interpreted as a threat. As the Klansmen gathered around a blazing cross, some thousand Lumbees emerged from the nearby woods screaming and firing guns; the Klansmen fled into the woods and ditches. Reports did not clarify whether or not fleeing Klansmen represented the best southern whites. A week later, a shaken but unrepentant Cole threatened to return to Robeson County with an army of Klansmen. Two months later, however, Cole and an associate were convicted and sentenced to eighteen to twenty-four months in prison for inciting a riot. North Carolina never hosted a statewide segregationist organization to oppose *Brown*.[37]

The Tennessee Federation for Constitutional Government and the North Carolina Patriots tried a moderate approach to prevent integration. But court fights were costly and often futile, and mailings usually went to the already converted. Despite the indifferent reception of both groups, no leader or organization emerged among whites to shape a program to integrate schools and open public accommodations. It would be 1960 before three students from North Carolina Agricultural and Technical College would sit down at a lunch counter in Greensboro and reset the clock of tradition.

10 The Best White Citizens

Every Negro in Selma who signed the petition for the desegregation of public schools has been the victim of all types of economic reprisal and any person who is known to be a member of the NAACP is also a victim.
—S. W. Boynton

You don't know what it's like to have to sleep with your gun in your hand, where every passing car might bring Death!
—Amzie Moore

When Mississippi governor Hugh White called a meeting to hear African Americans' opinions on segregation in July 1954, he expected hat-in-hand acceptance of segregation. He was shocked when T. R. M. Howard, a prominent surgeon, explained that his group had not come "to help work out any trick or plan to circumvent the decision of the Supreme Court outlawing segregation in the public schools." Praising the decision as "just and humane," Howard suggested the creation of a permanent committee of twenty-five blacks and an equal number of whites to discuss their mutual future. Settling problems along the color line, Howard implied, was a task for middle-class and elite blacks and whites. He rejected White's offer to upgrade black schools in return for maintaining segregation and expressed his hope that integration would come peacefully.[1]

Howard was one of a small but powerful group of African American leaders in Mississippi that included returning World War II veterans who were impatient for change. In 1951, Howard and other African American leaders had founded the Regional Council of Negro Leadership, which drew thousands of supporters to Mound Bayou for annual meetings. After World War II, African Americans in Mississippi had eagerly registered to vote and joined the National Association for the Advancement of Colored People (NAACP). Black voter registration rose from 2,500 in 1946 to between 20,000 and 25,000 in 1955. In 1954, the NAACP had 2,700 members in the state. Howard's suggestion that leading blacks and whites meet to discuss equal rights reflected his faith in African American leaders. But the *Brown* decision and Howard's call for interracial meetings unleashed white racial fears.[2] In Mississippi and throughout the South, the refusal of whites to join in a dialogue with African American leaders had profound consequences.

Instead of promoting harmony, whites formed Citizens' Councils, which used intimidation and economic power to attack African Americans who pushed for the vote or school integration. E. J. Stringer, a Columbus dentist and president of the Mississippi conference of NAACP branches, reported in October 1954 that every county in Mississippi had established "economic pressure groups called 'Citizen Committees' . . . for the purpose of forcing continued segregation by the careful application of economic pressure to Negroes and whites who favor integration." When blacks attempted to press the color line, the councils pressed back. In August, thirty Walthall County NAACP members filed an integration petition with the board of education; they were all subsequently investigated by a grand jury. The University of Mississippi imposed the absurd requirement that applicants had to submit character recommendations from five graduates of the university. Since "no Negro has ever graduated from the University of Mississippi," it was highly unlikely, in Stringer's opinion, that black applicants could meet the requirement. "Several of our branch officers have been intimidated, threatened and smeared and in one instance a branch meeting in Amite County was abruptly interrupted by the Sheriff and his deputies and the branch records confiscated," Stringer noted.[3]

Mississippi's black middle class and professionals were especially vulnerable to economic retaliation. The Citizens' Councils targeted a number of the 2,000 African Americans who attended the 1954 meeting of the Regional Council of Negro Leadership at Mound Bayou. Amos Robinson of Hollandale received a notice from his banker calling in the loan on his 120-acre farm. "We are not going to renew notes for any of you niggers in the Negro Council and the NAACP," the banker informed him. "We are going to use peaceful means but if that won't work, we shall use other means." Robinson appealed to the Federal Land Bank in Greenville, which agreed to loan him the money. Faced with losing a dependable customer, the Hollandale banker informed Robinson "that he was only joking when he intimated that his mortgage would not be renewed." An Indianola dentist who had attended the meeting watched his rural practice evaporate after planters stopped giving tenants vouchers to pay him. Planters in Columbus ostracized Stringer. White employers, the NAACP learned, "passed the word around not to let their servants go to Negro doctors who are active in the NAACP or the Negro Council."[4]

The Citizens' Councils attacked anyone suspected of membership in the NAACP, anyone who registered to vote, and anyone who signed a petition to integrate schools. C. N. Gray worked for the Delta Burial Insurance Company, but after he registered to vote in April 1955, his clientele disappeared when Indianola planters "forced the sharecroppers, tenant farmers and other laborers on their plantations to withdraw from the Delta Burial Insurance Company and join some other company in Indianola." When a planter told Mason Payne that he could stay on the planter's Humphreys County plantation the rest of his life if he would tear up his poll tax receipt, Payne refused and moved. Such pressure had its intended effect; by April 1955, all but 96 of the 400 African Americans who had registered to vote in Humphreys County had torn up their receipts.[5]

Citizens' Councils and other segregationist organizations spread throughout the South. By late 1955, Alabama's councils claimed 60,000 members. On November 29, 1954, 1,200 people attended a Citizens' Council organizational meeting in Selma. Mississippi congressman John Bell Williams gave the keynote address. One Selma speaker announced, "We intend to make it difficult if not impossible for any Negro who advocates desegregation to find and hold a job, get credit or renew a mortgage." Other speakers painted lurid pictures of black men and white women in integrated situations.[6]

In the fall of 1955, a member of the Southern Regional Council infiltrated a Citizens' Council organizational meeting in an unnamed Alabama county and reported that the meeting featured boring lectures, character assassination, and racist ideology. Speakers blamed "agitators from up North" for the crisis, described the NAACP's Walter White as a "mulatto" who was trying "to wipe out the white race" under communist direction, identified the bedroom as the NAACP's target, and speculated on the impact of black voting rights. Blacks would not simply vote, one speaker predicted, but also would "take over the running of your country." Despite their stranglehold on political and economic power, whites feared that blacks would somehow seize control.[7]

Throughout the South, whites understood the power of economic intimidation, and since they controlled state and local institutions, they could intimidate not only NAACP members but any suspected troublemaker. In the summer of 1955, the Selma Citizens' Council published the names of twenty-nine blacks who had signed a petition to integrate schools. Economic retaliation followed quickly. "Every Negro in Selma who signed the petition for the desegregation of public schools," NAACP leader S. W. Boynton revealed in July 1956, "has been the victim of all types of economic reprisal and any person who is known to be a member of the NAACP is also a victim." City officials tried to ruin Boynton's insurance business by not honoring his policies covering taxicabs.[8]

The Alabamian, a Citizens' Council newspaper started in the summer of 1956, fanned racial fears by featuring lurid stories of black rapists, demonizing the NAACP, and quoting documents from the House Un-American Activities Committee. The citation of congressional sources, committee hearings, official reports, and speeches by Senator James O. Eastland and others gave a patina of respectability to the paper's accusations. The paper's file on W. E. B. Du Bois, erroneously labeled "a Communist-sympathizing lawyer," contained eight single-spaced pages. Among others the paper condemned as un-American were Mary McLeod Bethune, Ralph Bunche, Norman Cousins, Gloster B. Current, Oscar Hammerstein, Ruby Hurley, Benjamin E. Mays, Wayne Morse, A. Philip Randolph, Walter Reuther, and Eleanor Roosevelt.[9]

To ensure that no act of the NAACP or other civil rights group went unobserved, Mississippi created a State Sovereignty Commission. Modeling itself on the Federal Bureau of Investigation (FBI) and employing former FBI agent Zack Van Landingham, the commission spied on civil rights organizations and compiled dossiers on suspected agitators. Over the years, it accumulated extensive files that contained rumor, innuendo, and detailed reports of civil rights meetings. Obviously the commission's spies had infiltrated black organizations. The commission worked closely with the Citizens' Councils.[10]

The participation of prominent southern politicians and civic leaders lent the Citizens' Councils and State Sovereignty Commission respectability. Reporter Murray Kempton penetrated the Citizens' Council member's disguise when he visited W. J. Simmons, the administrative director of the Citizens' Councils, in Jackson, Mississippi, in November 1955. Kempton described Simmons as "a tall, comfortable old-shoe fellow" who preferred "button-down collars." Simmons assured the reporter that the Citizens' Councils were nonviolent, but Kempton surmised that Simmons "would prefer not to be told what his tieless followers out in the delta are doing every day." Simmons was a kind man who "wouldn't harm a dog in the road," Kempton observed, but his "haunted eyes cry out that he represents a state that murders children." Kempton deftly uncovered the contradictions that made membership in the Citizens' Councils so disgraceful. Publicly they were the best white citizens who wrung their hands when African Americans were the targets of violence. "It is a state whose heroes are by necessity born Negroes in some unnamed patch," he judged, "and whose cowards are born gentlemen."[11]

On the same trip, Kempton visited J. B. Easterly, the head of Louisiana's Southern Gentlemen, which he described as "Louisiana's militant symbol of the counter-attack against racial integration." The organization had close ties with other segregationist groups, Kempton added, "ranging from the Citizens' Councils of Mississippi to the Apartheid Bund of South Africa." During Kempton's interview, several Southern Gentlemen visited Easterly's small backyard office (which Kempton labeled a "shed") and enlightened Kempton about their beliefs.[12]

Whereas the Citizens' Councils, Southern Gentlemen, North Carolina Patriots, and other groups offered the public a respectable face, other groups remained invisible. Elizabeth H. Cobbs's memoir provides a disturbing account of what went on inside several white Birmingham, Alabama, households. Cobbs grew up in Birmingham's Norwood community, and her family lived under a palpable cloud of fear sustained by her uncle, Robert Chambliss. "Like the rest of my family," Cobbs remembered, "I had lived all my life in the shadow of this man and his personal code, a law of life that he and his fellow Klansmen spoke of as 'the kiss of death.'" Chambliss's violent and unpredictable behavior kept family members off balance. He whistled "a long loud three-note whistle like you would use to call a New York cab" when he wanted his wife, nicknamed Tee, to serve him. Chambliss forbade his wife to wear slacks or smoke; he also physically abused her. After the worst episodes of abuse, Tee "would dress the dog in Robert's clothes, and as the dog walked on its hind legs, she would dance with it and carry on conversations, calling it insulting things in a very sweet tone of voice and smiling all the while." After the Chambliss household got a television set in 1950, "we heard him curse and rail whenever a black face appeared on the screen."[13]

As a child, Cobbs attended Ku Klux Klan meetings and often saw robed men in her uncle's house. The Klan meetings featured "Christian hymns and patriotic tunes." She recalled "The Old Rugged Cross," "Onward Christian Soldiers," "Dixie," and "America." Cobbs's family members, she recalled, were afraid of black people, especially men. This confused Cobbs, for most of the black men she encountered were old and polite. Even the aging black ice man left the heavy block of ice on the back porch for her mother to drag to the icebox because he was not allowed inside the house. Cobbs's family discouraged her dreams of college, and at age fifteen, she eloped with her sweetheart and then they returned to live with her parents. Six months later, she was pregnant. In the summer of 1956, her mother and aunts got the contract to make new Ku Klux Klan uniforms, and Chambliss hovered over the sewing women. She recalled that the women were not eager to sew the robes, but "participation was much easier than escape." She sat with the other women and "stitched Klan badges atop my huge pregnant stomach, and resented every minute of it." Three months after her son was born, she and her husband moved into an apartment, but her marriage was far from ideal. "Unfortunately the young man I had married was as immature as I was," she lamented, "and he expressed his frustration by beating me."[14]

Chambliss and his Klan friends were vigilantes and punished anyone who in their judgment had misbehaved. Chambliss bragged openly about beating and torturing black men. Klan members also disciplined white women who they claimed were sexually promiscuous. "Often the beatings of women were carried out by members of the Klan's women's auxiliary," Cobbs recalled, "who would hood up and go along on a night ride especially for that grisly purpose." Chambliss would "tell lies accusing females (and males) of promiscuity or loose morals whether there were any truth to the story or not." Cobbs found this hypocritical "because we all feared his wandering hands and eyes." Her mother warned her to avoid being alone with him. "At least two of my young cousins were victims of his inappropriate fondling, and a male cousin told me, 'I think he has tried to molest every child in the family—boys and girls.'"[15]

Cobbs suspected that Chambliss and his splinter group of Klansmen, the Cahaba Boys, were behind the rash of dynamite attacks in Birmingham's Fountain Heights community. The group, she learned, "operated with the approval of and often at the direction of the political power base." Chambliss's job in Birmingham's vehicle maintenance department "was said to be a reward for his efforts to prevent integration of housing in Fountain Heights." Chambliss and his friends even rode on patrols with the city police. Indeed, the most disturbing revelation in Cobbs's memoir is the connection between Klansmen such as Chambliss, city police, and politicians. Such license would lead Chambliss and his cohorts to plant a bomb at the Sixteenth Street Baptist Church on September 15, 1963, that killed four children. Cobbs later testified against Chambliss. Southern white leaders depended on men like Chambliss who would intimidate or kill anyone who showed softness on segregation.[16]

From Ku Klux Klan stalwarts like Chambliss to the Citizens' Councils, whites applied pressure on African Americans and white integrationists. State and local leaders eyed the federal government with apprehension. Like mischievous boys, they expected the righteous federal parent to discipline them. President Dwight D. Eisenhower, however, seemed uneasy and indecisive as the civil rights struggle intensified. The federal government drifted through the 1950s without a civil rights agenda as segregationists waged an aggressive battle against integration.

Because local elites controlled agricultural policy, the U.S. Department of Agriculture (USDA) became a segregationist tool. In early 1955, the Farmers Home Administration refused to grant loans to a number of black farmers in Mississippi. James Hargrove, who farmed near Tchula, had borrowed $5,115 in 1944 from the Farm Security Administration (the predecessor of the Farmers Home Administration) and still owed $4,491. When he applied for the customary loan in December 1954 to buy seeds, fertilizer, and food, the Farmers Home Administration "discovered" that J. W. McClintock held a mortgage on Hargrove's farm equipment (a tractor and plows) as well as his unplanted 1955 crop. The Farmers Home Administration refused to grant a loan without a nondisturbance agreement and a waiver from McClintock stating that he agreed not to seize Hargrove's equipment and crop prior to the Farmers Home Administration settlement. Hargrove's predicament demonstrated the vulnerability of African American landowners and exposed the USDA's institutional racism. Even though Hargrove owned his land, he still owed on it. The NAACP's Clarence Mitchell discovered that McClintock held similar mortgages on the crops and equipment of farmers Annie Ward and Cato Sample. Such liens apparently had presented no problem for the Farmers Home Administration before 1954, which led Mitchell to conclude that McClintock's mortgage gave the Farmers Home Administration "a good alibi for not making the loans." The Farmers Home Administration, of course, denied that the farmers' membership in the NAACP had anything to do with their credit problems.[17]

The NAACP attempted to help farmers targeted by the Citizens' Councils or denied credit by the Farmers Home Administration by directing them to the black-owned Tri-State Bank in Memphis. Farmers had difficulty meeting the bank's credit requirements, however, primarily because of their second mortgages. Most had previously relied on informal financial arrangements with either banks or credit merchants. The NAACP was in a quandary because of the confusion over the liens, and its Tri-State Bank plan faltered.[18]

Because local whites administered federal agricultural programs, retribution could be disguised as policy. Theodore Kennan Jr. had served as secretary of the Indianola branch of the NAACP and, along with many Sunflower County farmers, in 1955 applied to the Farmers Home Administration for disaster relief because of a wet growing season. Two days after being approved for a loan of $3,900, he and fourteen other claimants were told that the county had not been identified as a disaster area. Kennan's creditor, Walter Scruggs, a plantation owner and Ruleville banker, advised him to "cease his NAACP activities or leave." At that juncture, J. H. White, president of the Mississippi Vocational College at Itta Bena, volunteered to serve as intermediary. White had forbade the teachers at the college to belong to the NAACP, and he was rumored to be in the pay of the Citizens' Council. His negotiations between Kennan and Scruggs came with a price. To regain Scruggs's favor, Kennan must help neutralize NAACP activist Amzie Moore. Through White, Scruggs threatened to strip Kennan's credit, undermine his loyalty to the NAACP, and force him to suborn Amzie Moore.[19]

A World War II veteran and founding member of the Regional Council of Negro Leadership, Amzie Moore headed Cleveland's NAACP branch. In October 1955, Moore criticized the NAACP and especially Roy Wilkins, who during a visit to Cleveland gave the impression that he "knew very little about our problems and cared less." The Citizens' Councils desperately wanted to destroy the NAACP, Moore warned. "Hundreds are being let out of jobs, leaders are being threatened, one hundred farmers who are members of the Cleveland Branch who still owe for their land have no place to borrow money to operate their farms next year." Despite intimidation over the past ten months, Moore boasted, the NAACP in Cleveland had grown from 69 to 400 members. "You don't know what it's like to have to sleep with your gun in your hand," he reproached Wilkins, "where every passing car might bring Death!"[20]

The Farm Bureau's Boswell Stevens actively supported the Citizens' Councils. In June 1954, when African American county agent Charlie Burton from Greenville asked Stevens for $500 to fund Negro Delta Field Day, Stevens offered $100 and a lecture. Black Farm Bureau membership had declined, Stevens complained, and he warned Burton that black members were not doing their share. "As you know," Stevens blustered, "we are now contributing almost $2,000.00 to the various negro programs in the state." Burton apologized for the falling membership in Washington County. Neither man mentioned that the declining black membership might have been caused by the fact that machines and chemicals were replacing rural workers. Meanwhile, Stevens actively supported segregation. "I personally have made contributions and Farm Bureau has made some contributions in devious ways," he boasted. Stevens credited Reverend M. L. Young with "driving many Negro agitators out of the State." Young told Stevens that only two agitators were left and one of them had resigned from the NAACP. The other was Medgar Evers.[21]

Local and state agricultural leaders could manipulate USDA machinery to pressure black farmers while granting white planters sizable subsidies. Between 1956 and 1959, Senator James Eastland, a member of the Senate Agriculture Committee, received $275,000 in government subsidies and loans for his farm. The struggling black families that surrounded his plantation did not fare so well. Early in 1956, Medgar Evers and Mildred Bond, NAACP field secretaries, traveled 800 miles through the Mississippi Delta and visited seventy families. Away from the main roads, they found "innumerable sharecroppers and tenant farmers who are living on plantations and to whom we have absolutely no means of access." The problems of these black farmers were not the result of their association with the NAACP; they were caused by mechanization. Planters had replaced sharecroppers, who received food and lodging for the crop year, with day laborers, who had no claim on food or the crop. Evers and Bond heard "various tales" about "how these families are being driven from plantation to plantation as each owner resorts to cutting down on the cost of labor by getting cotton picking machines, planters, etc."[22]

Evers and Bond also found small farm owners whose life's work and possessions were jeopardized by belonging to the NAACP. Seventy-one-year-old Jake Tanner lived with his wife near Holly Bluff on a forty-acre farm he had owned

Boswell Stevens.
Boswell Stevens Papers,
Special Collections Department,
Mitchell Memorial Library,
Mississippi State University.

since 1917. The four-room house was valued at $1,800. Tanner customarily raised five acres of cotton, four of corn, and six of soybeans. In the winter of 1956, he needed $650 to finance planting. "Has been advised," Evers and Bond discovered, "that because of NAACP he'd better *not* even ask for loan or help." Near Shaw, they found fifty-nine-year-old Annie Baker, who also owned forty acres. The year before, she had produced sixteen bales of cotton on her ten-acre allotment. She owned a 1953 Ford tractor and needed $1,000 to cover the cost of planting. She headed a household consisting of an eighteen-year-old son, a daughter of twelve, and a daughter of three.[23]

At the same time that African Americans were struggling to make payments, survive as sharecroppers or day laborers, and take steps toward achieving first-class citizenship, Mississippi newspaper editor Hodding Carter championed the Delta Council's idea of whitening the state. "I think in the long run what will help Mississippi solve its problem is mechanization—mechanization which is encouraging the migration of Negroes to other sections of America," Carter wrote in March 1957. The downside of black flight, he admitted, was the fact that less money was spent in the small towns of the Delta, so he advocated the growth of industry "to keep up the purchasing power in the towns."[24]

Although Carter supported school segregation and black migration, he viewed the Citizens' Councils with suspicion and distrust. His March 1955 *Look* article reviewed the founding and expansion of the Citizens' Councils and re-called earlier Ku Klux Klan violence. Citizens' Council leader Robert B. Patter-

Medgar Evers.
LC-USZ62-119120,
*National Association
for the Advancement of
Colored People Papers,
Prints and Photographs
Division, Library of Congress,
Washington, D.C.*

son was closely connected with other fringe groups and had distributed a list of thirty publications that in Carter's opinion "represented as indecent and provocative a collection of bigoted publications as was ever compiled." Carter either ignored or was not informed of the Citizens' Councils' ironhanded economic sanctions.[25]

The responses to Carter's article open a window on public sentiment. Robert Patterson complained that although wealthy white people could afford to send their children to segregated private schools, poor white children "would be forced into associations that have always led to inter-racial marriages and strife." "Respectable" segregationists such as Patterson attempted to protect poorer whites from temptation. His argument implied that poorer whites were fond of blacks. Evidently, they were as likely to marry as to murder their black neighbors. It was from such unpredictable people that the Citizens' Councils distanced themselves. The NAACP's Roy Wilkins wrote to *Look's* editor thanking him for alerting people to the councils but faulting Carter for exposing the NAACP's role in obtaining credit for harassed farmers, repeating the rumor that the NAACP had communist links, and quoting a Mississippi legislator's comment that the NAACP's goal "is to open the bedroom doors of our white women to Negro men."[26] Both the NAACP and the Citizens' Councils had public relations problems, and increasingly both were portrayed as opposite extremes in the fight for equal rights. NAACP leaders resented this comparison, for they saw themselves as advocating obedience to the law whereas council members were outlaws.

Brave whites fought against discrimination as best they could. Jewell Mac-Daniel had served in the U.S. Army Nurse Corps in World War II. "It was there," she informed Carter, "that I learned that a person could be a good American whether he be black, yellow or white." In 1955, MacDaniel was head nurse in the Emergency Department at the University of Mississippi Medical Center in Jackson; her roommate, who cosigned the letter, was head nurse in the Colored Surgery Department. These women, who had been hardened by war, went about their professional duties with little regard for racial separation. Shed Hill Caffey observed that race relations in Philadelphia, Mississippi, were "bad enough," but he knew that in the Delta things were much worse. He had interned at the University of Virginia, where the clinics were integrated, "and there was no obvious animosity, jealousy or ill-will because this was taking place in the very back yard of Robert E. Lee." His wife, educated at Randolph-Macon College, knew young women who agreed that the South needed a "renaissance." In Philadelphia, Caffey was "appalled to learn the names of the people in our town who are on this Citizens Council Committee." He had spoken out against racism at a Rotary Club meeting and feared that as a result he had lost friends and patients. There were people in Mississippi, he ventured, who "would like to do the Christian thing but who are afraid to speak out."[27] Speaking out, as Caffey and others were learning, usually cost friends and jobs.

Jane C. Houck admitted to Carter that she wrote things in her letter that she feared to say in Greenwood, Mississippi, "except in a rather negative manner, by not agreeing or by disagreeing in minor points." Houck was surrounded by segregationists. "You see, I work for a member of the Citizens Council, and there is one member of our Bible Class who is a most rabid one." Robert H. Ahrens of DeRidder, Louisiana, asked, "What can I as a non-influential liberal (who is often considered a 'suspect' character) living in a comparatively intellectually primitive section—the 'Bible-belt' of La.—*do* to help save the South from itself?"[28] Jane Houck and Robert Ahrens fought lonely, conflicted, and silent battles as they weighed their convictions against the punitive weight of segregationists.

The Citizens' Councils and State Sovereignty Commission created a climate of suspicion and distrust. "I never thought I would ever see a whole population so obsessed with straight-out fear as the people of the delta are afflicted with today," J. W. Haddon wrote from Isola. The Delta had "many people with education and culture," but they casually employed "extreme economic pressure and physical force against people who have been responsible for most of the wealth in the delta." White segregationists at times seemed overzealous in policing the color line. In October 1956, the Monroe County Citizens' Council asked the Mississippi Public Service Commission "to request Southern Bell Telephone and Telegraph Company to place their white and Negro patrons on separate lines."[29]

Outraged that Carter had targeted them in a national magazine, the Citizens' Councils orchestrated a legislative condemnation of Carter. James W. Silver, a professor of history at the University of Mississippi, asserted that the state legislature "certainly made an ass of itself." He knew Carter well, he wrote to fellow historian Frank Owsley in April 1955; "he's a pretty nice guy and a sort of middle of the roader. . . . Certainly he's no radical." Silver was apprehensive. "More and more people are getting emotional as hell and I suppose the situation will get worse." He was to speak to the Greenville Rotary Club in two weeks, he added, "and I may end up in the Mississippi." Silver was under constant fire from legislators, the governor, and even congressmen. "Life is fairly exhilarating in Mississippi," he sighed, "though at times it gets tiresome."[30]

The legislative resolution condemning Carter elicited a compelling reaction from Fred Chaney, who had spent much of his life at Whitfield, a Mississippi institution for the insane. "To get the chance to become a *headline star career-psychopath* you don't locate in Whitfield," he joked to Carter, you go to the state legislature. "I hope you will write me something consoling because of all the time I have wasted at the wrong place," he lamented. In Chaney's opinion, the legislature's action sprang from "hysteria contained in the long exaggerated danger of social equality and mongrelization." The Citizens' Councils allowed their "fear and insecurity" to justify segregation and "their phobias" to sanction economic and political reprisals. Chaney called for common sense. "The way of sanity would be in giving the integrated school a trial at least in such places where there was no likelihood of violence." He dismissed the fear that voting or school attendance by blacks "carries the real threat of indiscriminate sexual relations, interracial marriages or the mongrelization of Southern society." Chaney recalled that when state authorities had ignored the findings of an investigation of Whitfield, the press had revealed "that many patients were slowly dying of starvation and that brutality in treatment was the commonly used method of handling the population." In that case, the press had helped "a segment of the population widely treated and thought of as being 'inferior,' 'different' and to be kept 'segregated.'" As much as any white Mississippian, Chaney understood the predicament of the state's black population. Whitfield, ironically, shielded him from the surrounding insanity.[31]

Despite the debate over his Citizens' Council article, Carter maintained his stand for continued segregation in Mississippi. When in early 1955 Citizens' Council finance chairman Ellett Lawrence berated Carter for favoring integration, he heatedly replied that he had "never advocated nor welcomed an end to separate public school systems in the South." He offered a stinging rebuttal to

Lawrence's claim that school integration meant mongrelization: "There has been far more miscegenation in the cotton houses than there would be in the school houses, as Deltans know as well as any." Carter dismissed Lawrence's suggestion that he leave Mississippi. "And lest you remain concerned that I have the 'inferiority complex' you mention," Carter concluded, "may I point out that as long as there are people like you in the world I could never feel inferior in the absolute sense."[32]

As whites bickered, African Americans continued to challenge segregation. In October 1955, NAACP field secretaries Ruby Hurley and Medgar Evers visited Yazoo City, where the Citizens' Council was tormenting everyone who had signed a petition to integrate schools. The council had obtained the names of the petitioners and published them in the local newspaper, and businesses had posted the lists in clear view. "Any of the petitioners and/or their relative who worked on plantations were driven from the cotton fields," Hurley discovered. Every person on the list who had held a job had been fired. No distributors sold to black store owners, and one man who received a government disability check could not get it cashed. The head of the Delta National Bank notified every account holder on the list "that the bank did not want to do business with them any longer."[33]

By January 1956, only fifteen of the fifty-three petitioners remained in Yazoo City. Pearlie Anderson had stayed behind while her husband went to Illinois to seek work after the white landlord ordered him off the farm. When he attempted to make a payment on his new tractor, the company refused his money and repossessed it. The fuel oil company would not sell to Anderson, so she used wood for heat. Perrine Stephens's employer fired her "after Citizens Council threatened reprisals if he did not." No gas company would service her butane tank (although they serviced her next-door neighbor's), so she too relied on wood for heating her house. She was living on the $82 a month she drew from social security as a widow.[34]

Whites boycotted Jasper Mims, a carpenter and president of the local NAACP branch. He could not even buy lumber. "Negroes no longer use his services due to W.C.C. pressure," Evers and Bond learned in January 1955. His rental houses stood empty. Whites made threatening phone calls to Mims and told him that the Tallahatchie River "will be locked with Negro bodies before any were permitted to vote" and that he should keep his poll tax receipt on him "so that it could be used for identification when his body was fished from the river."[35]

Many who signed the petition were hardworking people, but whites made no exceptions. Annie Mae Johnson's sixty-four-year-old husband went to Chicago looking for work but returned discouraged. Evers reported that Annie Johnson had been harassed by a man who ran the Sinclair Oil Station in Yazoo

City. After she found a job, a city councilman "told me if he sees me on job again he would shoot the hell out of me." The Johnsons were despised not because they were lazy and unindustrious, as so many whites characterized African Americans, but because they wanted equal rights and were determined to work. Evers and Bond concluded, "It is worse than being behind the Iron Curtain." Such stories prompted them to cite Yazoo City as "an example of the thoroughness and viciousness with which the Citizens Council operates without actually employing violence." Such pressure led to distrust in the black community, where informers kept the Citizens' Council up-to-date. "The atmosphere perhaps parallels that under the Gestapo," Evers and Bond judged.[36]

Aaron E. Henry, another black World War II veteran and a leading citizen of Clarksdale, Mississippi, publicized the firing of two Coahoma County Hospital employees. Gussie P. Young and Lurleander Johnson belonged to the NAACP and advocated school integration. Henry had been a friend of Patterson's as a child, but Patterson headed the Citizens' Councils, and Henry, in the words of sociologist Charles M. Payne, "was the closest thing there was to an official head of the resistance movement in Mississippi." Henry helped found the Clarksdale NAACP chapter in the early 1950s and in 1954 became president of the chapter. He secured affidavits from Young and Johnson and then issued a press release, mentioning that the hospital received federal funds. Reed Hogan, the hospital administrator, admitted that he had fired the women not because he found fault with their work but because the hospital board and the Citizens' Council had pressured him. Both women cited other problems at the hospital, including discrimination, discourtesy toward black patients, and unequal pay for the same work. Because it was useless to complain to the hospital board, Young argued, she was appealing to public opinion "in an attempt to keep these undemocratic, Unamerican and unchristian acts from continuing in the Coahoma County Hospital."[37]

When economic pressure and verbal threats failed, whites turned to violence. In Belzoni, Mississippi, the Citizens' Council mounted a particularly vicious campaign of intimidation. Reprisals started immediately after 400 African American residents paid their poll tax and registered to vote. Windshields were broken, stores were vandalized, and the Citizens' Council left warnings. There were no arrests. The violence produced the desired effect. All but 91 blacks tore up their poll tax receipts. On May 7, 1955, Reverend G. W. Lee, a fifty-one-year-old Baptist pastor who kept his voting credentials, was murdered while driving home. A convertible pulled up beside his car, three shotgun blasts were fired at Lee from the convertible, and Lee's car went out of control and struck a house. A. H. McCoy, a state NAACP leader, assisted in the autopsy. Buckshot from the shotgun blasts had killed Lee, and much of his head, ac-

Aaron E. Henry at Rust College. The Bearcat, *1964. Courtesy Leslie Burl McLemore.*

cording to McCoy, "gave the appearance of having gone through a hamburger grinder." McCoy retrieved six "irregular shaped pieces of lead resembling buck shots." At the inquest, he revealed, whites claimed that Lee's death could have been the result of "a scantling" or shock, that the lead could have been from a tooth filling, and that the alleged gunfire could have been "three tire blowouts." The press was equally shameless. In Mississippi, McCoy informed President Eisenhower, black people who complained of injustice were told to move. The Citizens' Councils had substantial support among whites, he pointed out, and the state attorney general "has specially deputized more than a thousand lawyers to aid in the circumvention of the Supreme Court decision." He asked for Eisenhower's help in this time of need.[38]

Ruby Hurley and Medgar Evers arrived in Belzoni for Reverend Lee's funeral and gathered more information on the shooting. When Pearleen Gray heard the gunfire two houses away, she thought her husband, who had been warned to stop his voter registration activities, had been shot. She saw what she thought was a 1953 Ford convertible speed away. Olivia Robinson, who lived across the street at the time and saw the attack, refused to discuss the incident and moved after some white men talked with her. Lee's car crashed into Katherine Blair's house. She had heard a noise and looked out the window in time to see a gun blast. Hurley and Evers uncovered rumors of the identities of the car's occupants but no proof. The NAACP activists in Belzoni feared not only racist whites but, in the words of Hurley and Evers, "'Uncle Toms.'" The Citizens' Council warned other NAACP members, including Gus Courts, that they were on the list of targets.[39]

Six months later, on November 25, 1955, sixty-five-year-old Gus Courts was wounded by shotgun blasts fired from a pickup truck as he stood in his grocery store making change. Courts headed the Belzoni NAACP chapter and was among some 8 or 10 registered black voters remaining of the original 400. FBI agents were asked to investigate, but given that one was from the Delta, the NAACP's Gloster Current questioned their objectivity. "The offering of a reward by the Belzoni Citizens' Council and resolutions which had been issued by the Council, Rotary and Kiwanis Clubs deploring the attack upon Courts is ludicrous," Current added. As Charles Payne concisely observed about Mississippi, "Those who wanted to work for change had to understand that they were challenging a system that could and would take their lives casually." After the Courts shooting, a number of prominent black leaders left the state, including T. R. M. Howard. NAACP membership declined. The Citizens' Council always distanced itself from violence, which it could handily attribute to the Ku Klux Klan, and used public relations to maintain its image as a group of upstanding community leaders. There was a division of duties. The Citizens' Council carried out "respectable" economic intimidation and blamed violence on the Ku Klux Klan.[40]

Although the Citizens' Councils did not advocate violence, at least publicly, Mississippi's African American population understood the risks of voter registration and other actions that undermined segregation. Whites refused to take seriously the murder of a prominent black clergyman and, even more unsettling, joked that his grave wounds could have been caused by an accident. Lee's death became an object lesson, a warning to other blacks who ignored threats. The attack on Courts added to the tension. After spending twenty-two days in the Mound Bayou hospital, Courts moved to Chicago. In January 1956, he defiantly mailed his $2 poll tax back to Humphreys County.[41]

Whites also pressured African American church congregations to give up support of the NAACP. On June 15, 1956, a Cleveland lawyer met with Reverend E. C. Smith, pastor of the New Hope Baptist Church, and asked him to stop holding weekly NAACP meetings in the church. Smith refused. The lawyer implied "that anything could happen to the New Hope Baptist Church" and advised Smith to buy more insurance. Smith talked over the issue with local NAACP leader Amzie Moore, and they decided the only thing they could do was

Gus Courts's grocery store, Belzoni, Mississippi. LC-USZ62-123835, *National Association for the Advancement of Colored People Papers, Prints and Photographs Division, Library of Congress, Washington, D.C.*

wait. For ten months, all was quiet. Then in May 1957, church members received anonymous phone calls warning them not to associate with the NAACP. On Thursday night, May 9, the NAACP held a membership drive that attracted 200 people. The meeting ended at 11:00 P.M.; the church burned at 4:00 A.M. It was a total loss. The fire chief blamed "loose connections," but the power switch had been turned off after the meeting. No other church in Cleveland would allow the NAACP to use its building, so the members of New Hope pledged to raise $7,000 to rebuild.[42]

The Citizens' Councils denied using violence and put a benign spin on the draconian economic pressures they employed. "Individuals who belong to councils may have persuaded Negroes to remove their names from school integration petitions by various means short of violence," the *Citizens' Council* newspaper explained. "These means could include firing employees, or refusing to renew leases for sharecroppers who have followed the NAACP line." The councils prevented bloodshed, the paper boasted. The Citizens' Council in Jackson was composed of "the best citizens in this capital city of 116,000 population." To project a responsible image, the Citizens' Councils produced television and radio programs. In June 1959, the executive producer of the radio and television program *Citizens' Council Forum* invited Congressman Tom Abernethy to appear on an eleven-minute segment. He was to be filmed in Con-

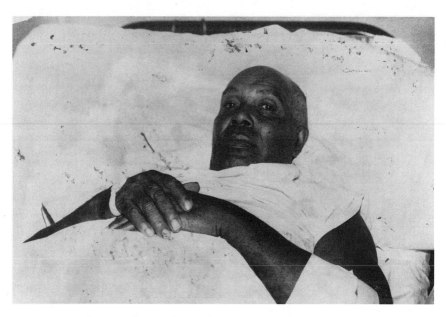

Gus Courts in the Mound Bayou hospital. LC-USZ62-123834. *National Association of Colored People Papers, Prints and Photographs Division, Library of Congress, Washington, D.C.*

gressman John Bell Williams's office. The Citizens' Councils not only blatantly used government offices to produce segregationist propaganda but also received $20,000 from the Mississippi State Sovereignty Commission in 1960 to fund the *Citizens' Council Forum*. Several of the state's newspapers questioned the arrangement and criticized Governor Ross Barnett for his cozy relations with the Citizens' Councils. The State Sovereignty Commission also subsidized two African American newspaper editors who championed segregation.[43]

Whites who stood up for decency faced constant pressure and harassment. The Delta and Providence Farms sheltered an aggregation of blacks and whites that was considered radical in Mississippi. In 1936, prominent evangelist Sherwood Eddy had bought a 2,000-acre tract of land in Bolivar County as a refuge for displaced tenant farmers. Leaders stressed the farm's Christian mission. Seminarian Eugene Cox arrived during the first months and helped shape the development of the farm, and in 1938, David Minter began his medical practice. On the farm, business meetings were integrated, churches welcomed blacks and whites, and the length of the term at black schools was the same as the length of the term at white schools. Although the farm had never been popular with its white neighbors, after the *Brown* decision, they regarded it as subversive. In September 1955, the Citizens' Council suggested that Cox and Minter leave the state. After fighting the council's harassment for a year, both left.[44]

Any opposition to segregation met with instant retribution. In Durant, Presbyterian minister Marshall Calloway lost his pulpit after denouncing segregation. Implement dealer A. D. Steward of Tchula, who had worked for the USDA, was forced to close his business after being accused of favoring desegregation. The Holmes County sheriff sued Hazel Brannon Smith, editor of the *Lexington Advertiser*, for libel after she reported that he had callously shot a black man.[45]

Amzie Moore, Aaron Henry, and Medgar Evers continued their activist work despite growing pressure from whites. They laid a solid foundation for civil rights workers who arrived in Mississippi in the 1960s. Their cause would later be taken up by members of the Student Nonviolent Coordinating Committee, who valued not only their elders' wisdom but also their network.[46]

The basis of white power, meanwhile, was undergoing a major transformation. With machines marching steadily through the fields displacing tens of thousands of black workers, planters no longer employed punitive methods of labor control. The Delta Council's master plan called for running off surplus black laborers as rapidly as possible, in part by denying blacks federal funds. Mechanization, chemicals, and the plan to whiten the state resulted in a decline in the number of black farm operators from 159,000 in 1940 to 38,000 in 1964. The demand for rural laborers decreased at the same time that planters became even more addicted to federal agricultural programs. Mississippi planters fed their own craving for federal aid while portraying blacks, who received a minute share of federal funds, as lazy and dependent on welfare. White politicians hoped to offset the black exodus, which was costing them national representation, by creating industrial jobs. The confusion in a modernizing Mississippi gave blacks who remained in the state enough space to continue their fight for equal rights.[47]

Mississippi's transition from labor-intensive agriculture to agribusiness, urbanization, and corporate development paralleled the emergence of the civil rights movement. White political and business leaders refused to share power with black citizens. Instead, the Citizens' Councils and State Sovereignty Commission encouraged Mississippi's modernization. When Medgar Evers likened the state's repression to conditions behind the Iron Curtain or under the Gestapo, he was close to the mark. In June 1963, Citizens' Council member Byron De La Beckwith shot the World War II veteran in the back. His sniper shot killed Evers but it failed to halt the movement for civil rights.[48]

11 The Sound of Silence

I was dumb with silence, I held my peace, even from good;
and my sorrow was stirred.
—*Psalms 39:2*

In fact, we have been so weak (all churches) in this matter that history will read
back and say that the armed forces, the effect of TV etc., and the power of the dollar
did more to solve the problem than we have had the courage to do in the church.
—*John Morris*

In August 1954, fifty-eight-year-old South Carolinian James McBride Dabbs attended a joint meeting of the Farm Bureau and the States' Rights League of Sumter County. Dabbs at various times had farmed, headed the Southern Regional Council, taught college English, and written provocative essays. He always spoke his mind. Hugh Agnew, president of the South Carolina Farm Bureau, gave the keynote speech and called for nullification of the *Brown* decision, a tirade Dabbs judged "mainly a tissue of illogicalities" and "nonsense." Agnew, like Boswell Stevens in Mississippi, used his Farm Bureau position to promote agribusiness, undermine unions, and enforce segregation. When Agnew asked South Carolinians to stand up and be counted, Dabbs obliged him and caused a commotion by condemning segregation as "an offense to Christian teachings." Boos and jeers drowned out his words. When the uproar subsided, Dabbs urged the crowd to "shake off the past and face the future." The civil rights struggle excited him, he admitted later. "It's a great fight; and I wouldn't have been born at any other time."[1]

Farm Bureau and States' Rights League members represented the white Sumter County middle class and elite. Those who heckled Dabbs, then, were respectable whites, although their lowdown cousins no doubt shared their segregationist sentiments. For the most part, working-class whites seemed more passive, or at least less vocal, about integration than middle-class whites, who assumed that they spoke for all southerners, black and white. They demanded conformity. Dabbs alone at the meeting voiced integrationist sentiments, but his words had a chilling effect. If working-class blacks and whites embraced

*James McBride Dabbs, 1935.
James McBride Dabbs Papers,
South Caroliniana Library,
University of South Carolina,
Columbia.*

school integration, they might challenge the elite's blueprint, which used race as the foundation of political, economic, and social control. At such meetings, the elite set the tone for white public sentiment following *Brown*.[2]

South Carolina's few white integrationists were well-educated professionals, and they expected support from people with similar backgrounds, especially educators, members of religious and political women's groups, and high-church clergy. They assumed that working-class whites were blindly devoted to segregation and wrote off the possibility of their support. African American integrationist leaders also came from the middle class. After *Brown*, integrated meetings necessarily focused on school integration. Because the agenda was no longer simply better race relations but an end to segregation, many moderate whites were at best uncomfortable. Many lacked conviction. Unlike Dabbs, they were loath to risk their neighbors' censure. Being a southern white integrationist in mid-fifties South Carolina required not only bravery but also resignation to being shunned. Although white integrationists found few white allies, they and their African American partners boldly canvassed the state for citizens willing to condemn segregation. Realizing that the South Carolina Council on Human Relations (SCCHR) needed recruits, Dabbs and other members searched for a field agent. They settled on Alice Norwood Spearman, executive director of the South Carolina Federation of Women's Clubs at the time. She was a brilliant choice.

Alice Norwood was born on March 12, 1902, in Marion, South Carolina. Although her mother pushed her to excel, her stern father was less supportive, causing what she described as "a terrific resentment . . . on a subconscious level for a long time." Precocious, competitive, tomboyish, curious, and rebellious, she excelled in both sports and scholarship. After she enrolled at Converse College in 1919, she was elected president of her class.[3]

Norwood was popular in college, but she showed little interest in courtship and none in marriage. She was drawn to the working class and taught Sunday school at the Spartan mill village. She attended "cutting edge" conferences at Blue Ridge, North Carolina, where young women who worked in the mills and college students exchanged experiences and ideas. Black women came to discuss the "racial situation." One summer, Norwood joined the student-in-industry Young Women's Christian Association (YWCA) project in Atlanta and worked in a sewing room, in a Vaudeville movie house, as an investigator of private employment agencies, and at the Fulton Bag and Cotton Mill. The women in the mills, she judged, "were finer, basically, than we college girls were, who were skimming the cream off of life." In 1926, she went to Columbia Teachers' College and, while completing an M.A. in religious education, took courses at Union Theological Seminary and YWCA courses on women's history.[4]

In 1930, a trip to England turned into an exciting and exceptional world tour. Norwood returned home in April 1932 and during the New Deal rose to district administrator in the Federal Emergency Relief Administration. She was also active in the Socialist Party. Norwood had liberated herself from the usual expectations of women of her class; she spurned marriage proposals in college, acquired an education, taught, worked, mixed with the working class, and traveled. In 1935, she married Eugene Spearman, who also worked in federal relief, and settled in Newberry. Alice Norwood Spearman then became a homemaker, a mother, and a community volunteer. During the New Deal, she met Modjeska Simkins, a black woman who was a member of the National Association for the Advancement of Colored People (NAACP), the Commission on Interracial Cooperation, and the Southern Conference for Human Welfare. Simkins recalled that Spearman "exemplified the bull in the china closet type."[5]

Spearman eagerly took control of the SCCHR in October 1954, using her finely honed talents, broad executive experience, and many contacts to fight for better race relations. Despite her vast experience among the working class, she focused on convincing black and white community leaders to join the SCCHR and to promote interracial meetings. Shortly after taking over as executive director, she invited her Charleston friend, Harriet Porcher Stoney Simons, the president of the League of Women Voters, to become an SCCHR board member. "In this critical time," she wrote Simons on January 10, 1955, "I do not see how we can do without you." Both women had attended the organizational meeting

Alice Norwood Spearman.
Alice Spearman Wright Papers,
South Caroliniana Library,
University of South Carolina,
Columbia.

of the SCCHR. Simons, however, had reservations about keynote speaker Marion A. Wright, a former president of the Southern Regional Council, an SCCHR board member, and an uncompromising integrationist. Wright's strong words pleased the SCCHR's African American members, but they alarmed cautious whites such as Simons. The increasing strain between blacks and whites over school integration had destroyed the Charleston Interracial Committee, and Spearman inquired whether Simons thought it would "remain dead," which seemed to be the consensus.[6]

Spearman confided to Simons that most white SCCHR members perceived NAACP members as militant and discouraged them from joining the board. Although this vacillating policy placated white moderates, it outraged black NAACP members, and both highly respected Modjeska Simkins and Robert Hinton resigned from the SCCHR board. By excluding NAACP leaders from the board, Spearman acknowledged, the SCCHR dismissed those most dedicated to ending segregation. For the remainder of the 1950s, Spearman tried to mend this racial divide. It proved a difficult and risky task. South Carolina moderates, for the most part, shied away from contact with blacks, and blacks tired of white equivocations. The conventional wisdom among whites contrasted idyllic pre-*Brown* race relations with dreaded integrationist pressure from the Supreme Court and the NAACP. South Carolina politicians erected legal barriers to prevent school integration and held out until 1963, longer than any other southern state.[7]

It took a month for Simons to sort out her feelings and reply to Spearman; she had a lot on her mind. Among Charleston's elite, issues of school integration and race relations were tangled with personalities and propriety. Simons dwelled on Marion Wright's keynote speech, which supported integration and praised Judge J. Waties Waring. After Waring's divorce and remarriage and his ruling ending the white primary, the Charleston elite had shunned him and his second wife.[8]

Wright's provocative address showed little regard for the sentiments of white Charlestonians in general and those of Simons in particular. Wright had served two terms as president of the Southern Regional Council and worked diligently to end segregation. "While I realize and accept that desegregation in the schools is inevitable," Simons confessed, "I am not anxious to hasten its progress." In her opinion, "this whole question of desegregation is so embedded in the most dangerous type of emotionalism that it is hard for the average person to be objective about anything connected with it." Simons decided she could not accept a position on the scchr board because she was "not in accord with the policy makers at the top level and I do not wish them to speak for me." Wright's talk had been decisive. Spearman soldiered on with her scchr mission and continued to woo Simons and the Charleston elite through 1956, insisting that she needed their help.[9]

Marion A. Wright brought keen intelligence and dedication to the scchr. Born in 1894, he grew up in Trenton, South Carolina, during the formative years of legal segregation. Senator Benjamin Tillman lived nearby, and the young Wright stayed with Mrs. Tillman and her daughter when the senator was away. Although he enjoyed reading the books in Tillman's library and credited the senator for implementing reforms, Wright denounced his belief in segregation. As a youngster, Wright had witnessed a racial incident that he "deeply resented." While Wright was working at a store, a well-dressed black man waiting for a train asked if he could wash his hands. After Wright directed him to a basin at the back of the store, the store owner went "berserk, almost." Grabbing a buggy whip, he "shouted something about a 'goddam nigger using my washpan' and ran the Negro out of the store." The owner then turned on Wright, but the stern lecture on segregation failed to erase from his mind the savage treatment of the black man. The incident remained vivid in Wright's memory a half century later.[10]

After a typical small-town childhood, Wright enrolled at the University of South Carolina in 1910, where, as an indifferent student, he split his time between newspaper reporting and the library. James McBride Dabbs was one of his classmates. After leaving school in 1914, Wright held a number of jobs before studying law. He moved to Conway and for years participated in a local interracial group whose members were "quite frank with each other." He served as president of both the South Carolina Committee on Interracial Cooperation and the Southern Regional Council, which, he recalled, stood for equal rights but not necessarily for integration. The extent of white opposition to integration surprised him, especially when people he considered "good citizens" joined the Citizens' Councils. Prejudice, he admitted, ran "deeper than I had thought." He met Alice Spearman and was "greatly impressed by her conversational gifts and also her fairly practical method of securing members and raising funds."[11]

Spearman admitted that her job produced "psychological stresses and strains." She knew that many whites were "overwhelmed with feelings of fear and resentment." Blacks, she discovered, expressed "considerable disillusionment . . . that they will be able to secure their rights through the efforts of white people." Spearman was confounded by the "reticence" of whites who failed to understand the "urgency of keeping open the lines of communication between the two races." A meeting between state NAACP leaders and whites in Florence, Spearman complained, only "served to widen the breach between the races." She feared that her remarks at the meeting went too far. Reverend Edward L. Byrd, pastor of the First Baptist Church in Florence, assured Spearman that her speech had been well received. Byrd suspected that Florence residents resented anyone from outside the town who suggested a course of action, even if it was one they might approve. Still, none of the city's white residents called for another meeting between blacks and whites.[12]

Spearman's recruiting was stymied by both increasing racial friction and an oppressive climate of fear and distrust. In late 1954 and early 1955, forty-five to sixty-seven people attended SCCHR meetings in Anderson, but then attendance declined. African American schoolteachers, Reverend Carl R. Pritchett reported, were "among the most influential leaders in the Negro community," but, fearing retaliation, they stayed away. The mayor expressed interest in attending meetings, but he hesitated because of the "severe political penalty exacted of any public man who shows any inclination to weaken the structure of segregation." Pritchett reserved his most bitter criticism for his fellow ministers. "One of our problems is the fact that so many of our ministers have just as much racial prejudice as anyone else," he charged. "The social penalty for nonconformity is still so high it discourages forthright thinking and outspoken Christian interpretation." Pritchett observed that southern whites "have had to protect their intelligence and conscience both from the Constitution of the United States and the Bible."[13]

In South Carolina and throughout the South, whites assumed that they could speak for African Americans. Only at rare meetings did whites listen attentively to ideas other than their own. Spearman felt that such white arrogance and presumption damaged her work among blacks. On March 30, 1955, she reprimanded David Carroll for not allowing African Americans meeting at Allen University to express "what use they would like to see made of such media as press, radio, and television, rather than telling them what to say." Two weeks later, she complained that his newspaper article on the gathering, by ignoring the "generous cooperation from the fine group of Negroes and from me," jeopardized her African American contacts. She stressed to Carroll that "to have maximum value it is necessary that we use with them a democratic precept which will allow them to *speak for themselves.*"[14]

Marion Wright, whose Charleston speech had offended Harriet Simons, continued to distress white moderates. As he was weighing an offer to head the SCCHR, Reverend J. Claude Evans placed Wright at one extreme of white opinion and Governor James Byrnes at the other. Speaking before the SCCHR executive board in late May 1955, Evans admitted that the separate-but-equal doctrine was a sham, but he urged a cautious approach to integration. Most whites, he acknowledged, saw their black neighbors as "low-class, poverty-bound, superstitious-laden." Evans seemed unsure what role the SCCHR should play. "Negatively, we are a non-political, non-pronouncement-making organization," he concluded. "We are not interested in making radical statements that follow an extremist point of view. Neither are we interested in doing nothing." He was unsure whether he was a suitable person to head the SCCHR.[15]

Spearman admitted that Wright's aggressive speeches upset people like Evans who realized that retribution could be swift. "Not only has he queered things both in Spartanburg and Charleston," Spearman complained of Wright, "but also he has shown considerable intolerance and lack of discrimination" in his attacks on politicians. Even if all politicians were "narrow, bigots, and deceitful," she confided to a friend, "I would still question the advisability or desirability of attacking them as he does."[16] Spearman feared that carefully cultivated white moderates would bolt the SCCHR. She still insisted that black and white people discuss issues together, but in a land where community standing and friendships were extremely important, many whites were unwilling to risk ostracism.

Despite the near collapse of cooperation between South Carolina's blacks and whites, Spearman never faltered. When black ministers from Newberry asked her to help analyze educational programs, she discussed plans with them until nearly daybreak. When she got phone calls that morale among black members was low, she immediately tried to inspire hope. She constantly traveled across the state, wrote hundreds of letters, and attended meetings, and her office became the headquarters for sorting out crises. As a woman who moved between the black and white communities, she was highly visible and controversial. "I think a lot of people thought I was going to get killed," she recalled later.[17]

Since her office became a clearinghouse for civil rights activity and reports of white retribution, Spearman's files bulged with significant but often overlooked cases. In April 1955, Chester C. Travelstead, dean of education at the University of South Carolina, attended Governor George Bell Timmerman Jr.'s address before the South Carolina Educational Association. The governor discussed parental rights, industrial expansion, and segregation. Stressing that he had lived in the South all his life except for two years during World War II, Travelstead disagreed "emphatically" with Timmerman's characterization of segregation's critics as "men of 'little character'" who were "cowardly." After encouraging the governor to abide by the *Brown* decision, Travelstead acknowledged that expressing integrationist sentiments exposed people to "possible embarrassment, ridicule, or reprisal." In August, Travelstead gave a bold talk to university faculty and students reiterating his belief in integration. Three weeks later, he received notification that his contract would not be renewed after the next academic year. He immediately accepted a position at the University of New Mexico.[18]

Travelstead's dismissal outraged Wright, and he upbraided university president Donald Russell for releasing the professor "for expressing in parliamentary language an opinion upon a question of public policy in the field of education." Wright suggested that the university had become a tool of state politicians and warned that failing to allow open discussion "is recreant to all its great traditions." In a literate society, Wright observed, Travelstead's opinions would "be regarded as commonplace, almost as platitudes." Travelstead's firing, Wright concluded, sent a message to students to "play it safe," stick with the majority, and march in "lock step."[19]

Across the South, professors courted retribution when they challenged segregation. In February 1957, Bud R. Hutchinson, an assistant professor of economics at Auburn University, publicly disagreed with an editorial in the school's newspaper, the *Plainsman*, that criticized integration in New York schools. In May, the board of trustees, offering Hutchinson no opportunity to defend himself, unanimously terminated his contract. Auburn president Ralph Draughon informed Hutchinson that his views clashed with community attitudes and that speaking out on the emotionally charged race issue "could not be tolerated." Hutchinson insisted that silence on such issues "leaves the students with the impression that their teachers are in complete agreement with the particular prejudices of Boards of Trustees." Hutchinson also received threatening phone calls warning him, "Get going out of Alabama while you're still healthy."[20]

Any South Carolinian who displayed "softness" or even compassion on race relations could suffer swift reprisals. Jay Clark, a Mullins teacher, basketball coach, and Baptist layman, spoke on February 8, 1956, at the Macedonia Methodist Church prayer meeting. He deplored the violence at the University of Alabama over the admission of Autherine Lucy and asked, "Was it un-American and unchristian to throw rocks at a student at the University of Alabama?" Clark offered the opinion that God "must be disappointed" at such behavior. After the prayer meeting, church and community leader Margaret Lipscomb asked him if he actually believed what he had said. When he replied, "I certainly do," she announced that "she'd have him fired by morning." She then called some school board members and charged that Clark was a communist. As Mullins resident Alice Edwards Lee put it, "Mrs. Lipscomb labeled him a Communist and insists that he must leave—that the board not make her out a liar." By the time Clark submitted his resignation, "*vicious* tales were circulating," including a rumor that he advocated intermarriage. The Methodist pastor claimed that he had a cold at the time and could not hear what Clark said. Clark's Baptist pastor stood up for him, but to no avail. According to Alice Edwards Lee, several Mullins women deplored Lipscomb's viciousness but feared her wrath.[21]

In the estimation of his pastor, Clark left teaching and coaching "a crushed boy." He "was grateful" to find a job at a furniture store near Myrtle Beach, according to Lee. Spearman wrote him a comforting note and assured him, "You are not alone in your concern about this matter."[22] For showing compassion and condemning the stoning of a black woman, sentiments that only a person such as Margaret Lipscomb could construe as unchristian or communist, Clark was driven out of town. His martyrdom went largely unremarked. Such powerful parishioners as Lipscomb, it seemed, thought nothing of offering a human sacrifice to enforce conformity on the race issue.

Although Clark was censured for remarks made outside the classroom, schoolteachers seemed particularly vulnerable to community pressure. William Denton, a Sumter, South Carolina, high school teacher, "was dismissed because of examination questions given by him which might be interpreted as reflecting an unacceptable point of view on race relations." He moved to Chapel Hill, North Carolina.[23]

Pastors as well as professors and teachers became targets of segregationists. Reverend George Jackson Stafford was called to the pulpit of the Batesburg Baptist Church in 1952. He had served in World War II as a marine pilot and then earned his bachelor of divinity degree at Southern Baptist Theological Seminary. By 1955, he had added 161 new members, completed a $100,000 auditorium, and doubled the church's budget. In a discussion at Judge John Bell Timmerman Sr.'s home in October 1954, Stafford admitted that at the Southern

Baptist Convention four months earlier he had voted for the resolution favoring the *Brown* decision. This information lay dormant for nine months. Then, in mid-July 1955, Timmerman, the governor's father, announced to Stafford, "You and I do not belong in the same church." The national Baptist position, in Timmerman's estimation, "has as an objective the abasement or mongrelization of my race." The judge was "sure that the 'reds' and the 'pinks' want this issue 'pussy-footed' until they get a stronger foothold in our churches." Stafford took exception to Timmerman's charges of communist influence and his insinuation that Stafford was, in essence, a communist dupe. Stafford, it turned out, had a Federal Bureau of Investigation security clearance dated June 25, 1955. He was hardly a security threat. Nor, he bristled, was he a "Communist dupe."[24]

Basing his defense on Baptist theology and the concept of religious freedom, Stafford challenged Timmerman and by extension his congregation. Since his ministry was not in question, Stafford assumed that two issues were involved: his right to vote his conscience at the Southern Baptist Convention and his right to a private opinion. A convention messenger was "never instructed as to how to vote on matters of morals and Christian principles, but is expected to vote in keeping with his conscience, convictions, and in the light of his interpretation of the Bible and the will of God." Stafford could not have voted the church's position, he argued, for it had never gone on record. He had prepared a report following the 1954 convention, supplied details in the church bulletin, and encouraged the congregation to read other literature.[25]

Upon his return from summer vacation, Stafford sent a letter to the congregation clarifying issues and citing scriptural support for his views on race relations. He denied that he advocated intermarriage, nor did he see it as a pressing issue. As to whether he favored admitting blacks into the congregation, he pointed out that this was not the pastor's decision but that of the congregation. "I cannot refuse my Christian fellowship to a person solely because of his race," he added. Stafford reviewed the persecution of Baptists and noted that it was two Baptist ministers who had influenced James Madison to pen the First Amendment, which guarantees religious freedom. "For additional scripture references on Christian race relations," he suggested, "you are urged to read the decisions of the early Christian church with reference to Christian fellowship with the Gentiles who must have composed a fair sample of the races of men surrounding the Mediterranean Sea at the time." He thoughtfully appended references and quotations.[26]

On October 23, 1955, Stafford offered his resignation as pastor. The congregation was faced with the dilemma of whether to support or denounce a young and popular pastor who had run afoul of a powerful political figure. Most church members were neither hot nor cold but lukewarm. Only 10 percent voted on the issue. Timmerman washed his hands of the affair, claiming to have had nothing to do with Stafford's departure. But the judge was not someone the congregation would lightly oppose, nor would they want him to carry out his threat to leave the congregation if Stafford remained. Denying Stafford the right to his own interpretation of the scriptures regarding segregation violated a fundamental Baptist belief, but the Batesburg congregation put segregation ahead of theology. Stafford had to be expunged lest he infect the congregation with a Baptist-like regard for independent thinking. He moved to Georgia and became a Veterans Administration chaplain, never completing his doctorate and never again subjecting himself to examination by a segregationist congregation.[27]

Benjamin E. Mays, an influential African American leader born near Ninety-Six, South Carolina, expressed grave misgivings about the role of churches in improving human relations. "I believe that throughout my lifetime, the local white church has been society's most conservative and hypocritical institution in the area of White-Negro relations," he judged. "Nor has the local black church a record of which to be proud." Many black churches, to their credit, admitted whites. After the 1954 *Brown* decision, three and a half years passed before eighty of Atlanta's white ministers made a statement of support. Mays, who was president of Morehouse College, devoted a chapter of his autobiography, *Born to Rebel*, to the role of the church in the civil rights movement.[28]

Spearman toured South Carolina asking white ministers and people of good will to meet with blacks and mend the racial divide, but she found whites hardening their hearts and blacks losing their patience. "I am sure that you are one of those persons who regret the bitterness and antagonism which is growing — spreading like a prairie fire — in South Carolina at the present," she wrote in September 1955 to Reverend Earl Cooper, pastor of the Earle Street Baptist Church in Greenville. She encouraged him to help bring black and white people together to discuss problems. Cooper replied that he was "not a firm believer in any kind of organization for this purpose, whether it be the Ku Klux Klan, or the White Citizens Council, or the South Carolina Council on Human Relations." James McBride Dabbs suggested that few ministers "frankly defend segregation." Most said nothing, but "the top-flight men, with very few exceptions, are opposed to segregation." No matter how daintily ministers skirted the segregation issue, Dabbs continued, white-supremacy groups "fear that the preachers are their worst enemy."[29] Cooper, like many of his neighbors, was intent on riding out the crisis in silence.

The Citizens' Councils only began organizing in South Carolina in August 1955, but they quickly absorbed other segregationist groups. Unlike white moderates, Citizens' Council members had no reluctance about meeting with blacks. A state senator felt compelled to meet with blacks to warn them that the

NAACP was attempting to dupe them. "The two sides sat on opposite sides of the room and talked," a Presbyterian minister reported of one such meeting. "The Nigras didn't have a lot to say." Citizens' Council members cautioned African Americans about using the courts to secure civil rights and warned that whites would close schools to prevent integration. Segregationist groups, like Protestant churches, seethed with strong opinions, and by 1959, turmoil among Citizens' Council leaders fractured the organization.[30]

On September 14, 1955, Spearman shared her frustrations with her friend Rebecca Reid, who had also graduated from Converse College. Reid had been an instructor at a Mississippi college, worked for the YWCA, and taught school in Sumter before being "run out" for teaching socialism. She was universally regarded as wise and fearless. Spearman complained to Reid that "my trip this week has been the most discouraging so far." Large parts of the state were in turmoil. She learned from a friend that in Hartsville a newcomer to town had driven off the Presbyterian minister and then formed a segregationist organization. Although residents of small southern towns resented visiting moderates who offered advice, they seemed quite willing to accept outsiders who brought segregationist tidings. "We have found a state of near hysteria in the Pee Dee District," Spearman wrote to another friend.[31]

In late March 1956, Spearman attended a meeting in Columbia that brought together black and white women "representing various denominations and faiths in South Carolina." Spearman considered many of the black women at the meeting close friends and was disturbed that other white women distanced themselves. Many black women were upset "at the lack of communication between the races," and Mrs. Morris S. Young of Anderson said she found it difficult to work with white women. She complained that they did not even want to receive mail "containing any reference to human relations as concerned in the integration problem." She hoped that contacting them in person would be better. Still, most South Carolina white women were reluctant to meet with black women or to discuss the issue that weighed on every South Carolinian's mind.[32]

A project by five moderate South Carolina pastors epitomized white caution regarding the color line. On June 9, 1956, John B. Morris, pastor of the Saint Barnabus Episcopal Church in Dillon, met with Reverends Ralph E. Cousins, Joseph R. Horn III, Larry A. Jackson, and John S. Lyles to plan a book that would put moderate views before the citizens of South Carolina. Morris's group contacted some 50 ministers and 150 laypeople throughout the state to ask them to consider writing essays. From the beginning, the group found it difficult to convince laypeople to participate. "To my surprise," H. Jack Flanders Jr. wrote from Furman University, "I did not seem to be able to think of a Baptist that I might be able to suggest for possible use in your program." Minister Harry R.

Mays echoed Flanders, explaining that there were several moderates in the Lancaster area but "few, if any, wish their views to be public knowledge." As Morris took the "pulse of the state" on the race issue, he realized that he was becoming more conservative and wondered if he was as courageous as he had been before.[33]

Writing openly about the race issue challenged prospective contributors to Morris's book. Harriet Simons, who earlier had shied away from Alice Spearman's enticements, drafted an essay but then had second thoughts. Publishing the essay, she explained to Morris, might end her effectiveness and "brand me as an out and out integrationist, which I am not." After discussing her concerns with her husband and friends, she withdrew the essay. "I've weakened the statement considerably," businessman John Clyde Barrington of Dillon informed Morris in June, "because of my *fear*!" Since segregationists denounced any wavering on the race issue, they forced moderates into the untenable position of being unable to embrace either segregation or integration. "There seems to be no middle ground on this issue," a Florence doctor complained to Morris.[34]

When people asked Morris why the church had come to favor integration, he carefully negotiated the minefield by explaining that whites had accepted segregation as part of southern culture but *Brown* had prompted the clergy to challenge old patterns. "In fact, we have been so weak (all churches) in this matter," he prophesied, "that history will read back and say that the armed forces, the effect of TV etc., and the power of the dollar did more to solve the problem than we have had the courage to do in the church."[35]

The book, *South Carolinians Speak: A Moderate Approach to Race Relations*, did not seem moderate to many South Carolinians. Most of the essays were cautious and timid, some were openly racist, and many embodied elite assumptions. The term "moderate" obviously covered a wide variety of beliefs. Columbia banker and Episcopal layman Robert Beverley Herbert described slaves as "savages" from a continent that "for untold centuries" had never contributed anything to civilization. He feared that blacks suffered from "venereal disease and illegitimacy" and was aghast at the idea of integration. Edgar Nelson Sullivan, a native of Stateburg who practiced medicine in Clinton, pleaded for gradualism. Helen Burr Christensen of Beaufort, an Episcopalian, spoke out "from the conviction that thousands of silent South Carolinians deplore the lack of constructive leadership in our state and long to find a reasonable solution to our problems." She regarded the integration of the armed forces as a positive step. Cheraw editor Andrew McDowd Secrest posed questions about integration and argued that a few blacks in a few schools "cannot create any real scholastic, educational, or social problems." The problems would come from "troublemakers."[36]

Georgetown lawyer Arthur Locke King observed that whites allowed black women to have a profound influence in rearing their children, so segregation "in public conveyances, court rooms, and other places, upon the theory that it is necessary to preserve race integrity, appears to be too absurd to command the respect of intelligent citizens." Julia Rees Reynolds, a Sumter English and history teacher and Episcopal church member, deplored the fact that black children lacked educational opportunities whereas "inferior whites, by virtue merely of color, have often assumed a position of superiority for which they seem not to have been designed 'by Nature and by Nature's God.'" Clyde Barrington urged both black and white leaders to "take the leadership away from agitators and dogmatists." John Moore, a retired professor from the Citadel, had eaten in dining cars with blacks and attended integrated classes at Cornell University in 1910. But, he argued, "enforced integration" in South Carolina "would be, at this time or in the foreseeable future, the worst thing that could befall the people of this section, all of them; and I therefore am unqualifiedly opposed to it."[37]

Claudia Thomas Sanders argued that "fear and ignorance" produced prejudice. "No longer is it popular to propose one law for men and another for women," she warned, "or even one for white and another for black." Sanders suggested that integration begin in the first grade. "Children are not born with prejudice," she explained. "If adults could only learn from children their ability to judge character and worth without regard to externals, our task would be immeasurably lighter." She dismissed fears of interracial marriage by asking whether the present segregated system "dooms" white children "to marriage with partners of different backgrounds, different ideals, different ideas of cleanliness and antagonistic religious concepts." All classes of whites mixed in the schools, she stressed, and such would be the case if schools were integrated. She advised leaders to move cautiously and stress Christian ideals.[38]

As most of the contributors to the book quietly adjusted to their notoriety, fifty-six-year-old Claudia Sanders was singled out for retribution. Well-educated and cultured, Sanders personified upper-class South Carolina society. An Episcopalian, she had graduated from Hollins College and then studied at Columbia University during the ascendance of anthropologists Franz Boas and Melville J. Herskovits. After a brief career in social work, she married James Henry Sanders and they settled in Gaffney.[39]

In November 1957, the local Ku Klux Klan targeted Sanders as a threat to white supremacy. Five Gaffney men met on November 17 to prepare a bomb to blow up the Sanders house because "Mrs. Sanders wrote an article in a book about the mixing of the races." After a Klan meeting on November 18, three members drove to the Sanders home. "We had this nine sticks of dynamite, alarm clock, battery in a nail keg, which we got at my house," one recalled. They placed the keg "beside the house" and left. The bomb did not go off. The next night, Klansmen threw three dynamite sticks into the Sanders yard at about 8:00 P.M. After they did not explode, the persistent Klansmen threw three more sticks of dynamite into the yard at 10:30 P.M., which did explode. The blast rocked the house, blew out windows, and cracked some walls, but the family escaped injury. Police found the twelve unexploded sticks of dynamite beside the house and, after arresting the suspects, discovered ninety-six more sticks of dynamite at a Klansman's house. Five Klansmen were arrested.[40]

Although many people sympathized with the Sanders family, the Ku Klux Klan held a rally in January 1958 at the Lonesome Pines Rodeo Grounds that used the bombing to recruit forty-five new members. "We do not wish Mrs. Sanders any harm," the Grand Dragon mocked. "If we could, we would send her back to Africa so she could be with her 'nigger' friends." The Klan showed the film *Birth of a Nation*, and then the Grand Dragon railed against selling liquor to minors and high school students who "smooched" before class. Obviously Klan members had family problems that resonated with their racial fears. Many children were in the audience. An observer noted that even the horses were hooded. A photograph showed a blazing cross, hooded figures, a film projector, and a record player (used for playing "The Old Rugged Cross"). The images were a curious and confusing jumble of the antiquated and the modern. Religion, race, changing values, and juvenile delinquency all blended together in the minds of Klan members.[41]

Almost unnoticed, Robert P. Martin Jr., who confessed to the bombing, did not live to stand trial. In February 1958 he was "crushed to death" when his automobile "apparently fell on him." Law enforcement officers declared the death accidental. In June, a magistrate ruled that only two men should stand trial for the bombing and that Martin's confession was inadmissible. On July 19, a jury returned a not guilty verdict.[42]

Claudia Sanders destroyed the hate mail she received. "I deplored the publicity and the feeling that I was hated," she remembered. "Both were new experiences for me." Her friends rallied at her side, which, according to Sanders, "more than made up for the anonymous and ugly telephone calls which persisted for a time." John Lyles was forced from his pulpit and moved to West Virginia. Few South Carolina whites publicly defended the book's editors or authors. It would take years for South Carolina to find more than a few voices of moderation or even civility. "The real issue in South Carolina is not segregation or desegregation," Morris wrote to a Dillon newspaper editor in November 1957, "but whether or not people may differ with one another."[43]

By contrast, reporter and rising Republican politician William D. Workman

Jr. gained widespread support for his 1960 book, *The Case for the South*. He reiterated the mythic story of Reconstruction and Redemption and described Citizens' Council members as upstanding people. Workman berated newspaper editors Ralph McGill and Hodding Carter and southern authors Erskine Caldwell, Lillian Smith, and Tennessee Williams and was especially vitriolic in chiding "'scribbling women' who prate of the joys of race-mixing with such fervor that they seem to have persuaded themselves that integration is the one way to happiness." Workman pointedly attacked African Americans. White southerners had trouble pronouncing the letter "r" in "Negro," he suggested, and "found it simpler, phonetically, to slide into the use of 'nigger' for Negro." Black people, he went on, had high rates of illegitimacy and venereal disease, bought cars beyond their means and decorated them with "fox-tails, and other unnecessary but gaudy appurtenances," and favored television sets over indoor plumbing. Only elite whites could keep their lowdown cousins—"unfortunate and frequently anti-social individuals"—under control, "except perhaps when inflamed by liquor, by fleeting passion, or by occasional mob psychology." Workman reported "documented occurrences of 'widespread sex orgies between white girls, Negro youths and perverts' in Milwaukee" and "riots and near-riots precipitated by inflamed emotions provoked by the wild abandon of 'rock-and roll' dance sessions attended by both races." Northern police officers, he promised, could vouch for "the disturbing effect of mixing whites, blacks, and primitive music." Except for their faulty enunciation, elite whites were the guardians of good taste and minimized the excesses of lowdown blacks and whites. Workman feared that "primitive music" would destroy segregationist barriers and fuel interracial sex. Working-class blacks and whites had to be kept separate at all costs.[44]

To prevent contact between blacks and whites, South Carolina white leaders demanded that all public spaces remain segregated or be closed. State officials closed Edisto Beach State Park in 1956 rather than integrate it and attempted through legislation and intimidation to prevent blacks from using other parks. In some instances, blacks quietly invaded segregated spaces. In April 1957, B. T. Matthews and his family visited Brookgreen Gardens near Georgetown. To Matthews's astonishment, several busloads of African Americans were enjoying a picnic there. He commented that "it made me feel real ashamed" to see blacks in the park. "Only about ten percent were white, which made it very embarrassing to walk around, a negro in front, one in back, and if you weren't careful they would walk right side of you, your wife or friends," he complained. "They acted as if you were black too." Matthews wrote to his state representative about the incident, which eventually came to the attention of the Citizens' Council. What most upset Matthews was not that African Americans were acting as if he

were black but that they were acting as if they were white. As African Americans shared public space with Matthews and his family, they erased his white privilege. Despite this incident, the state managed to prevent formal integration of its parks until 1966.[45]

Many South Carolina men fretted that upper-class white women were the driving force behind school integration. In March 1956, after the South Carolina legislature unanimously passed a bill that aimed at driving the NAACP out of the state, house member Charles G. Garrett of Greenville complained that activist white women had been the bill's primary opponents. "Most of the opposition," he confided to Congressman William Jennings Bryan Dorn, "is from the 'left wing' society element. (I think the change of life is working on quite a few high society women at present) so I take all opposition in stride."[46] Such was the state of political discourse in South Carolina in 1956.

Whites in Orangeburg used tactics similar to Mississippi Citizens' Councils to discourage blacks from signing school integration petitions. Day laborers were dismissed from their jobs, and sharecroppers' contracts were not renewed. White economic pressure forced half of the blacks who signed petitions to recant. Outraged blacks, Alice Spearman reported, retaliated "by boycotting many of the white store owners who have joined the citizens council." By mid-November 1955, the situation was at an impasse, but blacks were unwilling to end their integration activities. Spearman considered entering the dispute but feared she would be regarded as "the strike breaker in a labor dispute." J. E.

Roadside sign in Lexington County, South Carolina, advertising segregated rest rooms, spring 1956. W. D. Workman Jr. Papers, Modern Political Collections, South Caroliniana Library, University of South Carolina, Columbia.

Blanton, a black man from Cordova, wrote that he could think of only one white man who was not "on the 'Band Wagon' to ignore the Supreme Court's ruling." A white woman who had worked with him earlier, he wrote, "does not even know me when she passed me on the st." White men wanted to talk with blacks, Blanton assured Spearman, "but they want to pick the Negroes themselves, and you know how far they can get with that at a time like this."[47]

Whereas most South Carolina whites ignored the *Brown* decision as best they could, the African American community continued its steady and resolute opposition to segregation. In November 1955, the South Carolina Citizens' Committee, a black group organized in 1944, held its annual meeting at Allen University. The committee vowed to obey the law of the land, which included *Brown*, for "to circumvent or to deny the law is rebellion" and "to join others in so doing is criminal conspiracy." From the *Plessy v. Ferguson* decision in 1896 until 1954, African American citizens had "suffered deprivation and indignities," but they had not rebelled; instead, they had sought redress through the

Newspaper carriers preparing to deliver an issue of the Afro-American *featuring the lead story, "Boycott Spreads." John H. McCray Papers, South Caroliniana Library, University of South Carolina, Columbia.*

courts. "The struggle in which we are engaged is neither temporary nor futile," the committee announced; "we pledge ourselves one to another and in the presence of Almighty God to work forward to the inevitable triumph for good in our lives and in the lives of the children of this State."[48]

The Mississippi blueprint for economic retaliation had a South Carolina counterpart. In Orangeburg, Clarendon, and Sumter Counties, a group of African American ministers complained in 1955 that "it is impossible for a Negro to borrow any money with which to begin his farm work—unless he signs a statement that he does not belong to the NAACP, that he does not believe in its aims, that he does not believe in integration, and that he is perfectly satisfied with conditions as they are." The ministers reported that any farmer who signed a petition in support of black voting rights or school integration, even if he owned 350 acres or more of unencumbered land and was fully mechanized, could not borrow even $100.[49]

Such economic repression was not new to Clarendon County's African American farmers. One of the cases that was folded into the *Brown* decision, *Briggs v. Elliott*, had originated in the county in 1947, and whites had exacted retribution. Billie S. Fleming, a black undertaker, helped establish the Clarendon County Improvement Association, which secured small cash loans, fertilizer, seed, pesticides, and other supplies for farmers. In 1958, after two years of success, the association's credit dried up, and Fleming requested a $15,000 loan from the NAACP.[50]

A year later, Fleming testified before the Senate Subcommittee on Constitutional Rights and summarized white retaliation. When the *Briggs* case began, he claimed, whites tried to run off those who signed petitions. Even when signers removed their names, whites refused to restore their jobs. At that point, blacks organized the Improvement Association. When white farmers refused to rent them a combine to harvest soybeans, the United Automobile Workers gave the association funds to purchase one. When local implement dealers refused to sell to them, Improvement Association members crossed the county line to purchase implements from other dealers. When ginners in another part of the county refused to handle their cotton, they hauled it long distances. Fleming also testified that the local hospital would not call his funeral home to pick up the remains of deceased African Americans.[51]

In addition to suffering overt economic pressures, African American farmers suspected corruption in the Clarendon County Agricultural Stabilization and Conservation (ASC) committee. "The White farmers have been getting all the Cotton and Tobacco [allotments] they wanted," Billie Fleming explained, "while the Negro farmers had to accept what was left." In a speech in New York in late 1959, Fleming pressured the U.S. Department of Agriculture (USDA) to investigate the Clarendon County ASC committee, and the subsequent investigation substantiated his charges. "Although we now have a new County Committee," Fleming despaired, "we have not been able to get a Negro in the Office in any capacity whatsoever."[52] With little economic or political power, blacks used whatever weapons came to hand against unscrupulous whites.

After Ira Kaye, an attorney who worked with Spearman, met with USDA personnel in November 1961, he reported that the agency was unlikely to take any action to promote equal opportunity. He succinctly described the operations of the local, state, and federal components. "Their attitude seems to be that race problems are purely incidental to the program they administer and whatever the local power group decide is best for the community that is what is going to be done." Kaye protested that the segregated programs were not helping blacks and that the local agricultural committees were "composed of White Citizen Council members and other racist elements." He was shocked that discrimination was taken for granted. As long as whites controlled local, state, and federal institutions, African Americans stood little chance of receiving equal benefits.[53]

By 1957, the integration fight in Clarendon County was ten years old, and African Americans in the county had paid a high price. In 1947, six-year-old Harry Briggs Jr. had headed the plaintiff list in the case that went to the U.S. Supreme Court. A decade later, he lived with his grandmother and attended tenth grade in a segregated school. His parents had been frozen out of employment in the county and lived in Florida. Many of the 155 or more plaintiffs who joined in the case had lost their jobs. Blacks had fought a protracted battle of wills against county whites. After William Ragin pulled his truck full of tobacco into a filling station, the attendant pumped twenty-five gallons before telling him he would have to pay in cash. "Take every damned drop out," Ragin demanded. When the Ku Klux Klan left a warning in a black man's mailbox, he went to the sheriff's office. "I'm not here for any help," he told the sheriff. "I just want you to see this and get the word around that the first (—— ——) that puts his foot on my property, somebody is gonna tote him off, feet first." Ten years after the case began, integration remained an elusive goal.[54]

Whites tended to focus on generalities and ignored the daily lives of the black people who lived among them. That Clarendon County whites could so ruthlessly intimidate the *Briggs* plaintiffs illustrated white immunity from federal pressure. Across the South, African Americans faced retribution if they challenged segregation, registered to vote, boycotted segregationists' businesses, or belonged to the NAACP. White communities, for the most part, endorsed such harassment. As they had during Reconstruction, segregationists struck at both the bravest and the most vulnerable African Americans, believing that by making examples of them, they would intimidate the less strident.[55]

In April 1959, political leader and editor John H. McCray summed up what had occurred in South Carolina in the five years since the *Brown* case. Some people wanted better race relations, he admitted, but they "dare not speak out." Newspapers had "become propaganda sheets for intolerances." What had begun as opposition to the Clarendon County case "has blossomed out into a gyrating monster which sucks up just about every fundamental and basic right of a free State and a free people." The number of registered black voters had declined from nearly 200,000 to 60,000. When a lowcountry teacher and his wife insisted on registering, they lost their teaching jobs. "Unofficially," McCray revealed, "they were suspected of communistic ideas since they wanted to vote." In many communities, those "suspected of favoring desegregation are quickly and summarily fired from jobs, and barred from other employment by whites in the community." Even relatives suffered reprisals. "Similar cancellations are also made against any sympathetic white merchants, or wholesalers who allow credit to a Negro whose name has been placed on a list of persons the community undertakes to starve to death, or force out of the locality."[56]

As the fifties drew to a close, most blacks cooled toward the SCCHR. In November 1959, black minister D. M. Duckett addressed the SCCHR and declared that the movement for better race relations was "now at a stand-still." The "stalemate," he said, presented a particular dilemma: "Neither side is winning but both sides are losing." White people would not talk to blacks, he charged, and he suspected that not all members of the SCCHR believed in integration. "If we want to sell the idea of complete integration to any group we must believe in it ourselves," he insisted, "or else we will never get the car cranked to begin to go anywhere." Integration, he assured SCCHR moderates, "does not necessarily mean intermarriage," going to someone's home "for dinner or a cocktail," or even attending church. Integration meant equal job opportunities, equal access to housing and education, voting rights, and the opportunity to run for political office. He stressed that blacks and whites needed to talk and called on the clergy in particular to help end segregation. The Ku Klux Klan and Citizens' Councils, Duckett argued, "are surprisingly small groups" that lacked widespread support. He strongly recommended that blacks and whites "keep the line of communications open," but by this time, Duckett and other black ministers were weary of white timidity.[57]

By the fall of 1959, the SCCHR's financial woes led Spearman to reevaluate its role. "We hope to continue to coordinate our program with that of Penn Center, CORE, the NAACP, and the more conservative Negro organizations as well," she explained. She remained optimistic that the SCCHR "can make much progress." On December 1, 1959, Spearman complained to Ella Baker, executive director of the Southern Christian Leadership Conference (SCLC) in Atlanta, that the NAACP had become too controversial in the South. The SCLC, Spearman suggested, might reach blacks who "have been frightened by the aggressive role of the NAACP." Spearman not only "felt very much on the same wave length" as Baker but also confessed that she "was just wild about her." She had made arrangements with Baker for Martin Luther King Jr. to speak in South Carolina.[58]

By this time, Ella Baker was as impatient with the SCLC as she had been when she resigned her position with the NAACP after World War II. Such organizations were strangled by bureaucracy and ignored grassroots efforts. Reflecting on the role of the SCCHR, Spearman admitted that "it wasn't a thing but a symbol of faith." Both women were frustrated by missed opportunities, and as the 1950s ended, neither was optimistic that the movement could be accelerated. During the darkest days of the 1950s, James McBride Dabbs, James Hinton, John McCray, Modjeska Simkins, Alice Spearman, Marion Wright, and many other less well known South Carolinians never faltered. Their struggle to hold high ground would inspire and fortify the new generation.[59]

12 Bibles and Bayonets

*Everything is lovely. The year was one big success except that those
nine kids have been there and have been through hell every day.*
—J. O. Powell

*Walking up the steps that day was probably one of the biggest feelings
I've ever had.*
—Ernest Green

In the conventional telling of Little Rock's Central High School story, elite women and businessmen prevail over lower-class segregationists. But it took over a year after the crisis began in the summer of 1957 for elite women to find their voices and six more months and a teachers' purge to stir businessmen. The usual story features a pliant governor, a mob of rural rednecks, long-suffering black students, federal troops, noble teachers, and triumphant moderates. The crisis during the 1957–58 school year could more accurately be called a confrontation between Little Rock's working-class blacks and whites, who were competing for jobs, education, and respectability in a decade of great social change. The collision occurred in Little Rock because Governor Orval Faubus failed to ensure order during those treacherous times and because for a year, whether from fear or from complicity, nearly every white leader avoided supporting school integration.[1]

In his 1968 book, *Gothic Politics in the Deep South: Stars of the New Confederacy*, Robert Sherrill quoted an observation in the *London Economist* that Governor Orval Faubus's name, like that of the Roman general Fabian, might some day be associated with a particular strategy—"Faubian tactics, or the techniques of fighting a losing battle in such a way as to cause the greatest loss to all concerned." Yielding to his political ambitions, Faubus opposed a federal court order, encouraged violence, ignored opportunities to end the conflict, and permitted class and racial fissures to split the Little Rock community. As much as any incident in the 1950s, the Central High School crisis disclosed white working-class attitudes toward African Americans. The crisis was more than the last "Rebel yell." It provoked a strategic realignment of segregationist forces that sent women, ministers, and high school students to the front lines. For over a year, this segregationist coalition charmed the governor, initiated unrest inside Central High School, intimidated school administrators, and silenced Little Rock's business and civic leaders. Segregationists were especially clever at mixing defiance with portrayals of themselves as victims. By the end of the school year, nearly everyone in the city—black or white, old or young, male or female—claimed to be a victim of Faubian tactics.[2]

Central High School became the focus of black aspirations and white fears. Whatever their inner thoughts, few whites in Little Rock or elsewhere in the South publicly favored integration. Few blacks were consulted about what they thought. Little Rock seemed an unlikely battleground, for by 1957, Arkansas had integrated the state university, several colleges, some public schools, the Little Rock bus system, and several restaurants. Governor Faubus had appointed African Americans to the Democratic State Committee and to state boards and commissions. His son attended an integrated state college. The city's white community seemed prepared for, or at least resigned to, the fact that nine black students would enter Central High School.[3]

Despite a surface calm over Arkansas, a dedicated group of segregationists had strongly opposed school integration since the *Brown* decision. They hunted for a likely place to make a dramatic stand, and in July 1955, when the small town of Hoxie integrated its elementary school in the glare of national publicity, segregationists mobilized. Black elementary students had previously attended classes in a sagging building with outdoor toilets, a wood-burning stove, broken windows, and a leaking roof, and black high school students were bused twenty miles to Jonesboro. For the black children, the first day of classes at the integrated school, according to a *Life* magazine article, began with tension but ended in harmony: the early morning walk to the bus stop, the nervous ride to school, the cautious wait for class assignment, the acceptance by white teachers and pupils, and finally black and white girls romping across the school yard "arm in arm." A photograph of four white farmers sitting by the roadside sizing up the situation seemed the only cautionary note.[4]

A crowd of 200 Hoxie residents met on August 3 and denounced *Life*'s upbeat story. Soon a flood of segregationist literature deluged the community, and opportunists from outside Hoxie fanned racial fears. Two weeks later, Little Rock lawyer Amis Guthridge, legal counsel for the Capital Citizens' Council, presented a petition to the school board with 1,063 signatures that called for board members to resign. Guthridge and state senator Jim Johnson, who believed his political future was tied to the segregation issue, used inflammatory racist remarks and images to rouse a crowd at Walnut Ridge, the county seat. In November 1955, Johnson began publishing a monthly magazine, *Arkansas*

Amis Guthridge.
UPI Photograph.
J. N. Heiskell Historical
Collection, Archives and
Special Collections,
University of Arkansas,
Little Rock.

Faith, that sensationalized race and sex and occasionally strayed over the line of good taste. One subscriber complained about the use of the word "rectum" and other offensive terms in the magazine.[5]

The 1956 Democratic gubernatorial primary pitted incumbent Orval Faubus against Jim Johnson. Faubus saw Johnson's emotional racist campaign and the Arkansas congressional delegation's unanimous support for the Southern Manifesto as a united front against school integration. Johnson used *Arkansas Faith*, his name recognition from the Hoxie conflict, television spots, and support from outspoken southern segregationists in his campaign. Although he lost to Faubus, he was poised to run for governor again in 1958. In Faubus's calculations, southern political winds favored segregation, and he trimmed his sails accordingly. He desperately wanted a third term.[6]

Orval Eugene Faubus was an enigmatic and contradictory figure. A frail infant who barely survived childhood, he received a smattering of education in the Greasy Creek community in the Ozarks where he was raised. His father, John Samuel Faubus, was a member of the Socialist Party. After briefly enrolling at leftist Commonwealth College, Orval Faubus entered politics. He supported the New Deal and later joined Winthrop Rockefeller in advocating industrialism as the state's salvation. Still, hill country speech and manners clung to Faubus.[7]

Desegregation had apparently progressed too far in Arkansas to assume the emotional pitch it evoked in Mississippi and other Deep South states. On

Jim Johnson addressing a statewide segregationist rally. Margaret Jackson, president of the Mothers' League of Central High School, is seated behind Johnson to the right. UPI Photograph. J. N. Heiskell Historical Collection, Archives and Special Collections, University of Arkansas, Little Rock.

the surface, Little Rock residents seemed apathetic about school integration. School superintendent Virgil Blossom carefully planned the transfer of African American students from the all-black Horace Mann High School to Central High School. Disgruntled working-class whites complained that no black students had been transferred to the newly completed Hall High School, situated

Orval Faubus. Larry Obsitnik Collection, Special Collections Division, University of Arkansas Libraries, Fayetteville.

in a predominantly white, affluent section of West Little Rock. With little enthusiasm but grim determination, white city leaders and school officials began the countdown.[8]

Little Rock's segregationists refused to accept school desegregation as inevitable. In the summer of 1957, Amis Guthridge and Malcolm Taylor met with their pastor, James Wesley Pruden, to discuss strategy. Pruden decided to take an active role in the Capital Citizens' Council and during the summer of 1957 sponsored meetings, ran newspaper advertisements, and lobbied Governor Faubus to prevent the desegregation of Central High School. Guthridge and Pruden shaped a powerful strategy that reinvigorated the Capital Citizens' Council.

James Wesley Pruden, born in 1908, descended from an old Arkansas family. His middle name, Wesley, reflected the family's devout Methodist heritage. After winning a scholarship to Bethany College, a Nazarene school in Oklahoma, he converted to the Nazarene faith. Later, he held pastorates in Arkansas and Mississippi before settling in Little Rock. Early in his career, he established a radio program, *The Little Country Church*, and his success on the radio brought him an interdenominational following. Too old for the draft in World War II, Pruden spent the war years preaching at the interdenominational All Souls Church in Scott, just east of Little Rock. After being converted to the Baptist faith by the legendary Missionary Baptist preacher Ben N. Bogard, Pruden moved back to Little Rock and founded Broadmoor Baptist Church. He some-

James Wesley Pruden.
Courtesy Wesley Pruden Jr.

times preached at black churches, but like most white men of his generation, he did not accept black people as his social equals even when preaching the gospel. Segregation gave patriarchal white men one-way access to black society, but it prevented black men from associating with white women as social equals. School integration would fracture that crucial demarcation, and Pruden decided that whatever the risks to his career, he would lead the fight to preserve segregation.[9]

Pruden brilliantly conflated segregation and religion, capturing powerful symbols of Christianity. He invited prominent speakers to address the Capital Citizens' Council. In early August, Pruden targeted Superintendent Virgil Blossom by posing sexually loaded questions about the consequences of school integration in a newspaper advertisement. The advertisement asked whether black males and white females would dance together, whether black and white girls would shower in the same room, whether the PTA would be integrated, and whether black males and white females would enact "tender love scenes" in school dramas. The fact that a man of God posed such frank questions legitimized apprehensions about interracial sex. Patriarchy, anticommunism, resistance to federal intrusion, and control of women's sexuality were adorned in biblical vestments.[10]

Through his friend, Jimmy Karam, Faubus made overtures to the Citizens' Council. In July, the governor met with Guthridge, Pruden, and several others in the upper room above Karam's clothing store. He vaguely agreed to prevent the integration of Central High School in return for Citizens' Council support in the next gubernatorial contest. Faubus began the drift toward a confrontation with the federal government.[11]

Segregationists' power and respectability increased enormously when on August 20 some women in Pruden's congregation founded the Mothers' League of Central High School. Until this time, most southern white women had remained behind the scenes in the segregation crisis. A member of Broadmoor Baptist Church recalled that mothers organized because several had been unsuccessful in transferring their children from Central High School to the newly completed, suburban, and all-white Hall High School. They insisted that mostly working-class white students would mix with blacks. The fact that their children had been assigned to a school with African Americans suggested to these working-class parents that they were regarded as less respectable than the more affluent Hall High School parents.[12]

The Mothers' League was closely tied to both Broadmoor Baptist Church and the Citizens' Council. The first public meeting on August 27 opened and closed with a prayer. Pruden spoke and warned that black and white students were arming and preparing for violence. After a discussion of "inter-racial marriages and resulting diseases which might arise," the Mothers' League decided to petition the governor. Nadine Aaron was elected president, and Mary Thomason, recording secretary.[13]

On August 22, Governor Marvin Griffin of Georgia offered an impassioned defense of segregation at a fund-raising dinner attended by 350 members of the Capital Citizens' Council. Black waiters served. L. D. Foreman, pastor of Shiloh Missionary Baptist Church and head of the Missionary Baptist Seminary, presided. In addition to "Dixie," an organist played such sentimental favorites as "My Old Kentucky Home," "Carry Me Back to Old Virginny," and "Old Man River." The black waiters and sentimental songs evoked Citizens' Council members' vision of a harmonious and segregated past. At the end of the evening, Jim Johnson stood by the door shaking hands with the departing guests as his aide, Phil Stratton, assured them that Johnson would be running for governor. "He knows how to win now," Stratton told them.[14] Faubus interpreted Griffin's stridency, Johnson's persistence, and the Mothers' League's activism as a ground swell of segregationist support.

The Capital Citizens' Council and the Mothers' League presented a respectable public face, but segregationists also mounted an underground movement of intimidation. It was this invisible agenda that abruptly changed Daisy Bates's life. As head of Arkansas's National Association for the Advancement of Colored People (NAACP) state chapters, Bates was widely known and, among whites, extremely unpopular. On August 22, as she sat on her couch listening to the 11:00 P.M. news coverage of Griffin's speech, a rock was hurled through the living room window. An attached note read: "STONE THIS TIME. DYNAMITE NEXT." In the following days, two crosses were burned on the Bateses' front yard, and shots were fired into the house. Some white mothers who had children at Central High called Bates to offer support, but, she added, they "could not publicly express themselves." Bates and other African Americans who would have welcomed strident white support learned that moderate whites would not even endorse token integration.[15]

Daisy Bates's life had prepared her for her role in the Little Rock crisis. Born in Huttig, a small town in southern Arkansas, she discovered as a child that three white men had murdered her mother. She married L. C. Bates, an insurance salesman, and in 1941, they moved to Little Rock. L. C. Bates had majored in journalism at Wilberforce University, and in Little Rock, he edited a crusading newspaper, the *State Press*. Daisy Bates joined the NAACP, and in 1952, she was elected president of the state chapters. She had been an activist for years and faced the school crisis with determination. She followed a number of talented Arkansas black leaders who had struggled for years for equal rights.[16]

As segregationists whispered rumors of violence in Faubus's ear, local, state, and federal leaders pressured him to speak out for peaceful desegregation. Instead, haunted by the ghost of Jim Johnson's racist campaign, Faubus seized the "emotional issue" that he judged would assure him a third term as governor. He had decided that Johnson, the Capital Citizens' Council, the clergy, and the Mothers' League were too politically powerful to resist. Five days before school opened, Faubus testified on behalf of the Mothers' League in the court case it had initiated to postpone integration. Both Mothers' League officer Mary Thomason and Faubus warned of potential violence. The governor claimed to have evidence that blacks and whites were purchasing guns and knives. On August 29, U.S. District Court judge Ronald N. Davies dismissed the Mothers' League complaint and ruled that school should open as planned.[17]

Failing to halt integration through the courts, on Labor Day the Mothers' League instituted a telephone campaign urging women to gather in front of Central High the next morning at six o'clock for a "sunrise service." One woman who attended Broadmoor Baptist Church boasted that she had made some 200 calls. Working-class southern women marched in the front ranks of Little Rock's segregationists. To these women, civil rights initiatives created the specter of black males who could vote, attend schools with whites, and mix freely in white society. Such concerns went at least as far back as the Reconstruction era, when freedmen pursued the goal of manhood—the freedom to head a household, engage in politics, and participate equally in the economy. In the 1950s, whites realized that school integration opened interracial social

Daisy Bates.
WHi (x3) 52097,
State Historical Society
of Wisconsin, Madison.

space. According to the conventional wisdom among southern whites, a white woman who had a relationship with a black man was lowdown. School integration ruptured that assumption and made all students equal.[18]

The three black males who would attend Central High presented no real threat to white females, but in the minds of white segregationists, they represented the myth of black male equality and sexual prowess. Segregation laws were constructed in large part to prevent whites and blacks from sharing the same social space as equals. White men had customarily shielded their sexual encounters with black women, but school desegregation threatened to legitimize such relationships. Because whites attributed strong sexual urges to African American women, integration could also tempt white males to cross the color line. School integration could lead to interracial relationships, and southern society had no public space for color-line transgressions.

Pruden's active role, the prayers at the beginning and end of segregationist meetings, and the use of religious rhetoric such as "sunrise service" (a term associated with Easter and the Resurrection) clothed both the Citizens' Council and the Mothers' League in the protective mantle of religion. Many fundamentalist ministers seized on the crisis at Central High School to assume community leadership roles. In their minds, speaking out to preserve segregation enhanced their respectability. The merging of religious rhetoric, women's activism, and the emotional issue of integration invoked enormous power and potential. It would not be the last time the formula appeared.[19]

Wesley Pruden presiding over a Capital Citizens' Council meeting. LC-U9-1525-P #24, *Prints and Photographs Division, Library of Congress, Washington, D.C.*

No state or local leader stepped forward to remind citizens that the nine black students were painfully selected tokens, that the desegregation of Central High School set no state precedent, or that outright opposition to the Supreme Court's *Brown* decision raised serious legal questions. More important, no one dispelled the rumors of students arming themselves with knives, guns, and acid-filled water pistols. On Sunday, September 1, several moderate pastors urged their congregations to abide by the law, but few moderates publicly contested segregationists. Segregationists made threatening phone calls to school administrators and members of the Little Rock school board, a tactic they soon used against teachers and black parents.[20]

On Labor Day, the day before school opened, Governor Faubus announced on television at 10:15 P.M. that to preserve order and prevent violence he had called out the National Guard to prohibit the desegregation of Central High. After boasting of the state's progress in race relations, he condemned federal intrusion, justified state interposition, and reiterated the potential for violence. For those who had not received telephone calls from the Mothers' League, the governor helpfully announced that parents planned to "assemble peaceably" at six o'clock the next morning at the school. He predicted that caravans "will converge upon Little Rock from many points of the state." The governor, in effect, invited segregationists to rally at Central High and provoked the crisis that would touch so many lives in the coming year.[21]

In his interposition gambit, Faubus relied on President Dwight D. Eisenhower's ambivalence on federal civil rights legislation enforcement and on Texas and Tennessee precedents set a year earlier. Mansfield, Texas, much like Hoxie, Arkansas, had a small black population, an inadequate black elementary school building, and a single teacher for the eight grades at the school. Black high school students rode a bus twenty miles to Fort Worth. Mansfield whites defied a federal court order to integrate, and in late August, several hundred segregationists demonstrated in front of the high school. When local police were outnumbered, the NAACP requested protection from both Governor Allan Shivers, who sent Texas Rangers to support segregationists, and President Eisenhower, who ignored the crisis. With no state or federal support, the NAACP abandoned the fight. Black elementary students returned to their shabby building, and black high school students continued their twenty-mile bus ride for eight more years.[22]

Tennessee governor Frank Clement, on the other hand, had used state power to support integration in Clinton. The town's black high school students had formerly been bused to Knoxville, fifteen miles away, but on August 27, 1956, 12 black students attended school with 715 whites. On August 29, John Kasper, who had incited other demonstrations across the South, addressed a vicious mob of 1,000 people. When federal marshals took him into custody, North Alabama Citizens' Council leader Asa Carter arrived and stirred the mob to such a pitch that even the beefed-up Clinton police could not maintain control. To restore order, Governor Clement sent in the highway patrol and then the National Guard.[23]

As President Eisenhower evaded the crisis in Little Rock, Governor Faubus called out the National Guard, a direct challenge to federal authority. Faubus's predicted caravans and multitudes did not materialize at Central High School on September 3. Later, Jim Johnson would admit, "There wasn't any caravan." Segregationists, he slyly added, had convinced Faubus "that the sky was going to fall." The Citizens' Council, the Mothers' League, disgruntled parents, students, and pastors formed the crowd's core. Some students wore Confederate caps, and the Mothers' League's Mary Thomason led the crowd in singing "Dixie." Symbols of rebellion, including a Confederate flag, were in view, but even as the crowd flexed its muscles, it remained nonviolent. No black students attended school that day. Assistant Principal Elizabeth Huckaby, who was twice stopped by National Guardsmen on her way into the school, was irate to find soldiers at every door. "Shocking sell-out to the Segregationists!," she later confided to her diary.[24]

On September 4, Daisy Bates decided the time had come to test Central High School's color line. Seven of the nine students, along with several African American and white ministers, approached the school. "This school is off limits to Negro students and Negro Schools are off limits to white students," Colonel Marion E. Johnson of the National Guard told them. Another black student, Terrence Roberts, approached the school alone and stood at the entrance for a few minutes before a guard told him he could not enter. He then walked away.[25]

Fifteen-year-old Elizabeth Eckford had not received word of the rendezvous and took a public bus to school. "When I got to 14th Street on Park," she recalled, "I walked across the street to enter on the school grounds. I was stopped . . . by a member of the National Guard who was in uniform." He turned her away. All the while, white students on the school grounds and the mob outside the school were shouting, "Nigger go on to your own school, you have better schools than we do" and "Nigger go back to Africa." Mary Anita Sedberry of the Mothers' League claimed that she would have "snatched her hair out" if the National Guard had not been there. Amid the chaos surrounding her, Eckford walked to a bus stop and sat on a bench. As the television cameras rolled, still photographers snapped pictures, reporters posed questions, and the crowd screamed out epithets, Eckford outwardly maintained serene poise. Grace K. Lorch, the wife of a professor at Philander Smith College, stood nearby "intending to protect her if anyone should try to harm her." Lorch and *New York Times* reporter Benjamin Fine eventually accompanied Eckford to her bus, and she went to her mother's workplace. Despite the emotional turmoil of the white mob at Central High, no one was injured.[26]

Hazel Bryan came to school with her father but quickly joined her friend, Sammie Dean Parker, whose parents, Marie and J. D., were also in the crowd. Both girls joined the mob screaming at Eckford. Photographer Will Counts captured Bryan angrily shouting at Eckford, an image that appeared in *Life* magazine and evoked the tension and anger of the moment. Within a week, Bryan's parents transferred her to Fuller High School, which was closer to her home and safely away from the crisis.[27]

After being turned away from school, Melba Pattillo and her mother realized that the mob was focusing on Elizabeth Eckford. They knew they could do nothing to help, so they left. Mrs. Pattillo went to her teaching job, and Melba whiled away the time at home listening to Nat King Cole and Johnny Mathis records and reading *Seventeen* and *True Romance* magazines. Then she telephoned her friend, Minniejean Brown, and they decided to go to the commu-

Hazel Bryan. Courtesy Hazel Bryan Massery.

nity center, but Pattillo's grandmother insisted that she remain at home. Melba Pattillo, like the other black students, had been involved in many school activities and was accustomed to a teenager's hectic social life. It would take time to adjust to being a symbol instead of a typical high school student. The Pattillos, like the Parkers and Bryans, were hardworking upwardly mobile people. Their children were in many ways typical teenagers—until 1957, when they were swept into the turmoil at Central High School.[28]

All week, Elizabeth Huckaby observed the mob outside the school and occasionally spotted students among the crowd. On Thursday, she confided to her diary that Sammie Dean Parker, whom she described as "a twitchy little blonde," claimed that *New York Times* reporter Benjamin Fine had offered some boys $10 to start a fight. On Friday morning, Huckaby interviewed Parker and several National Guardsmen about Parker's accusation. Huckaby warned students to stay away from the crowd and was extremely upset on September 11 when she learned "that a group of eight or ten boys and girls had been dancing rock and roll in the street under the eyes of TV cameras, as school began." Huckaby cautioned one of the girls "to stay out of street scenes." The student explained that reporters had urged them to dance. Since the crowds had diminished, Huckaby suspected that the reporters were desperate for news. Confederate flags still waved occasionally, and strains of "Dixie" wafted into the open schoolroom windows.[29]

On September 9, the Council of Church Women of Little Rock and North

Elizabeth Huckaby.
The Pix, *1958. Archives
and Special Collections,
University of Arkansas,
Little Rock.*

Little Rock approved a resolution denouncing Faubus's actions and proclaiming that "enforced segregation of any group of persons because of race, creed or color is a violation of Christian principles." In the heated cauldron of Little Rock, this resolution vaporized, leaving hardly a trace. Most of Little Rock's white residents either supported Faubus or remained silent. The *Christian Century*, on the other hand, labeled Faubus's actions "treason."[30]

Under pressure to resolve the crisis, Faubus met with Eisenhower on September 14, and an opportunity to end the conflict arose. The president advised the governor to order the National Guard to escort the black students into Central High to preserve order. Instead, Faubus withdrew the National Guard on September 20 and left town to attend a governor's conference. City police took over the responsibility for crowd control, and schoolteachers and administrators arrived at school on September 23, in Assistant Principal Elizabeth Huckaby's words, "not knowing what to expect."[31]

The black students had gathered that morning at Daisy Bates's house. When they arrived together at Central High, ruffians in the crowd were chasing and beating four African American reporters. In the confusion, the black students entered the school almost unobserved through a side door. After a brief greeting from Principal Jess Matthews, they went to class. Segregationist students welcomed them with taunts, epithets, and shoves. In shorthand class, Melba Pattillo looked out at the crowd. "The ocean of people stretched farther than I could see—waves of people ebbing and flowing, shoving the sawhorses and the policemen who were trying to keep them in place." When word arrived that city police and state troopers could no longer hold back the crowd, the black students assembled in the principal's office. In the hasty tactical discussion, someone suggested sacrificing one of the black students to placate and divert the crowd. Chief of Police Gene Smith boldly took the students to the basement, put them in two cars, and instructed the drivers not to stop for any reason. Huckaby recorded a brief account of the day in her diary. "A scandalous and humiliating experience," she wrote. "I hope my worst day of teaching."[32]

A number of segregationist students had vowed to leave school if the black students entered. Sammie Dean Parker left the building with her books but returned several times to encourage other students to leave. Assistant Police Chief R. E. Glasscock apprehended her after she broke through police lines a fourth time despite being warned that "she was just inciting trouble." She was "screaming for everybody to get out," Glasscock remembered. Although she was not formally arrested, a ride to the police station in a paddy wagon and brief incarceration made Parker both a celebrity and a victim. J. D. Parker followed the paddy wagon and demanded his daughter's release.[33]

Daisy Bates, who was living under siege and paying private guards for protection during this time, coordinated the students' departure for school and counseled them when they returned. Many of her black neighbors feared that her actions endangered the community, and whites targeted her for abuse and possibly violence. On September 23, she telephoned NAACP leader Gloster B. Current and told him that the mob was "imported from the rural areas—real red necks." Bates did not want the students to go back to school the next day. "I am afraid the children may be killed," she said. "It's vicious down here." She suspected that Faubus was hoping for violence, which would fulfill his earlier predictions.[34]

Bates had correctly identified outsiders in the crowd. Amis Guthridge, among others, had actively recruited Arkansas segregationists. Some came armed and boasted that they could raise a segregationist regiment in several days. "Most of the rioters were laborers," television reporter John Chancellor wrote. "Many were in overalls, and reporters in the crowd were easy to identify." But few in the crowd fit the rural redneck mold. Neither photographs nor television footage captured many individuals in overalls. Most of the men and women were dressed casually but neatly; it was, at its core, a respectable-looking working-class crowd. Parents, pastors, students, and curiosity-seekers mixed with a few obvious troublemakers. At the height of the crisis, 250 reporters mingled with the crowd. "There was a definite feeling of Yankee vs. Rebel in Little Rock," Chancellor recalled thirty years later.[35]

People in the crowd were not of one mind. On September 9, the day school desegregation was attempted at North Little Rock High School, Mrs. Dale Richter took exception to "the use of bad language and irresponsible threats" by

The Little Rock nine and Daisy Bates. Left to right, standing: *Ernest Green, Melba Pattillo, Terrence Roberts, Carlotta Walls, Daisy Bates, and Jefferson Thomas;* sitting: *Thelma Mothershed, Minniejean Brown, Elizabeth Eckford, and Gloria Ray.* LC-USZ62-119154, *National Association for the Advancement of Colored People Papers, Prints and Photographs Division, Library of Congress, Washington, D.C.*

other segregationists and especially the vicious verbal abuse of *New York Times* reporter Benjamin Fine. An unidentified barmaid from the Ship Ahoy Bar had screamed, "Hey, Jew, why don't you go back to your nigger wife." When Richter objected to this language and claimed that "big mouths were hurting the segregationist cause," the barmaid called her "an obvious nigger lover." In the melee, someone punched Benjamin Fine in the ribs.[36]

Although the beatings and intimidation indicated that rough and violent people were in the crowd, the identities of the leaders have remained a mystery.

A *Life* magazine story placed businessman Jimmy Karam in the midst of the violence, nodding and whispering to "his burly aides." Karam was strategically positioned to make Faubus's prediction of violence come true. No matter where they came from, almost all of the people in the crowd considered school integration a major transgression of racial etiquette. Given the crowd's state of anxiety, any hothead could have set it off. Dissociating the mob from Little Rock and depicting it as rural and racist, which many reporters did, distanced the crisis from local residents, especially from the city's silently moderate whites. The mob members were portrayed as white trash from somewhere down the road.[37]

Fundamentalist ministers were among the most dedicated advocates of segregation, and one pastor counted twenty-two segregationist clergymen in the crowd. Pruden appeared every day. Corbett Mask, pastor of the Spring Creek Baptist Church in Benton, drove to Central High each morning (after his radio show) with another pastor. Mask had signed a resolution at a meeting of the State Association of Missionary Baptist Churches of Arkansas in November 1954 denouncing the *Brown* decision. L. D. Foreman, president of the Missionary Baptist Seminary in Little Rock, came to the school almost daily and readily admitted to *New York Times* reporter Benjamin Fine that he was a segregationist. He had signed a resolution supporting segregation at the Pine Bluff Missionary Baptist Convention in 1955 and regularly wrote articles for the *Missionary Baptist Searchlight*. After school opened, he deplored the erosion of states' rights and defended Faubus's use of the National Guard. He judged in-

Two women arguing in the crowd outside Central High School.
Photograph by Bern Keating. Prints and Photographs Division,
Library of Congress, Washington, D.C. Courtesy Black Star.

tegration "unscriptural, unscientific and unconstitutional." Foreman blamed
the NAACP and communists for stirring up the integration crisis. "We can say
what we want to," he wrote, "but those of us who know the colored race, also
know that the majority of them are backward and slow intellectually." He admitted exceptions but argued that mixing black and white students would
lower educational standards. Foreman articulated the beliefs of many Missionary Baptists.[38]

Other fundamentalist ministers rose to prominence almost overnight as segregationist spokesmen, writing letters to the editor, placing advertisements supporting Faubus, challenging moderate ministers to integrate their churches,
backing segregationist political candidates, and proselytizing among mainstream congregations. A 1959 study referred to fundamentalist ministers as
"sect pastors," but the authors warned that "it is a mistake to minimize the dis-
sident ministerial elements by saying that they are poorly educated, fanatical
pastors whose small flocks lack community influence." While most mainstream
clergy remained quiet during the crisis, fundamentalist pastors stridently

Men in the crowd outside Central High School.
Photograph by Bern Keating. Prints and Photographs Division,
Library of Congress, Washington, D.C. Courtesy Black Star.

supported segregation. They "gloated" when blacks were turned away by congregations whose ministers supported school integration. Their rhetoric and zeal elevated the segregationist fever in Little Rock. The more elite churches, the study explained, "prefer more tact, restraint and *savoir faire* than the segregationists characteristically demonstrate." But segregationists composed a large part of the congregations of even churches with moderate pastors. Most church members seemed quite willing to suspend the Golden Rule to preserve segregation.[39]

To most fundamentalists, integration was one of many assaults on their faith, which included questioning the Virgin birth, the deity of Christ, and the inviolability of the scriptures. Such deviations were manifestations of modernism that, in their terminology, polluted Christianity. On another level, working-class white families personified the tensions that haunted 1950s fundamentalism. Many were rising on the tide of 1950s prosperity, and whether rural or urban-born, they took pride in having good jobs and respectable homes. Their children embraced 1950s styles and music even when they conflicted with fundamentalist proscriptions, for dancing and black music were crucial ingredients of youth culture. Some parents turned their heads, while others more receptive to 1950s culture encouraged their children's mildly transgressive social activities.

Many working-class families saw school integration as a threat to upward mobility. Sammie Dean Parker's mother, Marie, operated a beauty parlor in her home that became a forum for gossip and speculation. J. D. Parker worked for the railroad. Upward mobility had taken the family from North Little Rock to a more respectable neighborhood near Central High School. His friends dropped by to chat and ruminate. As much as any Little Rock working-class family, the Parkers personified not only the hopes and fears of upwardly mobile whites but also the religious contradictions. Associating with African Americans on an equal basis undermined the dreams of such working-class white families as well as raising fears. At an integrated Central High, black and white students could dance together or even date. Religion, race, sex, and status fueled a combustible mixture of emotions.[40]

Little Rock residents waited anxiously after the crisis of September 23. The nine black students did not attend Central on September 24, nor did a third of the white students. Press coverage, especially television footage, raised the Little Rock crisis to national and then international importance, and newspapers and magazines featured stories about the crowd and the black students. President Eisenhower at last decided that enforcement of the federal court order necessitated military intervention, and he sent the 101st Airborne to Little Rock. Segregationists who had praised Faubus for calling out the National Guard now condemned the use of federal troops as an insulting abuse of power and a violation of states' rights. Federal intrusion opened a spigot of archaic southern rhetoric. To segregationists, the crisis recalled nullification, antebellum glory, secession, and their heroic version of the Civil War and Reconstruction.

The nine African American students arrived at the school on September 25 with a military escort. Melba Pattillo remembered hearing "that chillingly familiar but now muffled chant, 'Two, four, six, eight. We ain't gonna integrate.'" She also saw reporters lined up across the street and helicopters overhead. Pattillo walked up the main steps to Central High School, where, she remembered, "none of my people had ever before walked as students." Ernest Green shared the moment. "Walking up the steps that day was probably one of the biggest feelings I've ever had," he recalled. "I figured I had finally cracked it."[41]

Elizabeth Huckaby was impressed with the 101st. "Efficiency of troops remarkable after N.G.," she wrote in her diary. Commanding General Edwin A. Walker spoke to the assembled students and urged compliance with the law; soldiers and Federal Bureau of Investigation agents patrolled the halls. Principal Jess Matthews welcomed the black students, and then they went to class, escorted by the troops. Huckaby accompanied three of the black students to lunch. "They were invited to sit with white girls. About 75 kids left when Negroes came," she wrote in her diary. "Remaining pupils varied from friendliness to coldness toward them."[42]

Another opportunity for closure appeared. Despite organizing a hard-core group of segregationists, the Citizens' Council, the clergy, and the Mothers' League had failed to keep African Americans out of Central High School. The crowd had sung "Dixie," waved the Confederate flag, cursed the Supreme Court, and even beaten black reporters. Still, the nine black students were inside Central High School. Both sides could have declared victory as well as defeat. But closure would not come for years. The effort to get inside the building was only the first campaign in the Central High School war.

Many, perhaps most, students at Central High School were content to allow desegregation to proceed. After all, 9 black students could easily be assimilated into a student body of nearly 2,000 and even conveniently ignored. Were it not for a group of segregationist students who were determined either to drive the black students out or to provoke them into conflict, the first year of desegregation at Central might have gone smoothly. Supported and to some extent directed by the Capital Citizens' Council, the Mothers' League, and the clergy, segregationist students not only harassed black students but also intimidated white students who befriended them. The fact that a small gang of segregationist students could generate such disruption demonstrated the strength of their hateful strategy.

Fifteen-year-old Melba Pattillo, who kept a diary and later wrote *Warriors Don't Cry: A Searing Memoir of the Battle to Integrate Little Rock's Central High*, recorded the events of her first day tossing in a sea of white faces. Most white students ignored her, but others tormented her with a steady barrage of insults, slaps, shoves, and stares. In a restroom, away from the guards and teachers, white girls taunted Pattillo and her friends; "Nigger, go home" was written in lipstick on the mirror. She found Huckaby "hard to read" but "determined to carry out her duties." Even with a guard accompanying her, Pattillo was "confronted by a chorus of chants from sideburners." She speculated that these boys modeled their wardrobe and hairstyle on "James Dean and Elvis" and "fancied themselves to be 'bad boys.'" They knocked her books out of her hands and surrounded her and her guard. Other guards appeared and the "sideburners" left, muttering. Daisy Bates, teachers, and school administrators played down such incidents to preserve the notion that desegregation caused little friction.[43]

The James Dean and Elvis Presley look-alikes personified contradictions in style and substance. James Dean invariably played the role of the restless adolescent in rebellion against authority, including adults and especially parents, a "rebel without a cause." The Central High School "bad boys" enforced their parents' segregationist ideology; they were rebels of a lost cause. Elvis Presley dressed in Beale Street African American–style clothes, and, as much as any white musician, infused white culture with black style. The sideburners' tough demeanor thus was modeled on Hollywood-style rebellion filtered through James Dean and black culture as translated by Elvis Presley. During the crisis, Jerry Lee Lewis's "Whole Lot of Shakin' Going On" was climbing the charts, a blatant celebration of sexual expression. Popular culture had created sideburners' style and even musical preferences, but they rejected its message of cultural fusion. In their assault on the black students, they rebelled not against parents but against school staff and, in a larger sense, the federal government. The caption of John Vachon's photograph of nineteen-year-old Virginia Lemon in *Look* indicated that she "likes Elvis Presley and James Dean." The picture shows Lemon smiling warmly as she wears a Confederate cap and waves a Confederate flag. These Elvis Presley and James Dean wannabees dressed the dress and walked the walk, but they did not talk the talk. Style could serve many masters.[44]

Such style extended far beyond Central High. In August 1957, National Council of Churches activist Will D. Campbell reported on conditions in Nashville. He focused on John Kasper, who had formerly stirred up trouble in Clinton, Tennessee. "A word about Kasper's followers," he noted: "they are low income folk, the type generally called 'red-necks.' Some, his most intimate followers, are young men and women of the long-sideburn, ducktailed haircut set, bully-boys and girls who operate in packs." None of these folks were respectable, he concluded.[45]

The crisis sent shock waves throughout the country, but it especially incensed white southerners. They reacted with outrage to the use of federal troops and praised Governor Faubus for resisting integration. The image of citizens being threatened and poked with bayonets spread across the South. White southerners portrayed themselves as victims of federal power, just as they had nearly a century before during Reconstruction. Mounting opposition to the use of federal troops prompted the Eisenhower administration to take a less active role. Melba Pattillo, who had perceived growing friendliness among some white students, noticed a change on Tuesday, October 1, when the 101st turned over most of its duties to the federalized Arkansas National Guard. She heard more taunts, and when she saw guardsmen loitering in the hall, she felt alone. "During the afternoon, when I went into the principal's office several times to report being sprayed with ink, kicked in the shin, and heel-walked until the backs of my feet bled, as well as to report the name of my constant tormentor," she wrote, "the clerks asked why I was reporting petty stuff."[46]

Stamps commemorating the Little Rock crisis.
Thomas Abernethy Papers, Special Collections, University of Mississippi, Oxford.

Elizabeth Huckaby also noted the change when the 101st moved into the background, and she admitted that school administrators had underestimated the power of the segregationists, who, she judged, were "not people one would call the backbone of the community." They were not only tightly organized but also had the power of the state government behind them. Inside the massive school, discipline broke down completely. Huckaby reported that "the pack was chasing and harassing the Negro children as they got a chance." A white student admitted, "We chased them from one end of the school to the other." During the chaos, Pattillo spotted guardsmen "lounging against the walls like cats in sunlight." They stood around "with smug, grinning expressions on their faces." The next day, some 50 to 100 white students walked out of school to protest the presence of blacks.[47]

Melba Pattillo and Minniejean Brown asked Daisy Bates to demand protection, and she arranged a meeting with school administrators and National Guard leaders. Pattillo instantly disliked General Sherman Clinger, the head of the Arkansas National Guard. As he talked and the school administrators wrung their hands, Pattillo found the courage to speak up to white adults. She told Clinger they would leave unless they received protection, and the other students agreed. Clinger then assigned eighteen guardsmen to accompany the black students at all times. "Those Arkansas guardsmen were the biggest, dumbest, most disheveled hayseeds I'd ever seen," Pattillo remembered. "They looked as if they had slept in their rumpled uniforms." The guardsmen's appearance was so ridiculous that when the black students walked down the hall followed by the guardsmen, even the white students laughed. "For just one moment," Pattillo wrote later, "we all realized the ridiculous situation we were caught up in." In a less tense world not poisoned by racism, that moment would have had the potential to defuse the crisis, but at Central High, it merely passed.[48]

Because the black students were thrust into school as symbols and not individuals, most white students never got to know them. Rumors spread among segregationists that the NAACP had recruited several of the students from the North for special duty. School administrators apparently made no effort to dispel such rumors or to introduce the nine black students to the student body. Black students negotiated a narrow corridor between hostility and indifference. White students did not realize that most of the nine came from respectable middle- or working-class families, nor did they understand that these active, bright, and highly motivated students were sacrificing the opportunity to participate in extracurricular activities and high school social life to implement the *Brown* decision. The tragedy was not that whites and blacks were so different but that they did not realize how similar they were. To a large extent, they were all part of 1950s youth culture. They danced to the same music, listened to the same radio stations, read the same magazines (which rarely featured African Americans), dressed according to magazine and peer fashion cues, and dreamed similar teenage dreams. Perhaps teachers and administrators feared that knowledge of their shared interests would constitute a breach of the color line.

At Central High, the nine black students faced open hatred, guarded violence, and studied indifference. Years later, they would recall the occasional smile. Elizabeth Eckford endured the September 4 mobbing incident and resolutely continued at Central High. Even though at times she became deeply troubled by white hostility, she maintained her poise. Her father, like Sammie Dean Parker's, worked for the Missouri Pacific Railroad. Minniejean Brown was a tall, attractive, outgoing, and spirited eleventh-grader. She was a prime target of segregationist attacks intended to goad black students into striking back.[49]

Gradually, the black students emerged as individuals. Jefferson Thomas's tentative manner, Elizabeth Huckaby reasoned, provoked harassment from the school's bullies. Daisy Bates thought that next to Minniejean Brown, Thomas received most of the segregationists' unwelcome attention. Terrence Roberts was an excellent student. He almost quit Central at one point in February after being kicked viciously, but the next day, he resolutely continued. He did not want to hand the segregationists a victory.[50]

Thelma Mothershed, who had a heart condition, was barely five feet tall, and her fragile demeanor did not offer an inviting target even to the segregationists. She was the only one of the nine students who was born outside Little Rock. Fourteen-year-old Carlotta Walls, with her fast pace and "swinging, athletic gait," earned the honorary title, "the Ridge Runner." One day Walls turned on one of her tormenters, stomped on her foot, and called her names; the white student backed off. "You know, today was rather a nice day at school," she admitted to Daisy Bates. Gloria Ray was the youngest of three children, and her father, who had a heart condition, was a retired agricultural agent. Harvey Ray discovered that his daughter had agreed to attend Central High on September 4, when, during Elizabeth Eckford's ordeal, a television newscaster read the names of the black students.[51]

Ernest Green, the only senior in the group, endured harassment with an even disposition. When his father, a World War I veteran, passed away in 1953, Green became the head of the household. His mother taught elementary school. At times, his mother recalled, he would return home angry. He once told her he had been punched when he tried to stop an assault on Carlotta Walls. He confessed to his mother that "it makes me so mad that those morons continue to pick on us time and again and nothing is done about it." Because the black students were barred from participating in extracurricular activities, he was not allowed to play saxophone in the school band. Being the oldest and in some ways the most mature of the nine, Green was seen as the leader.[52]

The area's religious leaders, both those for and those against integration, sponsored a day of prayer for order and guidance on October 12. Some eighty-five churches participated, about twenty of them African American. The Capital Citizens' Council, meanwhile, ran newspaper advertisements that criticized ministers who favored school integration but did not accept blacks into their congregations. On the day of prayer, Reverend Wesley Pruden ran an advertisement asserting that "all races, kindreds and tongues are included in the Love of God" but warning that "race-mixing in our schools is a Communist Doctrine."[53]

Jim Johnson kept the crisis at the forefront of his efforts to achieve his political ambitions. He remained in close contact with Senator James O. Eastland and other leading segregationists, and he publicly threatened to attack Faubus if he showed weakness. "I can literally crucify Faubus in the next election," Johnson gloated to Eastland. To Johnson and his segregationist cohorts, the Central High crisis was a political weapon, and the more unrest there was both inside the school and in the streets, the better for their cause.[54]

On November 14, Hugh Williams "struck" Jefferson Thomas hard enough to knock him down. Williams was suspended. Rumors circulated that Gloria Ray, Melba Pattillo, and Ernest Green were slated next for violence. "Minnie in tears from hurt feelings," Huckaby wrote, "'tired of it all.' Certainly understandable." Daisy Bates considered the Thomas incident serious enough to warrant a meeting with the assistant principal for male students, J. O. Powell, and *Arkansas Gazette* editor Harry Ashmore. The *Gazette* did not carry the story. School administrators and Ashmore agreed to preserve the fiction that no serious harassment was taking place at Central. Privately, Bates claimed that "there was an organized group of students at the school of the White Citizens' Council; that they are only given a three-day suspension, a sort of small vacation and then they are free to return to school and again engage in similar incidents." Principal Matthews handled the segregationists with a velvet glove, refusing to act unless their actions were particularly outrageous and witnessed by a teacher.[55]

Accustomed to participating in extracurricular activities and having leadership roles, the nine black students endured being treated as pariahs at Central. For Minniejean Brown, the role of outcast became increasingly difficult to bear. When Brown asked to be allowed to try out for a talent contest on November 21, Huckaby replied, "You know as well as I do it wouldn't do, Minnie." Huckaby did not understand that performing had become crucial to Brown. "She had decided she would be accepted by white students if she could just show them how beautifully she sang," Melba Pattillo remembered. The Mothers' League was determined to prevent her from performing. Undaunted, Brown insisted on singing in the school Christmas program. Her mother and Daisy Bates argued with Matthews and Huckaby on December 9 that the program was a scheduled class activity. Matthews ruled that Brown could not participate.[56]

On December 17, Brown went over the edge. At lunchtime, as she made her way among crowded cafeteria tables toward her friends, some boys pushed chairs in front of her. "She had stopped dead in her tracks," Melba Pattillo remembered. "It was as though she were in a trance, fighting within herself." Brown's bowl of chili landed on two boys. Principal Matthews suspended Brown. "I can't help liking her natural reaction," Huckaby admitted, "which would be funny if it weren't tragic in its results. This bowl of chili no doubt has been heard around the world!" That afternoon, a new chant started, "One nigger down and eight to go."[57]

Minniejean Brown became the segregationists' target because she, more than her eight friends, refused to be submissive. Tall, outgoing, and aggressive, she challenged racial stereotypes. Elizabeth Huckaby tellingly described her behavior as "just acting too natural!" White female students remembered later that she had an attitude, that she was aloof, that she was overweight, that she "walked those corridors as if she belonged there," that she was easy to tease, that she was defiant, and that she "was a stereotype of a mammy." Amid these contradictions is the implication not only that Minniejean Brown was acting white but also that her aggressive behavior was unacceptable for a female of the 1950s.[58] In that sense, she and her female tormenters had crossed the same line. The double standard of behavior at Central High School implied that if black students could withstand daily torment, avoid fighting back, and give up all semblance of a normal high school life, they might be tolerated by administrators, teachers, and students.

As 1958 began, teachers and administrators perceived that the segregationist gang was out of control. On January 10, a guard saw Darlene Holloway shove Elizabeth Eckford, causing her to stumble down a stairway. He escorted both girls to Huckaby's office. "I took my books and shoved her," Holloway admitted. "I wouldn't *touch* her myself, or any of them." Huckaby suspended Holloway, who then claimed that Matthews "was afraid" to suspend Sammie Dean Parker. After school, a guard brought in James and Wanda Cole, Sammie Dean Parker, and Herbert Blount, accusing them of calling him names for apprehending Holloway. Huckaby noted increased tension after Holloway's suspension.[59]

On Monday, January 13, Minniejean Brown returned to school, and Huckaby commented on her nice appearance "in a new pink felt skirt and a white blouse." At noon, some students spilled ink on the skirt and ruined it. The next day, Elizabeth Eckford was knocked flat by an unknown girl, and Melba Pattillo was inked. After a large Citizens' Council meeting on January 14, white students stepped up their harassment. They arrived the next day with printed "Remember Little Rock" cards, and three of the black girls were inked. Calling cards containing hateful slogans became an underground segregationist currency. Huckaby entered in her diary, "We'll have to get rid of ring-leaders—Sammie Dean, David Sontag, etc." Despite her suspension, Holloway appeared at school wearing a "Remember Little Rock" button. When Huckaby took the badge and asked her to leave, Holloway petulantly replied that she would have to talk to Reverend Pruden, but she soon left.[60]

As Brown was eating with her friends during the second lunch period, David Sontag, Holloway's boyfriend, dumped a bowl of soup on her shoulders. A guard took her to Huckaby's office, where she was checked for burns and given clean clothes. The hall filled with students, and Huckaby observed that "they seemed, most of them, to have been attracted as people are by fires or accidents." Some cheered for Sontag. Mrs. Brown took her daughter home. Sontag's father arrived to meet with school administrators about his son's behavior. Brown had called him "white trash," he complained. A teacher replied, "So you had to prove it." He was expelled.[61]

On January 22, the board of education held a hearing on Holloway's suspension. Members of the Citizens' Council and Mothers' League filled the lobby, and as Huckaby passed them, she remembered, "their faces were full of hate." The board did not admit spectators to the hearing. Amis Guthridge represented Holloway and read aloud from Huckaby's report of the incident, punctuating it with careful inflection. Holloway denied Huckaby's version of events and claimed that she had only brushed against Eckford, who then gave her a dirty look and drew back to hit her. Sammie Dean Parker testified on her friend's behalf. Holloway returned to school. For Huckaby, the experience was humiliating. She described Guthridge as "ignorant, lying, hateful" and ended her diary entry that night with "horrible."[62]

What Huckaby and the other school administrators failed to understand was that the people in the lobby, as unruly as she may have imagined them to be, were seeking respectability. By attempting to undermine Blossom, Huckaby, and Matthews, they hoped to increase their own status. Guthridge met the school administrators as an equal and emphasized his equal status by improvising some dramatics as he read Huckaby's memorandum. The Mothers' League and the Citizens' Council saw school officials as evil enemies who had forced their children to attend school with black people. The crowd members were emotional, unscrupulous, shrill, and manipulative, characteristics that polite people dreaded. In their minds, they triumphed almost in direct proportion to the extent to which they insulted polite society.

For Sammie Dean Parker, the school year had been both stimulating and devastating. She had been photographed hugging the governor, interviewed by the press, and touted as a segregationist heroine. Energy that she might have devoted to her studies had been diverted to efforts to preserve segregation, and her dreams of taking senior drama classes and later attending college dissolved. Instead, she became a dramatic segregationist symbol. She was rumored to be Governor Faubus's eyes and ears inside the school, and she kept both her classmates and her teachers guessing about her movements. For the most part, she willingly yielded herself to the segregationist cause. Attractive and sassy, she eagerly embraced the role of segregationist superstar.

But Parker personified 1950s middle-class aspirations and, until the fall of 1957, was a typical teenager. She had been raised among fundamentalists and experienced conversion at a tender age. As a sophomore in high school, she was popular and active, dancing after school on *Steve's Show*, the Little Rock television sock hop. Proud of her father's upward mobility and doted on by her mother and father, who encouraged her dancing and socializing, Parker expected to continue making good grades and to develop her acting skills. These aspirations changed drastically during her junior year, when her elders, including the clergy, attacked the integration of Central High School. She responded as a true believer. By volubly and emotionally embracing segregation, she disturbed her less vocal, less visible, and more socially ambitious classmates. In some ways, she was the white counterpart of Minniejean Brown, who was seen as committed, articulate, sassy, impudent, and proud. Both teenagers violated proscriptions that relegated girls to the sidelines, and both pursued goals that involved great risks. The scales of history, however, have weighed their roles differently.

Segregationists kept constant pressure on the black students. Minniejean Brown became increasingly apprehensive and asked for a guard. For several days, Frankie Gregg and some of her friends had followed Brown "murmuring, 'Nigger, Nigger, Nigger!'" On February 6, the taunting continued. After Gregg ran into her, Brown paused at the homeroom door and said, "Will you please stop talking to me, white trash." Gregg claimed that she said, "Goodbye, paddy, White trash." Whatever she said, Gregg threw her purse at Brown. In Huckaby's office, Gregg expressed her outrage at being called "a name." Matthews pointed out that both girls were wrong and recommended that they avoid each other.[63]

The day quickly spun out of control. Both Sammie Dean Parker and Darlene Holloway professed a compelling need to leave school. Huckaby later wondered if the day's subsequent events had been orchestrated by the two absent students. After an anonymous caller told Terrence Roberts's mother that he had been injured, she rushed to the school. Many apprehensive white parents also showed up after receiving similar phone calls. Huckaby found Brown trembling in the hall and told her to go to lunch. In the cafeteria, a student dumped soup on her. Again a crowd gathered. Again Brown changed clothes in Huckaby's office and awaited her mother. Guards caught Herbert Blount and Dennis Milam kicking Carlotta Walls on the stairs on her way to lunch. In the cafeteria, Huckaby kept an eye on the remaining black students as a group of segregationists hovered around them. When Matthews, who had been at a Rotary meeting during the morning's events, returned, he expelled Brown for talking back to Gregg and provoking the purse-throwing incident. "The truth, of course, was that we could no longer run the school if Minnijean [sic] was there," Huckaby confided. The souping throwing and harassment would continue since she had become a prime target.[64] Brown was offered as a sacrificial lamb to appease the mob, thus fulfilling a suggestion that had been made on the black students' first day of school. Brown's influence did not end when she left Central High School. In the sixties, students carried on her legacy by continuing to spill soup and challenge white power.

School administrators and teachers kept a tight lid on what was happening at Central High School. As Huckaby confided her innermost thoughts to her diary, on April 23, J. O. Powell talked confidentially with Anti-Defamation League researcher May Anna Holden. His frustration with Matthews boiled over. He labeled the principal "a shaggy dog type—a big, happy man who wants everybody to be happy." Powell found it laughable that Matthews "is accused of being an integrationist." He and Huckaby reported segregationists' offenses day after day, but Matthews would suspend the students only if faculty witnessed the incidents. Powell estimated that some half dozen teachers were avid segregationists but stressed that the younger faculty members and veterans were more favorable to desegregation. He observed that as the year went by, most white Little Rock residents did not want to know what was going on at the school. In elite circles, the subject never came up. The problem, Powell insisted, "is keeping the white punks, the hulligans, from spitting on and kicking the Negro students." Powell argued that if Matthews had taken a strong stand against the segregationist students at the beginning of the school year, the harassment would have stopped. Matthews should have made examples of ten or fifteen students, Powell suggested. Powell quoted Matthews as saying, "If the white kids want to run them off next year, let them do it."[65]

In mid-February, after the parents of the black students met with the school board and complained of lax school discipline, Central High administrators were ordered to "get tough." One student was suspended for shoving Gloria Ray ("She's a nigger," he explained to Powell) and another for wearing a segregationist sign. At last, on February 17, Sammie Dean Parker was suspended for handing out "One Down—Eight to Go" calling cards at the end of the school day. "She cried. She sobbed. She shouted and bawled," Huckaby recorded. Then her father arrived, and the volume increased. "What a blow-up," Huckaby wrote in her diary.[66]

Minniejean Brown left for New Lincoln High School in New York City on February 21, 1958, the same day that the school board held hearings on Sammie Dean Parker's suspension. Amis Guthridge represented her, and the Mothers' League lent support. Huckaby recommended that Parker be readmitted if she agreed to cease her segregationist activities. On Wednesday night, February 26, Matthews, Huckaby, and Blossom met with the Parkers at the superintendent's office. Sammie Dean, Huckaby observed, was dressed in "a white wool dress, mouton jacket, high heels. She did not look like a schoolgirl." Sammie Dean dominated the meeting, complaining of her persecution at the hands of the administrators and insisting that she saw no reason to change her behavior at school. The way the meeting ended varies with the telling. Tempers flared and harsh words were exchanged between Huckaby and Marie Parker. "As the girl snatched the umbrella from my hand," Huckaby recalled, "her mother reached out and took off my glasses, saying, 'I'm going to hit you for what you have done to my daughter.'" Matthews stepped between them. On February 28, the school board expelled Sammie Dean, but J. D. Parker, vowing that she would return, filed a suit against Blossom, Matthews, and Huckaby.[67]

On March 4, Sammie Dean appeared on a special thirty-minute television program on KATV with her mother, Guthridge, and Pruden. She admitted that she had been wearing a "One Down—Eight to Go" button but insisted that three-fourths of the students had been wearing them. She broke down when Guthridge asked what her plans were for the future; she said she wanted to return to school. Marie Parker added that Sammie Dean had been an excellent student before integration began. "Race-mixing at Central High School is a failure," Pruden judged. He then asked for donations to the Capital Citizens' Council. In the same issue of the *Arkansas Gazette* that carried a report of the television program, two other stories disputed Sammie Dean's account of her confrontation with Huckaby and her ride in the paddy wagon in September. The Citizens' Council and the Mothers' League encouraged Sammie Dean's uncanny ability to stay at the center of controversy. If the segregationist plan called for creating trouble in school, Sammie Dean was a formidable tool. Marie Parker realized that the racial crisis had cost her daughter dearly, but the entire family basked in the glare of publicity.[68]

The crisis ended when Sammie Dean appealed to the board. "If you will reinstate me I promise in the future to conform to the rules," she wrote. On March 12, as she returned to school with her father, a television crew interviewed them in front of the school. "She wasted no time," Huckaby bristled, "in swishing about telling about how the School Board begged her to return, and how she didn't have to be responsible to Mrs. Huckaby any more."[69] Sammie Dean was caught in the headlights of the changing times. She and her friends did things that, in retrospect, they found difficult to justify. By choosing segregation, she was swept away in a historical current that would leave her marooned, ignored, or pilloried.

Segregationists failed to deter Ernest Green from his goal of graduating from Central High School. Despite the tension surrounding his pending graduation, the baccalaureate service on the Sunday night before graduation went off peacefully. On Tuesday night, Green graduated with 400 other Central High students. No incidents marred the occasion. Among the guests supporting Green was Martin Luther King Jr., who had spoken that morning at Arkansas Agricultural, Mechanical, and Normal College in Pine Bluff. Green's graduation symbolized a defeat for the segregationists. The school's annual cycle was complete, and it had included the presence of African Americans. The school year was a success, J. O. Powell sardonically judged. The football team had won its games, and *The Mikado* had been performed. "Everything is lovely. The year was one big success except that those nine kids have been there and have been through hell every day."[70]

On June 3, 1958, the endgame began when the Little Rock school board and superintendent petitioned a federal court to suspend desegregation in Little Rock until January 1961 because of the explosive atmosphere at the school. U.S. District Court judge Harry J. Lemley heard the case and paid special attention to reports of violence at the school. On June 20, Lemley ruled that the desegregation of Central High should be halted for two and half years.[71]

Even as the NAACP appealed Lemley's decision, Governor Faubus won the Democratic primary and was assured a third term. Jim Johnson, realizing that Faubus had co-opted his racial issue, won an Arkansas Supreme Court seat. On August 18, the Eighth Circuit Court of Appeals reversed Lemley's decision, and on September 12, the U.S. Supreme Court ordered Little Rock to comply with the decision. Yet another chance for closure appeared. Since Faubus had been assured his coveted third term and the Supreme Court stood firm, he could have given his blessing to the integration of the schools. Instead, Faubus immediately ordered all high schools in Little Rock closed for the coming academic year.[72] Parents began a chaotic scramble to place students with relatives outside Little Rock and to open private schools.

Only when the question came down to whether the white residents of Little Rock preferred no schools to desegregated schools did three elite white women, Adolphine Fletcher Terry, Vivian Brewer, and Velma Powell, organize the Women's Emergency Committee to Open Our Schools (WEC). "The men have failed," Terry announced to editor Harry Ashmore. "It's time to call out the women." On September 16, 1958, well-educated, influential, and resolute Adolphine Terry invited fifty women to her house to discuss the school issue. Except for the fact that they were all white, WEC members contrasted sharply with members of the Mothers' League. They had more education and higher family incomes, were active in civic organizations, and attended Methodist, Presbyterian, and Episcopal churches. WEC members saw themselves as opponents of the Capital Citizens' Council, the fundamentalist clergy, and the Mothers' League. "We had been disgraced by a group of poor whites and a portion of the lunatic fringe that every town possesses," Terry judged. The WEC organized to reopen the schools, not to integrate them. The first test came on September 27 when Faubus scheduled a special referendum on whether or not to integrate the schools. Although the WEC did not prevail, members obtained valuable organizational experience.[73]

In mid-November, Virgil Blossom's contract was bought out, and the entire school board resigned. The WEC played an active role in the next election and managed to stalemate the school board with three moderates to oppose the three segregationists. In May 1959, a major crisis erupted when a rump session of the school board fired forty-four teachers and administrators who allegedly favored integration. At last, the city's male leadership took action and founded the Committee to Stop This Outrageous Purge (STOP). The Citizens' Council and Mothers' League countered with the Committee to Retain Our Segregated Schools (CROSS), which encouraged boycotts of businessmen who joined STOP. The WEC worked behind the scenes and supported STOP in its successful sponsorship of moderates in the May 1959 school board vote. Throughout the crisis, whites fought each other but ignored black leaders. Many whites continued to regard the NAACP and Daisy Bates as radicals, and most whites, including the school board members, refused to meet with blacks to discuss options. In August 1959, Little Rock schools reopened with token integration. Segregationists gathered at the state capitol and started to march toward Central High School, but city police and firemen dispersed them.[74]

On the fortieth anniversary of the crisis, scholars, politicians, and former students, teachers, and administrators converged at Central High School for a retrospective conference. Hazel Bryan Massery, who was pictured screaming at Elizabeth Eckford, had apologized to Eckford several years after their picture appeared in *Life* magazine. But the two women did not meet again face to face until 1997. Will Counts, who took the 1957 photograph, convinced them to pose together in front of Central High School. It turned out that the women had much in common, and their mutual interests led to friendship. The National Council of Christians and Jews honored them with its humanitarian award.[75] This late-blooming friendship suggested the lost opportunities during the 1957–58 school year.

Such a friendship had no soil in which to grow in the 1950s. Segregationists policed the color line with a vengeance and intimidated any white person who deviated from their code. Although Little Rock high schools opened with token integration in the fall of 1959, segregationists throughout the state used the Central High blueprint to drive black students from integrated schools. By 1960, segregationists in Blinton, Russellville, Paris, Danville, Walnut Ridge, Clarksville, and Ozark had driven off black students, busing them to nearby black schools. The Citizens' Council's Little Rock strategy, which emphasized intimidation and segregationist solidarity, spread across the South. Litigation was useless, one newspaper argued, and blacks in small towns needed "peculiar courage, almost recklessness," to fight back.[76]

The human costs of Faubian tactics can never be fully tallied, but in one way or another, the crisis touched nearly everyone in Little Rock and had implications throughout the South. Divisions etched in 1957 and 1958 endure. Orval Faubus, for better or for worse, served six terms as governor of Arkansas. Author Robert Sherrill added a corollary to his discussion of Faubian tactics: "The costs of Faubus' action in 1957 were heavy indeed, but he was not the one who paid."[77]

13 Radical Departure

I didn't go down there to register for you. I went down to register for myself.
—Fannie Lou Hamer

The beginning of freedom summer in Mississippi is that three people are
missing and have been for forty-eight hours somewhere out in Neshoba County
where they say the sheriff killed six Blacks last year.
—Jane Stembridge

On February 1, 1960, four black freshmen from North Carolina Agricultural and Technical College (A&T) in Greensboro sat down at the white-only Woolworth's lunch counter and politely asked for service. They sat there for an hour without being served that Monday and then returned the next day. Their daring spontaneous protest kindled support. On Thursday, white women students from the University of North Carolina Women's College in Greensboro joined black students at the counter. On Saturday, downtown Greensboro filled with black students, including the A&T football team. White segregationists waved Confederate flags and heckled them. Sit-in demonstrations were held the next week in nearby Winston-Salem and Durham, then in Charlotte, then in Raleigh, and, in the following weeks, in over fifty cities across the South. By the end of the year, some 50,000 people had participated in sit-ins.[1]

The cutting edge of civil rights activity shifted from institutions and leaders to the younger generation. Free of institutional lethargy and caution, the sit-in demonstrators inspired one of the most explosive and significant movements of the century. Dismayed by the sit-ins, the National Association for the Advancement of Colored People (NAACP), Congress of Racial Equality (CORE), Southern Christian Leadership Conference (SCLC), and Urban League scrambled to take credit and gain control. The NAACP defined the sit-ins as "a student movement," provided counsel for those who were arrested, and took credit where it could. The national office sought "to regain a measure of control in this entire situation." Because sit-ins originated spontaneously, they presented both an opportunity and a threat to existing organizations.[2]

Alice Spearman, who only months earlier had suggested that the NAACP was too radical, quickly grasped the significance of sit-ins. When on February 12 students from Friendship Junior College in Rock Hill, South Carolina, began sit-ins at Woolworth's and McCrory's, Spearman realized that the participation of young blacks was shifting the movement "from low to high gear." The black community also supported the students. James H. Goudlock, president of Friendship Junior College, proclaimed that "the cause is just and if they are willing to help remedy conditions, their efforts should not be blocked." The Rock Hill African American community passed a resolution of support on February 29, but Goudlock complained that neither the Ministerial Alliance nor the local branch of the South Carolina Council on Human Relations (SCCHR) "made a statement." Spearman charged that white Christians "are like ostriches with their heads in the sand." She perceived that the sit-ins embodied a new spirit and were of "far more significance than appears on the surface." Black South Carolinians "are on the move and will no longer appear to be satisfied with discriminatory practices," she judged. By mid-March, Rock Hill students had protested at the bus station and city hall. Mass arrests followed. The SCCHR established a student defense fund to help defray court costs. Student enthusiasm and the support of President Goudlock challenged white privilege in a novel way.[3]

South Carolina segregationists assumed that they could crush the demonstrators. Three Methodist ministers who wrote letters to the editor in support of the Rock Hill sit-ins lost their pulpits. Black schoolteachers avoided meetings and demonstrations but still worried about job tenure. The mother of an Allen University student leader lost the teaching position she had held for thirty-five years. She was one year away from retirement. A report reached Spearman that Reverend W. P. Diggs, a sit-in leader, "was waylaid by four white men recently and threatened with death (they had a pistol) until he promised to have nothing further do to with these matters." Yet the demonstrations continued.[4]

As the press and television publicized the sit-ins, many southern whites were embarrassed by media images of white ruffians dumping ketchup and sugar on peaceful students, burning them with cigarettes, and in some cases striking them. The unflinching gaze of television transformed bullies into savages. The dignified black students sitting calmly at the lunch counters shamed many whites. Demonstrators seized the moral high ground, for peaceful students asking for service dramatically exposed the absurdity of segregation. Sit-ins also unleashed revolutionary energy. "The Southern butterfly can never return to its provincial cocoon," James McBride Dabbs judged; "it is adrift now on the winds of the world."[5]

As Dabbs suggested, the sit-ins generated a breeze of freedom that stirred young southerners. In the winter of 1960 at Union Theological Seminary in

New York, Jane Stembridge heard Martin Luther King Jr. discuss the sit-ins. She asked King if she could work with the SCLC during the summer. "He gave me the name of Ella J. Baker," Stembridge recalled. "The great Ella Baker." Connie Curry was in Greensboro visiting friends and family on February 1, but sensing the importance of the sit-ins, she quickly returned to her National Student Association (NSA) project in Atlanta. In Harlem, schoolteacher Bob Moses saw the determined faces of black students on television and decided to travel south during the summer. In Atlanta, Julian Bond and Ruby Doris Smith were immediately drawn to the sit-in movement, and in Nashville, Marion Barry, John Lewis, James Lawson, and Diane Nash took active roles. Around the country, sit-ins attracted diverse support. Young white southerners who were impatient with the slow pace of change and eager to make a statement joined black students at lunch counters.[6]

As young southerners flocked to lunch counters, segregationists viewed the sit-ins with alarm and took comfort in whatever victories they could achieve. In mid-March, Donald Davidson gloated to John Wade that Vanderbilt University chancellor Harvie Branscomb had "fired" Vanderbilt Divinity School student James Lawson. Davidson labeled him "the unruly Negro 'Reverend'" who had led "the sit-in demonstration of Negro students here." Liberals, Davidson continued, had complained to Branscomb "like a pack of howling hyenas, but are now, it seems, defeated—at least for the time being." But a sense of confusion, even doom, permeated Davidson's letter. The "civil commotions," he judged, were "unprecedented, except perhaps in Reconstruction days," and had "upset everything, everybody, and befuddled my mind for critical judgement, just at the time when I would like it to be most clear." Davidson had no plan for combating sit-ins and suspected that segregationists were weakening. Despite the collapsing morale among Davidson and other segregationists, southern politicians never wavered in their support of the neo–Lost Cause.[7]

In North Carolina, Wesley Critz George worried that "the integrationists here are even more aggressive than in the past." Many of the old North Carolina Patriots interpreted the sit-ins as part of a larger conspiracy. Segregationists rallied behind I. Beverly Lake in the gubernatorial election, and a friend warned George, "This will probably be our last chance to really defend our Southern way of life." After Lake lost, one segregationist attributed the loss partly to the fact that the University of North Carolina had hosted "a rash of Communist and/or radical speakers" that spring, including Martin Luther King Jr., Roy Wilkins, Linus Pauling, and Langston Hughes. He labeled this "shocking, utterly shocking," and asked how long the state's children would be "subjected to this filth and corruption." George's rhetoric took on a frantic edge that had been missing during the Patriot heyday. "But if we let the Congolese and the

Hottentots and the Harlemites make our decisions for us," he predicted, "I scarcely see how we can escape being a nation of Harlems."[8]

For white segregationists, the sit-ins exposed disturbing contradictions. While they taunted nonviolent demonstrators, they were wary of young blacks in the streets. They understood as little about black aspirations as they understood about the tradition of black self-defense and were surprised when black youngsters confronted white segregationists. "Hoodlums, some no more than 14 and 15 years of age," an observer wrote from Florida, had emerged from "the slums of Jacksonville and united as a confederation in order to retaliate against rumored or anticipated violence by whites." When whites, many of them Ku Klux Klan members, showed up with ax handles, an estimated 2,000 black youngsters arrived "loaded for bear," and "all hell broke loose." The police looked on. Similar confrontations took place in Chattanooga, Tennessee, and Greenville, South Carolina.[9]

The sit-ins alarmed white southerners primarily because they could not locate movement leaders. The fuse burned quickly between demonstration points, and student leaders independently called for sit-ins. The problem for segregationists was not the existence of a vast conspiracy but the lack of one. Segregationists stalled the NAACP with court challenges and intimidated adults with economic threats, but students seemed invulnerable because they willingly suffered abuse and went to jail. Segregationists could not find the off switch.

Ella Baker, more than any other civil rights leader, understood the significance of the sit-ins. In 1955, she had used her substantial organizational skills to help found In Friendship, a group that supported school integration and aided blacks who suffered reprisals. As the Montgomery bus boycott unfolded, she realized that it offered a focus for organizing and hoped that the Southern Christian Leadership Conference would empower local people in the South.[10]

In January 1958, Baker moved to Atlanta to bring order to the SCLC, which at the time lacked not only an office but also an organizational structure. Baker became an invaluable administrator and stayed on as executive secretary. She saw in the SCLC the potential to fan a grassroots fire that would burn away segregation. Mature, confident, outspoken, and experienced at organizing, Baker impatiently challenged King and the other ministers involved with the SCLC. Baker came to the realization that King was the SCLC. Instead of forging a grassroots movement, King seemed content to personify the organization and allow other ministers to play supporting roles. Although Baker had grown up in the church, by the 1950s, she was hardly devout. Her acquaintance with Harlem radicals eroded her patience for florid southern oratory, and her keen organizational mind revolted at the laxness—and chaos—that permeated the SCLC. Baker recognized the sit-ins' revolutionary potential and saw in grassroots or-

Ella Baker. Photograph by Danny Lyon. Courtesy Magnum.

ganizing a rare opportunity to destroy segregation. "Strong people don't need strong leaders," she judged.[11]

Often stymied by the institutions she had served, Baker saw in sit-in demonstrators the dedication and nerve that could achieve revolutionary change. Compiling names from newspaper sit-in coverage, she mailed announcements of a meeting at Shaw University in Raleigh on Easter weekend, April 15–17, 1960. Over 200 people attended. A carload of Union Theological Seminary students, including Jane Stembridge, drove down from New York. Connie Curry, the NSA leader, arrived from Atlanta. James Lawson, expelled from Vanderbilt Divinity School, impressed the audience not only with his knowledge of Ghandiism and radical Christianity but also with his criticism of mainline civil rights organizations. When it became apparent in a caucus that the SCLC leadership planned to control the young delegates, Baker walked out and then successfully urged the students to remain independent from all civil rights groups.[12]

In June, Jane Stembridge arrived in Atlanta to work with Baker, and they set up operations in a corner of the SCLC office on Auburn Avenue. SCLC ministers streamed in and out. Soon Baker insisted that Stembridge move across the street to maintain the student organization's separate identity. "It was a tiny little spot," Stembridge recalled. "You would open the door, and you were just practically on top of the desk." From then on, she insisted, the Student Nonviolent Coordinating Committee (SNCC) was "separate, totally, really separate." Stembridge put together a newsletter, the *Student Voice*. The SNCC office secured legal counsel for some students, bail for others. Stembridge recalls that Julian Bond from Morehouse College was the first student to offer help. She vividly remembered the arrival of Bob Moses from New York as a "turning point in my life." Moses had shown up unannounced intending to work with the SCLC, but neither Baker nor Stembridge had an assignment for him. Baker suggested that Moses go to Mississippi to encourage students to attend the October organizational meeting in Atlanta. The summer of 1960 was consumed with discussions and hard work. Stembridge sent the *Student Voice* to a growing list of people involved in sit-ins. At night, SNCC staff, volunteers, and friends would often eat in African American restaurants that would serve an integrated group and discuss strategy. Bond, Curry, Baker, King, Stembridge, and others frequently joined the group. The Atlanta Student Movement, meanwhile, sponsored demonstrations to integrate the restaurant at Rich's Department Store and other businesses. It was a summer of electric excitement.[13]

Since Stembridge's father was a Baptist minister, she understood the atmosphere of the SCLC and the background of King and other leaders. After her father held pastorates in South Carolina, Georgia, where Jane was born, Tennessee, and Kentucky, the Stembridges moved to North Carolina. Jane attended Meredith College, a Baptist women's college in Raleigh. Majoring in English and religion, she cherished the Meredith faculty's insistence that women develop their intellectual and leadership potential. To Stembridge and many other women in the mid-fifties, fraternity parties and dreams of marriage and family were of little interest. After graduating and sorting out her ambitions, Stembridge enrolled at Union Theological Seminary. It was there that she heard King's speech calling her back home. When she arrived in Atlanta, she met Connie Curry.[14]

Stembridge and Curry exemplified a new generation of southern white women who associated with African Americans as equals. Curry grew up in Greensboro, North Carolina, the daughter of first-generation Irish Americans. Curry's superior academic record, sense of humor, and charisma gained friends, although some classmates teased her for being "just too smart." She entered Agnes Scott College in Atlanta in 1952 and immediately became involved in the student movement. At her first NSA congress in Bloomington, Indiana, she roomed with a black woman, Aloa Collins. While attending a conference at the Butler Street Young Men's Christian Association in Atlanta, Curry, Collins, and several other students realized they could not eat together in downtown At-

Jane Stembridge and coworker. Photograph by Danny Lyon. Courtesy Magnum.

lanta. As they went their separate ways, Curry observed that segregation "ruined my way of life as well." Curry excelled at every activity—she was president of the student body, a member of the Phi Beta Kappa Society, and a Fulbright scholar in France after graduation.[15]

After a year in France, graduate studies at Columbia University, and work for the United Nations, in December 1959 Curry headed the NSA's Southern Human Relations Project in Atlanta. As it turned out, her project was largely diverted to SNCC work. Neither Stembridge nor Curry flinched at crossing the color line and working closely with African Americans. Their involvement with SNCC's predominantly black leadership—like white students' participation in sit-ins—signaled a significant attitudinal shift among many young southern whites.[16]

Changes in racial attitudes were more difficult for the older generation of southern white women. Columnist Margaret Long, whose daughter was active in civil rights, admitted in 1961 "that these Negro boys seem inordinately attractive." Rebellion against centuries of taboos, she suggested, would stir "young people who are brave and socially adventurous." The "sweet and vigorous sexuality" and "softness" of young black men, she admitted, "contrasted perhaps with a strain of ferocity and sadistic urge in more 'moral' Christian white boys, who, even now, approach their girls with hostility and guilt, along with the tenderness and desire." One of Long's friends had asked whether a local black professor "wasn't 'the sexiest man I ever saw.'" When Long admitted that it had not crossed her mind, her friend joked that something must be wrong with Long's glands. Long pondered whether her age or her inhibitions intruded, for she was "unable" or did not allow herself "to behold a Negro man 'like that.'"[17] Discussions of attractive black male students and professors seldom crept into white women's correspondence, but by the early sixties, the line that marked transgression had moved substantially, at least for some whites.

Ella Baker wanted to erase the color line. She believed that young peoples' spontaneity was the key to success. She encouraged young SNCC workers to remain unaffiliated with the NAACP, CORE, and the Urban League. When people criticized her confidence in young people, Baker replied that they were entitled to youthful mistakes. Unlike other movement leaders, she listened to young people, considered their suggestions, and offered sage advice. The decisions were their own. Her dream of a grassroots movement might come to pass through these brash and aggressive students. With her youthful spirit and wisdom, Baker became SNCC's unofficial leader. All her life, she had dreamed that some spark would kindle a mass movement to overthrow segregation; with SNCC, she hoped that the moment had arrived.[18]

Lillian Smith's vigil for civil rights also gained fresh inspiration from the sit-ins. In March 1957, she had insisted that it would be the younger generation that would force change. "We need to get the youngsters involved," she suggested. "They haven't got sense enough to know there is danger, so they'll go ahead and do what even you and I would gulp over." On October 16, 1960, she addressed a SNCC meeting in Atlanta. It is probable that she met Ella Baker at the meeting, but if so, the details have been lost. Smith warned SNCC delegates that for as long as she could remember southern white leaders had cherished a vision of "a new world" that they would purchase "with old Confederate Bills." Their world would not survive, she predicted. Smith was awed by the "spirit of self-sacrifice" among SNCC workers. She conceded that civil rights had become their fight, not hers. "We of the older generation cannot go on that great journey with you," she said, but she promised to lend her experience. "We can make of our lives, our knowledge, our failures, our experiences, our wisdom and hopes and faith and insight a *bridge*, a strong sure bridge, over which you can cross into the new unmade world."[19]

Shortly before she gave this speech, Smith had met Stembridge and invited her and other SNCC workers to her home on Old Screamer Mountain. Julian Bond, Marion Barry, and James Forman also made the trip. Smith observed that Stembridge "is so shrewd, so stable, so completely unified in her methods and her goals, so believing in real values." It was apparent that Smith saw in Stembridge a younger version of herself. "The fact that she is white, and is southern, and is so beautifully reared and educated gives her real influence and breeds respect among the young whites."[20]

On November 29, 1960, Stembridge described for Smith the continuing picketing in Atlanta, but she noted that she was disturbed after her last visit to Smith's home. "I left Ole' Screamer with great unhappiness Sunday," she admitted. At first, Smith had intrigued her. On later visits to Smith's home with her friend Donna McGinty, she had wanted to share more of Smith's life with Paula Snelling, wanted to help in the kitchen, become a part of the household. "I have the feeling," she confessed, "that you are not really interested in me or in Donna but that we make a good audience." She suspected that her opinions were unimportant to Smith. Spending time with Smith differed radically from her work with Ella Baker, who listened carefully and drew out her opinions. "Ole' Screamer represents a great deal to me," Stembridge confessed. "Truth in a way, Peace, Mountain, and Solitude." But she wanted her visits "to be real." She cringed when Smith bragged about her to others, identifying her as a writer and remarking on her courage. She asked Smith not to say such things "until you know that they might be true." Stembridge went to Old Screamer again in mid-December 1960. It was a good visit. "Among the talk, the dishes, the logs and within the mountain, something called redemption was present." The relationship between Smith and Stembridge lasted until 1964, and it ultimately personified the generational shift in white women's role in the battle for equal rights.[21] Despite her poor health, Smith not only paid close attention to the civil rights struggle but also continued to travel and speak out.

Smith offered an analysis of white southerners who passively accepted racial separation. "We must feel compassion for the poor, ignorant, sexually frustrated, spiritually frustrated whites who have been given the dope of White Supremacy for years," she wrote to author John Howard Griffin in 1962; "they are ADDICTS—how can we hate them or treat them as well men?" They were also "slaves to white supremacy, slaves to the ancient now breaking-up agricultural system; slaves to sexual puritanism; slaves to hollow souls and hollow minds never fed a creative, good, earthy peasant culture, but given nothing, nothing for a hundred and fifty years but the dope of white supremacy." The old order was collapsing, she observed, but the new order was far from completed.[22] From her mountaintop, Smith did not discern the "earthy peasant culture" that surrounded her, nor did many of her peers. Lowdown people offered so much to love and so much to detest that their contradictions were eagerly ignored.

A year later, Smith commented to Griffin on the similarities between women and blacks. "Do you realize, John," she began a January 1962 letter, "that women—white women—are discriminated against almost as much as are Negroes, except in the area of sex where they are pampered and petted?" Racial segregation, she argued, "is based firmly on this deeper sex segregation." When white women gained "full human rights," then such rights would follow for blacks. She raised the issue, she stressed, to point out that "racial segregation isn't the only evil we must grapple with." Discrimination against women and "all dark people," she concluded, "is all a deeply rooted evil of the patriarchal system."[23]

By the early 1960s, southern white women openly attacked white men's presumptions and fantasies. Eliza Heard, the nom de plume of a writer for the Southern Regional Council's publication, *New South*, asked women to unite "and in a very lady-like way tell our loud and valiant defenders that our virtue is in no danger, that we can protect it very well by ourselves." Heard had attended a Citizens' Council meeting and was outraged to hear men vowing to protect their daughters from black schoolmates or announcing that "the first colored grandchild they brought into my house will not be welcome." Wives and daughters blushed as men raved about interracial sex. White men had a problem, Heard suggested. "Are our white men so pale, so unattractive, so worthless, that the desegregated proximity of superior Negro men would inexorably draw all white females—even little sisters of five and six—away from their fathers, husbands and suitors?" Men had used such arguments to justify lynching. "I think it is about time we stopped permitting our name to be thus shamefully and senselessly bandied about." This stridency varied remarkably from the remarks of an earlier generation of women who in their campaign against lynching often did not see African Americans as their equals. White women redefined their role in southern society by supporting equal rights and working side by side with black men and women.[24]

Southern historians also felt the sting of the civil rights struggle. The consensus that had treated the Civil War as a lamentable but heroic interlude, had cast Reconstruction as diabolical federal intrusion, had portrayed African Americans as inferior, and had conflated the Lost Cause, segregation, and religion began to fracture in the 1950s. Portents of revision had emerged as early as W. E. B. Du Bois's *Black Reconstruction in America*, published in 1935. Historian James Silver's 1963 Southern Historical Association presidential address outraged many of the Old Guard. They not only resisted Silver's message but also were upset that he chose an emotional contemporary topic, "Mississippi, the Closed Society." A year earlier, Silver had witnessed the riot surrounding James Meredith's admission to the University of Mississippi. He decided that the time had come for southern historians to face the reality of segregation.[25]

Many academics denounced Silver, but his address inspired enthusiastic letters from former students. A woman from a small North Carolina town wrote that her husband was "quite a violent white supremacist." Until the civil rights movement began, she had not paid much attention to his rantings. "At first," she explained, "I couldn't help expressing how I felt about it." Her husband's vicious reaction silenced her, and she dejectedly "let him mutter and cuss the 'damn niggers.'" He "claimed that I must be part 'nigger' in order to 'take up for them,'" she said. For nine years, she had avoided bringing up controversial subjects. "So," she suggested, "a closed society can be a country, a state, a city or a family." Unsuccessful people, she ventured, needed someone outside their "personal orbit" to "belittle." For example, she observed, a member of the Citizens' Council "can feel much whiter if he exploits and emphasizes the blackness of the negro."[26]

Sensitive and provocative teachers such as James Silver lived both inside and outside the South. Although he played poker and hunted with his Oxford friends, Silver's beliefs placed him outside the chummy community circle. Such professors had a profound influence on students. In early 1964, former student Mildred W. Greear took her sixteen-year-old son to hear Silver speak in Georgia. She had taken one of Silver's history courses twenty years earlier. Although Greear could not recall the titles of the books she had read for the course, "I remember their flavor," she wrote, and that "they stretched my mind." More important, "since I was already a far gone radical as far as my contemporaries there were concerned, they [the books] gave me a vocabulary with which to voice some of my opinions." At the Georgia lecture, a student had asked Silver why he had remained in Mississippi. "I wanted to get up and answer for you," Greear explained. "It was for me, and hundreds of others."[27]

In the early 1960s, the civil rights movement preoccupied both blacks and whites, and television news dramatized the struggle. The John F. Kennedy administration juggled its desire to placate powerful southern politicians on the one hand and its hope to appear to support civil rights on the other. Federal power rarely permeated state and local crises, although the Federal Bureau of Investigation (FBI) usually had observers on hand. As demonstrations swirled through the South, Mississippi whites stood out as the most obstinate and violent in their protection of segregation. Black Mississippians clearly understood the risks of confronting registrars, signing school integration petitions, or defying segregation by word or deed. The possibility of retribution made their challenge even more remarkable.

The civil rights movement coincided with the emergence of southern agribusiness, and these revolutionary movements were tied together in contradictory but significant ways. The federal government gave far more support to southern white planters than to black farmers. U.S. Department of Agriculture

(USDA) programs encouraged mechanization and chemical applications. By 1967, only 5 percent of Mississippi's cotton was picked by hand, and herbicides had drastically reduced spring and summer hoe work. Planters paid hourly wages to tractor drivers and picking machine operators, increased herbicide use, and released surplus workers. In the Mississippi Delta, the number of sharecroppers declined from 17,563 in 1959 to 8,788 in 1964. Whites demeaned dispossessed farmworkers as lazy and worthless and honed USDA programs and federal commodity programs to a sharp punitive edge. Because they controlled local agricultural committees and welfare bureaucracies, planters were assured of maintaining economic supremacy. It was not that the powerful white Mississippians loathed the federal government; it was that they resented having to share federal funds, social space, and power with blacks.[28]

Machines, chemicals, and elite-controlled agricultural committees would have sufficed to decimate the rural working class, but there was more. A Tougaloo College professor, John R. Salter Jr., speculated in January 1963 that "this matter of automation has been pushed with great zeal by the landowners as a means of mass retaliation against Mississippi Negro efforts to secure basic American rights and to achieve human equality." Sponsored by the NAACP, he visited back roads in the winter of 1963 and found people living in shacks with no hope for jobs. Nor could they get government aid. "It is the general feeling in the Delta area," he wrote, "that this denial of welfare benefits is due to a wish, on the part of the white authorities, to 'massively retaliate' against the Negro civil rights movement."[29]

A 1963 National Sharecroppers Fund study revealed the extent of white control in South Carolina. In a nine-county area, no African Americans sat on county or local committees or review committees or were ever "employed as land surveyors, office clerks, or supervisors." It was customary that "Negro farmers do not participate in local committee elections." Black county agents and demonstration agents were excluded from meetings that discussed federal policy. "How much longer," the report asked, "must the federal government subsidize the largest segregated educational system in the world?"[30]

The administration of the South Carolina federal agricultural program mirrored the administration of the program throughout the South. The systematic exclusion of African American farmers (and poor whites) from agricultural committees began in 1933. As of 1964, the secretary of agriculture had never appointed an African American to a state committee in the South. In eleven southern states, no African American had ever been elected as a county committee member, and only 75 of 37,000 community committee members in the South were African American. In 1964, CORE's effort to encourage black farmers in Madison County, Mississippi, to run for Agricultural Stabilization and

Conservation Service county committees led to intimidation and violence. As long as county elites controlled allotments, acreage measurements, and the disbursement of federal agricultural funds, they could direct the evolution of agribusiness. Without cracking this institutional bias, African Americans and poor white farmers would never achieve equal opportunity to farm. The few African Americans who eventually won seats on local committees could affect little change. Poor whites seldom understood that their fates were in part tied to those of their black neighbors.[31]

White Mississippians changed the agricultural structure and even the landscape to suit agribusiness. As machines, chemicals, and government programs forced rural people off the land, the Delta Council tried to erase all evidence of their existence. Unsightly old houses and outbuildings left behind when workers moved created "an unfavorable impression of the State," a 1963 Delta Council resolution complained. Many planters simply burned or bulldozed old buildings after their inhabitants moved away.[32] Followed to its conclusion, such a policy could turn even the Mississippi Delta into an idyllic midwesternlike landscape.

The SNCC workers who walked southern back roads recruiting voters arrived at this crucial moment when farmworkers had become devalued. Planters no longer needed a reservoir of laborers to chop and pick cotton, and they turned on the people they had formerly employed and labeled them welfare addicts. When SNCC workers first arrived in a community, they alarmed both African Americans and whites. Attempting to vote, harboring SNCC workers, or attending meetings invited white retribution. Supporting SNCC seemed at best futile and at worst suicidal. Even if blacks registered to vote, the county agricultural offices and welfare programs were immune from direct political assault. White leaders also understood retribution. It was in this context that SNCC workers recruited potential voters in the Delta.

Despite the repressive climate of the South, SNCC's message resonated among poor blacks, in particular, who were willing to take risks to achieve justice. In August 1962, SNCC worker Charles McLaurin, a Mississippian, convinced over a dozen women, including Fannie Lou Hamer, to make the trip to Indianola to register to vote. Hamer filled out the forms but did not pass the test. When she returned home, landlord W. D. Marlowe demanded that she take her name off the registration form. Her reply has become the classic statement of black resistance: "I didn't go down there to register for you. I went down to register for myself." Marlowe put her off the plantation that very night.[33]

Leslie Burl McLemore met Hamer in 1962 when they traveled by bus to Dorcester, Georgia, to attend a citizenship workshop. McLemore had been unable to attend an integrated school as he had hoped in 1954 after he heard news

Fannie Lou Hamer, 1971.
Photograph by Pete Daniel.

of the *Brown* decision. Instead, he studied public speaking and pursued many extracurricular activities at Delta Center High School. He watched mechanical cotton harvesters idle many neighborhood farmers, whose only fieldwork was sporadic chopping and picking behind the still inefficient chemicals and machines. By the time McLemore enrolled at Rust College in Holly Springs, he had internalized the civil rights movement and soon became involved in a boycott of the segregated theater in Holly Springs. In 1962, he became president of the Rust College NAACP chapter and began working with SNCC.[34]

On the Georgia trip, McLemore recalled, Hamer "sang, literally, all the way there and all the way back." He believed that Hamer had a profound influence on the country "because so many women, black and white, identified with this poor sharecropper of a woman, unlettered, very articulate, very dynamic, very strong and courageous." Students and civil rights activists thought "she was touched in a special way by God." On Marlowe's plantation, she had not just been a sharecropper but had also held the responsible position of timekeeper, which included recording the weight of each worker's cotton. Fellow workers saw her as a leader both on the plantation and in church. When Marlowe evicted her from the plantation, McLemore observed, "he did her a favor and did the country a favor." In June 1963, she was arrested with several other women who asked for service at the lunch counter of the Winona bus station and then beaten in the Winona jail, an experience that she ultimately shared with the American public at the 1964 Democratic National Convention. In the same month, Medgar Evers was murdered in his driveway in Jackson. Such violence sent the message that blacks could be beaten or murdered with impunity. SNCC reacted by stepping up civil rights activity.[35]

At Rust College, Leslie McLemore was a leader and excellent student, but in 1962, when he attended his first SNCC meeting, he was surprised by the level of sophistication among people his own age. They knew about Africa, politics, philosophy, and tactics. Back on campus, he headed for the library. At the next meeting, he left his coat and tie in the dormitory and wore clothes that blended in with SNCC members' overalls and jeans. In the Mississippi Delta, then, leaders emerged from the grassroots, just as Ella Baker had predicted. The young men and women who worked for SNCC accepted the dangers as part of forcing change.[36]

When night fell in the Delta, SNCC workers often gathered around radios in Freedom Houses, debated tactics and the latest gains or losses, or went to nearby juke joints. Music became a vital part of SNCC, whether it was Hamer's inspiring songs, the radio, jukeboxes, or live music in juke joints. Jane Stembridge fondly recalled Joan Baez and Bob Dylan singing for SNCC workers. McLemore observed that dancing was important. "Whether you could dance or not it didn't matter," he joked, "but what would pass for dancing." He often talked with juke joint patrons about the blues, about music. It was something everyone had in common. "I had heard that music all my life," he said. He described a night at a Greenville juke joint. Local people watched the civil rights workers with "great admiration," he noticed; they enjoyed seeing "black folk and white folk together, some dancing and drinking and having a good time." Even the toughest blacks "admired the courage of the young people" and joined them to have fun.[37]

As significant events of the early sixties unfolded, SNCC workers lived in a world of potential violence and fierce retaliation. In Mississippi, they achieved incremental victories. In the fall of 1963, Stembridge settled in Greenwood, ground zero of the movement. She was jailed for supposedly running a stop sign. One of the jailers woke her up at five in the morning to ask if she was sleeping with one of the black SNCC workers. "It was buggin' him," she recalled. After she told them she had been born in Georgia, some of the police were nice to her—although some were not. The newspapers had reported that she was born in California, she wrote, "because they couldn't take it." Stembridge continued her friendship with Lillian Smith, writing numerous letters, calling her on the telephone, and visiting whenever possible. Stembridge's letters to Smith revealed her anguish and doubts. She practically begged Smith to acknowledge SNCC's good works. "Please drop a line whenever you can," she wrote in October 1963. "God knows we need it in this place."[38]

Leslie Burl McLemore. The Bearcat, 1964. Courtesy Leslie Burl McLemore.

On November 5, 1963, Stembridge wrote, "It's election day in Mississippi." She added, "That's a cruelty joke." But the Council of Federated Organizations, which included the NAACP, SNCC, CORE, and SCLC, organized an alternative election to demonstrate the potential of the disfranchised black electorate. Aaron Henry ran for governor and Ed King, the white chaplain at Tougaloo College, for lieutenant governor. Despite harassment, some 80,000 blacks voted. Stembridge was jailed for her participation in the protest election.[39]

The constant danger SNCC workers faced pared membership down to true believers. They lived in an environment so hostile that whites refused even to ask what they did. As winter approached, Stembridge feared that the movement was fraying under the strain. "Radio saying—Greenwood, Mississippi 960 on your dial," she wrote. "The sky is very gray and soon it will be very dark and between now and then," she despaired, "the revolution will not have been completed and I wonder if the sum total of field reports, clothes distribution, mass meetings, and voting will make us love each other more or if anything will or if it matters." If she were in Ruleville, she mused, she would eat pecans, drink coffee, and sing songs with Hamer. But there were bright spots. Freedom Schools attracted local children who were taught forbidden history that included the role of African Americans. On many afternoons, children crowded into the Greenwood Freedom House and eagerly read books, learned to play chess, and ate snacks. "If you should happen in some afternoon around three o'clock," Stembridge reported, "you would see thirty children waiting in line for books, especially about rockets and jets, and about other children."[40]

As Christmas approached, Stembridge's letters and reports recorded the unemployment, the harassment, and her rising frustration. "For here, there has been no breakthrough, not one scrap of evidence that we are overcoming," she admitted. "No lunchcounter in downtown Greenwood has opened to Negroes, no public school desegregation has occurred, no jobs have opened up and very very few people have been successful in their attempts to become registered voters." Even if black folks could sit at the Woolworth's lunch counter, few could afford a cup of coffee. "The masses are huddled around tiny gas stoves," she went on. "They are poor. They are hungry. And they are cold." She wanted to teach them, register them, and make up for "lost years."[41]

Stembridge wrote this letter less than twenty years after the end of World War II and the beginning of the atomic age. In Mississippi, it seemed to her, things were getting worse. But in those two decades, the southern cultural landscape had changed dramatically. From music and the progression of rhythm and blues, rock 'n' roll, and soul music to automobile racing and the triumph of NASCAR, southerners were dominating American culture. Millions of southerners, refugees from the land, had infiltrated other states and smuggled in their culture. Those left behind, as Stembridge understood so well, found life extremely hard. For many southerners, black and white, segregation remained a glaring reminder of the past. In their stubborn refusal to yield, southern politicians and segregationists not only provoked opposition but also increasingly appeared antiquated and backward. The federal government seldom challenged this intransigence. Mainstream civil rights groups had tested the limits of litigation and peaceful protest. By the summer of 1964, explosive tension had built up along the color line.

It was at this juncture that Stembridge and other SNCC workers began preparations for Freedom Summer. Some of the staff left to train volunteers, whereas others remained behind at the Greenwood office. "Our time is the time of revolt and the time it takes to put together a revolution," Stembridge wrote. She said she belonged to "the tragic generation" and wrote page after page to Smith explaining her feelings. She worried about violence but was equally disturbed by boredom. The SNCC workers stayed on, she felt, because they had to prove that they could live in Mississippi. In one letter to Smith, Stembridge described Hamer's role: "She is so brave and beautiful. She represents the dream . . . the reason we came and are staying." When Hamer visited the Greenwood office, they sang as the police watched outside with their dogs. Hamer improvised, "Ain't gonna let no dogs turn me roun."[42]

"The beginning of freedom summer in Mississippi," Stembridge wrote on June 23, "is that three people are missing and have been for forty-eight hours somewhere out in Neshoba County where they say the sheriff killed six Blacks last year." They waited anxiously for news of James Chaney, Michael Schwerner, and Andrew Goodman, but the next day, they learned of the "burned-out car on the edge of a swamp." By then, the three workers had been murdered and buried. Ten black churches were burned in Mississippi in June and July, along with other structures belonging to African Americans. SNCC workers took white volunteers into the field, and each white face compounded their danger. Stembridge hoped that in the future the bravery that marked those forsaken battlegrounds of Freedom Summer would be remembered.[43]

SNCC workers attacked entrenched white fortifications that possessed superior firepower and resources. They established a new category of bravery in the face of such odds. Their only allies were reporters, who could expose violence, and the cover of darkness, which improved their chances of defending themselves. Rural people customarily owned rifles and shotguns that they used for hunting. They did not hesitate to use their weapons for self-defense. Many SNCC workers appreciated the company of firearms, a fact not lost on the white community.[44]

It was Smith's disregard of Stembridge's risk and bravery that led to their split. In August, Stembridge wrote Smith that she had "decided to discontinue the letters." Their correspondence had been "dishonest," Stembridge explained, both because she disagreed with Smith over "the nature of the changing South" and because there was no dialogue. Her letters, she admitted, were confessional and needed someone to take them seriously. "You were not there," she wrote. "And so . . . neither have I been." Smith's silence on "the horror of this place" disappointed Stembridge. Even when she visited Old Screamer, she complained, Smith did not listen to her ideas. "I have written better poetry on the walls of johns in the Delta," she lashed out, "than in thirteen letters to you." Smith did not understand or care, it seemed. "Mississippi is hell. My life here has been hell—goddam fucking hell of a nowhere of death." She had never been so frank. Smith continued to write of her own work, her own career. Stembridge had felt like shaking her "because you do not have to justify your existence to anybody." Stembridge cared deeply for Smith but refused to be labeled "one of your admirers."[45]

Stembridge also noted ideological differences, and the shifting of generational plates could be felt in nearly every sentence. "I do not think we agree on the nature of the changes in the South, the solution to the problems, or the role of the artist in this," Stembridge wrote. Smith, she reasoned, was "within the system—America—and I am outside. I believe you uncovered the wound and I am within the wound." Smith had been "selective about those with whom you work," whereas Stembridge had "been thrown with the outsider, am an outsider, and am unwilling to stand away from any of the rest of the outsiders."

Whereas Smith believed that change could leave the structure intact, Stembridge argued that "a wide and deep revolution must occur which will radically alter the basic structure of the entire society: *before* justice, truth, love, and peace can really happen." In Mississippi, she saw how little the federal government cared about the most basic civil rights. "Whether the poets wish to deal with it or not," she insisted, "America is controlled by men who simply do not want justice: but who want power and—most of all—things to remain precisely as they are." She made an eloquent argument against "those institutions whose very existence has perpetuated the system of segregation."[46]

The artist could no longer remain in the coffeehouse, Stembridge reasoned, but "the place of the artist today is, of necessity, and because of responsibility—outside—and within the revolution." She had contempt for those who wrote about justice from afar. "The coffee house poet is only slightly more to be praised than the Reader's Digest writers." She acknowledged that Smith would "always speak of the white South and speak as no one else can. I will speak from the wound of the revolution." She left the door open. "I am here at the point of dialogue. I will remain here regardless. You are a beautiful person . . . the beauty reaches here. I see it."[47]

The strained friendship between Stembridge and Smith demonstrated the shift from Smith's intellectual radicalism of the forties and fifties to Stembridge's activist radicalism of the sixties. As both Smith and Stembridge understood, women's rights became an integral part of the civil rights movement, but the legacy of SNCC embraced all Americans who were outsiders. Stembridge witnessed the civil rights movement as a white woman in SNCC in Mississippi. It was a vantage point that more than once led her to admit, "I am sometimes angry with hot and red blindness." She understood that even the most daring and democratic movement could be co-opted and destroyed. Her dream, and that of most SNCC workers in 1964, was of a community that contained no boundaries or hierarchies but simply men and women and black and white people working and living together in harmony. Smith's silence lingers; she never revealed her reaction to Stembridge's ideas, but she preserved her letters.[48]

Stembridge witnessed the brunt of white hostility, and her frustration reflected the inability of SNCC and other civil rights groups to soften white prejudice. The press depicted them as idealistic outsiders. Although some whites registered misgivings about preserving segregation, without federal support, civil rights efforts splintered on the rock of white resistance and hostility. Local white elites refused to share power with African Americans, and whites in general hid behind segregationist tradition. An effort to organize whites in Biloxi, the White Folks Project, collapsed in less than a month. Still, SNCC workers continued to challenge segregation and push for voter registration.[49]

By the time Stembridge broke off her friendship with Smith, recent Rust College graduate Leslie McLemore was working with Ella Baker to seat the Mississippi Freedom Democratic Party (MFDP) at the 1964 Democratic National Convention in Atlantic City. Through grassroots organizing, SNCC had created a parallel Democratic Party that included both blacks and whites. It would challenge the regular segregationist Mississippi Democratic delegation. McLemore arrived by Greyhound bus in New York to discuss the mission on the day that the three civil rights workers disappeared in Mississippi. Baker, like Hamer, impressed McLemore, who had an affinity for strong women because of his mother's example. McLemore had been involved with the Freedom Vote Campaign in 1963 and the founding of the MFDP in April 1964. As a member of the "northern front," as he called it, he worked out of Washington with Baker, Frank Smith Jr., who had been active at Rust, Walt Tillow, and Charles Sherrod. The only staff member from Mississippi, McLemore found himself lobbying Congress and visiting delegations from across the country to explain in his unmistakable southern accent the MFDP challenge to the regular Democrats. Baker and her staff jointly conceived the party's strategy. "Miss Baker just simply had confidence in all of us," McLemore recalled. She gave him a map, a car, and his assignment. At other times, she would enthrall the staff with stories of her work with the NAACP, her acquaintance with W. E. B. Du Bois, or her involvement with the SCLC and Martin Luther King Jr. She also discussed the hostility of black and white males to her ideas. "She clearly was an equal among equals, and she saw herself as that," McLemore insisted. "The men didn't see her in that light." SNCC workers understood her wisdom and listened. "She sort of influenced the SNCC leadership and all of SNCC in a way that was not dogmatic, not dictatorial," he explained. She stirred the nerve of the fearless young men and women who were willing to give themselves to civil rights.[50]

With Baker's blessing, McLemore returned to Mississippi to attend the precinct meetings of the MFDP and was elected a delegate and vice chair of the party. Hamer became the voice of the party. "You had this wise political sage, Miss Baker; you had this very perceptive analytical philosopher, Bob Moses; and you had this earthy grassroots woman, Fannie Lou Hamer," McLemore said of the leadership. They worked well together. When discussions became muddled, Hamer would bring them back to earth. She understood the complexities and could "cut through the issues to get at the heart of the matter."[51]

When the MFDP arrived in Atlantic City in mid-August determined to be seated, it represented the culmination of grassroots organizing that had begun with the sit-ins in 1960. At the convention, neither President Lyndon B. Johnson nor his staff could successfully isolate or intimidate any member or clique of the MFDP delegation. The MFDP membership included blacks and whites, rich and poor people, old and young people, men and women, and highly educated and unlettered people. It repudiated discrimination, challenged violence, and demanded justice. Few events since the *Brown* decision in 1954 had offered the opportunity for national television coverage of a public debate over representative democracy. The MFDP challenged the all-white and segregationist regular Mississippi Democrats before the Credentials Committee of the convention. It was a defining moment in the history of equal rights, for the MFDP, born in crisis and reared amid violence and murder, epitomized reconciliation. It represented revolution from within, not federal imposition from without. If the committee voted to air the issue on the convention floor, not only would the MFDP stand an excellent chance of being seated but also the nation would learn of its members' bravery and ideas.

President Johnson, still basking in the afterglow of the signing of the 1964 Civil Rights Act on July 2, was determined that no demonstration, credentials fight, or floor debate mar his coronation. Civil rights and voting legislation would ultimately lead to vast changes in southern race relations, but Johnson refused to offer the magnanimous gesture that would acknowledge the MFDP and SNCC as legitimate representatives of democracy. Instead, he favored seating the all-white segregationist delegation, the very people who had made civil rights legislation necessary. The regular Mississippi delegation faced a determined MFDP composed of workers, educators, businesspeople, and sharecroppers. Johnson was so concerned about the MFDP's obstinate idealists that he ordered the FBI to shadow and eavesdrop on them.[52]

When the Credentials Committee met on August 22, Hamer's eloquence and passion overwhelmed listeners. As she neared the end of the story of her attempt to register to vote, her house being fired at, and her beating in Winona, she explained that she had prevailed because she wanted to be a first-class citizen. McLemore, who was standing close by, saw members of the Credentials Committee, "white men and white women crying like babies as she described the conditions in Mississippi." To co-opt television coverage, Johnson had called a press conference just as Hamer began her testimony, but that night, the networks featured her testimony on prime-time television. Johnson then let it be known that if the MFDP challenge went to the convention floor, Hubert Humphrey might be discarded as his vice presidential nominee. When Humphrey presented this dilemma to Hamer, she scolded him: "Well, Mr. Humphrey, do you mean to tell me that your position is more important to you than four hundred thousand black people's lives?"[53]

Johnson's staff exerted enormous pressure on MFDP delegates to accept a plan to seat the regular Mississippi delegation along with two MFDP members, Aaron Henry and Ed King. By accepting this offer, the MFDP would be subsumed into politics as usual. The offer provoked heated debate among delegates. But the heart of the delegation came from rural Mississippi, a place unfamiliar to most whites and most leaders of any color. Rural delegates, drawing on their experiences in Mississippi, distrusted leaders, especially whites. The MFDP was created outside institutional structures, which is why it appealed to poor people and made others uneasy. Many delegates believed Johnson's compromise represented an unwillingness to grant political power to African Americans. That affront would ultimately push SNCC to search for black power that excluded whites. Members of SNCC and the MFDP had not endured beatings, witnessed murders, stared down terror, registered to vote, challenged white power, and exerted political genius in order to accept a dubious settlement. "We didn't come all this way for no two seats," Hamer explained a few days later. The MFDP delegates refused to compromise and returned to Mississippi. When Freedom Summer ended, so did the promise of spontaneous grassroots revolution. The moment was lost.[54]

After Freedom Summer, the wind shifted. The civil rights movement did not alter course at once, but African Americans increasingly distrusted white promises. They were restless to control their own destiny, and many championed the black power movement. The struggle for civil rights later moved from the grass roots back to institutions. Still, laws slowly choked segregationists into angry submission.

The revolutionary possibilities that had emerged from World War II unraveled. The white elite engineered agribusiness, migration, and massive resistance, a counterrevolution that poisoned both the environment and race relations. Integration came not from good will or enlightened leadership but from laws and litigation, from reluctant compliance. Southern blacks and whites moved in an uneasy dance as the tension and violence of the age of segregation dissipated.

In the middle decades of the twentieth century, brave southerners opposed repression and united in the fight for equal rights. At the same time, stock car drivers and musicians embodied the hard gem of working-class spontaneity and genius. Before they were divided or tamed, these people redefined the South and established enduring cultural monuments.

Notes

ABBREVIATIONS

Manuscript and archival collections are abbreviated as follows.

Abernethy Papers
  Thomas Abernethy Papers, Special Collections, University of Mississippi,
  Oxford, Mississippi
ACES Papers
  Alabama Cooperative Extension Service Papers, Archives and Manuscripts
  Department, Auburn University, Auburn, Alabama
ACHR Papers
  Arkansas Council on Human Relations Papers, Special Collections Division,
  University of Arkansas Libraries, Fayetteville, Arkansas
Agricultural Extension Papers
  Agricultural Extension Papers, Louisiana State Collection, Louisiana State
  University, Baton Rouge, Louisiana
Alabama Farm Bureau Papers
  Alabama Farm Bureau Papers, Archives and Manuscripts Department,
  Auburn University, Auburn, Alabama
Anti-Defamation League Papers
  Anti-Defamation League Papers, Amistad Collection, Tulane University,
  New Orleans, Louisiana
ARS Records
  Records of the Agricultural Research Service, Record Group 310,
  National Archives and Records Administration, Washington, D.C.
ASCS Records
  Records of the Agricultural Stabilization and Conservation Service, Record Group
  145, National Archives and Records Administration, Washington, D.C.
Ashmore Papers
  Harry Ashmore Papers, Archives and Special Collections, University of Arkansas,
  Little Rock, Arkansas
BAE Records
  Records of the Bureau of Agricultural Economics, Record Group 83,
  National Archives and Records Administration, Washington, D.C.
Ball Papers
  William Watts Ball Papers, Rare Book, Manuscript, and Special Collections
  Library, Duke University, Durham, North Carolina
Baptist Historical Collection
  Baptist Historical Collection, Z. Smith Reynolds Library, Wake Forest University,
  Winston-Salem, North Carolina

Braden Papers
    Carl and Anne Braden Papers, State Historical Society of Wisconsin,
    Madison, Wisconsin
BSB&B Interviews
    "Beale Street Black and Blue," oral history transcripts, by Margaret McKee
    and Fred Chisenhall, box 57, Oral History Collection, Memphis Public Library,
    Memphis, Tennessee
Caldwell Papers
    Arthur B. Caldwell Papers, Special Collections Division, University of Arkansas
    Libraries, Fayetteville, Arkansas
Carter Papers
    Hodding Carter Papers, Special Collections Department, Mitchell Memorial
    Library, Mississippi State University, Mississippi State, Mississippi
CCPA Records
    Records of the Committee for Congested Production Areas, Record Group 212,
    National Archives and Records Administration, Washington, D.C.
Central High FBI Records
    Little Rock Central High Integration Crisis, FBI Records, Special Collections
    Division, University of Arkansas Libraries, Fayetteville, Arkansas
Charles Johnson Papers
    Charles S. Johnson Papers, Special Collections, Fisk University,
    Nashville, Tennessee
Clement Papers
    Frank Clement Papers, Tennessee State Archives, Nashville, Tennessee
Coody Papers
    Archibald S. Coody Papers, Mississippi Division of Archives and History,
    Jackson, Mississippi
Cooley Papers
    Harold D. Cooley Papers, Southern Historical Collection, Wilson Library,
    University of North Carolina, Chapel Hill, North Carolina
Cox Papers
    Allen Eugene Cox Papers, Special Collections Department, Mitchell Memorial
    Library, Mississippi State University, Mississippi State, Mississippi
D&PLC Records
    Delta and Pine Land Company Records, Special Collections Department,
    Mitchell Memorial Library, Mississippi State University, Mississippi State,
    Mississippi
Davidson Papers
    Donald Davidson Papers, Special Collections and University Archives,
    Heard Memorial Library, Vanderbilt University, Nashville, Tennessee
Dean of Women Papers
    Dean of Women Papers, Archives and Manuscripts Department,
    Auburn University, Auburn, Alabama
Dobbins Papers
    Charles G. Dobbins Papers, Archives and Manuscripts Department,
    Auburn University, Auburn, Alabama

Dorn Papers
>   William Jennings Bryan Dorn Papers, Modern Political Collection, South
>   Caroliniana Library, University of South Carolina, Columbia, South Carolina

Draughon Papers
>   Ralph B. Draughon Papers, Archives and Manuscripts Department,
>   Auburn University, Auburn, Alabama

Dwight D. Eisenhower Papers
>   Dwight D. Eisenhower Papers, Eisenhower Presidential Library, Abilene, Kansas

Edwards Papers
>   Charles W. Edwards Papers, Archives and Manuscripts Department,
>   Auburn University, Auburn, Alabama

Ervin Papers
>   Sam Ervin Papers, Southern Historical Collection, Wilson Library, University of
>   North Carolina, Chapel Hill, North Carolina

Faubus Papers
>   Orval Faubus Papers, Special Collections Division, University of Arkansas
>   Libraries, Fayetteville, Arkansas

Folsom Papers
>   James Folsom Papers, Alabama State Archives, Montgomery, Alabama

FWS Records
>   Records of the Fish and Wildlife Service, Record Group 22, National Archives and
>   Records Administration, Washington, D.C.

George Papers
>   Wesley Critz George Papers, Southern Historical Collection, Wilson Library,
>   University of North Carolina, Chapel Hill, North Carolina

Glover Library
>   C. N. Glover Library, Missionary Baptist Seminary, Little Rock, Arkansas

Graham Papers
>   Frank Porter Graham Papers, Southern Historical Collection, Wilson Library,
>   University of North Carolina, Chapel Hill, North Carolina

Hamilton Papers
>   Grace Towns Hamilton Papers, Atlanta History Society, Atlanta, Georgia

Hays Papers
>   Brooks Hays Papers, Special Collections Division, University of Arkansas
>   Libraries, Fayetteville, Arkansas

Huckaby Papers
>   Elizabeth Paisley Huckaby Papers, Special Collections Division, University of
>   Arkansas Libraries, Fayetteville, Arkansas

Jim Johnson Papers
>   Jim Johnson Papers, Arkansas History Commission, Little Rock, Arkansas

Lemley Papers
>   Harry J. Lemley Papers, Archives and Special Collections, University of Arkansas,
>   Little Rock, Arkansas

Long Papers
>   Russell Long Papers, Louisiana State Collection, Louisiana State University,
>   Baton Rouge, Louisiana

Lyndon B. Johnson Papers
> Lyndon B. Johnson Papers, Johnson Presidential Library, University of Texas, Austin, Texas

McCray Papers
> John H. McCray Papers, South Caroliniana Library, University of South Carolina, Columbia, South Carolina

Mason Papers
> Lucy Randolph Mason Papers, Rare Book, Manuscript, and Special Collections Library, Duke University, Durham, North Carolina

MFBF Papers
> Mississippi Farm Bureau Federation Papers, Special Collections Department, Mitchell Memorial Library, Mississippi State University, Mississippi State, Mississippi

Moore Papers
> Amzie Moore Papers, State Historical Society of Wisconsin, Madison, Wisconsin

Morehead Papers
> Richard M. Morehead Papers, Barker Center, University of Texas, Austin, Texas

Morris Papers
> John B. Morris Papers, South Caroliniana Library, University of South Carolina, Columbia, South Carolina

NAACP Papers
> National Association for the Advancement of Colored People Papers, Manuscript Division, Library of Congress, Washington, D.C.

NUL Papers
> National Urban League Papers, Manuscript Division, Library of Congress, Washington, D.C.

OHSA Interviews
> Oral History of Southern Agriculture Interviews, by Lu Ann Jones, National Museum of American History, Washington, D.C.

Owsley Papers
> Frank W. Owsley Papers, Special Collections and University Archives, Heard Memorial Library, Vanderbilt University, Nashville, Tennessee

Rock 'n' Soul Interviews
> Rock 'n' Soul Interviews, National Museum of American History, Washington, D.C.

Sanders Papers
> Claudia Thomas Sanders Papers, South Caroliniana Library, University of South Carolina, Columbia, South Carolina

SA Records
> Records of the Secretary of Agriculture, Record Group 16, National Archives and Records Administration, Washington, D.C.

Sarratt Papers
> Reed Sarratt Papers, Southern Historical Collection, Wilson Library, University of North Carolina, Chapel Hill, North Carolina

SCCHR Papers
  South Carolina Council on Human Relations Papers, South Caroliniana Library,
  University of South Carolina, Columbia, South Carolina
Sillers Papers
  Walter Sillers Papers, Delta State University Archives, Cleveland, Mississippi
Silver Papers
  James Silver Papers, Special Collections, University of Mississippi,
  Oxford, Mississippi
Smith Papers
  Lillian Smith Papers, Hargrett Rare Book and Manuscript Library, University of
  Georgia, Athens, Georgia
SOHP Collection
  Southern Oral History Program Collection, Southern Historical Collection,
  Wilson Library, University of North Carolina, Chapel Hill, North Carolina
Stevens Papers
  Boswell Stevens Papers, Special Collections Department, Mitchell Memorial
  Library, Mississippi State University, Mississippi State, Mississippi
Surgeon General's Records
  Records of the Army Surgeon General's Office, Record Group 112, National
  Archives and Records Administration, Washington, D.C.
Tureaud Papers
  A. P. Tureaud Papers, Amistad Collection, Tulane University, New Orleans,
  Louisiana
Workman Papers
  W. D. Workman Jr. Papers, Modern Political Collections, South Caroliniana
  Library, University of South Carolina, Columbia, South Carolina

CHAPTER ONE

1. The best analysis of the development of crop lien laws is Harold D. Woodman, *New
   South, New Law: The Legal Foundations of Credit and Labor Relations in the Post-
   bellum Agricultural South* (Baton Rouge, 1995). See also his "Post–Civil War Southern Agriculture and the Law," *Agricultural History* 52 (January 1979): 319–37. On
   labor laws, see William Cohen, *At Freedom's Edge: Black Mobility and the Southern
   White Quest for Racial Control, 1861–1915* (Baton Rouge, 1991), and Pete Daniel, *The
   Shadow of Slavery: Peonage in the South, 1901–1969* (Urbana, 1972).
2. *Historical Statistics of the United States, Colonial Times to 1970*, pt. 1 (Washington,
   D.C., 1975), series K 17–81, "Farm Population, Farmers, Land in Farms, and Value
   of Farm Property and Farm Products Sold by State, 1850 to 1969," 458; series K
   82–108, "Characteristics of Farm Operators, 1880 to 1969," 465; series K 109–153,
   "Farms, by Race and Tenure of Operator, and Acreage and Value, by Tenure of Operator, 1880 to 1969," 465; Donald Holley, "The Second Great Emancipation: The
   Rust Cotton Picker and How It Changed Arkansas," *Arkansas Historical Quarterly*
   52 (Spring 1993): 44–77. Primarily because of discriminatory U.S. Department of
   Agriculture (USDA) policies, African American farmers left agriculture at a higher

rate than white farmers. Had the rate been the same, 300,000 black farmers would have remained rather than less than 20,000 (William C. Payne Jr. to author, February 12, 1992).

3. Interview with Cauley Cortwright, Rolling Fork, Mississippi, December 20, 1973, by William M. Cash, Delta State University Archives, Cleveland, Mississippi.

4. A September 1942 draft report of the Southeast Region Post-War Planning Committee (representing most USDA agencies) proposed an agenda that would doom most small farmers. "Those who do not produce to exchange are lost to the economic system and to themselves," judged an almost biblical passage. The report applauded the exodus from farms and advocated doing "everything possible" to prevent those who left from returning to agriculture. See T. S. Buie, "A Program for the Study of Intermediate and Long-Time Agricultural Adjustments in the Southeast," September 15, 1942, box 867, William A. Hartman file, Regional Files, 1907–46, Southeast, BAE Records. See also Sidney Baldwin, *Poverty and Politics: The Rise and Decline of the Farm Security Administration* (Chapel Hill, 1968), and Richard S. Kirkendall, *Social Scientists and Farm Politics in the Age of Roosevelt* (Ames, 1982).

5. Robert Palmer, *Deep Blues* (New York, 1982), 3–7; Alan Lomax, *The Land Where the Blues Began* (New York, 1993), 405–22; interview 70, Coahoma County, Mississippi, August 25, 1944, Low-Income Farmer Survey, Division of Program Surveys, BAE Records; Walter W. Wilcox, *The Farmer in the Second World War* (Ames, 1947), 84–89.

6. Charles M. Payne, *I've Got the Light of Freedom: The Organizing Tradition and the Mississippi Freedom Struggle* (Berkeley, 1995), 29–31, 47, 56–57; Jenifer W. Gilbert, "The Civil Rights Movement in Cleveland, Mississippi, 1960, 1964," paper presented in Tim Tyson's class in African American history, University of Wisconsin.

7. Frank Alexander, "Current and Anticipated Rural Migration Problems of Coahoma County, Mississippi," February 19, 1945, Sample Counties Reconnaissance Surveys, box 250, General Correspondence, 1941–46, BAE Records. For examples of field agents' reports, see Rensis Likert to R. Keith Kane, memorandum, July 31, 1942; Donovan Senter to Waldemar A. Nielsen, memorandum, September 9, 1942, box 4, Division of Program Surveys; and Edward Moe, "The Problem of Increasing Race Tension in Augusta and Richmond County, Georgia," August 18, 1942, ibid.

8. The best treatment of southern racial violence during the war is James A. Burran III, "Racial Violence in the South during World War II" (Ph.D. diss., University of Tennessee, 1977).

9. Michael K. Honey, *Southern Labor and Black Civil Rights: Organizing Memphis Workers* (Urbana, 1993), 145–213, and "The Popular Front in the American South: The View from Memphis," *International Labor and Working-Class History* (Fall 1986): 44–58; Robert R. Korstad, "If You Beat the White Man at One Trick, He Will Try Another," paper presented at the Tulane-Cambridge Atlantic World Studies Program Conference, Sidney Sussex College, Cambridge University, March 24–26, 1999; Robert Korstad and Nelson Lichtenstein, "Opportunities Found and Lost: Labor, Radicals, and the Early Civil Rights Movement," *Journal of American History* 75 (December 1988): 786–811.

10. Moe, "Problem of Increasing Race Tension." See also "Race Tension and Farm

Wages in the Rural South," September 22, 1944, Manuscripts, 1940–46, box 1029, BAE Records.

11. Joanne Grant, *Ella Baker: Freedom Bound* (New York, 1998), 25–28, 45–83; Barbara Ransby, "Ella J. Baker and the Black Radical Tradition" (Ph.D. diss., University of Michigan, 1996), 85–132, 147–82; Payne, *I've Got the Light of Freedom*, 81–84; interview with Ella Baker, April 19, 1977, by Sue Thrasher and Casey Hayden, SOHP Collection.

12. Grant, *Ella Baker*, 7–20, 45–83; Ransby, "Ella J. Baker," 1–84, 147–82; Baker interview, April 19, 1977.

13. Grant, *Ella Baker*, 68–83.

14. Anne C. Loveland, *Lillian Smith: A Southerner Confronting the South* (Baton Rouge, 1986), 12–16, 22–79; Margaret Rose Gladney, "Personalizing the Political, Politicizing the Personal: Reflections on Editing the Letters of Lillian Smith," in *Carryin' On in the Lesbian and Gay South*, edited by John Howard (New York, 1997), 93–103; Margaret Rose Gladney, ed., *How Am I to Be Heard?: Letters of Lillian Smith* (Chapel Hill, 1993), xvi.

15. Interviews 51, 53, Tishomingo County, Mississippi, August 18, 1944, and interview 47, Tishomingo County, Mississippi, August 17, 1944, Low-Income Farmer Survey, Division of Program Surveys, BAE Records.

16. Interview 89, Pope County, Arkansas, August 31, 1944, ibid. The dislike of working among strangers was mentioned by several people. See, for example, interview 83, Chicot County, Arkansas, August 29, 1944, and interview 88, Pope County, Arkansas, August 31, 1944, ibid.

17. Interview 61, Lafayette County, Mississippi, August 22, 1944; interview 16, Randolph County, Arkansas, August 7, 1944; and interview 31, Randolph County, Arkansas, August 11, 1944, ibid.

18. Interview 70, August 25, 1944; William Watts Ball to Sarah B. Copeland, January 18, 1945, box 41, Ball Papers.

19. R. B. Peebles, "Scouting Survey Appraisal of Low Income Farmers' Reasons for Remaining on Their Farms," Harnett County, N.C., August 7–8, 1944, Low-Income Farmer Survey, Division of Program Surveys, BAE Records.

20. See Corrington Gill to Harold D. Smith, May 10, November 15, 1944, box 41, CCPA Records. For an overview of southern migration, see Jack Temple Kirby, *Rural Worlds Lost: The American South, 1920–1960* (Baton Rouge, 1987), 275–333. On the war in the South, see Pete Daniel, "Going among Strangers: Southern Reactions to World War II," *Journal of American History* 77 (December 1990): 886–911.

21. John Dos Passos, *State of the Nation* (Boston, 1944), 94.

22. Agnes E. Meyer, *Journey through Chaos* (New York, 1943), 198.

23. Interview with Lena Porrier Legnon, Jeanerette, Louisiana, May 30, 1988, by Lu Ann Jones, OHSA Interviews; interview with Cordell Jackson, Memphis, Tennessee, May 11, 1992, by Pete Daniel and David Less, and interview with Cordell Jackson, Memphis, Tennessee, May 19, 1992, by Pete Daniel, Charlie McGovern, and David Less, Rock 'n' Soul Interviews. See "Summary Statement on the Employment Situation in the Hampton Roads Area, Virginia," April 22, 1943, Hampton Roads, box 56, CCPA Records.

24. J. Clark Johnstone to Corrington Gill, July 26, 1943, box 72, and "Report on the Ad-

equacy of Services and Facilities in the Mobile Area," September 27, 1943, box 56, CCPA Records; Karen Tucker Anderson, "Last Hired, First Fired: Black Women Workers during World War II," *Journal of American History* 69 (June 1982): 82–97; Robin D. G. Kelley, *Race Rebels: Culture, Politics, and the Black Working Class* (New York, 1994), 55–75.

25. *Atlanta Journal,* December 14, 1944, and *Atlanta Constitution,* December 18, 1944, clippings in box 4, Hamilton Papers. For Atlanta's follow-through on equalizing facilities, see Esther Jones Protho, "A Study of Selected Community Organization Techniques Employed by the Atlanta Urban League in Stimulating Social Action on Behalf of the Equalization of School Facilities for Negroes in Atlanta, 1944–49" (M.A. thesis, Atlanta University, 1950), copy in ibid. For an overview of the racial situation in Atlanta, see Ronald H. Baylor, *Race and the Shaping of Twentieth-Century Atlanta* (Chapel Hill, 1996), and Lorraine Nelson Spritzer and Jean B. Bergmark, *Grace Towns Hamilton and the Politics of Southern Change* (Athens, 1997), 101–14.

26. Meyer, *Journey through Chaos,* 202, 209–10. See also C. Calvin Smith, "Diluting an Institution: The Social Impact of World War II on the Arkansas Family," *Arkansas Historical Quarterly* 39 (Spring 1980): 21–34, and Clayton R. Koppes and Gregory D. Black, *Hollywood Goes to War: How Politics, Profits, and Propaganda Shaped World War II Movies* (New York, 1987), 177–78.

27. Daniel, "Going among Strangers."

28. Allan Bérubé, *Coming Out Under Fire: The History of Gay Men and Women in World War Two* (New York, 1991).

CHAPTER TWO

1. Lillian Smith, "Growing Up in an Atomic Age: Let Us Think of Children," speech, 1946, series 1283A, box 42, Smith Papers. See Paul S. Boyer, *By the Bomb's Early Light* (New York, 1985). Five months after the war ended, William Watts Ball, editor of the *Charleston News and Courier,* admitted to his son, "To be sure, I cannot escape from the thought of the atomic bomb, and still, 'God's in his heaven'" (William Watts Ball to Philip Ball, January 6, 1946, box 42, Ball Papers).

2. John McCray to Theron L. Caudle, May 18, 1946; Caudle to McCray, May 28, 1946; McCray to Governor Ransome J. Williams, June 12, 1946; McCray to Thomas B. Pearce, May 29, 1946; McCray to E. R. Lewis, March 5, 1946, box 1; and "Memorandum: Batesburg, S.C., Police System," August 22, 1946, box 7, McCray Papers.

3. See E. Franklin Frazier, "Human, All Too Human," *Survey Graphic* 36 (January 1947): 74–75, 99–100, copy in box 6, Hamilton Papers, and Walter B. Weare, *Black Business in the New South: A Social History of the North Carolina Mutual Life Insurance Company* (Urbana, 1973).

4. Patricia Sullivan, *Days of Hope: Race and Democracy in the New Deal Era* (Chapel Hill, 1996), 134, 164–68, 218–19; Lorraine Nelson Spritzer and Jean B. Bergmark, *Grace Towns Hamilton and the Politics of Southern Change* (Athens, 1997), 109–14.

5. Junius Irving Scales and Richard Nickson, *Cause at Heart: A Former Communist Remembers* (Athens, 1987), 172.

6. Ibid.; James M. Hinton to William Watts Ball, December 1, 1947, box 7, and Ball to W. D. Workman Jr., February 24, 1948, box 44, Ball Papers (emphasis in original).

7. Chalmers Archer Jr., *Growing Up Black in Rural Mississippi: Memories of a Family, Heritage of a Place* (New York, 1992), 126–27. On the subversive nature of such resistance, see James C. Scott, *Weapons of the Weak: Everyday Forms of Peasant Resistance* (New Haven, 1985), and *Domination and the Arts of Resistance: Hidden Transcripts* (New Haven, 1990).

8. Charles S. Reid to William Watts Ball, July 19, August 30, 1948, box 44, Ball Papers.

9. Mary L. Dudziak, "Desegregation as a Cold War Imperative," *Stanford Law Review* 41 (November 1988): 61–120.

10. Numan V. Bartley, *The New South, 1945–1980* (Baton Rouge, 1995), 74–104; Michael K. Honey, *Southern Labor and Black Civil Rights: Organizing Memphis Workers* (Urbana, 1993), 245–77; James Dombrowski to Eleanor Roosevelt, May 31, 1946, April 23, 1947, box 20, Braden Papers.

11. Walter Sillers to Oscar F. Bledsoe, July 31, 1948, box 28, folder 16, Sillers Papers; Nadine Cohodas, *Strom Thurmond and the Politics of Southern Change* (New York, 1993), 154–93; John Egerton, *Speak Now against the Day: The Generation before the Civil Rights Movement in the South* (New York, 1994), 471–513; Sullivan, *Days of Hope*, 249–75; Anders Walker, "Legislating Virtue: How Segregationists Disguised Racial Discrimination as Moral Reform following *Brown v. Board of Education*," *Duke Law Journal* 47 (November 1997): 399–424.

12. Michael K. Honey, "Operation Dixie: Labor and Civil Rights in the Postwar South," *Mississippi Quarterly* 45 (Fall 1992): 440–43.

13. *Charlottesville Daily Progress*, November 20, 1948, and *New York Times*, November 21, 1948, clippings in box 22, Braden Papers; Egerton, *Speak Now against the Day*, 529–30.

14. Charles W. Edwards to William H. Bell, February 5, 1948; William F. Adams to Edwards, February 5, 1948; Edwards to Adams, February 7, 1948; and *Birmingham News-Age Herald*, February 15, 1948, clipping in box 3, Edwards Papers; Ralph B. Draughon, memorandum, February 16, 1948; Bell to Registrar, February 21, 1948; Edwards to Bell, February 24, 1948; and Jim [last name illegible] to Draughon, April 1, 1949, box 3, Draughon Papers.

15. Donald Jones to Walter White, January 23, 1948, Education, Student Attitudes in South, 1947–48, II A, box 247, NAACP Papers.

16. L. E. Austin to Walter White, February 7, 1947, ibid.

17. Arna Bontemps to Walter White, February 12, 1948, and Louise Young to Bontemps, March 25, 1948, ibid.

18. Donald Davidson to John Gould Fletcher, January 2, June 14, 1949, box 2, Davidson Papers; *Chronicle of the 20th Century* (Mount Kisco, N.Y., 1987), 631.

19. Sarah Patton Boyle, *The Desegregated Heart: A Virginian's Stand in Time of Transition* (New York, 1962), 22–23, 43, 53–59, 77–85; Joanna Bowen Gillespie, "Sarah Patton Boyle's *Desegregated Heart*," in *Beyond Image and Convention: Explorations in Southern Women's History*, edited by Janet L. Coryell, Martha H. Swain, Sandra Gioia Treadway, and Elizabeth Hayes Turner (Columbia, Mo., 1998), 158–68.

20. Wade F. Milam to William Watts Ball, October 1, 1948, box 44, Ball Papers. See also

Floride Gantt to Ball, July 7, 1949, and Ball to Virginia White, October 14, 1949, box 45, ibid.

21. Barbara S. Griffith, *The Crisis of American Labor: Operation Dixie and the Defeat of the CIO* (Philadelphia, 1988), 22–45, 72, 74, 161–76; Honey, "Operation Dixie," 440–52; Honey, *Southern Labor*, 214–44.

22. Lucy Randolph Mason to David S. Burgess, April 19, 1949; Mason to Natalie Bunting, March 5, 1949, box 6; and James A. Crain to Mason, July 13, 1950, box 7, Mason Papers (emphasis in original); Honey, "Operation Dixie," 441–42. For a discussion of working-class faiths, see Paul Conkin, *American Originals: Homemade Varieties of Christianity* (Chapel Hill, 1997), 110–61, 276–315.

23. Lucy Randolph Mason to Kent Ruth, October 19, 1948, box 6, Mason Papers.

24. Tuskegee Civic Association, C. A. Walwyn, president, William P. Mitchell, secretary, telegram to editor, *Montgomery Examiner*, June 29, 1949, box 12, Dobbins Papers.

25. See Richard Kluger, *Simple Justice: The History of "Brown v. Board of Education" and Black America's Struggle for Equality* (New York, 1975).

26. "President's Annual Address," May 15, 1952, and "Committee Reports," Delta Council Annual Report, 1951–52, Early C. Ewing Jr., D&PLC Records. When Hodding Carter surmised in a *Reader's Digest* article in 1954 that the black population of the South would probably decrease as mechanization lessened the need for rural laborers, he received a barbed reply from Pauli Murray, who criticized his "thinning out" idea (Murray to Carter, August 16, 1954, Correspondence, 1954, Carter Papers).

27. Archer, *Growing Up Black in Rural Mississippi*, 117.

28. Myles Horton to Charles S. Johnson, July 1, November 27, 1953, July 2, 1954, box 86, Charles Johnson Papers.

29. "Facts Forum, State of the Nation," September 14, 1953, transcript in H-37, box 4, file 1, Correspondence, August–September 1953, Ashmore Papers (emphasis in original).

30. T. R. Montgomery to Frank Clement, September 14, 1953, and Clement to Montgomery, September 29, 1953, box 37, Clement Papers; Walker, "Legislating Virtue," 406–24.

31. Mrs. M. Lafayette Jones to Frank Clement, December 6, 1953, box 37, Clement Papers (emphasis in original).

32. Lella M. Galvoni to Frank Clement, March 13, 1954; F. K. Lashbrook to Clement, September 15, 1953; Mrs. Martin C. Hunt to Clement, October 8, 1953; and R. K. Pruitt to Clement, October 19, 1953, ibid. (emphasis in original).

33. Kate Steel to Frank Clement, December 2, 1953, ibid. (emphasis in original).

34. Hodding Carter to Tom Karsell, August 11, 1953, Correspondence, 1953, Carter Papers; Kluger, *Simple Justice*, 717–18.

CHAPTER THREE

1. Harry Crews, *A Childhood: The Biography of a Place* (New York, 1978), 128–29.

2. On class structure during the 1930s and 1940s, see Arthur F. Raper, *Preface to Peas-*

antry: A Tale of Two Black Belt Counties (New York, 1968), and "Cultural Reconnaissance, Greene County, Georgia," September 18, 1944, and Frank D. Alexander, "Cultural Reconnaissance Survey of Coahoma County, Mississippi," n.d., Farm Population and Rural Welfare Sample Counties, Reconnaissance Surveys, box 250, BAE Records. On the domestic allotment program, see Harold F. Breimyer, "Agricultural Philosophies and Policies in the New Deal," *Minnesota Law Review* 68 (1983–84): 338–39, 343–44; Anthony J. Badger, *Prosperity Road: The New Deal, Tobacco, and North Carolina* (Chapel Hill, 1980), 89–94, 125–26, 220–29; Richard S. Kirkendall, *Social Scientists and Farm Politics in the Age of Roosevelt* (Ames, 1982), 92, 100–102; Pete Daniel, *Breaking the Land: The Transformation of Cotton, Tobacco, and Rice Cultures since 1880* (Urbana, 1985), 101–2; and Donald H. Grubbs, *Cry from the Cotton: The Southern Tenant Farmers' Union and the New Deal* (Chapel Hill, 1971), 3–61.

3. David Ray James, "The Transformation of Local, State, and Class Structures and Resistance to the Civil Rights Movement in the South" (Ph.D. diss., University of Wisconsin, 1981), 263–88; Breimyer, "Agricultural Philosophies," 347–48; Deborah Fitzgerald, *The Business of Breeding: Hybrid Corn in Illinois, 1890–1940* (Ithaca, 1990); James C. Cobb, *The Most Southern Place on Earth: The Mississippi Delta and the Roots of Regional Identity* (New York, 1992), 206.

4. David Westfall, "Agricultural Allotments as Property," *Harvard Law Review* 79 (April 1966): 1188–89; Neil E. Harl, *Agricultural Law* (New York, 1998), vol. 11, sec. 91.02[3], "Transfers of Allotment." For a recent analysis of the Agricultural Stabilization and Conservation Service (ASCS), see Neil D. Hamilton, "Legal Issues Arising in Federal Court Appeals of ASCS Decisions Administering Federal Farm Programs," *Hamline Law Review* 12 (Fall 1989): 633–48. On rice allotments, see Murray R. Benedict and Oscar C. Stine, *The Agricultural Commodity Programs: Two Decades of Experience* (New York, 1956), 141–44, and Daniel, *Breaking the Land*, 276–77, 280–81. On the reorganization of USDA programs, see Gladys L. Baker, Wayne D. Rasmussen, Vivian Wiser, and Jane M. Porter, *Century of Service: The First One Hundred Years of the United States Department of Agriculture* (Washington, D.C., 1963), 482–83, 487. For a discussion of the changes in the cotton plan in 1965, see Brainerd S. Parrish, "Comment: Cotton Allotments—Another 'New Property,'" *Texas Law Review* 45 (March 1967): 734–53. On credit arrangements, see "Mortgages on Future Crops as Security for Government Loans," *Yale Law Journal* 47 (November 1937): 98–111, and Keith G. Meyer, "Potential Problems Connected with the Use of 'Crops' as Collateral for an Article 9 Security Interest," *Agricultural Law Journal* 3 (1981–82): 115.

5. U.S. Department of Agriculture, *Agricultural Statistics, 1967* (Washington, D.C., 1967), table 85, "Cotton: Acreage, Yield, Production, Value, and Foreign Trade, United States, 1866–1966," 74, and *Agricultural Statistics, 1977* (Washington, D.C., 1977), table 78, "Cotton: Area, Yield, Production, and Value, United States, 1959–76," 59.

6. See Paul D. V. Manning to Ezra Taft Benson, May 5, 1953; Joe E. Culpepper to Benson, May 26, 1953; Culpepper to K. A. Spencer, April 24, 1953; and John A. Davis to J. Earl Coke, June 2, 1953, Research Work, Regional Field Laboratories, 1953, SA Records; James, "Transformation of Local, State, and Class Structures," 267–88;

Harold Hoffsommer, "The AAA and the Cropper," *Social Forces* 13/14 (1935): 496–97; Badger, *Prosperity Road*, 125–26, 220–23; James C. Cobb, "'Somebody Done Nailed Us on the Cross': Federal Farm and Welfare Policy and the Civil Rights Movement in the Mississippi Delta," *Journal of American History* 77 (December 1990): 914–15; Karen Sorlie Russo, "Farm Clients Beware of ASCS Mysteries," *Compleat Lawyer* 8 (Winter 1991): 57–60; John H. Davidson, ed., *Agricultural Law* (Colorado Springs, 1981), vol. 1, sec. 1.25, "Appeal Regulations"; Robert Earl Martin, "Negro-White Participation in the AAA Cotton and Tobacco Referenda in North and South Carolina: A Study in Differential Voting and Attitudes in Selected Areas" (Ph.D. diss., University of Chicago, 1947), 242–43, 259–60, 263, 267; and *Lee v. De Berry et al.*, 65 S.E.2d 775 (1951). I am indebted to Anthony Badger for bringing the Martin study to my attention.

7. On the consequences of state planning that has ignored rural culture, see James C. Scott, *Seeing Like a State: How Certain Schemes to Improve the Human Condition Have Failed* (New Haven, 1998), 183–306.

8. For examples of farmers' knowledge, see Theodore Rosengarten, *All God's Dangers: The Life of Nate Shaw* (New York, 1974), and J. M. Spicer, *Beginnings of the Rice Industry in Arkansas* (Stuttgart, Ark., 1964).

9. Arthur Raper, "Uses Being Made by Rural Families of Increased Wartime Income," January 1946; Frank D. Alexander and Edward B. Williams, "Some Postwar Social Trends in the Rural Southeast, March 1946"; Theo L. Vaughn, "Some Postwar Social Trends in the Rural West-South-Central States," March 1946, General Correspondence, 1941–46, Farm Population and Rural Welfare, Sample Counties, Reconnaissance Survey, box 250; and J. P. Cavin and Nathan Koffsky, "Business Conditions in Alabama," December 10, 1948, General Correspondence, 1946–53, Economic Stabilization, BAE Records.

10. Oscar Johnston to Walter Sillers, April 24, 1947, box 32, folder 14, Sillers Papers; statements and president's reports, March 31, 1947, March 31, 1948, March 31, 1949, March 31, 1950, series II, box 4, and Basil J. Young diary, 1949, 1950, D&PLC Records. See also interviews with James Hand, F. H. "Slim" Holiman, and Jere Nash, Greenville, Mississippi, July 3, 1974, by William M. Cash, Delta State University Archives, Cleveland, Mississippi. In 1953, the D&PLC placed 7,220 bales of cotton (valued at $1,269,493) under loan. Only the California firm of Giffen, Inc., placed more cotton under loan (7,314 bales). See "Producers with Largest Quantity of Cotton and Rice under Loan, 1953 Crop, Mississippi," Commodity Stabilization Service, Records of the Deputy Administrator, Price Support, 1935–57, ASCS Records. On contemplated aid to southern farmers evicted by mechanization, see Bradford Jordan to Walter White, January 15, 1947; Madison Jones to White, memorandum, March 25, 1947; and Lester B. Granger to White, April 14, 1947, Labor, Agriculture, Wage Ceiling, 1945–48, II B, box 85, NAACP Papers; and J. Lewis Henderson, "In the Cotton Delta," *Survey Graphic* 36 (January 1947): 51, 111.

11. Early C. Ewing Jr. to W. N. Bangham, June 27, 1950, Ewing Correspondence, D&PLC Records; T. M. Patterson to Secretary of Agriculture, January 30, 1953, Committee, Mobilization, Mississippi, SA Records; interview with Cauley Cortwright, Rolling Fork, Mississippi, December 20, 1973, by William M. Cash, Delta State University Archives, Cleveland, Mississippi; *Historical Statistics of the United*

States, Colonial Times to 1970, pt. 1 (Washington, D.C., 1975), series K 17–81, "Farm Population, Farmers, Land in Farms, and Value of Farm Property and Farm Products Sold by State, 1850 to 1969," 458.

12. Claude A. Barnett, "Address before the Conference of Presidents of Negro Land Grant Colleges, Washington, D.C., October 18, 1951," and John W. Davis to R. B. Atwood, June 20, 1951, Negroes, General Correspondence, SA Records; Emmett Sizemore to Bailey Hill, May 16, 1950, box 58, ACES Papers.

13. John B. Jordan to J. R. Otis, February 29, 1948, and Otis to P. O. Davis, July 9, 1948, box 358, ACES Papers; *Pittsburgh Courier*, December 15, 22, 1951, clippings in Negroes, Correspondence, 1940–55, SA Records.

14. P. O. Davis to Walter Randolph, October 19, 1949, box 56; Davis to Edward O'Neal, November 8, 1949; O'Neal to Davis, December 3, 1949, box 57; Davis to A. H. Barnett, April 15, 1950, box 56; Davis to Senator Lister Hill, May 1, 1950; and O'Neal to Davis, February 3, 1950, box 57, ACES Papers. For insight into the politics in the Extension Service office at Auburn University, see Howard C. Smith to Charles G. Dobbins, April 24, 1947, box 12, Dobbins Papers. For a critique of the Farm Bureau and Extension Service, see John Salmond, *A Southern Rebel: The Life and Times of Aubrey Williams, 1890–1965* (Chapel Hill, 1983), 198–218.

15. Gladys Tappan to P. O. Davis, January 16, 1950, box 58 (emphasis in original); Mrs. Walter Mastin to Davis, February 24, 1950; Davis to Mastin, February 28, 1950; Mattie Jo Barber to Davis, March 10, 1950; Mastin to Davis, April 6, 1950; Davis to Mastin, April 15, 1950; Barber to Davis, April 21, 1950; and Davis to Barber, April 25, 1950, Correspondence, 1949–50, A–E, box 56, ACES Papers.

16. U.S. Bureau of the Census, *Census of Agriculture, 1964*, vol. 2, *General Report*, table 3, "Number of Farms by Color and by Tenure of Operator, and Land in Farms by Tenure of Operator, by Regions and States, 1880–1964," 756; table 4, "Number of Negro and Other Nonwhite Farm Operators, by Regions and States, 1900 to 1964," 761. See also Craig Heinicke, "African-American Migration and Urban Labor Skills, 1950 and 1960," *Agricultural History* 68 (Spring 1994): 185–98.

17. Edward L. Schapsmeier and Frederick H. Schapsmeier, "Eisenhower and Agricultural Reform: Ike's Farm Policy Legacy Appraised," *American Journal of Economics and Sociology* 51 (April 1992): 147–59; Ezra Taft Benson, *Cross Fire: The Eight Years with Eisenhower* (Garden City, 1962).

18. L. N. Flippo Jr. to Dwight D. Eisenhower, February 16, 1953, Farming 2, Family Farming, SA Records.

19. M. G. Mann to Ezra Taft Benson, March 26, 1953, Cotton, Acreage Allotments, Marketing Quotas, SA Records; Harold Cooley to Mann, November 12, 1954, box 41, Cooley Papers.

20. Ezra Taft Benson to Donald Paarlberg, July 23, 1953, Farm Program, SA Records.

21. On Benson's understanding of the complexities of the farm program, see interview with Herschel D. Newsom, Washington, D.C., session 1, March 21, 1968, by Ed Edwin, Dwight D. Eisenhower Papers. "He couldn't understand that the free market had been tampered with and interfered with wisely, in my judgment," Newsom said of Benson, "to the point that it was just sheer nonsense to talk about reverting to a free market."

22. Boswell Stevens to James O. Eastland, October 16, 1953, Subject Files, Eastland,

1953–62, Stevens Papers; Jamie Whitten to Ezra Taft Benson, October 12, 1953; Benson to Whitten, November 2, 1953; Whitten to Benson, November 21, 1953; Karl Loos to Benson, November 27, 1953; and Gerald L. Dearing to Benson, December 3, 1953, Cotton, Acreage Allotments, Marketing Quotas, SA Records. Solicitor Karl Loos confidentially informed Benson that he did have the authority to declare an emergency. See Loos to Benson, November 27, 1953; Whitten to Benson, December 5, 1953; A. Van Wagenen Jr. to Loos, December 4, 1953; Benson to Whitten, December 21, 1953; Whitten to Benson, January 6, 1954; and Benson to Whitten, January 15, 1954, ibid. On the power of western growers, see John F. Reuther to F. Marion Rhodes, March 12, 1954, ibid.

23. *Hawkins v. State Agriculture Stabilization and Conservation Committee*, 149 F.Supp. 681 (1957), 681–88; *Fulford v. Forman*, 245 F.2d 145 (1956), 145–53.

24. On the number of complaints, see *Fulford v. Forman*, 245 F.2d 145 (1956), 152, n. 20, and Stephen Pace to D. W. Brooks, December 2, 1953, and Brooks to Ezra Taft Benson, December 3, 1953, Cotton, Acreage Allotments, Marketing Quotas, SA Records.

25. Alex Noflin to Congressman James H. Morrison, December 14, 1953; Salvadore Miletello to Morrison, December 16, 1953; Ted C. Jackson to Morrison, December 14, 1953; Harry Himel to Russell Long, March 2, 1954; R. G. Lamb to John L. McClellan, December 11, 1953; and Ross Rizley to McClellan, January 4, 1954, Cotton, Acreage Allotments, Marketing Quotas, SA Records.

26. Walter Sillers to Gerald L. Dearing, August 12, 1955, box 25, folder 8, Sillers Papers.

27. James N. Cundiff to Ezra Taft Benson, April 22, 1954, and Carl L. Burton to Benson, July 15, 1954, Tobacco, box 6, ASCS Records.

28. J. True Hayes to Ezra Taft Benson, July 15, 1954; J. J. Todd to Hayes, July 24, 1954; Hayes to Benson, August 6, 1954; and Benson to Hayes, August 30, 1954, Tobacco, Acreage Allotments, Marketing Quotas, SA Records.

29. Mrs. Clyde V. Collier to Ezra Taft Benson, December 6, 1954, Records of the Tobacco Division, box 5, ASCS Records.

30. Estes Kefauver to Marvin L. McLain, July 18, 1957, Tobacco, Acreage Allotments, Marketing Quotas, SA Records. See also Iris Blitch to Ezra Taft Benson, August 12, 1957; McLain to Blitch, October 4, 1957; Mrs. Van Smith to McLain, October 10, 1957; and John C. Watts to Benson, February 7, March 3, 14, 1958, ibid.

31. Deputy Administrator for Production Adjustment to Chairman, Arkansas State ASC Committee, memorandum, June 23, 1955, Rice, ASCS Records.

32. U.S. House, Subcommittee on Rice, Committee on Agriculture, *National Acreage Allotments—Rice: Hearing on H.R. 7367*, 84th Cong., 1st sess., July 21, 25, 1955, 51.

33. Elizabeth May to Ezra Taft Benson, September 3, 1955, and Pauline Lowry to Sherman Adams, September 20, 1955, Farming 2, Family Farming, SA Records.

34. Basil L. Whitener to Marvin L. McLain, June 6, 1957, and True D. Morse to Whitener, June 14, 1957, Acreage Allotments, Marketing Quotas, SA Records.

35. *J. W. Paul v. United States*, 222 F.Supp. 102 (1963).

36. Mrs. J. O. Lawson to Ezra Taft Benson, April 16, 1953; Benson to Lawson, May 13, 1953, Farming 2, Family Farming; and Henry J. Smith to Benson, August 15, 1953, Farming 4, *Farm Journal* Survey, SA Records. Benson replied that he had lived on a "family-size dairy farm" and was familiar with some of her problems.

37. Norman L. Hicks to Ezra Taft Benson, December 26, 1955, Farm Program, and W. N. Andrews to Benson, n.d. (reply, January 24, 1956), Economics 2, Cost Squeeze, ibid.

38. Mrs. Leigh Kelly to Ezra Taft Benson, April 1953, Farm Program, and M. E. Cousins Jr. to Benson, September 19, 1953, Farming 4, *Farm Journal* Survey, ibid.

39. Gene R. Andrew to Dwight D. Eisenhower, February 20, 1954; Francis L. McLaine to Andrew, March 22, 1954; Andrew to Ezra Taft Benson, January 26, 1956; and Lloyd N. Case to Andrew, March 28, 1956, Rice, ASCS Records.

40. W. O. Vaughn to Ezra Taft Benson, February 17, 1958, Farm Program, SA Records.

41. Mrs. Aron Sanders to Ezra Taft Benson, January 6, 1956, Farming 2, Family Farming, ibid. (emphasis in original).

42. R. Douglas Hurt, *American Agriculture: A Brief History* (Ames, 1994), 353–54.

43. Otis A. O'Dell to Olin D. Johnston, October 18, 1956, and Marvin L. McLain to Johnston, November 7, 1956, Farm Program 2, SA Records. See also J. O. Lollis to William Jennings Bryan Dorn, February 4, 1958, Cotton, Acreage Allotments, Marketing Quotas; Ellis E. Randle to John C. Stennis, September 12, 1956; McLain to Stennis, October 5, 1956, Farm Program; and True D. Morse to Allen J. Ellender, January 28, 1957, Farm Program 3, ibid.

44. Hollis W. Walton to Lyndon B. Johnson, June 9, 1958; Marvin L. McLain to Johnson, July 9, 1958; Walton to Arthur C. Perry, July 11, August 9, 1958; True D. Morse to Johnson, September 8, 1958; Walton to Johnson, September 20, 1958; and McLain to Johnson, October 21, 1958, Commodities, Acreage Allotments, Marketing Quotas, ibid.

45. Linda Flowers, *Throwed Away: Failures of Progress in Eastern North Carolina* (Knoxville, 1990), 59–60; Mrs. W. D. Lewis to Senator Lister Hill, March 25, 1957, and True D. Morse to Hill, May 3, 1957, Farm Program 3, SA Records.

46. W. G. Buie III to Dwight D. Eisenhower, March 17, 1958, Cotton, Acreage Allotments, Marketing Quotas, SA Records.

47. A. W. Todd to Ezra Taft Benson, February 15, 1957, Farm Program 2, Soil Bank, ibid.

48. Claude O. Vardaman to Clyde Wheeler, January 22, 1958, Cotton, Acreage Allotments, Marketing Quotas; George Hoback to Ezra Taft Benson, February 5, 1958, Commodities, Acreage Allotments, Marketing Quotas; George Andrews to Benson, January 29, 1958; and Leonard T. Smith to Lindley Beckworth, February 7, 1958, Cotton, Acreage Allotments, Marketing Quotas, ibid.; James, "Transformation of Local, State, and Class Structures," 288.

49. Mrs. A. A. Luckenbach to Lyndon B. Johnson, March 16, 1958, Subject File, 1958, Agriculture, Soil Conservation, Soil Bank, box 583, Lyndon B. Johnson Papers.

50. C. P. Quincy to Dwight D. Eisenhower, March 13, 1958, Farm Program, SA Records.

51. Marvin L. McLain to John J. Sparkman, April 15, 1959, Commodities, 5-1, Storage, ibid. See also McLain to Herman Talmadge, June 25, 1959, ibid.

52. E. Spech to Secretary of Agriculture, May 4, 1959, Farm Program, ibid.

53. J. P. Kimbrell to Ezra Taft Benson, July 20, 1953, Farming 4, *Farm Journal* Letters, ibid. Kimbrell provided one of the rare glimpses of anti-Semitism in letters to the USDA. He charged that Jews formulated the agricultural programs and intended to take control "when the dirty work is done" and farmers were "reduced to serfdom."

54. Grady West to whom it may concern, July 1959, Farm Credit, ibid. Another Texan, Preston Laws, complained to Ezra Taft Benson that it had cost him $2,000 a year "for you to hold office. I think your program for the cotton farmer was designed with bankruptcy for the farmer in mind" (Laws to Benson, September 17, 1959, Cotton, ibid.).

55. Roy B. Davis to Boswell Stevens, May 11, 1961, Subject Files, Freeman Farm Bill, Stevens Papers.

56. U.S. Bureau of the Census, *Census of Agriculture, 1964*, vol. 2, *General Report*, table 4, "Number of Negro and Other Nonwhite Farm Operators, by Regions and States, 1900 to 1964," 761. As late as October 1998, the USDA's Civil Rights Office was in disarray with no resolution of 616 complaints from African American farmers (*Washington Post*, October 2, 1998, A21).

CHAPTER FOUR

1. On the mind-set that insisted on science and technology, see James C. Scott, *Seeing Like a State: How Certain Schemes to Improve the Human Condition Have Failed* (New Haven, 1998), 4–6, 262–306. Scott labels one element of such thinking "high-modernist ideology," which he carefully differentiates from legitimate scientific inquiry. Although Scott is analyzing other agricultural systems, many of the four ingredients he discusses — "administrative ordering of nature and society," "high-modernist ideology," "an authoritarian state," and "a prostrate civil society" — were relevant in U.S. policy.

2. See James Whorton, *Before "Silent Spring": Pesticides and Public Health in Pre-DDT America* (Princeton, 1974); Scott R. Baker and Chris F. Wilkinson, eds., *The Effects of Pesticides on Human Health* (Princeton, 1990); James E. Davies and R. Doon, "Human Health Effects of Pesticides," in *"Silent Spring" Revisited*, edited by Gino J. Marco, Robert M. Hollingsworth, and William Durham (Washington, D.C., 1987), 113–24; and Colman McCarthy, "Strawberry Fields and Pesticides," *Washington Post*, March 9, 1996, A21.

3. See, for example, Thomas R. Dunlap, *DDT: Scientists, Citizens, and Public Policy* (Princeton, 1981); Robert L. Rudd, *Pesticides and the Living Landscape* (Madison, 1964); and Frank Graham Jr., *Since "Silent Spring"* (Boston, 1970). A USDA estimate put insect damage in 1938 at $1.6 billion. See F. C. Bishopp, "The Tax We Pay to Insects," in *Science in Farming: The Yearbook of Agriculture, 1943–1947* (Washington, D.C., 1947), 614.

4. Edmund P. Russell III, "'Speaking of Annihilation': Mobilizing for War against Human and Insect Enemies, 1914–1945," *Journal of American History* 82 (March 1996): 1505–29, and "War on Insects: Warfare, Insecticides, and Environmental Change in the United States, 1879–1945" (Ph.D. diss., University of Michigan, 1993); Dunlap, *DDT*, 17–25; H. L. Haller and Ruth Busbey, "The Chemistry of DDT," 616–17, and R. W. Harned, "Insecticides for Cotton," 655–57, both in *Science in Farming*.

5. Russell, "'Speaking of Annihilation,'" 1515; Dunlap, *DDT*, 25–31; Donovan Webster, "A Reporter at Large: Heart of the Delta," *New Yorker*, July 8, 1991, 49–54; Eldon W.

Downs and George F. Lemmer, "Origins of Aerial Crop Dusting," *Agricultural History* 39 (July 1965): 123–35; Douglas Helms, "Technological Methods for Boll Weevil Control," *Agricultural History* 53 (October 1979): 286–99; Corley McDarment, "The Use of Airplanes to Destroy the Boll Weevil," *McClure's Magazine* 57 (August 1924): 90–102.

6. *Hammond Ranch Corporation v. Dodson*, 136 S.W.2d 484 (1940), 484–87; Dunlap, *DDT*, 39–55. See also interview with Leo Murphree, Greenwood, Mississippi, October 17, 1987, by Lu Ann Jones, OHSA Interviews.

7. Harry Crews, *A Childhood: The Biography of a Place* (New York, 1978), 39–40.

8. Russell, "'Speaking of Annihilation,'" 1505–29; Haller and Busbey, "Chemistry of DDT," 616–22; Dunlap, *DDT*, 59–63; Rudd, *Pesticides and the Living Landscape*, 10–21.

9. For more information on pesticide brand names and chemical composition, see Donald E. H. Frear, ed., *Pesticide Handbook, 1963* (State College, Pa., 1963).

10. Charles F. Brannan to Edwin Arthur Hall, October 11, 1945, Chemicals, SA Records. See Bishopp, "The Tax We Pay to Insects," 613–15; Haller and Busbey, "Chemistry of DDT," 616–22; Randall Latta and L. D. Goodhue, "Aerosols for Insects," 623–27; Bernard V. Travis, "New Insect Repellents," 628–31; E. F. Knipling, "Pests That Attack Man," 632–42; L. S. Henderson, "DDT in the Home," 643–47; W. A. Baker, "Control of Forage Pests," 651–54; Harned, "Insecticides for Cotton," 655–58; B. A. Porter, "Orchard Insecticides," 659–62; W. H. White, "Insecticides for Vegetables," 663–69; and E. W. Laake and W. G. Bruce, "Controlling Pests of Stock," 670–73, all in *Science in Farming*. On inadequate testing during World War II, see S. Bayne-Jones to R. R. Spencer, March 27, 1946; H. B. Andervont to Spencer, April 8, 1946; and Spencer to Bayne-Jones, April 8, 1946, entry 29, General Subject File, 1945–46, box 641, Medicinal Drugs and Chemicals, file 441, DDT, 1946, Surgeon General's Records. I am indebted to Edmund Russell for sharing his notes from the Surgeon General's Records.

11. Dunlap, *DDT*, 63–66; Virginia Scott Jenkins, *The Lawn: A History of an American Obsession* (Washington, D.C., 1994); Chalmers Archer Jr., *Growing up Black in Rural Mississippi: Memories of a Family, Heritage of a Place* (New York, 1992), 93–94.

12. Webster, "Reporter at Large," 56–57; Downs and Lemmer, "Origins of Aerial Crop Dusting," 133.

13. Rachel Carson, *Silent Spring* (Boston, 1962). On the health implications of pesticides, see Baker and Wilkinson, *Effects of Pesticides*, and Rudd, *Pesticides and the Living Landscape*, 141–56.

14. *Southwestern Bell Telephone Company v. Smith*, 247 S.W.2d 16 (1952); A. J. Loveland to W. Lee O'Daniel, October 11, 1948; Charles F. Brannan to J. W. Fulbright, June 21, 1948; and Brannan to Wayne Morse, July 9, 1948, Chemicals, SA Records; John W. Mitchell, "Plant Growth Regulators," in *Science in Farming*, 256–66.

15. On the emerging law, see George C. Chapman, "Crop Dusting: Scope of Liability and a Need for Reform in the Texas Law," *Texas Law Review* 40 (April 1962): 527–41; "Crop Dusting: Legal Problems in a New Industry," *Stanford Law Review* 6 (December 1953): 69–90; "Liability for Chemical Damage from Aerial Crop Dusting," *Minnesota Law Review* 43 (January 1959): 531–44; and Webster, "Reporter at Large,"

63. On Mississippi, see Stuart W. Turner to Harold Lyons, February 7, 1962, and Lyons to Walter Sillers, March 1, 1962, box 63, folder 13, Sillers Papers. Tara Zachary brought these letters to my attention.

16. *Chapman Chemical Company v. Taylor,* 222 S.W.2d 820 (1949), 820–28. See also *Burns v. Vaughn,* 224 S.W. 2d 365 (1949), 365–66, and *Gotreaux v. Gary,* 94 So.2d 293 (1957), 293–95.

17. *Heeb v. Prysock,* 245 S.W.2d 577 (1952), 577–80. See also *Alexander v. Seaboard Air Line Railroad Company,* 71 S.E.2d 299 (1952), 299–305.

18. *Southwestern Bell Telephone Company v. Smith,* 247 S.W.2d 16 (1952), 16–19. USDA studies claimed that 2,4-D was safe to use around animals. "Tests on some farm animals showed that 2,4-D was not poisonous to cows and sheep even when the animals were fed the acid, or when they ate pasturage sprayed with it. The acid is considered to have little, if any, bad effect on humans" (Mitchell, "Plant Growth Regulators," 262).

19. Hoyt B. Lamm to Alton A. Lennon, September 19, 1960; Lennon to Ezra Taft Benson, September 22, 1960; C. M. Ferguson to Lennon, October 14, 1960, Insecticides, Aeronautics; C. S. Baker to Lyndon B. Johnson, October 6, 1960; and Ferguson to Johnson, October 27, 1960, Insecticides, SA Records; Carson, *Silent Spring,* 76–78; John L. George, *The Pesticide Problem: A Brief Review of Present Knowledge and Suggestions for Action* (New York, 1957), 31.

20. D. H. Janzen to Director, August 3, 1950, box 22; Oscar L. Chapman to Charles F. Brannan, August 14, 1950; and B. L. Hutchinson to Chapman, August 1, 1950, box 24, Correspondence, Insecticides, 1949–60, Division of Wildlife Research, FWS Records; Baker and Wilkinson, *Effects of Pesticides,* 15–18. Most of the 152 accidental deaths attributed to pesticides in 1956, for example, were caused by exposure to such inorganic compounds as arsenic and cyanide or gross disregard for instructions for the application of other compounds.

21. *Kentucky Aerospray v. Mays,* 251 S.W.2d 460 (1952), 460–62. See also Carson, *Silent Spring,* 39–42.

22. See George, *Pesticide Problem,* 6–8, 14–24; Carson, *Silent Spring*; Russell J. Hall, "Impact of Pesticides on Bird Populations," in Marco, Hollingsworth, and Durham, *"Silent Spring" Revisited,* 85–111; and Pete Daniel and Louis Hutchins, "Pesticides on Trial: Miracle Chemicals or Environmental Scourge?," pamphlet for "Science, Power, and Conflict" exhibition, National Museum of American History, Washington, D.C., 1988.

23. M. J. Funchess to L. O. Brackeen, June 7, 1950, and enclosed article, "Government-Farmer Program Needed," *Southern Farmer,* June 1950, box 57, ACES Papers. Eradication dreams died hard. A Texas effort to eradicate boll weevils with malathion in 1995 killed wasps and other beneficial insects and prompted an invasion of beet army worms that feasted on cotton plants. A 1993 Texas law had created the Texas Boll Weevil Eradication Foundation, which assessed farmers $12 to $18 per acre to fund the malathion program. See *New York Times,* August 4, 1996, 24.

24. M. R. Clarkson to E. D. Burgess, October 26, 1956, Plant Pest Control Division, no. 376, and Clarkson, memorandum for the files, September 10, 1957, Regulatory Crops 1, no. 752, ARS Records; A. L. Gray to Walter Sillers, September 26, 1963, box 19, folder 28, Sillers Papers. On Hayes, see Dunlap, *DDT,* 70–71. On Rachel Car-

son's regard for Hayes, see Linda Lear, *Rachel Carson: Witness for Nature* (New York, 1997), 334–35.

25. Robert S. Roe to M. R. Clarkson, January 24, 1957, and Paul A. Clifford, "Pesticide Residues in Fresh Milk Survey of 1955–1956," December 1956, Pesticide Residues in Fresh Milk, 1957, no. 709, ARS Records (emphasis in original). In 1947, the USDA recommended spraying cows daily with a solution containing 0.2 percent DDT, as well as dusting, or dipping, animals in suspensions of DDT. See Laake and Bruce, "Controlling Pests of Stock," 670–73. On how DDT accumulates in human fat, see Dunlap, *DDT*, appendix C, 249–50, and Rudd, *Pesticides and the Living Landscape*, 159–71, 248–67.

26. T. C. Byerly to M. R. Clarkson, February 8, 1957, Pesticide Residues in Fresh Milk, 1957, no. 709, ARS Records.

27. W. I. Patterson, "Report on Food and Drug Administration, USDA, Conference on Spray Residue in Milk," March 7, 1957; M. R. Clarkson to T. C. Byerly, memorandum, March 27, 1957; and A. R. Miller to Clarkson, memorandum, n.d., ibid.

28. A. R. Miller to B. T. Shaw, February 2, 1959, Insecticides, SA Records. See Laake and Bruce, "Controlling Pests of Stock," 670–73, and Dunlap, *DDT*, 68.

29. Herrell DeGraff to Ervin L. Peterson, February 2, 1959, and DeGraff to John Marble, January 31, 1959, Insecticides, SA Records (emphasis in original).

30. T. C. Byerly, memorandum on conference with Herrell DeGraff, enclosed with A. R. Miller to B. T. Shaw, February 2, 1959, and Herrell DeGraff to John Marble, confidential memorandum, January 31, 1959, no. 709, ARS Records.

31. Donald Paarlberg to General Wilton B. Persons, draft confidential memorandum, October 10, 1959; Paarlberg to Ezra Taft Benson, October 12, 1959; Aled P. Davies to Miller Shurtleff, October 12, 1959; True D. Morse to Paarlberg, November 2, 1959; and W. L. Popham to Homer C. Lyon, November 6, 1959, Insecticides, SA Records. See Carson, *Silent Spring*, 178–84.

32. Hart Stilwell, "Farm Fallout Can Kill You!," *True Magazine*, March 1960, copy enclosed with Aled P. Davies to Ervin L. Peterson, March 4, 1960, Insecticides, Publications, SA Records.

33. Ibid.; Justus C. Ward to W. L. Popham, July 14, 1960, Regulatory Crops, no. 252, ARS Records. See also Boswell Stevens to Ross E. Hutchins, February 14, 1961, Subject Files, Ross E. Hutchins, 1955–61, Stevens Papers.

34. E. D. Burgess to B. T. Shaw (through W. L. Popham), January 16, 1957, and M. R. Clarkson to Burgess, March 15, 1957, Regulatory Crops, no. 752, ARS Records; Lear, *Rachel Carson*, 369–70; Dunlap, *DDT*, 73–75, table E-2, 254; George, *Pesticide Problem*, 10.

35. W. L. Popham to B. T. Shaw, January 12, 1960, Regulatory Crops, no. 253, ARS Records.

36. Margaret Till to USDA, June 2, 1959; Homer G. Lyon Jr. to Estes Kefauver, June 25, 1959; and Louise Bankton to Albert Gore, February [?], 1959, Insects, SA Records.

37. "Comparison of 1961 Estimated Availability and 1962 Budget Estimates for Regulatory Programs," n.d., General Correspondence, Regulatory Crops, 1961, no. 396, ARS Records. See Styles Bridges to Ezra Taft Benson, June 30, 1953; Benson to Bridges, July 14, 1953; "Work Performed for, or in Conjunction with, the Department of Defense, Fiscal Year 1953"; Deputy Administrator to J. Earl Coke, memo-

randum, "Program of Animal Disease Research at Plum Island," July 8, 1953; and other material in Reports, Research Work, SA Records.

38. Dunlap, *DDT*, 76–97; Rudd, *Pesticides and the Living Landscape*, 22–41, 64.

39. See Pete Daniel, "A Rogue Bureaucracy: The USDA Fire Ant Campaign of the Late 1950s," *Agricultural History* 64 (Spring 1990): 99–114. Since the publication of this article, additional material emerged that is incorporated into this shortened discussion. I am indebted to Louis Hutchins for helping with research on this project, which was done in conjunction with two exhibits at the National Museum of American History, "Science, Power, and Conflict" and "Science in American Life."

40. E. V. Smith, P. O. Davis, Coyt Wilson, and J. L. Lawson, "The Alabama Polytechnic Institute and the Imported Fire Ant," March 21, 1957, box 2, Draughon Papers; Walter R. Tschinkel, "History and Biology of Fire Ants," n.d., draft furnished by Maureen K. Hinkle; Louisiana Extension Entomologist, *Annual Narrative Report*, 1952, Entomology, December 1, 1951, through November 30, 1952, vol. 586; *Annual Narrative Report*, 1953, Entomology, December 1, 1952, through November 30, 1953, vol. 586; *Annual Narrative Report*, 1954, Entomology, December 1, 1953, through November 30, 1954, vol. 586; *Annual Narrative Report*, 1955, Entomology, December 1, 1954, through November 30, 1955, vol. 586; *Annual Narrative Report of Entomology*, 1956, December 1, 1955, through November 30, 1956, vol. 587; *Annual Narrative Report of Entomology*, 1957, December 1, 1956, through November 30, 1957, vol. 587, Agricultural Extension Papers.

41. Tschinkel, "History and Biology of Fire Ants."

42. Interview with Earl L. Butz, January 15, 1968, by Ed Edwin, Dwight D. Eisenhower Papers.

43. Jeff Hester to James Folsom, March 26, 1957; Jeanette Brown to Folsom, April 13, 1957; and Loretta S. Sullivan to Folsom, April 23, 1957, box SG 13877, Folsom Papers.

44. Smith, Davis, Wilson, and Lawson, "Alabama Polytechnic Institute and the Imported Fire Ant"; J. Lloyd Abbot to E. V. Smith, October 24, 1958, box 2, Draughon Papers.

45. Dunlap, *DDT*, 36–37. On the comparative toxicity of DDT and other chemicals, see George, *Pesticide Problem*, 22–23.

46. Evelyn Reid Griffith, "Fire Ants on the March," *Progressive Farmer*, July 1957, 26, and Patsi Farmer, "Our Ant Problem," *Shreveport Times*, August 18, 1957, copies in box 89, Long Papers.

47. Kirby L. Hays, "The Present Status of the Imported Fire Ant in Argentina," *Journal of Economic Entomology* 51 (February 1958): 111–12. See also Kirby L. Hays, "The Present Status of the Imported Fire Ant, *Solenopsis saevissima richteri Forel*, in Argentina," n.d., box 2, Draughon Papers. An Extension entomologist at Auburn complained that although Congress had appropriated $2.4 million to spray for fire ants in 1957, it had appropriated nothing for research. See W. A. Ruffin to Ralph B. Draughon, April 29, 1958, ibid. In 1994, USDA workers visited Envira, Brazil, and reported a "booming population of fire ants." A USDA team began an attack on the ants. See "Fighting the Fire Ant," *Agricultural Research* 42 (January 1994): 4–9.

48. Ross Laffler to Ezra Taft Benson, December 2, 1957, box 22, Correspondence, 1957–60, Fire Ants, Division of Wildlife Research, FWS Records; Ervin L. Peterson to Laffler, December 16, 1957, Insects, Cooperation, SA Records. On the role of

chemical companies, see K. T. Karabatsos to W. L. Popham, August 29, 1957, Regulatory Crops, Fire Ants, no. 752, ARS Records, and E. D. Burgess to M. R. Clarkson, November 7, 1957, and Homer G. Lyon Jr. to Karabatsos, December 5, 24, 1957, Insects, SA Records.

49. B. T. Shaw to Ernest Swift, December 3, 1957; W. L. Popham to Samuel H. Ordway Jr., December 26, 1957, no. 752; Popham to Rachel Carson, January 28, 1958, no. 944; Popham to M. R. Clarkson, July 1, 1958; and Popham, office memorandum, October 3, 1958, no. 943, Regulatory Crops, Fire Ants, ARS Records; Lear, *Rachel Carson*, 342–43. Representatives of Velsicol Chemical Corporation also appeared in Decatur County and, according to a wildlife researcher, asked "what we knew about heptachlor, one of the company's products" (C. Edward Carlson to Chief, Branch of Wildlife Research, March 18, 1958, Division of Wildlife Research, FWS Records).

50. J. Lloyd Abbot to Kirby L. Hays, June 5, 1958; Abbot to F. S. Arant, June 10, 1958; Abbot to Hays, June 21, 1958; E. V. Smith to Byron Shaw et al., memorandum, July 18, 1958; and Abbot to Ralph B. Draughon, September 22, 1958, box 2, Draughon Papers.

51. For examples of criticism and its impact on ARS personnel, see L. F. Curl to W. L. Popham, May 13, 1958; M. R. Clarkson to D. H. Janzen, June 4, 1958, no. 944; Clarkson to Ervin L. Peterson, June 10, 1958, no. 272; and Homer G. Lyon to Peterson, June 16, 1958, no. 944, Regulatory Crops, ARS Records; Charles H. Callison to Frank Boykin, May 23, 1958; Boykin to Ezra Taft Benson, May 26, 1958; and Peterson to Boykin, June 10, 1958, Federal-State Relations, SA Records; Sterling G. Clawson, "Fire Ant Eradication and Quail," *Alabama Conservation* 30 (December 1958–January 1959): 14–15, 25, copy in box 5, Record Group 543, Alabama Farm Bureau Papers; National Audubon Society, "The Hazards of Broadcasting Toxic Pesticides: As Illustrated by Experience with the Imported Fire Ant Control Program," November 10, 1958, and Dan Lay, "Count Three for Trouble," *Texas Game and Fish*, July 1958, Insecticides, Publications, SA Records; Stilwell, "Farm Fallout Can Kill You!"; "The Program to Eradicate the Imported Fire Ant: Preliminary Observations," The Conservation Foundation, Division of Wildlife Research, FWS Records; and Clarence Cottam to Miller Shurtleff, October 14, 1958, Insects, Fire Ant; Cottam to Shurtleff, November 19, 1958; Shurtleff to Cottam, December 3, 1958; Cottam to Shurtleff, December 19, 1958; and unidentified to Cottam, December 15, 1958, Insecticides, SA Records. On intimidation of fieldworkers, see Rachel Carlson to Director, Bureau of Sport Fisheries and Wildlife, October 6, 8, 1958, Division of Wildlife Research, FWS Records.

52. Lansing J. Parker to Assistant Secretary for Fish and Wildlife, confidential, February 20, 1959, Division of Wildlife Research, FWS Records; Richard H. Stroud to Ervin L. Peterson, March 17, 1959; Peterson to Stroud, April 22, 1959, and enclosed draft; and Fairfield Osborn to Peterson, May 13, 1959, Insects, SA Records; George S. Langford to W. L. Popham, June 24, 1959, no. 113, Regulatory Crops, Fire Ants, ARS Records; Lear, *Rachel Carson*, 343–44.

53. E. D. Burgess to James C. Davis, December 8, 1959; Clarence Cottam to Miller Shurtleff, February 15, 1960, Insecticides; and Clarence Cottam, "Pesticides and Wildlife," speech given at the Ninth Annual Texas Agriculture-Aviation Conference, College Station, Texas, February 21–23, 1960, Pesticides, SA Records.

54. Miller Shurtleff to Clarence Cottam, January 28, 1960; R. C. "Red" Bamberg to Ervin L. Peterson, January 13, 1960; and Peterson to Bamberg, March 1, 1960, Insects, ibid.; "Testimony of ARS on Imported Fire Ants before the Senate Agriculture Appropriations Subcommittee," April 19, 1960, copy in Fire Ants, Division of Wildlife Research, FWS Records.

55. "Testimony of ARS on Imported Fire Ants before the Senate Agriculture Appropriations Subcommittee," April 19, 1960, copy in Fire Ants, Division of Wildlife Research, FWS Papers. See also Rudd, *Pesticides and the Living Landscape*, 268–79; Tschinkel, "History and Biology of Fire Ants"; and *Jackson (Mississippi) Clarion Ledger*, March 8, 1982.

56. Carolyn Lochhead, "It's War! And the Fire Ant Is Winning," *Washington Times*, May 31, 1989, F8; Elizabeth F. Shores, "The Red Imported Fire Ant: Mythology and Public Policy, 1957–1992," *Arkansas Historical Quarterly* 53 (Autumn 1994): 331, 334–35. See Ervin L. Peterson to Secretary, January 15, 1960, and "Notice to Registrants of Heptachlor Regarding Revised Directions for Use," February 9, 1960, Insecticides, SA Records; and "States Protest End of USDA Eradication Program," *Agricultural Chemicals* (April 1965): 48–49, 121–23.

57. Shores, "Red Imported Fire Ant," 320–39; Maureen K. Hinkle, "Impact of the Imported Fire Ant Control Programs on Wildlife and Quality of the Environment," n.d.; R. L. Metcalf, "A Brief History of Chemical Control of the Imported Fire Ant," n.d.; Tschinkel, "History and Biology of Fire Ants." I am indebted to Maureen K. Hinkle for providing drafts of these papers relating to recent research on fire ants.

58. Tschinkel, "History and Biology of Fire Ants"; Jesse Grantham to Dusty Dunstan and Maureen Hinkle, memorandum, November 15, 1988, copy in author's possession; Lochhead, "It's War!"; "Fire Ants Infest Parts of S. California," *Washington Post*, December 20, 1998, A28.

59. B. F. Smith to Delta Council members, October 3, 1962, and Smith to Delta Council board of directors, November 2, 1962, box 32, folder 10, Sillers Papers. On the legal fight against DDT, see Dunlap, *DDT*, 129–245.

60. Report of meeting of Delta Council board of directors, Cleveland, Mississippi, November 27, 1962, box 32, folder 10, Sillers Papers.

61. Walter Sillers to Archie Lee Gray, September 23, 1963, box 19, folder 28, ibid.

62. Archie Lee Gray to Walter Sillers, September 26, 1963, ibid. I am indebted to archivist Tara Zachary for assistance in relocating the Sillers-Gray letters.

CHAPTER FIVE

1. Jack Temple Kirby touched on many of these issues in *The Countercultural South* (Athens, 1995). Will Campbell made a strong point that rednecks are not by definition racists in "Elvis Presley as Redneck," in *In Search of Elvis: Music, Race, Art, Religion*, edited by Vernon Chadwick (New York, 1997), 93–101. On poor whites, see Charles Bolton, *Poor Whites of the Antebellum South: Tenants and Laborers in Central North Carolina and Northeast Mississippi* (Durham, 1994); Bill Cecil-Fronsman, *Common Whites: Class and Culture in Antebellum North Carolina* (Lexington, 1992); J. Wayne Flint, *Poor but Proud: Alabama's Poor Whites* (Tuscaloosa,

1989); Grady McWhiney, *Cracker Culture: Celtic Ways in the Old South* (Tuscaloosa, 1988); and I. A. Newby, *Plain Folk in the New South: Social Change and Cultural Persistence, 1880–1915* (Baton Rouge, 1989). On policing racial categories, see Victoria E. Bynum, "'White Negroes' in Segregated Mississippi: Miscegenation, Racial Identity, and the Law," *Journal of Southern History* 64 (May 1998): 247–76.

2. Rick Bragg, *All Over but the Shoutin'* (New York, 1997), 153; I. F. Stone, *The Haunted Fifties* (New York, 1969), 251. On community attitudes toward poverty and welfare, see Pete Daniel, *Breaking the Land: The Transformation of Cotton, Tobacco, and Rice Cultures since 1880* (Urbana, 1985), 65–90. On white trash, see Roxanne A. Dunbar, "Bloody Footprints: Reflections on Growing up Poor White," 73–85; Annalee Newitz, "White Savagery and Humiliation, or, A New Racial Consciousness in the Media," 131–54, and other essays in *White Trash: Race and Class in America*, edited by Matt Wray and Annalee Newitz (New York, 1997).

3. William Alexander Percy, *Lanterns on the Levee: Recollections of a Planter's Son* (New York, 1953), 149. For excellent examples of lowdown southern speech, see Roy Wilder Jr., *You All Spoken Here* (New York, 1984). On the power of unofficial language, see Mikhail Bakhtin, *Rabelais and His World* (Bloomington, 1984), 145–95.

4. Bragg, *All Over but the Shoutin'*, 7, 58. See also Paul Hemphill, *Wheels: A Season on NASCAR's Winston Cup Circuit* (New York, 1997), 118. Much of the discussion on southern working-class culture is informed by recent writing on white trash. See John Hartigan Jr., "Name Calling: Objectifying 'Poor Whites' and 'White Trash' in Detroit," 48, 50, and Constance Penley, "Crackers and Whackers: The White Trashing of Porn," 90, both in Wray and Newitz, *White Trash*.

5. See Jack Temple Kirby, *Rural Worlds Lost: The American South, 1920–1960* (Baton Rouge, 1987), 204–15.

6. Kim Chapin, *Fast as White Lightning: The Story of Stock Car Racing* (New York, 1981), 48–49, 51. See also Tom Wolfe, "The Last American Hero Is Junior Johnson—Yes!," in *Esquire: The Best of Forty Years* (New York, 1973), 156.

7. Chapin, *Fast as White Lightning*, 46–52; Hemphill, *Wheels*, 83–101.

8. Smokey Yunick, "One Hell of a Racer," *Autoweek*, April 5, 1999, 10; Peter Golenbock, *American Zoom: Stock Car Racing, from the Dirt Tracks to Daytona* (New York, 1993), 49–68, 113–23.

9. Peter Golenbock, *The Last Lap: The Life and Times of NASCAR's Legendary Heroes* (New York, 1998), 45, and *American Zoom*, 58.

10. Jerry Bledsoe, *The World's Number One, Flat-Out, All-Time Great Stock Car Racing Book* (New York, 1975), 34. Bledsoe closely linked musicians to stock car drivers: "Stock car racing and country music had a lot in common. They had been created out of isolation and rejection by southern working-class whites—rednecks, as the intellectuals had tagged them. This sport, this music provided not only entertainment and a means of expression, but a dream as well. . . . You could be poor and uneducated and scorned by society, but if you could learn to pick a guitar or drive a car, you just might luck out and find that glory, that pot of gold at Darlington or Nashville." On the centrality of laughter as a counter to authority and official culture, see Bakhtin, *Rabelais and His World*, 59–144. Bakhtin's description of carnivals suggests that stock car races are also places of eating, drinking, cursing, fighting, and fornicating.

11. See Walter Benjamin, *Illuminations* (New York, 1968), 176, and John Kasson, *Amusing the Million: Coney Island at the Turn of the Century* (New York, 1978), on repetitive activities. I am indebted to Elspeth Brown for pointing out the relevance of Benjamin's and Kasson's works.

12. Golenbock, *American Zoom*, 58; Wolfe, "Last American Hero," 146. See also Richard Pillsbury, "A Mythology at the Brink: Stock Car Racing in the American South," in *Fast Food, Stock Cars, and Rock 'n' Roll: Place and Space in American Pop Culture*, edited by George O. Carney (Lanham, Md., 1995), 239–48.

13. Chapin, *Fast as White Lightning*, 46; Bledsoe, *Stock Car Racing Book*, 39–45, 80; Golenbock, *Last Lap*, 15; interview with Ned Jarrett, Hickory, North Carolina, December 19, 1996, by Pete Daniel.

14. Bledsoe, *Stock Car Racing Book*, 47–50.

15. Greg Fielden, *Forty Years of Stock Car Racing*, vol. 1, *The Beginning, 1949–1958* (Surfside Beach, S.C., 1992), 9–10, 18; Larry Fielden, *Tim Flock: Race Driver* (Pinehurst, N.C., 1991), 69–76; Robert Cutter and Bob Fendell, *The Encyclopedia of Auto Racing Greats* (Englewood Cliffs, 1973), 211; Hemphill, *Wheels*, 119–21; Golenbock, *Last Lap*, 1; Robert G. Hagstrom, *The NASCAR Way: The Business That Drives the Sport* (New York, 1998), 28–29.

16. Greg Fielden, *The Beginning*, 5–9; Bledsoe, *Stock Car Racing Book*, 47–58, 70, 75; Larry Fielden, *Tim Flock*, 93–94; Cutter and Fendell, *Encyclopedia of Auto Racing Greats*, 224–28; Charles P. Pierce, "Junior Johnson Has Left the Building," *GQ* 66 (July 1996): 71.

17. Al Pearce, "Master of the Minnow Pond," *Autoweek* 46 (April 1, 1996): 44–45; Bledsoe, *Stock Car Racing Book*, 51–52; "Darlington's Labor Day Race," *South Carolina Magazine* (August 1956): 11–22; "A Day at the Southern 500," *The State Magazine*, October 1, 1950, 8–9; Greg Fielden, *The Beginning*, 32–34; Golenbock, *American Zoom*, 55; Hagstrom, *NASCAR Way*, 94.

18. Richard Pillsbury, "Carolina Thunder: A Geography of Southern Stock Car Racing," in Carney, *Fast Food, Stock Cars, and Rock 'n' Roll*, 229–38. See also Mark D. Howell, *From Moonshine to Madison Avenue: A Cultural History of the NASCAR Winston Cup Series* (Bowling Green, 1997).

19. Larry Fielden, *Tim Flock*, 11–34; Chapin, *Fast as White Lightning*, 42–43.

20. Larry Fielden, *Tim Flock*, 27–30; Chapin, *Fast as White Lightning*, 73.

21. Bledsoe, *Stock Car Racing Book*, 77–85, 90–92; Larry Fielden, *Tim Flock*, 11–34, 41, 45, 121; Cutter and Fendell, *Encyclopedia of Auto Racing Greats*, 211–13.

22. Larry Fielden, *Tim Flock*, 62–64, 88, 105–14; Chapin, *Fast as White Lightning*, 73, 89.

23. Jarrett interview, December 19, 1996.

24. Larry Fielden, *Tim Flock*, 117–20, 122–28; Chapin, *Fast as White Lightning*, 90–91; Cutter and Fendell, *Encyclopedia of Auto Racing Greats*, 215. The encyclopedia includes an entry for Jocko Flocko.

25. Larry Fielden, *Tim Flock*, 126–45; Cutter and Fendell, *Encyclopedia of Auto Racing Greats*, 213–14.

26. Chapin, *Fast as White Lightning*, 90–91, 99; Bledsoe, *Stock Car Racing Book*, 77–86, 185–205; Jarrett interview, December 19, 1996.

27. Greg Fielden, *The Beginning*, 10, 11, 13; Larry Fielden, *Tim Flock*, 54–58; Cutter and Fendell, *Encyclopedia of Auto Racing Greats*, 132–33.

28. "S.C. Queen of the Speedway," *The State Magazine*, August 27, 1950, 15; Cutter and Fendell, *Encyclopedia of Auto Racing Greats*, 133, 563–64. On women's roles in racing as beauty queens and drivers, see Bledsoe, *Stock Car Racing Book*, 87–101.

29. Greg Fielden, *Forty Years of Stock Car Racing*, vol. 2, *The Superspeedway Boom, 1959–1964* (Surfside, S.C., 1988), 140, 184, 233, 243, 290; Bledsoe, *Stock Car Racing Book*, 225–35; Cutter and Fendell, *Encyclopedia of Auto Racing Greats*, 544–45. Women were not allowed in the pits again until 1973, when a woman photographer threatened to bring suit.

30. Interview with Junior Johnson, June 4, 1988, by Pete Daniel, SOHP Collection; Jarrett interview, December 19, 1996. Both Wendell Scott and Louise Smith were inducted into the International Motorsports Hall of Fame in 1999. See *Washington Post*, October 22, 1998, E2.

31. Bob Zeller, "Life in the Fast Lane," *Greensboro News and Record*, October 16, 1993, A1, 6.

32. Ibid.

33. Johnson interview, June 4, 1988; Jarrett interview, December 19, 1996; Bledsoe, *Stock Car Racing Book*, 39–45.

34. Johnson interview, June 4, 1988.

35. Wolfe, "Last American Hero," 153; Johnson interview, June 4, 1988; Jarrett interview, December 19, 1996. On Lee Petty, see Cutter and Fendell, *Encyclopedia of Auto Racing Greats*, 475–76.

36. Bob Zeller, "Fast Ride: Johnson Finally Gets Caught," *Greensboro News and Record*, October 17, 1993, C1, 12; Golenbock, *American Zoom*, 20–22.

37. Johnson interview, June 4, 1988; Wolfe, "Last American Hero," 145. See also Cutter and Fendell, *Encyclopedia of Auto Racing Greats*, 339–40.

38. Wolfe, "Last American Hero," 145; Johnson interview, June 4, 1988; Kim Chapin, "The Autumn of the Patriarch," *Autoweek*, June 10, 1995, 21–25; Bob Zeller, "Junior Johnson Keeps Paying Long after Stills Dry Up," *Greensboro News and Record*, October 18, 1993, C1, 8; Hemphill, *Wheels*, 187–94. In 1970, when the Department of Energy encouraged gasohol production during the fuel crisis, Junior Johnson and some associates applied unsuccessfully for federal support to produce alcohol.

39. Chapin, *Fast as White Lightning*, 110–14, 136–42; Bledsoe, *Stock Car Racing Book*, 64–65.

40. Chapin, *Fast as White Lightning*, 110–14, 136–42; Cutter and Fendell, *Encyclopedia of Auto Racing Greats*, 509–10; Golenbock, *Last Lap*, 134–36, 139–43.

41. Jarrett interview, December 19, 1996.

42. Ibid.; Bledsoe, *Stock Car Racing Book*, 52; Cutter and Fendell, *Encyclopedia of Auto Racing Greats*, 331–32.

43. Chapin, *Fast as White Lightning*, 102–8; Jarrett interview, December 19, 1996.

44. Jarrett interview, December 19, 1996.

45. Chapin, *Fast as White Lightning*, 39–41, 43–44, 52–53, 85–86; Bledsoe, *Stock Car Racing Book*, 53–54; Larry Fielden, *Tim Flock*, 40; Golenbock, *Last Lap*, 20, 22, 36.

46. Chapin, *Fast as White Lightning*, 23–24.

47. Ibid., 76–77; Bledsoe, *Stock Car Racing Book*, 53–54; Cutter and Fendell, *Encyclopedia of Auto Racing Greats*, 649–50.

48. Bledsoe, *Stock Car Racing Book*, 185–86; Larry Fielden, *Tim Flock*, 40, 157–64; Cut-

ter and Fendell, *Encyclopedia of Auto Racing Greats*, 615–17; Hemphill, *Wheels*, 38. Turner died in an airplane crash on October 5, 1970.

49. Bledsoe, *Stock Car Racing Book*, 57–58; Chapin, *Fast as White Lightning*, 91, 100, 121. See also Bakhtin, *Rabelais and His World*, 59–144. The crowds at stock car races were preoccupied with inverting society and insulting propriety with humor, obscenity, and sexual innuendo.

50. Jarrett interview, December 19, 1996.

51. Bledsoe, *Stock Car Racing Book*, 23, 261–335; Hagstrom, *NASCAR Way*, 11–12. For a more recent commentary on the Darlington infield, see Blanche McCrary Boyd, *The Redneck Way of Knowledge: Down-Home Tales* (New York, 1982), 21–32. For insight into the collective memory of such events, see Benjamin, *Illuminations*, 159–60.

52. Jarrett interview, December 19, 1996; Bledsoe, *Stock Car Racing Book*, 215–24; Hemphill, *Wheels*, 151–69; Hagstrom, *NASCAR Way*, 32, 38–39, 47–73. The wildness was also incorporated into a tamed legend that treated infield outrages as good old boy hormonal surges. On how insurgents are rhetorically tamed, see Ranajit Guha, "The Prose of Counter-Insurgency," in *Selected Subaltern Studies*, edited by Ranajit Guha and Gayatri Chakravorty Spivak (New York, 1988), 45–86.

53. Jarrett interview, December 19, 1996; Richard Homan, "You Read It Here First," *Road and Track* 48 (June 1997): 125; Pierce, "Junior Johnson Has Left the Building," 69, 71–72, 81. Family ties continue to be strong in NASCAR racing as well as in other types of racing. Dale Jarrett, Kyle Petty, and Dale Earnhardt come from a racing heritage, and the Waltrip, Bodine, Burton, Labonte, and Wallace brothers carry on the Flock family tradition.

54. Johnson, remarks after interview, June 4, 1988.

CHAPTER SIX

1. See George Lipsitz, *Class and Culture in Cold War America: "A Rainbow at Midnight"* (South Hadley, Mass., 1981), 198, and Nick Tosches, *Country: Living Legends and Dying Metaphors in America's Biggest Music* (New York, 1977), 25–27.

2. On blues and country musicians, see Robert Palmer, *Deep Blues* (New York, 1982); Alan Lomax, *The Land Where the Blues Began* (New York, 1993); Peter Guralnick, *Searching for Robert Johnson* (New York, 1989); Nolan Porterfield, *Jimmie Rodgers: The Life and Times of America's Blue Yodeler* (Urbana, 1979); Colin Escott, *Hank Williams: The Biography* (Boston, 1994); Bill C. Malone, *Country Music, U.S.A.* (Austin, 1985); Bruce Bastin, *Red River Blues: The Blues Tradition in the Southeast* (Urbana, 1986); and Samuel Charters, *The Blues Makers* (New York, 1991). Bill C. Malone, in "Writing the History of Southern Music: A Review Essay," *Mississippi Quarterly* 45 (Fall 1992): 385–404, argues that both southern black music and southern white music were largely ignored by scholars until the 1980s and 1990s.

3. Interview with Ashley Thompson, Ripley, Tennessee, October 27, 1973, and interview with Sam Chatmon, Memphis, Tennessee, November 13, 1973, BSB&B Inter-

views. See Margaret McKee and Fred Chisenhall, *Beale Black and Blue: Life and Music on Black America's Main Street* (Baton Rouge, 1993), 181–90.

4. Interview with Arthur Crudup, Exmore, Virginia, September 27, 1973, BSB&B Interviews. See also McKee and Chisenhall, *Beale Black and Blue*, 205–14.

5. See Pete Daniel, *Breaking the Land: The Transformation of Cotton, Tobacco, and Rice Cultures* (Urbana, 1985); Gilbert C. Fite, *Cotton Fields No More: Southern Agriculture, 1865–1980* (Lexington, 1984); Jack Temple Kirby, *Rural Worlds Lost: The American South, 1920–1960* (Baton Rouge, 1987); Nan Elizabeth Woodruff, "Mississippi Delta Planters and Debates over Mechanization, Labor, and Civil Rights in the 1940s," *Journal of Southern History* 60 (May 1994): 263–84; and Gavin Wright, *Old South, New South: Revolutions in the Southern Economy since the Civil War* (New York, 1986). On southern migration, see Kirby, *Rural Worlds Lost*, 275–333. On the evolution of music during this time, see Malone, *Country Music*; Bill C. Malone, *Southern Music, American Music* (Lexington, 1979); and Lipsitz, *Class and Culture*, 195–225.

6. Christopher Silver and John V. Moeser, *The Separate City: Black Communities in the Urban South, 1940–1968* (Lexington, 1995), 31–41, 62–63, 132–34, 145–46. For a thorough analysis of the Memphis working class, see Michael K. Honey, *Southern Labor and Black Civil Rights: Organizing Memphis Workers* (Urbana, 1993). For descriptions of housing patterns, see Laura Helper, "Whole Lot of Shakin' Going On: An Ethnography of Race Relations and Crossover Audiences for Rhythm and Blues and Rock and Roll in 1950s Memphis" (Ph.D. diss., Rice University, 1997), 34–35, 70–142, 258–61.

7. Silver and Moeser, *Separate City*, 86–96, 181; Honey, *Southern Labor*, 245–77. See also Michael J. Klarman, "How *Brown* Changed Race Relations: The Backlash Thesis," *Journal of American History* 81 (June 1994): 81–118.

8. For an excellent account of working in segregated Memphis in the mid-1920s, see Richard Wright, *Black Boy* (New York, 1966), 228–88.

9. See Michael K. Honey, *Black Workers Remember: Segregation, Unionization, and the Freedom Struggle* (Berkeley, 1999), interview with Clarence Coe.

10. Ibid., interview with George Holloway.

11. Ibid., interview with Leroy Boyd.

12. See Helper, "Whole Lot of Shakin' Going On," 147–68.

13. Silver and Moeser, *Separate City*, 50–51, 84–85, 91–101.

14. Robert Gordon, *It Came from Memphis* (Boston, 1995), 32–46; interview with Jim Dickinson, Memphis, Tennessee, August 4, 1992, by Pete Daniel and Charles McGovern, Rock 'n' Soul Interviews. The Rock 'n' Soul Interviews were financed by the Special Exhibitions Fund of the Smithsonian Institution. For the "Rock 'n' Soul: Social Crossroads" exhibit, a team including Charles McGovern, Peter Guralnick, David Less, Lee Woodman, Kip Lornell, and Pete Daniel conducted twenty-seven audio and/or video interviews with people from the Memphis area who were involved in the music industry in the 1950s and 1960s.

15. See interview with Ford Nelson, Memphis, Tennessee, August 10, 1992, by Kip Lornell, Rock 'n' Soul Interviews; Brian Ward, *Just My Soul Responding: Rhythm and Blues, Black Consciousness, and Race Relations* (Berkeley, 1998), 29–42; Brian Ward and Jenny Walker, "'Bringing the Races Closer'?: Black-Oriented Radio in the

South and the Civil Rights Movement," in *Dixie Debates: Perspectives on Southern Cultures*, edited by Richard H. King and Helen Taylor (New York, 1996), 132; and B. B. King, with David Ritz, *Blues All Around Me: The Autobiography of B. B. King* (New York, 1996), 184.

16. On Dewey Phillips, see Gordon, *It Came from Memphis*, 14–26; interview with John Novarese, Memphis, Tennessee, August 10, 1992, by David Less and Charles McGovern, Rock 'n' Soul Interviews; McKee and Chisenhall, *Beale Black and Blue*; Louis Cantor, *Wheelin' on Beale: How WDIA-Memphis Became the Nation's First All-Black Radio Station and Created the Sound That Changed America* (New York, 1992), 7–77, 164–69; Peter Guralnick, *Last Train to Memphis: The Rise of Elvis Presley* (Boston, 1994), 38–39; and Honey, *Southern Labor*, 148, 166–67, 206. Radio assumed enormous importance, and the clear channel stations that could be heard for hundreds, sometimes thousands, of miles spread the latest hits. See Paul Hemphill, *Leaving Birmingham* (New York, 1993), 187.

17. On the jukebox business, see Novarese interview, August 10, 1992; interview with Morse Gist, Helena, Arkansas, May 15, 1992, by Pete Daniel and Charles McGovern, and interview with George Sammons, Memphis, Tennessee, August 4, 1992, by Pete Daniel and Charles McGovern, Rock 'n' Soul Interviews. On Poplar Tunes, see Helper, "Whole Lot of Shakin' Going On," 44–51, 55, and Gordon, *It Came from Memphis*, 18.

18. Gordon, *It Came from Memphis*, 79–80; Dickinson interview, August 4, 1992.

19. Helper, "Whole Lot of Shakin' Going On," 184–88, 242–67; Gordon, *It Came from Memphis*, 48–54; Dickinson interview, August 4, 1992.

20. Interview with Calvin Newborn, Memphis, Tennessee, August 7, 1992, by Pete Daniel and Charles McGovern, Rock 'n' Soul Interviews.

21. Ibid.

22. Interview with Willie Mitchell, Memphis, Tennessee, August 5, 1992, by Pete Daniel and Charles McGovern, Rock 'n' Soul Interviews. See this interview for Mitchell's insight into Hi Records and Al Green, the Memphis Horns, and other musicians.

23. Interview with Fred Ford, Memphis, Tennessee, May 20, 1992, by Pete Daniel, David Less, and Charles McGovern, ibid.

24. Martha Bayles, *Hole in Our Soul: The Loss of Beauty and Meaning in American Popular Music* (Chicago, 1994), 127–38; Charles White, *The Life and Times of Little Richard: The Quasar of Rock* (New York, 1984), 16–17; Nick Tosches, *Hell Fire: The Jerry Lee Lewis Story* (New York, 1982), 33–51, 72–74.

25. Interview with Willie Gordon, Memphis, Tennessee, August 6, 1992, by Pete Daniel and Charles McGovern, Rock 'n' Soul Interviews.

26. Interview with James Blackwood, Memphis, Tennessee, May 21, 1992, by Peter Guralnick, Rock 'n' Soul Interviews; Gordon interview, August 6, 1992.

27. Blackwood interview, May 21, 1992.

28. Interview with Sam Phillips, Memphis, Tennessee, May 22, 1992, by Pete Daniel, Charles McGovern, and Peter Guralnick, Rock 'n' Soul Interviews; Peter Guralnick, *Lost Highway: Journeys and Arrivals of American Musicians* (Boston, 1979), 328–29; Tosches, *Country*, 41.

29. Colin Escott and Martin Hawkins, *Good Rockin' Tonight: Sun Records and the Birth of Rock 'n' Roll* (New York, 1991), 1–242.

30. Interview with Rufus Thomas, Memphis, Tennessee, August 5, 1992, by Pete Daniel and Charles McGovern, Rock 'n' Soul Interviews.

31. King, *Blues All Around Me*, 6, 11, 23, 34–36, 72, 94–95, 98, 101, 110–15, 123–31, 135–37, 141, 145–46, 151–76.

32. Arthur Crudup, who wrote "That's All Right, Mama," made the connection in a 1973 interview when he said that a planter had cheated him out of over $1,500 and immediately mentioned $60,000 in back royalties still owed him. See Crudup interview, September 27, 1973. See also McKee and Chisenhall, *Beale Black and Blue*, 205–14.

33. Tosches, in *Country*, 29–44, traces the emergence of rhythm and blues and upbeat country.

34. Guralnick, *Last Train to Memphis*, 67–95; John Shelton Reed, "Elvis as Southerner," in *In Search of Elvis: Music, Race, Art, Religion*, edited by Vernon Chadwick (New York, 1997), 75–91.

35. Guralnick, *Last Train to Memphis*, 57–125; interview with Scotty Moore, Memphis, Tennessee, August 13, 1992, by Pete Daniel and Charles McGovern, Rock 'n' Soul Interviews; Scotty Moore, as told to James Dickerson, *That's Alright, Elvis: The Untold Story of Elvis's First Guitarist and Manager, Scotty Moore* (New York, 1997), 1–59; Reed, "Elvis as Southerner," 75–91.

36. Guralnick, *Last Train to Memphis*, 93–125; Moore interview, August 13, 1992; Moore, *That's Alright, Elvis*, 59–68. On historians' treatment of Presley, see Simon Frith, "The Academic Elvis," in King and Taylor, *Dixie Debates*, 114. There are different versions of who "discovered" Elvis Presley. See Bruce Feiler, "If Elvis Could Hear Him Now," *New York Times*, August 10, 1997, H28–29, and Richard Harrington, "The King and Him," *Washington Post*, August 10, 1997, G1, 6.

37. Guralnick, *Last Train to Memphis*, 57–125; Phillips interview, May 22, 1992. Nick Tosches wrote, "What made rockabilly such a drastically new music was its spirit, a thing that bordered on mania" (*Country*, 58). On Presley and how the musical parts fitted together, see Guralnick, *Lost Highway*, 93–95, 118–41.

38. Phillips interview, May 22, 1992; Moore, *That's Alright, Elvis*, 61–65.

39. Guralnick, *Lost Highway*, 333; Lipsitz, *Class and Culture*, 216; Robert K. Oermann and Mary A. Bufwack, "Rockabilly Women," *Journal of Country Music* 8 (May 1979): 65–71.

40. Interview with Carl Perkins, Memphis, Tennessee, May 20, 1992, by Pete Daniel and Charles McGovern, Rock 'n' Soul Interviews.

41. Ibid.; Carl Perkins and David McGee, *Go, Cat, Go: The Life and Times of Carl Perkins, the King of Rockabilly* (New York, 1996), 33–50.

42. Perkins interview, May 20, 1992.

43. Ibid. See Tom Piazza, "Elegy for Carl Perkins," *Oxford American*, no. 23, 73–75.

44. Interview with Billy Lee Riley, Memphis, Tennessee, May 13, 1992, by Pete Daniel and Charles McGovern, and interview with Billy Lee Riley, Newport, Arkansas, May 21, 1992, by Pete Daniel, Charles McGovern, and Peter Guralnick, Rock 'n' Soul Interviews; Jeannie Whayne, "Interview with Billy Lee Riley," *Arkansas Historical Quarterly* 55 (Autumn 1996): 298–308. When he was nine years old, his childhood sweetheart owned a Sears and Roebuck guitar that she hung on the wall. In those days, Riley recalled, "they used to come around and spray your houses

with DDT for insects and things. . . . They sprayed right over the guitar. It caused all the finish to just come off. So I bought it from her, my dad did, for ten bucks. And that's my guitar. That's what I learned on."

45. Whayne, "Interview with Billy Lee Riley," 314–16. Novelist Harry Crews remembered that he and his black playmate would peruse the Sears and Roebuck catalog constructing feuds among the models: "The Sears, Roebuck catalogue was much better used as a Wish Book [than in the outhouse], which it was called by the people out in the country, who would never be able to order anything out of it, but could at their leisure spend hours dreaming over it" (*A Childhood: The Biography of a Place* [New York, 1978], 53–57).

46. Riley interviews, May 13, 21, 1992; Whayne, "Interview with Billy Lee Riley," 298–318.

47. Riley interviews, May 13, 21, 1992.

48. Ibid.

49. Interview with Charlie Rich, Memphis, Tennessee, August 12, 1992, by Pete Daniel and Charles McGovern, Rock 'n' Soul Interviews; Guralnick, *Lost Highway*, 145.

50. Rich interview, August 12, 1992.

51. Interview with Stan Kesler, Memphis, Tennessee, May 13, 1992, by Pete Daniel and Charles McGovern, Rock 'n' Soul Interviews.

52. Ibid.

53. Perkins interview, May 20, 1992.

54. Phillips interview, May 22, 1992.

55. Ibid. Phillips told Peter Guralnick that his "greatest contribution . . . was to open up an area of freedom within the artist himself, to help him to express what *he* believed his message to be" (Guralnick, *Lost Highway*, 330 [emphasis in original]). There was also a reaction against rock 'n' roll among country musicians. See Neil V. Rosenberg, "Bluegrass, Rock and Roll, and 'Blue Moon of Kentucky,'" *Southern Quarterly* 22 (Spring 1984): 66–78.

56. Guralnick, *Lost Highway*, 334–35 (emphasis in original). Kesler also offered insight into Phillips, who, he said, "is close to being a genius in his working with people. He had a way of making you want to do your best." During a session, Phillips would sit in the control room and only occasionally come out to comment: "He always did it in a way that made you feel better and want to do better." See Kesler interview, May 13, 1992. Greil Marcus, in *Dead Elvis: A Chronicle of a Cultural Obsession* (New York, 1991), 60–66, comments on the role of Phillips, the rural background of Sun's artists, and the failure of some to reach stardom.

57. Interview with Paul Burlison, Memphis, Tennessee, May 5, 1992, by Pete Daniel and Charles McGovern, Rock 'n' Soul Interviews.

58. Dickinson interview, August 4, 1992.

59. Ibid.; Gordon, *It Came from Memphis*, 32–48.

60. Interview with Jim Stewart, Memphis, Tennessee, May 19, 1992, by Pete Daniel, Peter Guralnick, David Less, and Charles McGovern, Rock 'n' Soul Interviews.

61. Rob Bowman, *Soulsville, U.S.A.: The Story of Stax Records* (New York, 1997), 1–29; Gordon, *It Came from Memphis*, 58–70; interview with David Porter, Memphis, Tennessee, August 7, 1992, by Pete Daniel and Charles McGovern, Rock 'n' Soul Interviews; Stewart interview, May 19, 1992.

62. Bowman, *Soulsville*, 30–192; Bayles, *Hole in Our Soul*, 158–59; Dickinson interview, August 4, 1992; Stewart interview, May 19, 1992; Porter interview, August 7, 1992.

63. Moore interview, August 13, 1992.

CHAPTER SEVEN

1. See Bill C. Malone, *Southern Music, American Music* (Lexington, 1979), 96–97. Malone mentions Marlon Brando and James Dean, "whose shrugs, confused postures, inarticulate mumblings, and antiauthoritarian stances paralleled their own gropings. The dress, hairstyles, and demeanor of the method actors, combined with the rocking beat of American grass roots music, provided the volatile ingredients of Rock 'n' Roll."

2. Bill C. Malone, *Singing Cowboys and Musical Mountaineers: Southern Culture and the Roots of Country Music* (Athens, 1993), 94–116, and "Country Elvis," in *In Search of Elvis: Music, Race, Art, Religion*, edited by Vernon Chadwick (New York, 1997), 3–18; Johnny Cash, with Patrick Carr, *Cash: The Autobiography* (New York, 1997), 73; interview with Billy Lee Riley, Memphis, Tennessee, May 13, 1992, by Pete Daniel and Charles McGovern; interview with Billy Lee Riley, Newport, Arkansas, May 21, 1992, by Pete Daniel, Charles McGovern, and Peter Guralnick; interview with Charlie Rich, Memphis, Tennessee, August 12, 1992, by Pete Daniel and Charles McGovern; and interview with Bernard Lansky, Memphis, Tennessee, August 15, 1992, by Pete Daniel, Rock 'n' Soul Interviews. The photograph is in Colin Escott and Martin Hawkins, *Good Rockin' Tonight: Sun Records and the Birth of Rock 'n' Roll* (New York, 1991), 58. On the centrality of black style in fifties culture, see Norman Mailer, "The White Negro: Superficial Reflections on the Hipster," in *Advertisements for Myself* (New York, 1959), 302–22, and W. T. Lhamon Jr., *Deliberate Speed: The Origins of a Cultural Style in the American 1950s* (Washington, D.C., 1990), 39.

3. Lansky interview, August 15, 1992; Rich interview, August 12, 1992; Cash, *Cash*, 73.

4. Peter Guralnick, *Last Train to Memphis: The Rise of Elvis Presley* (Boston, 1994), 119, 137, 138–39, 171–72, 174, 223, 238, 284, 303; Scotty Moore, as told to James Dickerson, *That's Alright, Elvis: The Untold Story of Elvis's First Guitarist and Manager, Scotty Moore* (New York, 1997), 39. See Gael Sweeney, "The King of White Trash Culture: Elvis Presley and the Aesthetics of Excess," in *White Trash: Race and Class in America*, edited by Matt Wray and Annalee Newitz (New York, 1997), 249–63, and Marjorie Garber, *Vested Interests: Cross-Dressing and Cultural Anxiety* (New York, 1992), 363–74. Simon Frith, in "The Academic Elvis," in *Dixie Debates: Perspectives on Southern Cultures*, edited by Richard H. King and Helen Taylor (New York, 1996), has argued that academics either ignored or trivialized Presley because he "was trashy and/or politically incorrect" (100). See ibid., 99–114, and *Sound Effects: Youth, Leisure, and the Politics of Rock 'n' Roll* (New York, 1981), 218–24.

5. Moore, *That's Alright, Elvis*, 71, 73; Malone, "Country Elvis," 3; U.S. House, Judiciary Committee, Hearings, *Monopoly Problems in Regulated Industries*, 84th Cong., 2d sess., 1956, 4426.

6. Interview with D. J. Fontana, Memphis, Tennessee, August 13, 1996, by Pete Daniel and Charles McGovern, Rock 'n' Soul Interviews.

7. Jann S. Wenner, "Jagger Remembers," interview with Mick Jagger, *Rolling Stone*, December 14, 1995, 98; Garber, *Vested Interests*, 367–68; Guralnick, *Last Train to Memphis*, 128; Moore, *That's Alright, Elvis*, 95.

8. Charles White, *The Life and Times of Little Richard: The Quasar of Rock* (New York, 1984), 20–57.

9. Ibid.

10. Escott and Hawkins, *Good Rockin' Tonight*, 253–54; Martha Bayles, *Hole in Our Soul: The Loss of Beauty and Meaning in American Popular Music* (Chicago, 1994), 139–41; interview with Cordell Jackson, Memphis, Tennessee, May 11, 1992, by Pete Daniel and David Less, and interview with Cordell Jackson, Memphis, Tennessee, May 19, 1992, by Pete Daniel, Charles McGovern, and David Less, Rock 'n' Soul Interviews.

11. Interview with Bobby Manuel, Memphis, Tennessee, May 19, 1992, by Pete Daniel and Charles McGovern, Rock 'n' Soul Interviews.

12. *Arkansas Gazette*, September 2, 1957.

13. Robert Armstrong Andrews to Harry Ashmore, December 22, 1958, box 8, file 4, Ashmore Papers (emphasis in original).

14. Calvin Kytle and James A. Mackay, *Who Runs Georgia?* (Athens, 1998), 246–53.

15. Beth L. Bailey, *From Front Porch to Back Seat: Courtship in Twentieth Century America* (Baltimore, 1988).

16. John Howard, "The Library, the Park, and the Pervert: Public Space and Homosexual Encounter in Post–World War II Atlanta," *Radical History Review* 62 (Spring 1995): 166–87, reprinted in *Carryin' On in the Lesbian and Gay South*, edited by John Howard (New York, 1997), 107–31. See also John Howard, *Men Like That: A Southern Queer History* (Chicago, 1999).

17. See John Howard, "Introduction," 1–12; William Armstrong Percy III, "William Alexander Percy (1885–1942): His Homosexuality and Why It Matters," 75–92; James T. Sears, "Race, Class, Gender, and Sexuality in Pre-Stonewall Charleston: Perspectives on the Gordon Langley Hall Affair," 164–200; and Donna Jo Smith, "Queering the South: Constructions of Southern/Queer Identity," 370–85, all in Howard, *Carryin' On*; White, *Little Richard*, 20–42; James T. Sears, *Lonely Hunters: An Oral History of Lesbian and Gay Southern Life, 1948–1968* (New York, 1997), 110–14.

18. Bob Swisher, "One Big Community," *Southern Exposure* 16 (Fall 1988): 29.

19. See Allan Bérubé, *Coming Out Under Fire: The History of Gay Men and Women in World War Two* (New York, 1991).

20. Sears, *Lonely Hunters*, 12–107; James A. Schnur, "Closet Crusaders: The Johns Committee and Homophobia, 1956–1965," in Howard, *Carryin' On*, 132–63; John Loughery, "Hunting Gays in Gainesville," *Harvard Gay and Lesbian Review* (Winter 1996): 17–19.

21. Florida Legislative Investigation Committee, "Homosexuality and Citizenship in Florida" (Tallahassee, 1964), reprinted in *Government versus Homosexuals*, edited by Jonathan Katz (New York, 1975). I am indebted to David K. Johnson for calling Loughery's article, "Hunting Gays in Gainesville," and the government report to my attention.

22. Anne C. Loveland, *Lillian Smith: A Southerner Confronting the South* (Baton

Rouge, 1986), 12–16; Margaret Rose Gladney, "Personalizing the Political, Politicizing the Personal: Reflections on Editing the Letters of Lillian Smith," in Howard,
Carryin' On, 93–103; Margaret Rose Gladney, ed., *How Am I to Be Heard?: Letters of
Lillian Smith* (Chapel Hill, 1993), xvi; Lillian Smith, *Killers of the Dream* (New York,
1963), 17. For autobiographical sketches, see Lillian Smith to Miss Morehouse, June
6, 1956, series 1283A; Smith to Joan Titus, n.d., series 1283A, box 1; and Smith to
Sarah Patton Boyle, August 14, 1962, series 1283, box 5, Smith Papers.

23. Smith, *Killers of the Dream*, 69–73. On how young southerners were initiated into
segregation and how some came to oppose it, see Melton McLaurin, "Rituals of
Initiation and Rebellion: Adolescent Responses to Segregation in Southern Autobiography," *Southern Cultures* 3 (Summer 1997): 5–24.

24. Lillian Smith to Denver Lindley, March 19, 1957, series 1283, box 17, and Lawrence S.
Kubie to Smith, October 14, 1955, series 1283A, box 2, Smith Papers. During World
War II, Kubie worked for the National Research Council and penned a paragraph,
"Sexual Perversions," that was used by the U.S. Army for antihomosexual screen-
ing. See Bérubé, *Coming Out Under Fire*, 19.

25. Eleanor Roosevelt to Lillian Smith, October 17, 1961; Smith to Roosevelt, October
31, 1961, series 1283A, box 3; and Pat Watters to Smith, November 7, 1961, series 1283,
box 26, Smith Papers.

26. Jane Xenia Harris Woodside, "The Womanless Wedding: An American Folk
Drama" (M.A. thesis, University of North Carolina, Chapel Hill, 1987); Leslie H.
Carter, "The Womanless Wedding: A Burlesque Entertainment" (San Francisco,
1926); "Mock Marriage in Rhyme" (1931); "Womanless Wedding at Wilson Tonight," *Osceola Times*, March 15, 1935; "Womanless Wedding," *Marked Tree Tribune*, May 3, 1918; Lewis Nordan, *The Sharp-Shooter Blues* (Chapel Hill, 1997), 152.
Michael Taft, a Canadian folklorist, reported that mock weddings were an integral
part of social life on the Canadian prairie. In Canadian ceremonies that sometimes
commemorated a twenty-fifth wedding anniversary, men dressed as women and
women as men. See Michael Taft, *Discovering Saskatchewan Folklore: Three Case
Studies* (Edmonton, 1983). Jeannie Whayne furnished the Wilson and Marked Tree
newspaper articles. The *Krispy Kreme News*, August 1962, reported that its dough-
nuts were served at a womanless wedding in Jacksonville, Florida.

27. See Garber, *Vested Interests*, 277–78; Bérubé, *Coming Out Under Fire*, 67–97. John
Howard generously offered me important suggestions on interpreting the Wilson,
Arkansas, photographs.

28. Daneel Buring, "Softball and Alcohol: The Limits of Lesbian Community in Memphis from the 1940s through the 1960s," in Howard, *Carryin' On*, 203–23.

29. Interview with Bettye Berger, Memphis, Tennessee, August 6, 1992, by Pete Daniel
and Charlie McGovern, Rock 'n' Soul Interviews.

30. Ibid.

31. Ibid. See Laura Helper, "Whole Lot of Shakin' Going On: An Ethnography of Race
Relations and Crossover Audiences for Rhythm and Blues and Rock and Roll in
1950s Memphis" (Ph.D. diss., Rice University, 1997), 175–88.

32. Interview with Hazel Bryan Massery, Little Rock, Arkansas, January 29, 1996, by
Pete Daniel and Elizabeth Jacoway.

33. "Civil War in Alabama's Citizens' Councils," *Reporter*, May 17, 1956, 19; *National*

Guardian, April 23, 1956, 5, copy in box 1, Cox Papers; *Tampa Morning Tribune*, March 30, 1956, clipping in White Citizens' Council, Ku Klux Klan, III A, box 292, NAACP Papers.

34. Unidentified newspaper, July 21, 1958, and *Memphis Press-Scimitar*, October 20, 1959, clippings in box 1, Cox Papers.

35. Archibald S. Coody to John U. Barr, September 22, 1955, box 4, Coody Papers.

36. Robert B. Patterson to Ed White, March 3, 1955, box 44, folder 24, Sillers Papers. See also Nick Tosches, *Country: Living Legends and Dying Metaphors in America's Biggest Music* (New York, 1977), 8, and Annalee Newitz, "White Savagery and Humiliation, or, A New Racial Consciousness in the Media," in Wray and Newitz, *White Trash*, 135.

37. *Pittsburgh Courier*, December 22, 1956. See also Margaret McKee and Fred Chisenhall, *Beale Black and Blue: Life and Music on Black America's Main Street* (Baton Rouge, 1993), 94–96.

38. McKee and Chisenhall, *Beale Black and Blue*, 239. In 1959, Mary Ann Mobley from Brandon, Mississippi, won the Miss America title, and Lynda Lee Mead from Natchez won in 1960. Cheryl Piewitt from Ackerman won in 1980, and Susan Akin from Meridian won in 1986. All attended the University of Mississippi. See "What's Ole Beauty," *Life*, August 25, 1961, 58–61, 64. Debbie Doyle supplied the Miss America information.

39. Interview with Sandra Scarbrough Kramer, Natchez, Mississippi, February 3, 1996, by Pete Daniel. See also Berger interview, August 6, 1992.

40. Ben E. Bailey, "The Red Tops: The Orchestra That Covered the Delta," in *The Black Perspective in Music*, 177–85; Jim Cleveland, "Blues Archive Celebrates Red Tops," n.d.; Linda Temple, "Top of the Pops," *Jackson Clarion-Ledger*, November 14, 1993; Deidre Tyler, "Giving Tribute to My Father and the Red Top Band," n.d. These sources were generously shared by Nadine Cohodas. See also "The Red Tops Return," *Southern Register* (Winter 1999): 7, and *Red Tops*, liner notes, Center for the Study of Southern Culture, University of Mississippi.

41. Kramer interview, February 3, 1996.

42. Ibid.

43. W. L. Harrison to Chairman of the Joint Temperance Committee, Jackson, February 24, 1960, box 45, folder 3, Sillers Papers.

44. Kramer interview, February 3, 1996.

45. Karal Ann Marling, *Graceland: Going Home with Elvis* (Cambridge, 1996), 36.

46. Anne Rivers Siddons, *Heartbreak Hotel* (New York, 1993), 53, 101, 173–235, 83–84; Paul Hemphill, *Leaving Birmingham* (New York, 1993), 102.

47. Katharine Cater to Sam Brewster, January 7, 1947, and Cater to Ralph B. Draughon, memorandum, November 1, 1947, box 6, Dean of Women Papers.

48. Katharine Cater to Ralph B. Draughon, March 9, 1959, ibid.

49. Lillian Smith to Lawrence S. Kubie, January 30, 1957, series 1283, box 15, Smith Papers.

50. Lillian Smith to Mozell Hill, March 11, 1957, series 1283, box 3, ibid.

51. *Winston-Salem Journal*, November 21, 1957; *Winston-Salem Sentinel*, November 21, 23, December 10, 1957; and *Life*, October 7, 1957, 32–33, copies in Controversies and Episodes, Baptist Historical Collection. A poll showed that 96 percent of the stu-

dent body approved of dancing, and the student legislature passed a resolution to allow on-campus dancing. See also *Raleigh News and Observer*, November 16, 1957.

CHAPTER EIGHT

1. Pauli Murray to Lillian Smith, May 25, 1954, series 1283, box 19, Smith Papers; Pauli Murray, *The Autobiography of a Black Activist, Feminist, Lawyer, Priest, and Poet* (Knoxville, 1989), 302 (emphasis in original), and *Proud Shoes: The Story of an American Family* (New York, 1956).
2. Interview with Leslie Burl McLemore, Washington, D.C., October 26, 1984, by Pete Daniel.
3. Hollinger F. Barnard, ed., *Outside the Magic Circle: The Autobiography of Virginia Foster Durr* (Tuscaloosa, 1985), 274; Carrine Newton to Frank Clement, June 13, 1954, and Josephine Winbush to Clement, June 14, 1954, box 38, Clement Papers.
4. George S. Mitchell to Charles S. Johnson, June 1, 1954, box 111, Charles Johnson Papers; Wilma Dykeman and James Stokely, *Neither Black nor White* (New York, 1957), 19.
5. Lillian Smith to Henry Hart Crane, April 2, 1956, series 1283, box 7, Smith Papers.
6. See Samuel S. Hill, ed., *Encyclopedia of Religion in the South* (Macon, 1997).
7. Mark Newman, "Getting Right with God: Southern Baptists and Race Relations, 1945–1980" (Ph.D. diss., University of Mississippi, 1993), 84–132, 318; *Biblical Recorder* 120 (May 29, 1954): 5, 8, 20.
8. See *Arkansas Baptist* 53 (May 27, 1954): 13, (June 3, 1954): 11; *Religious Herald* (Virginia) 127 (May 27, 1954): 10, 11; *Baptist and Reflector* (Tennessee) 120 (June 3, 1954): 2, 3; and *Baptist Courier* (South Carolina) 86 (June 3, 1954): 2, 24. All Baptist periodicals can be found in the Baptist Historical Collection. For accounts of pastors who supported integration, see Jack H. Manley, "The Next Step in Racial Adjustment," *Religious Herald* 127 (July 1, 1954): 4–5, 24; Charles M. Jones, "The Church and the Supreme Court Decision: What the Church Can Do," May 30, 1954, copy of sermon in box 47, folder 33, Graham Papers; W. C. Laney to Alice Spearman, October 12, 1949, box 1, SCCHR Papers; and *Biblical Recorder* 118 (April 26, 1952): 23; 120 (May 29, 1954): 20, (November 27, 1954): 18; 121 (November 19, 1955): 15.
9. *Alabama Baptist* 119 (May 27, 1954): 3; "Proud of the South," *Biblical Recorder* 120 (June 5, 1954): 5; "Southern Baptist Leaders Call for Calm Appraisal of Court Ruling," and D. E. Earnhardt and Millard M. Johnson, "Resolution Passed in Clinton Ministerial Association, Monday, May 24, 1954," *Biblical Recorder* 120 (June 12, 1954): 23; Tennessee Delegation of the Tennessee Methodist Student Movement, meeting at Lake Junaluska, North Carolina, to Frank Clement, June 12, 1954, box 38, Clement Papers. For the reaction of Baptist ministers, see *Arkansas Baptist* 53 (June 3, 1954): 11. See also *Religious Herald* 127 (May 27, 1954): 10–11; *Baptist Courier* 86 (June 3, 1954): 2; and *Baptist and Reflector* 120 (June 3, 1954): 2, 3.
10. *Rocky Mount Evening Telegram*, November 25, 27, 28, 1952; *Biblical Recorder* 120 (May 22, 1954): 5; "Too Much 'Bang-Bang' TV for the Kiddies," *Biblical Recorder* 120 (May 22, 1954): 5, 8; *Biblical Recorder* 120 (June 5, 1954): 21. Fundamentalists were not the only critics of the Revised Standard Version of the Bible. See Dwight

Macdonald, *Against the American Grain* (New York, 1952), 262–88. Alice Hildreth, reference librarian at the Thomas Hackney Braswell Memorial Library in Rocky Mount, furnished the *Rocky Mount Evening Telegram* references.

11. Newman, "Getting Right with God," 321–24; *Christian Index* (Georgia) 133A (June 10, 1954): 9; *Religious Herald* 127 (June 10, 1954): 14–15; *Biblical Recorder* 120 (June 19, 1954): 17, 20. See also *Alabama Baptist* 119 (June 10, 1954): 4; *Baptist Courier* 86 (June 17, 1954): 24, (June 24, 1954): 7, 19; *Baptist Record*, June 10, 1954, 3; July 22, 1954, 4. The *Free Will Baptist* did not mention the *Brown* case during the spring and summer of 1954.

12. Newman, "Getting Right with God," 324–25; Joel L. Alvis Jr., *Religion and Race: Southern Presbyterians, 1946–1983* (Tuscaloosa, 1994), 57–58.

13. Arthur C. Allen to Frank Clement, June 27, 1954, box 38, Clement Papers.

14. Hodding Carter to Harry M. Wilson, November 26, 1954, and Wilson to Carter, December 1, 1954, Correspondence, 1954, Carter Papers.

15. Daniel L. Durway to Nat R. Griswold, January 11, 1957, series 1, box 5, ACHR Papers.

16. Frank Porter Graham to Clarence Poe, May 26, 1954, box 47, folder 41, Graham Papers. On Graham's attempts to confront segregation, see Graham to Jim Farley, February 2, 1954, box 46, folder 25, ibid.

17. Elizabeth DeVane Worth to Frank Porter Graham, June 21, 1954; Graham to Worth, July 2, 1954; Worth to Graham, July 7, 1954; and Graham to Worth, July 9, 1954, box 47, folder 51, ibid.

18. Junius Irving Scales and Richard Nickson, *Cause at Heart: A Former Communist Remembers* (Athens, 1987), 172–73.

19. Lillian Smith to Frank W. Spencer, March 8, 1956, series 1283, box 24, and Smith to Henry Hart Crane, series 1283, box 7, Smith Papers; Lillian Smith, *Now Is the Time* (New York, 1955), 48.

20. Lillian Smith to Frank W. Spencer, March 8, 1956, series 1283, box 24, Smith Papers. See also Smith to Hallock Hoffman, July 28, 1955, in *How Am I to Be Heard?: Letters of Lillian Smith*, edited by Margaret Rose Gladney (Chapel Hill, 1993), 176–78. Lucy Randolph Mason shared Smith's distrust of Ralph McGill. She confided to Aubrey Williams that she had "utterly lost trust in him" and insisted that "he has garbled and changed information given him." See Mason to Williams, March 11, 1950, and Mason to Hugh A. Brimm, April 18, 1950, box 7, Mason Papers.

21. Lillian Smith to Lawrence S. Kubie, October 10, 1957, in Gladney, *How Am I to Be Heard?*, 217–21. For insight into Smith's thinking on being ignored, see Homer A. Jack, "Lillian Smith of Clayton, Georgia," *Christian Century* 74 (October 2, 1957): 1166–68.

22. Lillian Smith to Don Seawell, July 16, 1959, series 1283, box 22A; George L. White to Smith, June 11, 1959, series 1283, box 27; and Smith to Eugenia Rawls, November 18, 1959, series 1283A, box 3, Smith Papers.

23. Wilma Dykeman Stokely to Lillian Smith, December 18, 1957, series 1283, box 24, ibid. (emphasis in original); Dykeman and Stokely, *Neither Black nor White*. "By this title," Dykeman explained in her letter, "we meant that our problems here in the South are red, the color of human blood which flows the same color in all our veins, green, the color of the money we need and the grass on our hills, and grey— the color of fear and drab conformity."

24. Dykeman and Stokely, *Neither Black nor White*, 39, 77.

25. Lillian Smith to Wilma Dykeman Stokely, December 21, 1957, series 1283A, box 4, and Smith to John Howard Griffin, December 3, 1961, series 1283A, box 2, Smith Papers.

26. Lillian Smith to Dorothy Canfield Fisher, March 10, 1956, series 1283, box 10, ibid. See also Smith to Gilbert Harrison, March 15, 1956, series 1283A, box 2, and Smith to Dorothy Norman, April 11, 1956, series 1283, box 20, ibid.

27. Hodding Carter, "The Court's Decision and the South," *Reader's Digest*, September 1954, 51–56, copy in *Reader's Digest* Article, 1954, Carter Papers. On Carter's ideology, see John T. Kneebone, "Liberal on the Levee: Hodding Carter, 1944–1954," *Journal of Mississippi History* 49 (May 1987): 153–62, and Dykeman and Stokely, *Neither Black nor White*, 61.

28. C. W. R. to Hodding Carter, September 8, 1954, *Reader's Digest* Article, 1954, Carter Papers.

29. Dykeman and Stokely, *Neither Black nor White*, 22.

30. Nancy MacLean, *Behind the Mask of Chivalry: The Making of the Second Ku Klux Klan* (New York, 1994), 52–74. On the NAACP's urgency, see Adam Fairclough, *Race and Democracy: The Civil Rights Struggle in Louisiana, 1915–1972* (Athens, 1995), 165–72; Liva Baker, *The Second Battle of New Orleans: The Hundred Year Struggle to Integrate the Schools* (New York, 1996), 233–57; and A. P. Tureaud to Thurgood Marshall, June 2, 1954, series 3, box 10, Tureaud Papers.

31. Frank Smith, *Congressman from Mississippi* (New York, 1964), 105; Dykeman and Stokely, *Neither Black nor White*, 57–58.

32. Mrs. Hugh C. Day to Frank Clement, May 18, 1954, and Clement to Day, July 13, 1954, box 38, Clement Papers.

33. W. W. Malone to Congressman Bob Jones, July 18, 1956, box 247, Abernethy Papers; Hattie Daly to Frank Clement, May 22, 1954, box 37, Clement Papers.

34. Margaret Trotter to Frank Clement, May 25, 1954, box 37, Clement Papers (emphasis in original).

35. Margaret E. Poole to P. O. Davis, August 17, 1954, box 70, ACES Papers.

36. Mrs. L. G. Baker to President Dwight D. Eisenhower, [ca. May 1954], copy in series 15, subseries 4, box 541, Faubus Papers.

37. Harry P. Gamble to Hodding Carter, [ca. August 1954], *Reader's Digest* Article, 1954, Carter Papers.

38. Lillian Smith to Marvin Rich, December 11, 1965, series 1283, box 22, Smith Papers.

CHAPTER NINE

1. Thomas Pickins Brady to Hodding Carter, n.d. (reply, May 24, 1954), Correspondence, 1954, Carter Papers; J. Robertshaw to Boswell Stevens, May 25, 1954, Subject Files, General, MFBF Papers.

2. Robert B. Patterson to editor, May 18, 1954, copy in box 37, Clement Papers; Neil R. McMillen, *The Citizens' Council: Organized Resistance to the Second Reconstruction, 1954–64* (Urbana, 1994), 15–23; Hodding Carter, "A Wave of Terror Threatens the South," *Look*, March 22, 1955, 32–36; Paul Anthony, "Pro-Segregation Groups' His-

tory and Trends," *New South*, January 1957, 4–6, copy in White Citizens' Council—Financial Support file, and H. L. Mitchell, "On the Rise of the White Citizens Council and Its Ties with Anti-Labor Forces in the South," confidential, January 30, 1956, Ku Klux Klan file, Cox Papers.

3. Walter Sillers to Dewey Mayhew Jr., July 19, 1955, and Robert B. Patterson to Sillers, November 2, 1955, box 5, folder 8, Sillers Papers.

4. Mitchell, "On the Rise of the White Citizens Council."

5. Ibid.

6. H. L. Mitchell to A. E. Cox, January 25, 1956, White Citizens' Council—H. L. Mitchell—Labor Unions file; Murray Kempton, "The New Subversion," *New York Post*, March 25, 1955, and "Loyalty Test," *New York Post*, February 15, 1956; "Threats to Unions in South Depicted," *New York Times*, May 7, 1956; and H. L. Mitchell, "The White Citizens Councils vs. Southern Trade Unions," March 12, 1956, White Citizens' Council—Labor Unions file, Cox Papers. A list of the members of the Advisory Committees for the state chapters of the Federation for Constitutional Government was attached to Mitchell's report.

7. Paul Conkin, *The Southern Agrarians* (Knoxville, 1988), 1–31; Donald Davidson, *The Big Ballad Jamboree* (Knoxville, 1996).

8. John Donald Wade to Donald Davidson, August 8, 1954, box 11, Davidson Papers (emphasis in original); Conkin, *Southern Agrarians*, 64–65.

9. Conkin, *Southern Agrarians*, 32–164; Donald Davidson to John Mebane, September 19, 1960, box 2, Davidson Papers.

10. Donald Davidson to John Donald Wade, August 4, 1955, box 2, Davidson Papers.

11. Ibid.; Donald Davidson to Russell Kirk, July 13, 1955, and Davidson to John Mebane, September 19, 1960, box 2, Davidson Papers; McMillen, *Citizens' Council*, 107–11.

12. Donald Davidson to Floyd Watkins, June 3, 11, 1956, box 2, Davidson Papers.

13. Henry L. Swint to Frank Owsley, May 15, 1956, box 5, Owsley Papers. Swint faulted the NAACP's strategy. Had it moved for integration "in private colleges such as Berea, Chattanooga, Maryville, etc. they would have encountered little opposition." But by attacking the most stubborn targets first, it guaranteed stiff opposition.

14. William H. Chafe, *Civilities and Civil Rights: Greensboro, North Carolina, and the Black Struggle for Freedom* (New York, 1980), 4–10, 52, 56–66.

15. Mitchell, "On the Rise of the White Citizens Council"; Wesley Critz George to Mr. French, December 2, 1954, series 1.2, box 2, George Papers. Many white writers dismissed black achievements. See Lucius Graham Wilkes to Sam Ervin, June 11, 1955, box 11, Ervin Papers. See Steven Niven, "Wesley Critz George: Scientist and Segregationist," *North Carolina Literary Review*, no. 7 (1998): 39–41.

16. Felix Hichenson to Wesley Critz George, November 18, 1954; Minnie McIver Brown to George, November 21, 1954, series 1.2, box 2; and H. H. Palmer to George, February 21, 1956, series 1.3, folder 22, George Papers.

17. Mary B. Gilson to Wesley Critz George, November 18, 1954, and Jennifer Hauk Ogle to George, November 19, 1954, series 1.2, box 2, ibid.

18. Dallas E. Gwynn to Wesley Critz George, November 19, 1954; Rufus S. Jones to George, November 19, 1954; and A. B. Nimitz to Dwight D. Eisenhower, January 25, 1956, series 1.3, folder 21, ibid.

19. F. W. Avant to Wesley Critz George, November 29, 1954, series 1.2, box 2, ibid.

20. Ibid. On the legal position of light-skinned African Americans, see Victoria E. Bynum, "'White Negroes' in Segregated Mississippi: Miscegenation, Racial Identity, and the Law," *Journal of Southern History* 64 (May 1988): 247–76.

21. Anonymous to Wesley Critz George, February 2, 1956, series 1.3, folder 22, George Papers.

22. Wesley Critz George to [John W.] Clark, April 21, 1955, series 1.3, box 2, ibid.

23. Chester Davis, "The Patriots of North Carolina: Will the State Follow Their Lead?," *Winston-Salem Journal-Sentinel*, June 3, 1956, copy in series 1.3, folder 26, ibid.

24. W. C. George, "Human Progress and the Race Problem," speech given at Dartmouth College, October 12, 1956, series 1.3, folder 26, ibid. See also W. C. George, "What about 'Middle Ground' in Our Race-School Problem?" (1956), series 1.3, folder 32, ibid.

25. W. C. George, "Race, Heredity, and Civilization," n.d., copy in series 21, folder 99, ibid.

26. Wesley Critz George to Chalmers G. Davidson, June 10, 1955, series 1.3, box 2, ibid. George mentioned Roger John Williams, *Free and Unequal* (1953); Henry Pratt Fairchild, *Race and Nationality* (1947); and J. D. Sayers, *Can the White Man Survive?* (1929).

27. Wesley Critz George to David Clark, July 7, 1955, and Harry P. Gamble Sr. to George, April 6, 1955, series 1.3, box 2, George Papers; Walter Sillers to Marie B. Whittin, October 30, 1952, box 28, folder 26, Sillers Papers.

28. Paul D. Hastings to Wesley Critz George, January 3, 1956; Eugene A. Hood to Allison James, January 21, 1956; Hood to Fielding L. Fry, April 22, 1956; Hastings to William B. Rodman Jr., January 12, 1956; and Paul D. Hastings, "Basic Principles Involved in the Supreme Court's Decision on Segregation," speech given to Leaksville, N.C., Rotary Club, January 10, 1956, series 1.3, folder 21, George Papers.

29. Luther H. Hodges, *Businessman in the State House: Six Years as Governor of North Carolina* (Chapel Hill, 1963), 90–91; Chafe, *Civilities and Civil Rights*, 83–84; Benjamin E. Mays to Reed Sarratt, September 15, 1955, series 1, box 1, Sarratt Papers.

30. Paul D. Hastings to Wesley Critz George, April 19, 1956, series 1.3, folder 21, and Erwin A. Holt to George, February 24, 1957, series 1.3, folder 33, George Papers.

31. Paul D. Hastings to William C. Cannon, June 19, 1956, series 1.3, folder 26, ibid.

32. Reed Sarratt to Bill Sharpe, June 5, 1956, and Sharpe to Sarratt, June 7, 1956, series 1, box 1, Sarratt Papers; Sharpe to James T. Dees, November 18, 1957, series 1.3, folder 36, and J. Bruce Eure to Wesley Critz George, July 9, 1956, series 1.3, folder 27, George Papers.

33. William D. Anderson to W. D. Lewis, June 29, 1956, series 1.3, folder 26, George Papers. See also Frank Hough to Wesley Critz George, August 1, 1956, series 1.3, folder 28, ibid.

34. W. C. George, "Report for Annual Meeting of Patriots," Greensboro, N.C., August 25, 1956, series 1.3, folder 29, ibid. See also Paul D. Hastings to Horace McCall, November 29, 1956, series 1.3, folder 31, ibid., for developments after the Greensboro meeting and factional disputes.

35. Wesley Critz George to Luther Hodges, August 20, 1957, series 1.3, folder 35, ibid.

36. James Dees to editor, *Raleigh News and Observer*, October 4, 1958, copy in series 1.4,

folder 40, and Wesley Critz George to W. J. Simmons, February 20, 1958, series 1.4, folder 38, ibid.; Dees to Reed Sarratt, March 12, 1959, series 1, box 3, Sarratt Papers.

37. Unidentified newspaper, January 27, March 10, 14, 15, August 20, 1958, clippings in Ku Klux Klan file, Cox Papers. On the growth of the Ku Klux Klan after the *Brown v. Board of Education* decision, see Fletcher Knebel and Clark Mollenhoff, "Eight Klans Bring New Terror to the South," *Look*, April 30, 1957, 59–60, clipping in ibid.

CHAPTER TEN

1. T. R. M. Howard, "The Mississippi Negro's Stand on Segregation in the Public Schools of Mississippi," speech given at governor's conference, July 30, 1954, Desegregation, Schools, Mississippi, II A, box 227, NAACP Papers; Numan V. Bartley, *The Rise of Massive Resistance: Race and Politics in the South during the 1950s* (Baton Rouge, 1969), 76.

2. Charles M. Payne, *I've Got the Light of Freedom: The Organizing Tradition and the Mississippi Freedom Struggle* (Berkeley, 1995), 24–28, 31; Neil R. McMillen, *The Citizens' Council: Organized Resistance to the Second Reconstruction, 1954–64* (Urbana, 1994), 15–40. J. H. White, president of Mississippi Vocational College in Itta Bena, considered the address "not only out of place, but . . . rather a blow to the goodwill of the people of the State." White, eager for better facilities, favored the separate-but-equal offer. See J. H. White to E. J. Stringer, August 25, 1954, Desegregation, Schools, Mississippi, II A, box 227, NAACP Papers. On J. H. White's role as a white ally, see B. F. Smith to Hugh L. White, April 22, 1955, box 15, folder 10, Sillers Papers.

3. E. J. Stringer to Thurgood Marshall, October 7, 1954, Desegregation, Schools, Mississippi, II A, box 227, NAACP Papers.

4. Gloster B. Current to Roy Wilkins, "Report on Mississippi Situation," December 13, 1954, Mississippi Pressures, box 424, ibid.

5. Ruby Hurley to Roy Wilkins, April 8, 1955, ibid.

6. Paul Anthony, "Pro-Segregation Groups' History and Trends," *New South*, January 1957, 6–7, copy in White Citizens' Council—Financial Support file, Cox Papers.

7. "How White Citizens' Councils Came to Alabama," *New South*, December 1955, 9–12, copy in box 33, SCCHR Papers. The author remained anonymous.

8. "The Selma, Alabama, Report," September 11, 1955, Reprisals, Alabama, II A, box 508; affidavit of S. W. Boynton, July 26, 1956; affidavit of Otis Washington, July 28, 1956; affidavit of H. W. Shannon, July 28, 1956; and affidavit of Daniel Stevens, July 29, 1956, Reprisals, Alabama, 1956–59, III A, box 272, NAACP Papers.

9. *Alabamian*, July 1956, copy in box 36, Davidson Papers.

10. John Dittmer, *Local People: The Struggle for Civil Rights in Mississippi* (Urbana, 1994), 60; "Sovereignty Groups Files Packed with Information," *Jackson State Times*, September 19, 1959, A2.

11. Murray Kempton, "Pride in Their Words, Shame on Their Faces," *New York Post*, November 13, 1955, copy in White Citizens' Council—Mississippi file, Cox Papers.

12. Murray Kempton, "The Southern Gentlemen," unidentified newspaper, November 14, 1955, clipping in White Citizens' Council—Labor Unions file, ibid. For a vivid

description of an organizational meeting in Erath, Louisiana, see *Lafayette Daily Advertiser*, December 2, 1955, clipping in White Citizens' Council—Louisiana file, ibid.

13. Elizabeth H. Cobbs/Petric J. Smith, *Long Time Coming: An Insider's Story of the Birmingham Church Bombing That Rocked the World* (Birmingham, 1994), 25–29, 35. In 1977, Cobbs testified against Robert Chambliss at his trial for murder in the bombing of the Sixteenth Street Baptist Church on September 15, 1963. In December 1981, Cobbs legally became a man and took the name of Petric J. Smith.

14. Ibid., 38–43, 84.

15. Ibid., 52–54.

16. Ibid., 56–57, 61–63, 74–75; "Summary of Reports for Week Ending Sunday, May 22, 1949," H. Browne and Associates Report, II B, box 84, NAACP Papers.

17. Clarence Mitchell to Medgar Evers, memorandum, February 18, 1955, and R. B. McLeaish to Kenneth L. Scott, February 25, 1955, Mississippi Pressures, II A, box 422, NAACP Papers.

18. Ruby Hurley to Roy Wilkins, April 8, 1955, Mississippi Pressures, II A, box 424, ibid.

19. Mildred Bond to Roy Wilkins, memorandum, January 25, 1956, Mississippi Pressures, A–L, 1956–64, III A, box 230, ibid.

20. Amzie Moore to Roy Wilkins, October 11, 1955, Mississippi Pressures, II A, box 422, ibid.

21. J. Robertshaw to Boswell Stevens, May 25, 1954; J. B. Cunningham to Stevens, June 29, 1955; Stevens to Cunningham, July 8, 1955; Charlie Burton to Stevens, June 14, 1954; Stevens to Burton, June 28, 1954; Burton to Stevens, July 1, 1954, Subject Files, General; and Stevens to James O. Eastland, May 28, 1959, Subject Files, Eastland, 1953–62, Stevens Papers.

22. *Washington Daily News*, June 23, 1959; unidentified newspaper, June 23, 1959, clipping in Senator James O. Eastland file, Cox Papers; Medgar Evers and Mildred Bond to Gloster B. Current, January 23, 1956, "Farmer Information Sheets," confidential, Mississippi Pressures, Relief Fund, 1956–63, III A, box 233, NAACP Papers.

23. Medgar Evers and Mildred Bond to Gloster B. Current, January 23, 1956, "Farmer Information Sheets," confidential, Mississippi Pressures, Relief Fund, 1956–63, III A, box 233, NAACP Papers (emphasis in original). See also Fay Bennett to John A. Morsell, January 8, 1957, and Gloster B. Current to Morsell, January 21, 1957, Mississippi Pressures, Cases, M–Y, 1956–63, box 230, ibid. For a discussion of sharecropping, government programs, and harassment by planters for political participation, see Constance Curry, *Silver Rights* (Chapel Hill, 1995).

24. Hodding Carter to Jack Dale, March 6, 1957, Correspondence, 1957, Carter Papers.

25. Hodding Carter, "A Wave of Terror Threatens the South," *Look*, March 22, 1955, 32–36.

26. Robert B. Patterson, open letter to *Look*, March 8, 1955, Correspondence, 1955, *Look* Article, Carter Papers; Roy Wilkins to editor, *Look*, March 17, 1955, White Supremacy, White Citizens' Council, II A, box 672, NAACP Papers.

27. Jewell MacDaniel and Christine Sappington to Hodding Carter, March 9, 1955, and Shed Hill Caffey to Carter, April 2, 1955, Correspondence, 1955, *Look* Article, Carter Papers.

28. Jane C. Houck to Hodding Carter, December 12, 1955, and Robert H. Ahrens to Carter, April 1, 1955, ibid. (emphasis in original).

29. J. W. Haddon to Hodding Carter, March 30, 1955, ibid.; *Citizens' Council*, October 1956, copy in box 36, Davidson Papers.

30. James W. Silver to Frank Owsley, April 3, 1955, box 4, Owsley Papers.

31. Fred Chaney to Hodding Carter, Easter Sunday, 1955, Correspondence, 1955, Carter Papers (emphasis in original).

32. Hodding Carter to Ellett Lawrence, February 28, 1955, ibid.

33. Ruby Hurley to Roy Wilkins, October 7, 1955, Mississippi Pressures, II A, box 422, and unsigned statement, [1955], Desegregation, Schools, Mississippi, box 227, NAACP Papers. See Curry, *Silver Rights*, 49–50.

34. Medgar Evers to Roy Wilkins, September 12, 1956, III A, box 233, NAACP Papers.

35. Ibid.

36. Annie Mae Johnson to Roy Wilkins, February 20, 1956; Wilkins to Medgar Evers, July 31, 1956; Johnson to Wilkins, July 12, 1956, February 24, 1957; Evers to Wilkins, September 12, 1956, III A, box 233; and Evers and Mildred Bond to Gloster B. Current, January 24, 1956, Mississippi Pressures, Cases, M–Y, 1956–63, III A, box 230, ibid.

37. Aaron E. Henry to Roy Wilkins, February 4, 1956; affidavit of Gussie P. Young, February 1, 1956; affidavit of Lurleander Johnson, February 1, 1956; and "School Petitioners Fired at Federally-Aided Hospital," press release, February 9, 1956, Mississippi Pressures, A–L, 1956–64, III A, box 230, ibid.; Payne, *I've Got the Light of Freedom*, 56–60.

38. A. H. McCoy to Dwight D. Eisenhower, May 10, 1955, and Ruby Hurley, "Investigation of Death of Reverend G. W. Lee, Belzoni, Mississippi," memorandum, May 13, 1955, Mississippi Pressures, II A, box 422, NAACP Papers. See also Jack Mendelsohn, *The Martyrs: Sixteen Who Gave Their Lives for Racial Justice* (New York, 1966).

39. Ruby Hurley, "Investigation of Death of Reverend G. W. Lee, Belzoni, Mississippi," memorandum, May 13, 1955, Mississippi Pressures, II A, box 422, NAACP Papers.

40. Gloster B. Current to Henry Lee Moon, December 1, 1955, ibid.; Payne, *I've Got the Light of Freedom*, 15, 36–40.

41. Gertrude Gorman to Roy Wilkins, November 1, 1956; Gus Courts to Wilkins, April 18, 1957; Wilkins to Courts, April 22, 1957; and Courts to Wilkins, May 6, 1957, Mississippi Pressures, Cases, Courts, 1956–57, III A, box 230, NAACP Papers. Documents relating to Courts ended up in U.S. senator Sam Ervin's office. Marginal notes indicated that Ervin's staff pondered whether or not Courts had paid income tax and questioned the nature of his wounds. See notes on Courts's testimony, box 388, Ervin Papers.

42. Affidavit of E. C. Smith, June 1957, box 6, Moore Papers.

43. *Citizens' Council*, October 1955, copy in box 36, Davidson Papers; Payne, *I've Got the Light of Freedom*, 40–43; Richard D. Morphew to Tom Abernethy, June 17, 1959, box 246, Abernethy Papers; *Jackson Daily News*, January 27, 1960, and unidentified newspaper, July 28, 1960, clippings in Ross Barnett—Mississippi file; and *Jackson State Times*, September 19, 1959, clipping in Mississippi Sovereignty Commission file, Cox Papers.

44. Jerry W. Dallas, "The Delta and Providence Farms: A Mississippi Experiment in Cooperative Farming and Racial Cooperation, 1936–1956," *Mississippi Quarterly* 40 (Summer 1987): 283–308.

45. H. L. Mitchell, "On the Rise of the White Citizens Council and Its Ties with Anti-Labor Forces in the South," confidential, January 30, 1956, Ku Klux Klan file, Cox Papers.

46. Payne, *I've Got the Light of Freedom*, 101.

47. U.S. Bureau of the Census, *Census of Agriculture, 1964*, vol. 2, *General Report*, table 4, "Number of Negro and Other Nonwhite Farm Operators, by Regions and States, 1900 to 1964," 761.

48. Dittmer, *Local People*, 165–66.

CHAPTER ELEVEN

1. Thomas Lindemann Johnson, "James McBride Dabbs: A Life Story" (Ph.D. diss., University of South Carolina, 1980), 371–77, 416; James McBride Dabbs to Roy Wilkins, November 11, 1956, Desegregation, Public Opinion, C–D, 1956–58, III A, box 96, NAACP Papers. See also James McBride Dabbs, *The Southern Heritage* (New York, 1958) and *The Road Home* (Philadelphia, 1960). For an overview of race relations in South Carolina, see Orville Vernon Burton, "The Black Squint of the Law," in *The Meaning of South Carolina History: Essays in Honor of George C. Rogers Jr.*, edited by David R. Chesnutt and Clyde N. Wilson (Columbia, S.C., 1991), 161–85.

2. On the transition from small farms to agribusiness and industrialization in South Carolina, see T. S. Buie, "From Cotton to Cattle," *South Carolina Magazine*, March 1959, 8–10, 26–27; Sara Reese Sullivan, "Peacetime Uses of Atomic Energy," *South Carolina Magazine*, October 1958, 9; and L. N. Schilling, "Poultry," *South Carolina Magazine*, December 1956, 4–5.

3. Interviews with Alice Spearman Wright, February 28, August 8, 1976, by Jacquelyn Dowd Hall, SOHP Collection; Marcia G. Synnott, "Alice Norwood Spearman Wright: Civil Rights Apostle to South Carolina," in *Beyond Image and Convention: Explorations in Southern Women's History*, edited by Janet L. Coryell, Martha H. Swain, Sandra Gioia Treadway, and Elizabeth Hayes Turner (Columbia, Mo., 1998), 186–88.

4. Alice Spearman Wright interviews, February 28, August 8, 1976; Synnott, "Alice Norwood Spearman Wright," 187–89.

5. Alice Spearman Wright interview, August 8, 1976; interview with Modjeska Simkins, November 15, 1974, by Jacquelyn Dowd Hall, SOHP Collection; Synnott, "Alice Norwood Spearman Wright," 184–92.

6. Alice Spearman to Harriet Simons, January 10, 1955, box 1, SCCHR Papers; Synnott, "Alice Norwood Spearman Wright," 192–93.

7. Alice Spearman to Harriet Simons, January 10, 1955, box 1, SCCHR Papers; Alice Spearman Wright interview, August 8, 1976; Maxie Myron Cox Jr., "1963 — The Year of Decision: Desegregation in South Carolina" (Ph.D. diss., University of South Carolina, 1992), 7–8.

8. Harriet Simons to Alice Spearman, February 7, 1955, box 1, SCCHR Papers.

9. Ibid. See also Alice Spearman to Josephine Pinckney, September 7, 1955; Spearman to Harriet Simons, November 17, 1955; and Spearman to George Mitchell, May 8, 1956, box 1, SCCHR Papers; Synnott, "Alice Norwood Spearman Wright," 192–97.

10. Interview with Marion A. Wright, March 11, 1976, by Arnold Shankman, and interview with Marion A. Wright, March 8, 1978, by Jacquelyn Dowd Hall, SOHP Collection. On Wright's personal life and court decisions, see John Egerton, *Speak Now against the Day: The Generation before the Civil Rights Movement in the South* (New York, 1994), 407–9, 524–25.

11. Marion A. Wright interview, March 11, 1976.

12. Alice Spearman to Edward L. Byrd, January 10, 1955; Spearman to Iola Jones, January 10, 1955; and Byrd to Spearman, January 13, April 2, 1955, box 1, SCCHR Papers.

13. Carl R. Pritchett to Alice Spearman, February 22, 1955, ibid.; Alice Spearman Wright interview, August 8, 1976.

14. Alice Spearman to David Carroll, March 30, April 14, 1955, and Carroll to Spearman, April 16, 1955, box 1, SCCHR Papers (emphasis in original).

15. J. Claude Evans, "Statement to the S.C. Council on Human Relations," executive board meeting, May 29, 1955, copy in ibid.

16. Alice Spearman to Rebecca Reid, June 6, 1955, ibid.

17. Alice Spearman Wright interview, August 8, 1976.

18. Chester C. Travelstead to Governor George Bell Timmerman Jr., May 2, 1955, and Alice Spearman to George S. Mitchell, October 26, 1955, box 1, SCCHR Papers; Cox, "1963—The Year of Decision," 71–78.

19. Marion A. Wright to Donald Russell, November 26, 1955, box 33, SCCHR Papers.

20. Bud R. Hutchinson to editor, *Lee County Bulletin*, May 16, 1957, and *Opelika News*, May 15, 16, 1957, clippings in box 34, Draughon Papers.

21. Alice Edwards Lee to Alice Spearman, February 11, March 2, 1956; Spearman to Lee, March 7, 1956; Lee to Spearman, March 9, 1956; and Spearman to Jay Clark, March 13, 1956, box 1, SCCHR Papers (emphasis in original).

22. Alice Edwards Lee to Alice Spearman, March 9, 1956, and Spearman to Jay Clark, March 13, 1956, ibid.

23. Alice Spearman to Allan J. Sindler, February 9, 1960, box 2, ibid.

24. John Bell Timmerman to George Jackson Stafford, July 13, 29, 1955, and Stafford to "Dear Fellow Worker in Christ," July 31, 1955, box 24, ibid.; Tandy McConnell, "Religion, Segregation, and the Ideology of Cooperation: A Southern Baptist Church Responds to the *Brown* Decision," *Southern Studies* 4 (Spring 1993): 19–20, 31–32.

25. George Jackson Stafford to "Dear Fellow Worker in Christ," July 31, 1955, box 24, SCCHR Papers; McConnell, "Religion, Segregation, and the Ideology of Cooperation," 33–34.

26. George Jackson Stafford to "Dear Fellow Worker in Christ," August 9, 1955, box 24, SCCHR Papers.

27. George Jackson Stafford, memorandum, September 7, 1955, and *The State*, November 1, 1955, clipping in ibid.; McConnell, "Religion, Segregation, and the Ideology of Cooperation," 33–34.

28. Benjamin E. Mays, *Born to Rebel: An Autobiography* (Athens, 1987), 241–64.

29. Alice Spearman to Earl Cooper, September 2, 1955, and Cooper to Spearman, September 5, 1955, box 1, SCCHR Papers; Dabbs, *Southern Heritage*, 252–53.

30. James L. Atkinson, "Citizens Councils of South Carolina, 1955–1961" (honors thesis, University of South Carolina, 1987), 9–14, 34, 38–40, 83.

31. Alice Spearman to Rebecca Reid, September 14, 1955; Spearman to James M. Dabbs, September 14, 1955; and Spearman to Carl Pritchett, September 15, 1955, box 1, SCCHR Papers; Alice Spearman Wright interview, August 8, 1976.

32. Alice Spearman to John B. Morris, March 30, 1956, and Mrs. Morris S. Young to Spearman, May 3, 1956, box 1, SCCHR Papers; Alice Spearman Wright interview, August 8, 1976; Synnott, "Alice Norwood Spearman Wright," 201.

33. Harry R. Mays to John B. Morris, April 24, 1957, and Morris to Joe, Larry, John, and Ralph, June 5, 1957, box 1, SCCHR Papers.

34. Harriet Simons to John B. Morris, June 11, 1957; John Clyde Barrington to Morris, June 27, 1957; and M. R. Mobley to Morris, June 25, 1957, ibid. (emphasis in original).

35. John B. Morris to Jack Frost, May 9, 1957, ibid.

36. John B. Morris to Larry, Ralph, Joe, and John, August 24, 1957, ibid.; Ralph E. Cousins, Joseph R. Horn III, Larry A. Jackson, John S. Lyles, and John B. Morris, comps., *South Carolinians Speak: A Moderate Approach to Race Relations* (n.p., 1957), 3, 4, 10, 18, 19, 22, 31, 32, copy in box 1, Morris Papers. The authors were Robert Beverley Herbert, Columbia; Edgar Nelson Sullivan, Clinton; Helen Burr Christensen, Beaufort; Andrew McDowd Secrest, Cheraw; J. Emmett Jerome, Rock Hill; Julia Rees Reynolds, Sumter; Prentiss McLeod Kinney, Bennettsville; Andrew Peeples, Bamberg; Arthur Locke King, Georgetown; John Clyde Barrington, Dillon; Claudia Thomas Sanders, Gaffney; and John Moore, Mount Pleasant.

37. Cousins et al., *South Carolinians Speak*, 50, 51, 56, 62–68, 76–89.

38. Ibid., 70–73.

39. For a complete account of Claudia Thomas Sanders's role in the preparation of the book and the subsequent bombing, see Tim Tyson, "Dynamite and 'The Silent South': A Story from the Second Reconstruction in South Carolina," n.d., paper in author's possession.

40. Confession of Robert P. Martin Jr., December 6, 1957, copy in Sanders Papers; *Spartanburg Herald*, November 20, 1957, and *Spartanburg Journal*, November 20, 21, 1957, clippings in ibid.; John B. Morris to Larry Jackson, November 29, 1957, box 1, Morris Papers.

41. *Spartanburg Herald-Journal*, January 12, 1958, clipping in Sanders Papers.

42. *Charleston News and Courier*, February 28, 1958, clipping in box 32, SCCHR Papers; *Gaffney Ledger*, June 28, July 15, 19, 1957, and *Charlotte Observer*, June 29, 1958, clippings in Sanders Papers.

43. Claudia Sanders to Thomas Johnson, March 19, 1974, Sanders Papers; John B. Morris to W. D. Workman Jr., August 22, 1958, and Morris to J. D. Blizzard, November 22, 1957, box 1, Morris Papers.

44. William D. Workman Jr., *The Case for the South* (New York, 1960), 13, 47–67, 139, 165, 216.

45. B. T. Matthews to George Sam Harrell, April 29, 1957, box 19, Workman Papers. See also C. N. Dennis to George Sam Harrell, April 29, 1957, and W. D. Workman Jr. to

T. D. Keels, June 18, 1957, ibid.; Cox, "1963—The Year of Decision," 259–345; and "State Parks and Segregation," *South Carolina Magazine*, January 1956, 3.

46. Charles G. Garrett to William Jennings Bryan Dorn, March 21, 1956, box 42, Dorn Papers.

47. Alice Spearman to J. E. Blanton, November 17, 1955, and Blanton to Spearman, November 20, 1955, box 1, SCCHR Papers; I. A. Newby, *Black Carolinians: A History of Blacks in South Carolina from 1895 to 1968* (Columbia, S.C., 1973), 346–47; Johnson, "James McBride Dabbs," 396–97.

48. "Negro Group States Policy, Objectives," *Columbia Record*, November 10, 1955, copy of typescript in box 1, SCCHR Papers.

49. M. D. McCollom, Henry L. Parker, E. E. Richburg, and Alfred Isaac, "An Open Letter," [1955], Reprisals, South Carolina, II A, box 508, NAACP Papers.

50. Billie S. Fleming to John Morsell, December 1, 1958, Reprisals, South Carolina, 1958–61, III A, box 279, ibid.; Cox, "1963—The Year of Decision," 145–59.

51. "Statement of Billie S. Fleming, President of the Clarendon County, South Carolina, Improvement Association," Senate Subcommittee on Constitutional Rights, April 16, 1959, Reprisals, South Carolina, 1958–61, III A, box 279, NAACP Papers.

52. Billie S. Fleming to John Morsell, April 5, 1961, ibid. See also Alice Spearman to James E. Pierce, February 1, 1960, box 2, SCCHR Papers.

53. Ira Kaye to Alice Spearman, November 9, 1961, box 25, SCCHR Papers.

54. John H. McCray, "The Clarendon County Story," April 12, 1957, typescript in box 5, McCray Papers.

55. In 1960, Alice Spearman told of "an old Negro couple who have been dispossessed of their holdings, bodily injured in their own home and put into the county jail." She added, "all of us know that the practice of foreclosing on persons whose land is desired by others is not an uncommon practice." See Spearman to James E. Pierce, February 1, 1960, box 2, SCCHR Papers.

56. John H. McCray, "Statement on Civil Rights," Senate Subcommittee on Constitutional Rights, April 16, 1959, copy in box 1, McCray Papers; John Morsell to Henry Lee Moon, February 10, 1960, Reprisals, South Carolina, 1960–65, III A, box 279, NAACP Papers.

57. D. M. Duckett, speech, October 11, 1959, and Alice Spearman to Hawley Lynn, [early 1960], box 2, SCCHR Papers.

58. Alice Spearman to Paul Rilling, October 3, 1959, and Spearman to Ella Baker, December 1, 1959, ibid.; Alice Spearman Wright interview, August 8, 1976.

59. Alice Spearman to Ella Baker, December 1, 1959, box 2, SCCHR Papers; Synnott, "Alice Norwood Spearman Wright," 202.

CHAPTER TWELVE

1. On how such conflicts are constructed to serve the elite, see Ranajit Guha, "The Prose of Counter-Insurgency," in *Selected Subaltern Studies*, edited by Ranajit Guha and Gayatri Chakravorty Spivak (New York, 1988), 78–82.

2. Robert Sherrill, *Gothic Politics in the Deep South: Stars of the New Confederacy* (New York, 1968), 76. On the international implications of the crisis, see Azza Salama

Layton, "International Pressure and the U.S. Government's Response to Little Rock," *Arkansas Historical Quarterly* 56 (Autumn 1997): 257–72. For a discussion of the philosophical implications of the crisis through the eyes of Hannah Arendt, see Richard H. King, "American Dilemmas, European Experiences," *Arkansas Historical Quarterly* 56 (Autumn 1997): 314–33.

3. Virgil T. Blossom, *It Has Happened Here* (New York, 1959), 1–7, 16–18. On integration in Fayetteville, see Julianne Lewis Adams and Thomas A. DeBlack, *Civil Obedience: An Oral History of School Desegregation in Fayetteville, Arkansas, 1954–1965* (Fayetteville, Ark., 1994).

4. "A 'Morally Right' Decision," *Life,* July 25, 1955, 29–31.

5. Mildred Bond to Thurgood Marshall, August 5, 1955, and Bond to Roy Wilkins, memorandum, August 6, 1955, Desegregation, Hoxie, II A, box 226, NAACP Papers; Cabell Phillips, "Integration: Battle of Hoxie, Arkansas," *New York Times Magazine,* September 25, 1955, clipping, and transcript of rally, September 17, 1955, Walnut Ridge, series 1, box 16, ACHR Papers; Nat R. Griswold, "The Second Reconstruction in Little Rock," unpublished manuscript, [1968], lent to author by John Kirk; interview with Jim Johnson, Conway, Arkansas, January 27, 1966, by Pete Daniel and Elizabeth Jacoway; Willis E. Ayers Jr. to Jim Johnson, February 5, 1956, box 2, folder 10, Jim Johnson Papers. Johnson charged that the Federal Bureau of Investigation (FBI) intimidated Hoxie whites, and he interpreted J. Edgar Hoover's *Masters of Deceit* and the writings of Dan Smoot as warnings of a conspiracy by the federal government to strip away peoples' rights. He praised Hoover and damned the FBI in the same breath.

6. See Amis Guthridge to Jim Johnson, November 7, 1955; James O. Eastland to Johnson, December 20, 1955, box 30, folder 10; Johnson to Guthridge, November 9, 1955; Phil Stratton to Johnson, n.d.; Johnson to Sam Englehart, April 18, 1957, box 10, folder 11; and Malcolm Taylor to Johnson, July 5, 1956, box 30, folder 12, Jim Johnson Papers. On Johnson's overall strategy, see Stratton to H. R. Cullen, April 22, 1957, ibid. For insight into how the Southern Manifesto affected the Little Rock crisis, see Tony Badger, "'The Forerunner of Our Opposition': Arkansas and the Southern Manifesto of 1956," *Arkansas Historical Quarterly* 56 (Autumn 1997): 353–60.

7. Roy Reed, *Faubus: The Life and Times of an American Prodigal* (Fayetteville, Ark., 1997) and "Orval E. Faubus: Out of Socialism into Realism," *Arkansas Historical Quarterly* 54 (Spring 1995): 13–29. On Faubus and the context of the 1957 crisis, see David L. Chappell, *Inside Agitators: White Southerners in the Civil Rights Movement* (Baltimore, 1994), 97–121; Sherrill, *Gothic Politics,* 74–117; David Halberstam, *The Fifties* (New York, 1993), 667–92; and Numan V. Bartley, *The Rise of Massive Resistance: Race and Politics in the South during the 1950s* (Baton Rouge, 1969), 251–69.

8. Blossom, *It Has Happened Here,* 1–7, 16–18; Sara Alderman Murphy, *Breaking the Silence: Little Rock's Women's Emergency Committee to Open Our Schools, 1958–1963* (Fayetteville, Ark., 1997), 34–41.

9. Interview with Wesley Pruden Jr., December 6, 1995, by Pete Daniel; Reed, *Faubus,* 189.

10. "Events, Information, Statements, etc., prior to September 3, 1957," and interview with Bryce Miller, September 7, 1957, by Francis Finley and Gilbert W. Strickland, Central High FBI Records; Blossom, *It Has Happened Here,* 33–36, 41–42.

11. Reed, *Faubus*, 193–96.

12. Interview with Margaret Jackson, September 6, 7, 1957, by Paul R. Scott and John R. Brett; interview with Margaret Ann Stephens, September 5, 1957, by Paul L. Scott and John R. Brett; and interview with Mrs. John W. McCauley, September 7, 1957, by George A. Barron Jr. and John M. Moore, Central High FBI Records. Many women used their husband's name, but their given names are cited when available. See also Arthur B. Caldwell, memorandum, August 30, 1957, ibid., which summarizes the testimony of Orval Faubus and Mrs. Clyde Thomason in Chancery Court, August 29, 1957. Thomason claimed that thirty-seven women were founding members of the Mothers' League.

13. Interview with Mrs. John Harden, September 8, 1957, by Vincent H. Lammers and Larry C. Boyer; interview with Eva Sample, September 8, 1957, by J. Robert Meigs and Walden L. Green; and "Events, Information, Statements, etc., prior to September 3, 1957," Central High FBI Records; *Arkansas Gazette*, August 24, 1957.

14. *Arkansas Gazette*, August 23, 1957; Fletcher Knebel, "The Real Little Rock Story," *Look*, November 12, 1957, 31–32.

15. Daisy Bates, *The Long Shadow of Little Rock* (Fayetteville, Ark., 1986), 4, 110–11; interview with Daisy Bates, September 8, 1957, by Roy N. Osborn and Edward G. Stork, Central High FBI Records.

16. Bates, *Long Shadow of Little Rock*, 2–3, 6, 11, 15, 21, 23, 33, 47; Carolyn Calloway-Thomas and Thurmon Garner, "Daisy Bates and the Little Rock School Crisis: Forging the Way," *Journal of Black Studies* 26 (May 1996): 616–28; John A. Kirk, "The Little Rock Crisis and Postwar Black Activism in Arkansas," *Arkansas Historical Quarterly* 56 (Autumn 1997): 286–93.

17. "Resume of Testimony in Mothers' League Hearing," Central High FBI Records; Reed, *Faubus*, 203–4. For background on the sentiment in Little Rock, see Irving J. Spitzberg Jr., *Racial Politics in Little Rock, 1954–1964* (New York, 1987), 31–58.

18. Stephens interview, September 5, 1957; interview with Mrs. O. R. Aaron, September 5, 1957, by William C. Rupp Jr. and James L. Pugh; Jackson interview, September 6, 7, 1957; interview with Mary Anita Sedberry, September 7, 1957, by Roy M. Osborn and Edward G. Stork; and interview with Mrs. Hodge Alves, September 5, 1957, by Roy M. Osborn and Edward G. Stork, Central High FBI Records. See Martha Hodes, "The Sexualization of Reconstruction Politics: White Women and Black Men in the South after the Civil War," *Journal of the History of Sexuality* 3 (January 1993): 402–17.

19. Thomas F. Pettigrew and Ernest Q. Campbell, "The Christian Minister and Little Rock: A Research Report," [1959], box 2, Anti-Defamation League Papers, and *Christians in Racial Crisis: A Study of Little Rock's Ministry* (Washington, D.C., 1959), 36–38, 45.

20. Blossom, *It Has Happened Here*, 62, 65–66, 70–71, 90; Reed, *Faubus*, 200; *Arkansas Gazette*, September 2, 7, 1957; Warren Olney III to Attorney General, September 13, 1957, box 5, folder 2, Caldwell Papers; *Dallas Morning News*, September 16, 1957, clipping in box 3G432, Morehead Papers; Pettigrew and Campbell, "Christian Minister and Little Rock."

21. Governor Orval E. Faubus, "Mobilization of Arkansas National Guard," speech, September 2, 1957, Central High FBI Records. See also Tony A. Freyer, "The Little

Rock Crisis Reconsidered," *Arkansas Historical Quarterly* 56 (Autumn 1997): 361–70; Reed, *Faubus*, 207–8; Knebel, "Real Little Rock Story," 32–33; Sherrill, *Gothic Politics*, 86, 89, 100–105; Halberstam, *The Fifties*, 666–75; Harry S. Ashmore, *Hearts and Minds: A Personal Chronicle of Race in America* (Cabin John, Md., 1988), 251–59; interview with Brooks Hays, Washington, D.C., June 28, 1970, by John Luter, Columbia University Oral History Program. The FBI found no unusual numbers of purchases of knives and guns in Little Rock. See Warren Olney III to Attorney General, September 13, 1957, box 5, folder 2, Caldwell Papers.

22. Craig R. Anderson, "Before Little Rock: The Desegregation Crises at Mansfield, Texas, and Clinton, Tennessee" (M.A. thesis, Utah State University, 1995), 33–63.

23. Ibid., 64–89.

24. Blossom, *It Has Happened Here*, 81; *Arkansas Gazette*, September 4, 1957; Elizabeth Huckaby diary, September 3, 1957, Huckaby Papers; Reed, *Faubus*, 213.

25. Interview with W. H. Bass, September 6, 1957, by Thomas J. Morton Jr. and Eugene G. Douglass; interview with James W. Gallman, September 6, 1957, by Paul L. Scott and John R. Brett; and interview with Colbert L. Cartwright, September 4, 1957, by Thomas J. Bader and Estes G. Coleman, Central High FBI Records; Murphy, *Breaking the Silence*, 151–53.

26. Interview with Elizabeth Eckford, September 4, 1957, by Robert E. Hickam and Gilbert W. Strickland; interview with Lieutenant Marion E. Johnson, Arkansas National Guard, September 6, 1957, by William G. Rawls and Harry W. Hankinson; Sedberry interview, September 7, 1957; and interview with Grace K. Lorch, September 8, 1957, by Paul L. Scott and John R. Brett, Central High FBI Records.

27. Interview with Hazel Bryan Massery, Little Rock, Arkansas, January 29, 1996, by Pete Daniel and Elizabeth Jacoway.

28. Melba Pattillo Beals, *Warriors Don't Cry: A Searing Memoir of the Battle to Integrate Little Rock's Central High* (New York, 1994), 46–59.

29. Elizabeth Huckaby, *Crisis at Central High: Little Rock, 1957–58* (Baton Rouge, 1980), 27; Blossom, *It Has Happened Here*, 85; Elizabeth Huckaby diary, September 6, 1957, Huckaby Papers; interview with Captain Alan Templeton, September 8, 1957, by Herman E. Tickel, Central High FBI Records.

30. Mrs. Carl Frick to Orval Faubus, September 4, 1957, and Ronald A. May to Faubus, September 6, 1957, series 14, subseries 8, box 520, Faubus Papers; *Christian Century* 74 (September 18, 1957): 1091–92; "Hats Off to the Women of Little Rock," *Christian Century* 74 (October 2, 1957): 1155–56.

31. Chappell, *Inside Agitators*, 112–13; Reed, *Faubus*, 217, 219–23; Elizabeth Huckaby diary, September 12, 16, 20, 22, 1957, Huckaby Papers; Hays interview, June 28, 1970. For an account of the meeting with Eisenhower, see interview with Orval Faubus and Brooks Hays, June 4, 1976, by John Ward, series 3, subseries 1, box 45, Hays Papers.

32. *Arkansas Gazette*, September 24, 1957; "The Little Rock Crisis, 1957–1958," in Henry Hampton and Steve Fayer, *Voices of Freedom: An Oral History of the Civil Rights Movement from the 1950s through the 1980s* (New York, 1990), 44–46; Elizabeth Huckaby diary, September 23, 1957, Huckaby Papers; Beals, *Warriors Don't Cry*, 108–15; Huckaby, *Crisis at Central High*, 34–39; Murphy, *Breaking the Silence*, 56. Virgil Blossom never thought that the students were in danger. See Blossom, *It Has Happened Here*, 103–9.

33. *Arkansas Gazette*, March 5, 1958. For a reporter's description of the crowd, see Relman Morin, "Events at Central High School, September 23, 1957," *Sacramento Bee*, September 23, 1957, in *Little Rock, U.S.A.: Materials for Analysis*, edited by Wilson Record and Jane Cassels Record (San Francisco, 1960), 59–63.

34. Telephone transcript, Gloster B. Current and Mrs. L. C. Bates, September 23, 24, 1957, Desegregation, Little Rock, 1956–57, III A, box 97, NAACP Papers. Like other black activists, the Bateses suffered an "economic squeeze" after the *Brown* decision that threatened L. C. Bates's newspaper, the *State Press*. Advertising sales decreased, and a newsprint company refused to fill orders. Even the Internal Revenue Service investigated their tax records and billed them for $1,300. See Daisy Bates to Gloster B. Current, September 9, 1957, and Bates to Roy Wilkins, September 12, 1957, ibid. On Daisy Bates's views on self-defense and the ideology and extent of self-defense, see Timothy B. Tyson, "Robert F. Williams, 'Black Power,' and the Roots of the African American Freedom Struggle," *Journal of American History* 85 (September 1998): 540–70.

35. Eldon C. Williams, "Integration in Public Schools in Little Rock," interviews with Emmett E. Miller, L. R. Luker, and Hugh Lynn Adams, September 13, 1957, copy in Central High FBI Records. On the composition of the crowd, see Hays interview, June 28, 1970; John Chancellor, "Radio and Television Had Their Own Problems in Little Rock Coverage," *The Quill*, December 1957, 9–10, 20–21, and "White Hysteria in Little Rock," *The Quill*, November 1987, 48–50, and Ray Mosley, "Northern Newsmen Withstood Mob's Abuse to Report Little Rock Story," *The Quill*, December 1957, 8, 18, copies in box 3G434, Morehead Papers; and Reed, *Faubus*, 224–27.

36. Bern Keating, photograph caption attached to contact sheet, *U.S. News and World Report* file, LC-U9-1015, A–E, Prints and Photographs Division, Library of Congress, Washington, D.C.

37. "A Historic Week of Civil Strife: Governor with an Assistant Agitator for Promoting Trouble," *Life*, October 7, 1957, 37–48; interview with Larry Obsitnik, September 7, 1957, by Francis Finley and Gilbert W. Strickland, Central High FBI Records; *Arkansas Gazette*, September 8, 1957, clipping in box 3G432, Morehead Papers; Griswold, "Second Reconstruction in Little Rock"; "Arkansas 'Right to Work' Agitator in Midst of Little Rock Agitation," September 30, 1957, file S2B22, NUL Papers; Murphy, *Breaking the Silence*, 49; "Members of the Mob," *Look*, November 12, 1957, 35–37; Reed, *Faubus*, 227; I. F. Stone, *The Haunted Fifties* (New York, 1969), 205–7.

38. Pettigrew and Campbell, "Christian Minister and Little Rock" and *Christians in Racial Crisis*, 36–37, 45, 110; interview with Corbett Mask, September 7, 1957, by Roy M. Osborn and Edward G. Stork, Central High FBI Records; L. D. Foreman, "National Guardsmen at Central High," *Missionary Baptist Searchlight*, September 10, 1957, Glover Library. On Foreman's career, see Alta Payne, "Worthy of Double Honor," *Missionary Baptist Searchlight*, September 28, 1984. On the segregationist stand of Mask and Foreman, see "Minutes of the State Association of Missionary Baptist Churches of Arkansas," November 4, 5, 1954, 29, 30, and "Minutes of the Ninety-second Session of the Pine Bluff Missionary Baptist Association," October 14, 15, 1955, 20, Glover Library. See Council of Church Women of Little Rock and North Little Rock, memorandum, September 9, 1957, series 1, box 6, ACHR Papers. Nine moderate Little Rock pastors lost their pulpits during the year.

39. Pettigrew and Campbell, "Christian Minister and Little Rock" and *Christians in Racial Crisis*, 24–39, 45.

40. Pettigrew and Campbell, *Christians in Racial Crisis*, 46; Massery interview, January 29, 1996; Templeton interview, September 8, 1957.

41. Beals, *Warriors Don't Cry*, 132–33; "Little Rock Crisis, 1957–1958," 48.

42. Elizabeth Huckaby diary, September 25, 1957, Huckaby Papers; Huckaby, *Crisis at Central High*, 40–47; "From a Talk to the Student Body of Central High School, September 25, 1957," *San Francisco Bee*, September 26, 1957, in Record and Record, *Little Rock, U.S.A.*, 70–71.

43. Beals, *Warriors Don't Cry*, 134–43; telephone transcript, Daisy Bates and Clarence Laws in Little Rock and Gloster B. Current in New York, September 25, 1957, Desegregation, Little Rock, 1956–57, III A, box 97, NAACP Papers.

44. Beals, *Warriors Don't Cry*, 134–43; *Arkansas Democrat*, September 24, 1957; *Cash Box*, September 21, 1957, 24; "Members of the Mob," *Look*, November 12, 1957, 37.

45. Will D. Campbell to "All Human Relations Personnel in the South," August 20, 1957, Desegregation, Schools, Tennessee, 1956–63, III A, box 105, NAACP Papers.

46. Beals, *Warriors Don't Cry*, 161, 163, 165. For reaction to the crisis, see, for example, Israel Lafleur to Orval Faubus, September 27, 1957, and I. Beverly Lake to Faubus, September 26, 1957, series 14, subseries 8, box 505, Faubus Papers; John R. Mayes to James Folsom, October 3, 1957, box 13908, Folsom Papers; Don Blasingame to Lyndon Johnson, October 5, 1957; Sue C. Baxter to Johnson, September 27, 1957; J. D. Christian to Johnson, September 25, 1957; and Earl Dunkin to Johnson, n.d., Senate Papers, Legislative file, Faubus file, Opposing Eisenhower, box 394, Lyndon B. Johnson Papers; Lillian Smith to Ruth Nanda Anshen, October 8, 1957, series 1283, box 2, Smith Papers; and "Faubian Tactics," *America* 97 (September 28, 1957): 667. Of the letters to Johnson regarding the Little Rock crisis, 300 opposed Eisenhower and 23 supported him.

47. Elizabeth Huckaby diary, October 1, 2, 1957, Huckaby Papers; Huckaby, *Crisis at Central High*, 51–52, 54; Beals, *Warriors Don't Cry*, 167; *Arkansas Democrat*, October 2, 1957. For an overview of the first few months of school, see Spitzberg, *Racial Politics in Little Rock*, 59–81.

48. Beals, *Warriors Don't Cry*, 170–71; Elizabeth Huckaby diary, October 2, 7, 8, 10, 1957, Huckaby Papers; Huckaby, *Crisis at Central High*, 54–57.

49. Bates, *Long Shadow of Little Rock*, 116–22, 133–34.

50. Elizabeth Huckaby diary, October 2, 1957, Huckaby Papers; Bates, *Long Shadow of Little Rock*, 122–30, 138–39.

51. Bates, *Long Shadow of Little Rock*, 130–32, 134–38, 139–45.

52. Ibid., 145–51; Huckaby, *Crisis at Central High*, 72.

53. *Arkansas Democrat*, October 4, 6, 10, 12, 1957; "All Prayers for Little Rock Prayers," *Christian Century* 74 (October 16, 1957): 1219, (October 23, 1957): 1251; Ernest Q. Campbell and Thomas F. Pettigrew, "Men of God in Racial Crisis," *Christian Century* 75 (June 4, 1958): 663–65; James McBride Dabbs, "Manners into Morals," *Christian Century* 75 (October 29, 1958): 1237–38.

54. Jim Johnson to James O. Eastland, October 15, 1957, box 30, folder 13, Jim Johnson Papers.

55. Elizabeth Huckaby diary, November 14, 20, 1957, Huckaby Papers; telephone tran-

script, Daisy Bates and Gloster B. Current, November 13, 1957, Reprisals, Arkansas, 1956–57, III A, box 274, NAACP Papers. See also Elizabeth Huckaby, re: Gloria Ray, n.d., box 2, folder 18, Huckaby Papers. Virgil Blossom minimized the extent of the harassment and insisted that only a small percentage of white students were troublemakers and that the teachers had the situation under control. See Blossom, *It Has Happened Here*, 133–46, 156–75.

56. Elizabeth Huckaby diary, November 21, December 6, 9, 10, 1957, Huckaby Papers; Huckaby, *Crisis at Central High*, 81, 87, 92–95; Beals, *Warriors Don't Cry*, 193, 202.

57. Elizabeth Huckaby diary, December 17, 1957, Huckaby Papers; Huckaby, *Crisis at Central High*, 103–4; Beals, *Warriors Don't Cry*, 219–20.

58. Beth Roy, *Bitters in the Honey: Tales of Hope and Disappointment across Divides of Race and Time* (Fayetteville, Ark., 1999); Clarence A. Laws to Roy Wilkins, December 18, 1957, Reprisals, Arkansas, 1956–57, III A, box 274, NAACP Papers. See also "Student and Teacher Opinion in December 1957" and "The Negro Students in December 1957," *Southern School News*, January 1958, in Record and Record, *Little Rock, U.S.A.*, 84–87.

59. Huckaby, *Crisis at Central High*, 109–10, 117–18, 121–22; Elizabeth Huckaby diary, January 2, 7, 9, 10, 1958, Huckaby Papers; Huckaby, memorandum, January 17, 1958; Huckaby, re: Melba Pattillo, January 9, 1958; J. O. Powell, "Summary of Guard's Statement," [January 10, 1958]; Huckaby, "Report to Mr. Blossom on Darlene Holloway" (emphasis in original); and Huckaby, re: Melba Pattillo, January 10, 1958, box 2, folder 18, Huckaby Papers.

60. Elizabeth Huckaby diary, January 15, 1958, and Huckaby, re: Melba Pattillo, January 15, 1958, box 2, folder 18, Huckaby Papers; Huckaby, *Crisis at Central High*, 125–26.

61. Elizabeth Huckaby diary, January 16, 18, 19, 20, 21, 1958; Huckaby, re: Sammie Dean Parker, January 15, 1958; and Huckaby, re: Minniejean Brown, January 16, 1958, box 2, folder 18, Huckaby Papers; Huckaby, *Crisis at Central High*, 126–32.

62. Elizabeth Huckaby diary, January 22, 1958, Huckaby Papers; Huckaby, *Crisis at Central High*, 133–37.

63. Huckaby, *Crisis at Central High*, 145–46; Elizabeth Huckaby diary, February 3, 1958; Huckaby, re: Minniejean Brown, February 4, 1958; Huckaby, re: Minniejean Brown, Frankie Gregg, February 6, 1958; and Frankie Gregg's account, February 6, 1958, box 2, folder 18, Huckaby Papers.

64. Elizabeth Huckaby, re: Sammie Dean Parker, February 6, 1958; Huckaby, re: Minniejean Brown, February 6, 1958; memorandum on soup throwing, n.d.; Huckaby, re: Judy Atkinson, February 6, 1958; and Huckaby, re: Carlotta Walls, Herbert Blount, Dennis Milam, February 6, 1958, box 2, folder 18, Huckaby Papers; Murphy, *Breaking the Silence*, 52.

65. Interview with J. O. Powell, April 23, 1958, by Anna Holden, box 2, folder 11, Anti-Defamation League Papers.

66. Elizabeth Huckaby diary, February 17, 1958, Huckaby Papers; Huckaby, *Crisis at Central High*, 163–64.

67. Elizabeth Huckaby diary, February 21, 26, 1958, Huckaby Papers; Huckaby, *Crisis at Central High*, 167–75; Beals, *Warriors Don't Cry*, 246–47.

68. *Arkansas Gazette*, March 5, 1958.

69. Huckaby, *Crisis at Central High*, 170–75, 181–85; Elizabeth Huckaby diary, March 13, 16, February 26, 1958, Huckaby Papers.

70. Elizabeth Huckaby diary, May 25, 1958, Huckaby Papers; Huckaby, *Crisis at Central High*, 208–17; Powell interview, April 23, 1958.

71. The case is discussed in Dale Alford and L'Moore Alford, *The Case of the Sleeping People: Finally Awakened by Little Rock School Frustrations* (n.p., 1959), 9–50. On the reaction to Lemley's ruling, see Sterling Hutcheson to Harry J. Lemley, June 24, 1958; Esther R. Coady to Lemley, June 22, 1958; J. B. Milham to Lemley, June 24, 1958; Thomas A. Bledsoe to Lemley, July 22, 1958; and Grace Weld Mart to Lemley, June 30, 1958, box 2, file 2, Lemley Papers.

72. Elizabeth Jacoway, "Taken by Surprise: Little Rock Business Leaders and Desegregation," in *Southern Businessmen and Desegregation*, edited by Elizabeth Jacoway and David R. Colburn (Baton Rouge, 1982), 30; Lorraine Gates, "Power from the Pedestal: The Women's Emergency Committee and the Little Rock School Crisis," *Arkansas Historical Quarterly* 55 (Spring 1991): 27; Alford and Alford, *The Case of the Sleeping People*, 51–57; Murphy, *Breaking the Silence*, 65–66; "Saints in the Basement," *Christian Century* 75 (September 17, 1958): 1050–52.

73. Gates, "Power from the Pedestal," 26–43; Murphy, *Breaking the Silence*, 67–90; Karen Anderson, "The Little Rock School Desegregation Crisis and the Reproduction of a White Body Politic, 1957–1960," paper presented at the Organization of American Historians convention, April 17, 1997, San Francisco, California, copy in author's possession; Elizabeth Jacoway, "Down from the Pedestal: Gender and Regional Culture in a Ladylike Assault on the Southern Way of Life," *Arkansas Historical Quarterly* 56 (Autumn 1997): 345–52.

74. Jacoway, "Taken by Surprise," 31–41; Gates, "Power from the Pedestal," 36–57. Sara Murphy contended that even when men took an active role in opening the schools, "they remained segregationists emotionally" (*Breaking the Silence*, 60).

75. The photograph of Hazel Bryan and Elizabeth Eckford ran on the front page of the *New York Times* on September 21, 1997. Both women appeared on television, and Hazel Bryan Massery announced publicly that she did not want to be identified forever with that moment in 1957. She explained that she had practiced tolerance, raised a family, and been active in humanitarian causes since that time.

76. *Arkansas Gazette*, July 16, 1960, clipping enclosed with Nat R. Griswold to A. H. Rosenfeld, July 19, 1960, series 1, box 6, ACHR Papers. For a concise summation of the significance of the Central High School crisis, see Adam Fairclough, "The Little Rock Crisis: Success or Failure for the NAACP?," *Arkansas Historical Quarterly* 56 (Autumn 1997): 371–75. For how such tactics were employed in Mississippi, see Constance Curry, *Silver Rights* (Chapel Hill, 1995).

77. Sherrill, *Gothic Politics*, 76.

CHAPTER THIRTEEN

1. William H. Chafe, *Civilities and Civil Rights: Greensboro, North Carolina, and the Black Struggle for Freedom* (New York, 1980), 98–141; August Meier and Elliott Rudwick, *CORE: A Study in the Civil Rights Movement, 1942–1968* (New York, 1973),

101–31; Howard Zinn, *SNCC: The New Abolitionists* (Boston, 1965), 16–31; Clayborne Carson, *In Struggle: SNCC and the Black Awakening of the 1960s* (Cambridge, 1995), 9–18. For a segregationist view of white women students' participation in sit-ins, see Bill Sharpe to Gordon Blackwell, March 11, 1960, series 1.4, folder 47, George Papers.

2. Gloster B. Current to Roy Wilkins, memorandum, February 16, 1960, Reprisals, North Carolina, 1956–65, III A, box 279, NAACP Papers; Adam Fairclough, *Race and Democracy: The Civil Rights Struggle in Louisiana, 1915–1972* (Athens, 1995), 273–76. In Louisiana, Southern University students notified NAACP leader A. P. Tureaud on March 3 that they were planning demonstrations in Baton Rouge and invited him to a meeting. He accepted. See Major Johns to Tureaud, March 3, 1960, series 3, box 11, Tureaud Papers.

3. Alice Spearman to Mrs. St. Julian Childs, February 17, 1960; Spearman to Maurice Sheen, March 1, 1960; James H. Goudlock to Charlotte A. Hickman, February 18, 1960; Spearman to Goudlock, February 27, 1960; Goudlock to Spearman, March 2, 1960; Spearman to David S. Gruber, February 18, 1960; Spearman to James D. Murphy, April 1, 1960; and J. E. Blanton to Spearman, May 20, 1960, box 2, SCCHR Papers. For an overview of the sit-ins in South Carolina, see I. A. Newby, *Black Carolinians: A History of Blacks in South Carolina from 1895 to 1968* (Columbia, S.C., 1973), 314–30.

4. Christine White to Alice Spearman, April 15, November 15, 1960; Spearman to White, November 26, 1960; White to Spearman, December 1, 1960; and Spearman to Courtney Siceloff, August 2, 1960, box 2, SCCHR Papers.

5. James McBride Dabbs, "Dime Stores and Dignity," *The Nation*, April 2, 1960, clipping in box 33, ibid.

6. Telephone interview with Jane Stembridge, December 5, 1996, by Pete Daniel; interview with Connie Curry, Washington, D.C., January 17, 1997, by Pete Daniel; Zinn, *SNCC*, 16–19.

7. Donald Davidson to John Wade, March 18, 1960, box 2, Davidson Papers.

8. Wesley Critz George to I. Beverly Lake, February 24, 1960; Paul D. Hastings to James P. Dees, March 9, 1960, series 1.4, folder 47; W. N. Jefferies to Members of the Board of Trustees, University of North Carolina, July 22, 1960; George to "Dear Bill," August 13, 1960, series 1.4, folder 51; and George to Jefferies, March 6, 1961, series 1.4, folder 54, George Papers.

9. Nate Perlmutter to Arnold Forster, September 6, 1960, box 1, Anti-Defamation League Papers; Numan V. Bartley, *The New South, 1945–1980* (Baton Rouge, 1995), 303; Newby, *Black Carolinians*, 324; Timothy B. Tyson, "Robert F. Williams, 'Black Power,' and the Roots of the African American Freedom Struggle," *Journal of American History* 85 (September 1998): 540–70.

10. Joanne Grant, *Ella Baker: Freedom Bound* (New York, 1998), 100–103; Barbara Ransby, "Ella J. Baker and the Black Radical Tradition" (Ph.D. diss., University of Michigan, 1996), 187–96; Charles M. Payne, *I've Got the Light of Freedom: The Organizing Tradition and the Mississippi Freedom Struggle* (Berkeley, 1995), 91.

11. Grant, *Ella Baker*, 105–24; Ransby, "Ella J. Baker," 186–216; Payne, *I've Got the Light of Freedom*, 91–92; interview with Ella Baker, April 19, 1977, by Sue Thrasher and Casey Hayden, SOHP Collection.

12. Grant, *Ella Baker*, 127–31; Zinn, *SNCC*, 32–35; Stembridge interview, December 5, 1996; Curry interview, January 17, 1997; Baker interview, April 19, 1977.

13. Stembridge interview, December 5, 1996; telephone interview with Jane Stembridge, September 17, 1997, by Pete Daniel; Grant, *Ella Baker*, 132–34.

14. Stembridge interviews, December 5, 1996, September 17, 1997.

15. Curry interview, January 17, 1997.

16. Ibid.; Stembridge interviews, December 5, 1996, September 17, 1997; Carson, *In Struggle*, 25; Zinn, *SNCC*, 35.

17. Margaret Long to Lillian Smith, [late 1961], series 1283A, box 3, Smith Papers.

18. Grant, *Ella Baker*, 131–34.

19. Lillian Smith to Mozell Hill, March 11, 1957, series 1283, box 3, and Lillian Smith, "Are We Still Buying a New World with Old Confederate Bills?," speech given in Atlanta, Georgia, October 16, 1960, series 1283A, box 42, Smith Papers (emphasis in original).

20. Lillian Smith to Jane Stembridge, October 20, 1960, series 1283, box 24, ibid.; Smith to Stembridge, October 22, 1960, in *How Am I to Be Heard?: Letters of Lillian Smith*, edited by Margaret Rose Gladney (Chapel Hill, 1993), 257–58; Smith to Anna Grace Sawyer, October 31, 1960, series 1283, box 22A, Smith Papers; Smith to Stembridge, November 21, 1960, in Gladney, *How Am I to Be Heard?*, 258–61; Stembridge interview, September 17, 1997; Baker interview, April 19, 1977.

21. Jane Stembridge to Lillian Smith, November 29, December 10, 19, 1960, series 1283A, box 4; Smith to Stembridge, November [1960], series 1283, box 24; and Smith to Anna Grace Sawyer, October 31, [November or December] 1960, March 21, 1961, series 1283, box 22A, Smith Papers.

22. Lillian Smith to John Howard Griffin, September 25, 1962, series 1283A, box 2, ibid. For Smith's comments on Griffin's *Black Like Me*, see Smith to Griffin, December 3, 1961, ibid.

23. Lillian Smith to John Howard Griffin, January 1962, ibid.

24. Eliza Heard, "In the Name of Southern Womanhood," *New South*, November–December 1962, 16–18, copy in box 33, SCCHR Papers. See Jacquelyn Dowd Hall, *Revolt against Chivalry: Jessie Daniel Ames and the Women's Campaign against Lynching* (New York, 1979), 149–57, 250–53.

25. James Silver to Elizabeth Silver, October 2, 1962, box 7, folder 3, Silver Papers. See also Phil Mullen to James Silver, November 21, 1963, box 35, folder 4, ibid. For Silver's presidential address, see "Mississippi: The Closed Society," *Journal of Southern History* 30 (February 1964): 3–34.

26. Helen M. McKinney to James Silver, November 16, 1963, box 35, folder 2, Silver Papers.

27. Mildred W. Greear to James Silver, January 15, 1964, box 35, folder 6, ibid.

28. James C. Cobb, *The Most Southern Place on Earth: The Mississippi Delta and the Roots of Regional Identity* (New York, 1992), 254–59.

29. John R. Salter Jr., "Exploratory Report Re: Economic Destitution of Rural and Urban Negro Families in the Delta Region of the State of Mississippi," enclosed with Gloster B. Current to Wilkins, Carter, Morsell, Mitchell, Moon, and Delany, January 31, 1963, Mississippi Pressures, General, 1963–65, III A, box 231, NAACP Papers.

30. "Statement on Discriminatory Practices Affecting Programs of the U.S. Department of Agriculture," enclosed with National Sharecroppers Fund to Orville Freeman, August 29, 1963, Government, National, USDA, 1958–64, III A, box 145, ibid.

31. "The Federal Agricultural Stabilization Program and the Negro," *Columbia Law Review* 67 (June 1967): 1121–36; U.S. Commission on Civil Rights, *Equal Opportunity in Farm Programs: An Appraisal of Services Rendered by Agencies of the United States Department of Agriculture* (Washington, D.C., 1965), 90; Meier and Rudwick, *CORE*, 81, 342; "Current Membership of ASCS County Committeemen by Ethnic Groups," 1989, USDA, Office of Advocacy and Enterprise. On more recent problems in the USDA, see Ward Sinclair, "Old-Boy Network Still Haunts Agriculture's Problem Child," *Washington Post*, September 21, 1987, A13; "Agriculture Dept. Lags on Blacks' Complaints," *Washington Post*, October 24, 1997, A25; "Soiled Legacy," *Wall Street Journal*, May 1, 1998, A1, 8.

32. "Resolution on Cotton Policy," [1963], Delta Council Correspondence, box 32, folder 18, Sillers Papers; Cobb, *Most Southern Place on Earth*, 256.

33. Kay Mills, *This Little Light of Mine: The Life of Fannie Lou Hamer* (New York, 1993), 34–39, 119; interview with Leslie Burl McLemore, Washington, D.C., October 26, 1984, by Pete Daniel.

34. McLemore interview, October 26, 1984; interview with Leslie Burl McLemore, Washington, D.C., September 28, 1997, by Pete Daniel; minutes, Delta Council Labor Committee meeting, March 27, 1961, and Delta Council Board of Directors meeting, November 27, 1962, box 32, folder 10, Sillers Papers.

35. McLemore interview, October 26, 1984; Payne, *I've Got the Light of Freedom*, 227–28, 287–89.

36. McLemore interview, September 28, 1997; Mills, *This Little Light of Mine*, 46; Payne, *I've Got the Light of Freedom*, 176–77. On SNCC activity in Holly Springs, see Frank Smith, report, July 26, 31, 1962, box 7, Moore Papers.

37. McLemore interview, September 28, 1997; Stembridge interview, September 17, 1997.

38. Jane Stembridge to Lillian Smith, October 31, 1963, series 1283A, box 4, Smith Papers.

39. Jane Stembridge, field report, Greenwood, Miss., November 5, 1963, ibid.; Payne, *I've Got the Light of Freedom*, 204–6, 295–97.

40. Jane Stembridge, field report, Greenwood, Miss., November 20, 1963, series 1283A, box 4, Smith Papers; McLemore interview, September 28, 1997.

41. Jane Stembridge, field report, Greenwood, Miss., December 6, 1963, series 1283A, box 4, Smith Papers.

42. Jane Stembridge to Lillian Smith, May 9, 1964, ibid. (ellipses in original).

43. Jane Stembridge to Lillian Smith, June 23, 24, 1964, June 1964, ibid.; Grant, *Ella Baker*, 171–72.

44. Tyson, "Robert F. Williams."

45. Jane Stembridge to Lillian Smith, August 3, 1964, series 1283A, box 4, Smith Papers (ellipses in original); Carson, *In Struggle*, 122.

46. Jane Stembridge to Lillian Smith, August 3, 1964, series 1283A, box 4, Smith Papers (emphasis in original).

47. Ibid. (ellipses in original). Smith summed up her role in attempting to improve race relations in Lillian Smith to Norman Cousins, February 3, 1966, series 1283, box 7, ibid.

48. Jane Stembridge to Lillian Smith, August 3, 1964, series 1283A, box 4, ibid.

49. Bruce Maxwell, "Report on the White Project," September 1964, box 7, Moore Papers; Carson, *In Struggle*, 118–19.

50. McLemore interview, September 28, 1997.

51. Ibid.

52. Ibid.; Grant, *Ella Baker*, 174–79; Mills, *This Little Light of Mine*, 105–33.

53. Mills, *This Little Light of Mine*, 105–33; Carson, *In Struggle*, 111–29.

54. Carson, *In Struggle*, 126; Mills, *This Little Light of Mine*, 105–33.

Index

cotton culture, 57; and urban areas, 124

Environmental issues, 1, 84, 85, 87

Equal rights: and discrimination, 1, 10–11, 17–18, 24, 26, 30, 125, 293; and whites, 2, 27, 292, 293; and Ella Baker, 12, 13; and politics, 28; and Wade Milam, 33; and religion, 185; and segregationist organizations, 222, 248; and agriculture, 227; and Southern Regional Council, 233; and integration, 249; and Mississippi Freedom Democratic Party, 304

Eure, J. Bruce, 207

Evans, J. Claude, 234

Evers, Medgar, 10–11, 216–17, 221–23, 227, 298

Ewing, C., Jr., 44

Faubus, John Samuel, 253

Faubus, Orval Eugene, 251–53, 256–58, 260–61, 264–65, 267–68, 270, 272, 275, 278, 282–83

Faulkner, William, 171–72, 186, 189

FBI. *See* Federal Bureau of Investigation

FDA. *See* Food and Drug Administration

Feathers, Charlie, 143, 145

Federal Bureau of Investigation (FBI), 224, 270, 294, 304

Federal government: and politics, 2, 11; agricultural programs of, 7, 9–10, 36, 39, 41–42, 47–60, 214–15, 227, 294–96; and urban growth, 16, 19; and African Americans, 37; and segregationist organizations, 214; and integration, 257, 300

Federal Insecticide, Fungicide, and Rodenticide Act, 69, 77

Federation for Constitutional Government, 197, 200–201

Fine, Benjamin, 262, 263, 266, 267

Flanders, H. Jack, Jr., 239

Fleming, Billie S., 247

Flock, Tim, 91, 97, 98, 102–3, 114, 116

Flock family, 98, 100–102, 107, 109

Florida, 83, 84, 97–99, 156, 287

Flowers, Linda, 57

Fontaine, Joan, 165

Fontana, J. D., 151

Food and Drug Administration (FDA), 71, 73–74, 84

Ford, Fred, 130

Foreman, L. D., 257, 267–68

Forman, James, 291

France, William Clifton, 99

France, William Henry Getty, 97–99

Frizzel, Lefty, 140

Frost, Robert, 200

Funchess, M. J., 70–71

Garrard, W. M., Jr., 86

Garrett, Charles G., 244

Garroway, Dave, 187

Gays, 19, 152, 155–57

George, Wesley Critz, 198, 201–5, 207–8, 286–87

Georgia, 36, 51, 54, 81, 84, 95, 97, 101, 257

Gilson, Mary B., 202

Glasscock, R. E., 265

Goodman, Andrew, 301

Gordon, Roscoe, 132

Gordon, Willie, 130–31

Gore, Albert, 78

Goudlock, James H., 285

Graham, Frank Porter, 25, 185–86, 188, 189

Graves, John Templeton, 24

Gray, Archie Lee, 86

Gray, C. N., 210

Gray, Pearleen, 223

Greear, Mildred W., 294

Green, Ernest, 251, 270, 275, 281

Gregg, Frankie, 279

Griffin, John Howard, 292–93

Griffin, Marvin, 257, 258

Guralnick, Peter, 135, 151

Guthridge, Amis, 252, 255–56, 265, 277–78, 280

Gwynn, Dallas E., 202, 204, 208

Haggard, Merle, 118

Hamer, Fannie Lou, 284, 296–300, 303–5

Hammerstein, Oscar, 212
Hampton, Lionel, 129
Haney, Bette, 77
Hargrove, James, 214–15
Harris, Wynonie, 134
Hastings, Paul D., 205, 206
Hayes, Isaac, 150
Hayes, Wayland J., Jr., 71
Hays, Kirby L., 81
Health, Education, and Welfare, U.S. Department of, 77
Health care, 16, 18, 19, 30, 123
Heard, Eliza, 293
Hedgeman, Anna Arnold, 12
Heeb, Franklin, 67–68
Height, Dorothy, 12
Henry, Aaron E., 11, 222, 227, 299, 304
Herbert, Robert Beverley, 240
Hichenson, Felix, 201
Higgins, Tom, 99
Hinton, James M., 22, 25–26, 250
Hinton, Robert, 231
Hitler, Adolf, 22
Hoback, George, 58
Hodges, Luther, 205–6
Hogan, Reed, 222
Holden, May Anna, 279
Holland, Spessard L., 84
Holloway, Darlene, 277–78, 279
Holloway, George, 125
Holman, John, 112
Homosexuality, 19, 152, 154–60
Honey, Michael K., 33, 124, 125
Horn, Joseph R., III, 239
Horton, Myles, 36
Houck, Jane C., 219
House Un-American Activities Committee, 211
Housing, 13, 19, 30, 35, 37, 123, 214
Howard, John, 154–55
Howard, T. R. M., 209, 224
Hoxie, Arkansas, 252–53, 261
Huckaby, Elizabeth, 261, 263–65, 270–71, 273–74, 276–81
Hughes, Langston, 286
Humphrey, Hubert, 304

Hunt, Blair T., 123
Hurley, Ruby, 212, 221, 223–24
Hutchinson, Bud R., 235
Hux, Martin Luther, 183

Integration: and education, 2, 32, 34, 36, 126, 183–84, 190, 200–201, 204–6, 208, 210–11, 220; and Lillian Smith, 14; and whites, 21, 30, 124, 186, 188, 193, 196, 201, 214, 226, 228–29, 234–36, 272; and Communist Party, 24; and politics, 28–29, 231, 234, 237; and unionism, 33, 197, 206; and Supreme Court, 34; and communism, 38, 208, 211, 236–37, 249, 268; and urban areas, 125–26; and interracial mixing, 153–54, 158–59, 201, 203–5, 208, 211, 218, 220, 241, 243, 249, 256, 258–59, 293; and music, 165, 174

Jackson, Al, Jr., 145
Jackson, Cordell, 17, 148, 153
Jackson, Larry A., 239
Jackson, Wayne, 146
Jagger, Mick, 152
Janzen, D. H., 69
Jarrett, Ned, 97, 102, 104, 106–7, 109–13, 117, 119, 120
Javonich, Bill, 187
Jefferson, Thomas, 30
Jewish faith, 182, 196
Johns, Charley E., 156
Johnson, Annie Mae, 221–22
Johnson, Charles S., 181
Johnson, Fred, 107, 110
Johnson, Jim, 252–53, 257, 258, 261, 275, 282
Johnson, Junior, 91, 97, 106–11, 113, 120
Johnson, L. P., 107, 110
Johnson, Lora Money, 107, 110
Johnson, Lurleander, 222
Johnson, Lyndon B., 57, 58, 69, 303, 304–5
Johnson, Marion E., 262
Johnson, Robert Glenn, Sr., 107–8
Johnston, Jack, 154
Jones, Booker T., 145, 146

Rose, Billy, 151
Rural areas: culture of, 1, 7–8, 21, 42, 93; and migration, 7, 15, 19–20, 38, 312 (n. 4); and language, 8, 91–94; and music, 8–9, 38, 91, 94, 121, 138–39, 143–44, 198, 300, 305; and postwar era, 9–10, 42–43
Russell, Donald, 235
Russell, Richard, 84
Ruth, Kent, 34

Salter, John R., Jr., 295
Sanders, Claudia Thomas, 241–42
Sanders, James Henry, 241
Sarratt, Reed, 207
Scales, Junius, 24, 25, 29, 186
Scarbrough, Sandra, 169–71, 175
SCCHR. See South Carolina Council on Human Relations
SCEF. See Southern Conference Education Fund
SCHW. See Southern Conference for Human Welfare
Schwerner, Michael, 301
SCLC. See Southern Christian Leadership Conference
Scott, Wendell, 104–7, 117
Scruggs, Walter, 215
Secrest, Andrew McDowd, 240
Sedberry, Mary Anita, 262
Segregation: and whites, 1–3, 18, 22–26, 29–30, 32–33, 37–38, 181, 184, 188, 190–94, 292, 302; and politics, 2, 22–23, 28–29, 181, 183, 190, 200, 205, 207, 244; and Citizens' Councils, 2, 181, 195–97; and color line, 9, 11–14, 21–22, 32, 60, 123, 126, 131, 148, 165–67, 169, 175, 191, 193–94; and migration, 9, 16; and urban areas, 9, 17–18, 123–24, 126; and World War II, 11, 22; and separate-but-equal myth, 18, 26, 234; and African Americans, 24–26, 30, 123, 189, 202, 209, 221; and diplomacy, 27; and religion, 33–34, 38, 181–86, 188, 233, 256, 259, 263–64, 267–69, 271, 275; and working class, 33–34, 92, 123, 179;

and music, 124, 126, 128, 165–69; and women, 157; and sexual behavior, 160–61; and education, 180–81, 189, 193, 209, 239; and segregationist organizations, 195–208, 211–28, 238–39, 247–48, 252, 255–56, 258–62, 265–66, 271, 273, 275–79, 281–83, 285–87; and southern historians, 293; and SNCC, 300
Sharecroppers: migration of, 1, 22, 122–23; replacement of, 8, 9, 44, 295; and culture, 8, 94; and defense work, 10; and New Deal, 40; and federal agriculture policy, 42, 49, 216; and music, 134, 137, 139, 141, 175; and economic retaliation, 211, 225, 244
Sharpe, Bill, 206–7
Shaw, Byron T., 77, 84
Sherrill, Robert, 251, 283
Sherrod, Charles, 303
Shivers, Allan, 261
Siddons, Anne Rivers, 172
Sillers, Walter, 28, 52, 86, 196, 205
Silver, James W., 220, 293–94
Simkins, Modjeska, 230–31, 250
Simmons, W. J., 208, 212
Simons, Harriet Porcher Stoney, 230–32, 234, 240
Smith, Bruton, 99, 115
Smith, E. C., 224
Smith, F. B., 86
Smith, Frank, 191
Smith, Frank, Jr., 303
Smith, Gene, 265
Smith, Hazel Brannon, 227
Smith, J. A., 68
Smith, Jack, 94
Smith, Lillian, 14, 22–23, 156–57, 173, 180–82, 186–88, 243, 291–93, 298, 300–303
Smith, Louise, 104
Smith, Ruby Doris, 286
Smith, Warren, 145
Smith v. Allwright (1944), 12, 23
SNCC. See Student Nonviolent Coordinating Committee